LABOR-BASED CONTRACTS: BUILDING EQUITY AND INCLUSION IN THE COMPASSIONATE WRITING CLASSROOM

PERSPECTIVES ON WRITING
Series Editors, Susan H. McLeod and Rich Rice

The Perspectives on Writing series addresses writing studies in a broad sense. Consistent with the wide ranging approaches characteristic of teaching and scholarship in writing across the curriculum, the series presents works that take divergent perspectives on working as a writer, teaching writing, administering writing programs, and studying writing in its various forms.

The WAC Clearinghouse, Colorado State University Open Press, and University Press of Colorado are collaborating so that these books will be widely available through free digital distribution and low-cost print editions. The publishers and the Series editors are committed to the principle that knowledge should freely circulate. We see the opportunities that new technologies have for further democratizing knowledge. And we see that to share the power of writing is to share the means for all to articulate their needs, interest, and learning into the great experiment of literacy.

Recent Books in the Series

Mark Sutton and Sally Chandler (Eds.), *The Writing Studio Sampler: Stories About Change* (2018)

Edited by Kristine L. Blair and Lee Nickoson (Eds.), *Composing Feminist Interventions: Activism, Engagement, Praxis* (2018)

Mya Poe, Asao B. Inoue, and Norbert Elliot (Eds.), *Writing Assessment, Social Justice, and the Advancement of Opportunity* (2018)

Patricia Portanova, J. Michael Rifenburg, and Duane Roen (Eds.), Contemporary Perspectives on Cognition and Writing (2017)

Douglas M. Walls and Stephanie Vie (Eds.), *Social Writing/Social Media: Publics, Presentations, and Pedagogies* (2017)

Laura R. Micciche, *Acknowledging Writing Partners* (2017)

Susan H. McLeod, Dave Stock, and Bradley T. Hughes (Eds.), *Two WPA Pioneers: Ednah Shepherd Thomas and Joyce Steward* (2017)

Seth Kahn, William B. Lalicker, and Amy Lynch-Biniek (Eds.), *Contingency, Exploitation, and Solidarity: Labor and Action in English Composition* (2017)

Barbara J. D'Angelo, Sandra Jamieson, Barry Maid, and Janice R. Walker (Eds.), *Information Literacy: Research and Collaboration across Disciplines* (2017)

Justin Everett and Cristina Hanganu-Bresch (Eds.), *A Minefield of Dreams: Triumphs and Travails of Independent Writing Programs* (2016)

LABOR-BASED GRADING CONTRACTS: BUILDING EQUITY AND INCLUSION IN THE COMPASSIONATE WRITING CLASSROOM

By Asao B. Inoue

The WAC Clearinghouse
wac.colostate.edu
Fort Collins, Colorado

University Press of Colorado
upcolorado.com
Louisville, Colorado

The WAC Clearinghouse, Fort Collins, Colorado 80523-1040

Printed for the WAC Clearinghouse by University Press of Colorado, Louisville, Colorado 80027

ISBN 978-1-64215-021-6 (PDF) | 978-1-64215-022-3 (ePub) | 978-1-60732-925-1 (pbk.)

Printed in the United States of America

Library of Congress Cataloging-in-Publication Data

Names: Inoue, Asao B., author.
Title: Labor-based grading contracts : building equity and inclusion in the compassionate
   writing classroom / by Asao B. Inoue.
Description: Fort Collins, Colorado : The WAC Clearinghouse, 2019.
   | Series: Perspectives on writing | Includes bibliographical references.
Identifiers: LCCN 2018057432 | ISBN 9781607329251 (pbk : alk. paper)
   | ISBN 9781642150223 (epub)
Subjects: LCSH: College students—Rating of. | Grading and marking (Students)
   | Educational tests and measurements. | Academic writing—Evaluation.
Classification: LCC LB2368 .I66 2019 | DDC 378.1/98—dc23 LC record available at
   https://lccn.loc.gov/2018057432

Copyeditor: Don Donahue
Designer: Mike Palmquist
Series Editors: Susan H. McLeod and Rich Rice
Cover Image: Ljupco Smokovs / Shutterstock.com. Used with permission.

This book is printed on acid-free paper.

The WAC Clearinghouse supports teachers of writing across the disciplines. Hosted by Colorado State University, and supported by the Colorado State University Open Press, it brings together scholarly journals and book series as well as resources for teachers who use writing in their courses. This book is available in digital formats for free download at wac.colostate.edu.

Founded in 1965, the University Press of Colorado is a nonprofit cooperative publishing enterprise supported, in part, by Adams State University, Colorado State University, Fort Lewis College, Metropolitan State University of Denver, Regis University, University of Colorado, University of Northern Colorado, Utah State University, and Western State Colorado University. For more information, visit upcolorado.com. The Press partners with the Clearinghouse to make its books available in print.

CONTENTS

ACKNOWLEDGMENTS

I wish to humbly thank so many people in my professional and personal life for helping me in the writing of this book. First, I thank my editors, Sue McLeod and Rich Rice, as well as Mike Palmquist, all of whom have been supportive, helpful, and thoughtful colleagues. I feel blessed to have such good people working to help my book become public. I thank my wife and partner, Kelly Inoue, for all of her labors each day that allow me to sit in peace and do the labors of writing and revising. And when I needed to just talk about an idea, she has always given me her ear and time. Along with those precious gifts, Kelly has given me her trust, love, and presence, things I could not live without, and are essential ingredients in my ability to write this book.

I'm thankful to several colleagues who read earlier versions of this book, Chris Knaus from University of Washington, Tacoma, my brother in antiracist work, and Norbert Elliot, a friend, colleague, and always careful, kind reader. I extend a special thank you to Virginia (Gin) Schwartz, a Ph.D. student at the University of Wisconsin and long-time grading contract user, who read an earlier version of the book and gave me valuable and extensive, page by page, comments and ideas. She was an important part of making this book possible in its current form. Of course, I'm also, as always, thankful and grateful to my mentor, Victor Villanueva, who still helps, guides, and supports me. He is my academic father, and often I am mindful of his gifts to me, gifts of time and presence, of words of encouragement and kindness, and sometimes, just a smile and laugh. I am indebted to the two anonymous reviewers of the book, who each read thoughtfully, carefully, and compassionately, providing me with insightful and helpful suggestions, many of which I took, particularly in rethinking parts of the Introduction and the order of the last few chapters.

And lastly, I wish to thank all of my students at California State University, Fresno, and the University of Washington, Tacoma, for helping me with my labor-based grading contracts over the years. This book has been at least ten years in the making, and that labor started and ended in my classrooms, places that required open, compassionate students to help me think, labor alongside them, and do our social justice work together. My students have been, and continue to be, my main source of encouragement, inspiration, and joy. Thank you.

LABOR-BASED GRADING CONTRACTS: BUILDING EQUITY AND INCLUSION IN THE COMPASSIONATE WRITING CLASSROOM

INTRODUCTION.
LABORING TOWARD GRADING CONTRACTS AND THE INNER DIKES

If you are picking up this book because you're interested in learning about grading contracts for your English or writing classroom, or you have used them and want to think more deeply about them or revise your practice, you got the right book. But this book is also about grading literacy performances more broadly— that is, I think, a teacher can learn something about any grading practice from this book even if they decide not to use labor-based grading contracts. Doing grading well, either at the secondary or postsecondary level, is not simply about finding the best practice, method, or mechanism. It is about understanding the various ways that the nature and function of grades might be constructed in a classroom, and the variety of consequences to learning that are possible. What I'm saying is that designing fair and meaningful grading practices is about cultivating with our students an ecology, a place where every student, no matter where they come from or how they speak or write, can have access to the entire range of final course grades possible.

This book focuses on one kind of grading contract, one that calculates final course grades purely by the labor students complete, not by any judgments of the quality of their writing. While the qualities of student writing is still at the center of the classroom and feedback, it has no bearing on the course grade. Why take our judgments of quality out of the tabulation of course grades and progress in a course? Because all grading and assessment exist within systems that uphold singular, dominant standards that are racist, and White supremacist when used uniformly. This problem is present in any grading system that incorporates a standard, no matter who is judging, no matter the particulars of the standard. Thus, in the chapters that follow, I critique hybrid grading contracts, such as those advocated by Danielewicz and Elbow, and Ira Shor ("Critical Pedagogy" and *Empowering Education*), that use notions of quality in order to determine the higher grades possible. In my experience and research, a grading contract based only on labor is better for all students and undermines the racist and White supremacist grading systems we all live with at all levels of education. But using labor as the only way to grade my students allows my classroom assessment ecologies to engage in larger social justice projects, ones that make up an important agenda of mine, ones that interrogate and attempt to dismantle White language supremacy in schools and society. This project is one that builds equity and inclusion in writing classrooms while also engaging students with the politics of language. It turns out that engaging with diverse ways of languaging and judging in the right kinds of assessment ecologies offers flexible and critical rhetorical training that can prepare students for a wide variety of communication situations.

When grading is done well, it offers opportunities to address the politics of the judgment of language, which is vital in negotiating any rhetorical situation in and out of school. Some call this critical pedagogy, but I think the minute writing teachers move the discussion to pedagogy, to teaching, to lessons and readings, most teachers ignore or forget about assessment and grading. Or maybe, many of us feel that the grading part of a course can be separated from the learning part, or the critical part. Most of us don't grade first drafts anyway, right? But that isn't enough. It is often believed falsely that grading is just an institutional necessity, something we can ask students to ignore, at least while they are learning. But to attempt to do that is to ignore the way grades work in classrooms, how they shape many aspects of the entire ecology, how they influence students' and teachers' actions. Not thinking of assessment first, or at least simultaneously with pedagogy, is a mistake. And our students who do not already come to us embodying a dominant English will pay for it, even when our intentions are to help those very students.

At its best, the practice of grading writing can be a cyclical, self-conscious, evolving practice informed by reflection on that practice and dialogue. That is, it can be just as much a learning practice for the teacher as it is meant to be for students. It can be an ongoing loop of paying attention to what we are doing when we grade, or when we think we are supposed to be grading, and letting those insights inform how we do assessment together with our students tomorrow. Most of all, it can be about deeply attending to our students, not to correct but to understand and grow ourselves and allow them to understand and grow. The goal of the kind of assessment ecology I'm calling for in this book is one that makes the means of grading also its ends. Why? Well, the book will explain in a number ways. But in short, because the means, our processes of laboring, are all we have and all our students can have for their learning. I hope that short answer will become richer as you read on.

UNDERMINING WHITE LANGUAGE SUPREMACY

One main goal I have for this book about labor-based grading contracts for secondary and postsecondary writing classrooms is simple. I wish to change the rules of the grading game in writing classrooms. I know that most writing teachers hate grading, and know intuitively how bad it is for their students' learning. It is a distraction that pulls students away from the real dialogues and discussions about their writing that we want to have. It isn't formative in nature. A grade on a paper is a red herring to most students. But there is a more sinister problem with grading, one that may make some teachers very uncomfortable, because it is going to sound like a personal attack, or a reason to be permissive and lax about standards. It may even sound like a way not to prepare our students for future success with language. I want to assure you that this is far from what I mean and far from what I've seen in my own classrooms.

What is this more sinister problem with grading? Grading, because it requires a single, dominant standard, is a racist and White supremacist practice. There is no way around it. Let me back up and come at this claim from some known premises. Grading is almost always employed in order to control students (and sometimes their teachers), force students to be accountable (and sometimes their teachers), and measure or rank students (and sometimes their teachers), either against each other or against a single standard. Each of these purposes for grading in writing classrooms is detrimental to learning generally, and more harmful to many students of color and raciolinguistically diverse students. This is because "diverse students" means "not White students," or students who use varieties of English that are not the standardized version used in the schools.[1] Raciolinguistically diverse students come to our classrooms with *habitus* (or linguistic, bodily, and performative dispositions) that do not match the White racial *habitus* embodied in the standard of the classroom. In short, the traditional purposes and methods used for grading writing turn out to be *de facto* racist and White supremacist. Grading by a standard, thus, is how White language supremacy is perpetuated in schools.

Let me pause for a moment and explain why I will be using the terms, "White supremacy" and "White language supremacy," since I know they can be triggers for many, especially White people. I use these terms compassionately as a way to help teachers of all political stripes confront their Whiteness and stay in the discomfort that the term generates when associated with our own grading practices, with our own values and habits, with our bodies. When we associate the things we hold dear with something like White supremacy, it can sound like an attack on your person. It can be uncomfortable. Yes, I want you to feel uncomfortable because it can help you *feel the problem*, not intellectualize it, or see it, or hear it. You need to feel it if you want to change systems.

---

1   I realize that race does not equal language practice. All White students do not use the dominant standardized version of English expected in their classrooms, but that is the dominant pattern in the US. Black, Latinx, Asian, and indigenous students may also use the dominant English, but that is not the pattern in the US.

In fact, this tactic itself is one way I resist the rhetorical pull to produce a text that both assumes a cool, calm, and rational tone and expects its readers to have the same disposition as they read. This disposition to be calm and rational is a part of the academic dispositions that Thaiss and Zawacki contend, in their interdisciplinary study of writers, may be universal in all academic writing (5–6). This disposition also is deeply rooted in a White racial *habitus*.[2] It's part of the dominant "standard" for good writing. So, I'm compassionately asking you, my reader, to feel something as you read, even if that feeling is anger, defensiveness, or guilt. I ask this of you because I believe we all can come to great insights and knowledge about ourselves and others through this kind of discomfort, if we sit long enough in it, and interrogate why we feel the way we do about terms like, "White supremacy."

But I have another reason for using these trigger words. It is compassionate to suffer with others, like the suffering that so many of our students feel when a standard that is not of their own is used against them. Staying a while in your discomfort that my use throughout this book of the terms "White language supremacy" and "White supremacy" bring is an important part of a critical, Freirean, problematizing practice that I'll discuss in Chapter 1. The terms are a constant reminder of pain, our own and our students'. Sometimes our work as teachers and scholars cannot be cool, objective, unemotional, and purely reasoned. Sometimes it must hurt, cause us some discomfort, so that we really change. If it helps, remember this when you feel misrepresented or blamed by my use of the terms: You think you're misunderstood? You think you are unfairly judged because you are an alley in the struggle for racial equality? What do you think your students of color feel? Suffer with us.

My use of these terms also draws on my interpretation of methodologies from Critical Race Theory (CRT), which discuss counter storytelling as important to disrupting White supremacist and racist narratives that become naturalized in institutions and society as normative, often non-racial, and neutral (Solórzano and Yosso "Critical Race and LatCrit"; "Critical Race Methodology"; "Critical Race Counterstory"). I wish by repetition to create a kind of counter languaging, or counter rhetoric, that calls our standards for writing and their grading practices what they really are, which are the ways teachers, courses, programs, departments, schools, disciplines, and society perpetuate White language supremacy. By using these terms I look to produce in readers a bodily response that I hope will urge you to pause, notice, and reflect. And so, I must name the thing we are really talking about and not shy away from it by using neutered euphemisms in order that my audience might skip the very problematizing of

---

2   To see how the literature on Whiteness has identified the disposition of reason and neutrality, see Brookhiser, Myser, Frye, and McGill and Pearce.

their own subject positions and *habitus* that are assumed in their standards, ways of judging language, and grading practices. It is not my job to make you comfortable. In fact, I believe it is quite the opposite.

But my use of these terms in this book is also meant to be a compassionate invitation to all readers to sit in discomfort with your complicity to unfair systems, to urge you to feel seriously about changing those systems. And I say that this is a compassionate invitation because I firmly believe that compassion is suffering with others and helping them grow in areas in which they want to grow. If you've picked up this book, then you have already expressed that desire to grow. As Chapter 6 will discuss, compassion is an important part to my labor-based grading contracts because it is an important way that my students and I set ground rules for the difficult conversations about language, race, racism, Whiteness, and White language supremacy we have.

What do I mean by "White supremacy"? I'm most taken by Derald Wing Sue's definition of the term. He links it closely to White privilege, and through his discussion, also to institutional racism. Drawing on Peggy McIntosh and others, Sue explains that White privilege is a set of "unearned advantages and benefits that accrue to White folks by virtue of a system normed on the experiences, values, and perceptions of their group"; furthermore, these invisible privileges are "premised on the mistaken notion of individual meritocracy and deservingness (hard work, family values, etc.) rather than favoritism . . . [and are] deeply embedded in the structural, systemic, and cultural workings of U.S. society" (*Overcoming* 137). These advantages and benefits are automatically conferred, such as using a standard for writing in a course in which some students have considerably more contact with it outside of the course (or school) than others. These students' good grades seem to be due simply to hard work and merit, but this is only so because their White racial *habitus* and the *habitus* that informs the standard for good writing agree with one another.

Sue explains that White privilege needs White supremacy as a system to exist at all. There's no way around it. Larger structures are the only things that can create privileges for a group of people so consistently, not individual racist acts or people, not anomalies in the system. Thus

> White supremacy is a doctrine of racial superiority that justifies discrimination, segregation, and domination of persons of color based on an ideology and belief system that considers all other non-White groups inferior (J. M. Jones, 1997) . . . it resides in the very institutional and cultural foundations of our society . . . To maintain conformance and silence of persons of color, White supremacy as a doctrine and belief is instilled

7

> through education and enforced by biased institutional poli-
> cies or practices that punish those who dare raise their voices
> in objection to their second-class status. (*Race Talk* 155)

White supremacy, then, is institutional racism. It's structural, seems natural, thus is normalized such that many of us cannot see it as such in our classrooms, in our disciplines, in our ways of reading and valuing student texts. We cannot see, for instance, how holding one standard in our grading practices reinforces White supremacy since all such standards have historically come from one racial formation on the globe. We cannot see clearly how our own grading practices are linked to historically White supremacist ideology and practices, laws and customs, all of which have been maintained and policed primarily by White racial formations and those who embody a White racial *habitus* in our society, schools, and disciplines of study.

Sue quotes James M. Jones' important work on the subject, his 1997 edition of *Prejudice and Racism*. In defining institutional racism, which I'm offering as one way to define White supremacy, Sue quotes Jones, saying that institutional racism—and so White supremacy—are "those established laws, customs, and practices which systematically reflect and produce racial inequalities in American society," and these customs, laws, and practices are what Sue identifies as our "standard operating procedures" or SOPs (Sue, *Race Talk* 90). For instance, the privileges that a White racial *habitus* confer in classrooms where language is graded by a single standard gives some unearned privileges, yet those standards are a part of our SOPs in school. How are we to determine a student's progress? How else are students going to be motivated to do work? Isn't it only fair to have one standard and apply it to all students equally? Jones continues: "If racist consequences accrue to institutional laws, customs, or practices, the institution is racist whether or not the individuals maintaining those practices have racist intentions" (Jones 438; qtd. in Sue, *Race Talk* 90). So if our SOPs and the standards for language use within them privilege a White racial *habitus*, then no matter who controls that system, it still produces unfair results, i.e., White supremacist results. The system and its standards are White supremacist by design and results.

So how would I define White supremacy in one sentence? White Supremacy is a product or effect of systems and structures, our SOPs (standard operating procedures), despite anyone's intentions, that produce political, cultural, linguistic, and economic dominance for White people. This means that White language supremacy can be defined as a product or effect of assessment systems and structures, our SOPs in classrooms and other places where language is judged, despite anyone's intentions, that produce political, cultural, linguistic, and economic dominance for White people. The use of labor-based grading contracts, I believe, changes the rules of the grading game in such a way that White language supremacy can not only be seen for what it is, but effectively countered. This makes for a fairer, more equitable, and inclusive language classroom.

EDUCATION AS INNER DIKES

So in our current society and educational systems, regardless of who you are, where you came from, or what your intentions or motives are as a teacher, if you use a single standard to grade students' language performances, you are directly contributing to the racist status quo in schools and society. Language only moves in groups of people and people are racialized in a variety of ways in society and history. This is how language exists and how race is a part of our politics of language. Language exists because racialized people communicate among each other, and their languages are always in historical processes that associate those languages with particular social and racial formations in society. While linguists and other scholars agree that there is no single way to communicate effectively, judgments of effectiveness and correctness of language are contingent and contextual. What this really says in a U.S. educational context is that effectiveness and correctness of language is racialized. It has come from White racialized groups in our histories (Ignatiev; Jacobson; Roediger). White people and Whiteness as a set of raciolinguistic dispositions and habits, or White *habitus*, are the context and contingency for effectiveness, or "goodness," or appropriateness, or excellence.

This means all standards for good writing are deeply informed by a White racial *habitus*, which makes grading by such standards White supremacist. I am not saying that you (the teacher) are a bad person, but grading by a standard does make your grading methods and your grading ecology in your classroom racist, and White supremacist. I've argued elsewhere how this is the case (Inoue, *Antiracist*), so I won't repeat those arguments here. Instead, I point to the legal literature on the history of Whiteness as property in the US to further argue the point that grading by a single standard is White supremacist.

Cheryl L. Harris' comprehensive legal account of the ways that laws and the courts in the US defined and maintained Whiteness as property extends to education and literacy, particularly as seen in the *Brown v. Board of Education* decisions (1954 and 1955), which were an extension of the *Plessy v. Ferguson* decision (1896) (Harris 1746–57). These judicial decisions hinge on questions of Whiteness as property. Harris explains in her conclusion about the Brown decisions:

> Whiteness as property continues to perpetuate racial sub-
> ordination through the courts' definitions of group identity

9

> and through the courts' discourse and doctrine on affirma-
> tive action. The exclusion of subordinated "others" was and
> remains a central part of the property interest in Whiteness
> and, indeed, is part of the protection that the court extends to
> Whites' settled expectations of continued privilege. (1758)

What Harris shows in her discussion over and over in various legal ways and through court decisions in various realms of U.S. society is the way Whiteness has functioned and been used as property for the benefit of those deemed to be racially White. Whiteness is the property that even a poor, uneducated, or jobless White man can have that has value. Furthermore, Harris argues that "Whiteness and property share a common premise—a conceptual nucleus—of a right to exclude" (1704). Whiteness as property is, therefore, about exclusion. This point is critical in educational settings because most of us proclaim or promote inclusion. Our schools, programs, and even pedagogies proclaim to include raciolinguistically diverse students, but our grading practices, standards, and assumptions function to exclude. And the direction this exclusion takes is a racialized one.

In *Literacy and Racial Justice: The Politics of Learning After* Brown v. Board of Education, Catherine Prendergast argues convincingly that historically in the US the courts have worked from a fundamental premise that "literacy is first and foremost White property," and the logic goes "that no attempt should therefore be made to redistribute the best goods" (167). She looks closely at the logics and consequences of *Brown v. Board, Washington v. Davis* (1976), and *The Regents of the University of California v. Bakke* (1978), all of which demonstrate what Prendergast calls "the economy of literacy as a White property," or a dynamic rooted in figurative or literal "White flight" in places where people of color begin to accumulate. She explains the dynamic: "literacy standards are perceived to be falling or in peril of falling" when too many people of color, often African-American, are included or presence in the place in question, be it a school, police department, community, etc. (41). Where do we find the most calls around "literacy crises"? Schools and communities that are made up of increasing numbers of people of color. What do schools and classrooms have at their disposal to remedy such perceptions of falling literacy standards among their students? Grading mechanisms and standards. Remember the primary goals of grading by a standard are control, enforced accountability, and measurement. Thus, grading is a great way to protect the White property of literacy in schools, while never mentioning race. It's a great way to maintain the White supremacist status quo without ever being White supremacist, yet such standards are White language supremacy.

So if literacy has been, and continues to be, a White property in the US, and if the nature of White property is the right to exclude, and if grading by a standard is always about control, accountability, and measurement, then grading by a single standard is how most, if not all, schools and writing classrooms exercise the historical right to exclude in order to protect literacy as White property, all the while exclaiming and even believing that they are helping their students of color. And how well has that helping really worked out?

Put more directly, in all schools, grades are the means of discrimination, the methods of exclusion, not inclusion, no matter what else we may think they do for our students. Therefore, this book argues to change the rules of the grading game in writing and literacy classrooms, so that your grading mechanisms stop trying to be fair to everyone (i.e., treat everyone as if they are White, as if they have the same proximity to a White racial *habitus*), and start trying *NOT to be unfair*, not to be White supremacist. This latter purpose for grading ecologies in classrooms stems from an assumption that the literacy practices promoted in schools and colleges have and still are conceived of as White property, and that the standards and grading practices we all inherit, or that are forced upon us by principals, disciplines, departments, and programs, are White supremacist and seek to exclude, not include, by their nature and function, by default, regardless of how we justify them or who uses them. Trying not to be unfair is the only way one can ensure equitable and inclusive practices in inherently unfair systems that are by their nature inequitable and exclusive.

I'm reminded of the noted eugenicist and advocate for racial segregation, Lothrop Stoddard and his 1920 book, *The Rising Tide of Color: The Threat Against White World Supremacy*. Stoddard was a White supremacist. In the book, he argues that increasing populations of peoples of color around the world threaten the White geographical, economic, and political center. White settlements are being taken over, he argues, by various people of color, and this is a bad thing. Strategically, Stoddard notes, there are inner and outer dikes. The outer dikes of civilization are those places in the world that contain mostly people of color, but the inner are those places on the globe that are White settlements in which people of color are increasing, and those areas must be protected. Just like the logic behind redlining to protect real estate property from Black Americans, the White settlements—the White property—that Stoddard speaks of are understood as crucial dikes that need protecting because they are the last defense of the White centers. Education, schools, and literacy in the US are inner dikes.

Stoddard's introduction to this discussion is instructive in how it so easily maps to arguments about holding or raising standards and the logic within the calls about literacy crises in the US today, most of which are attached to grades:

> The inner dikes (the areas of White settlement), however, are
> a very different matter. Peopled as they are wholly or largely
> by Whites, they have become parts of the race-heritage, which
> should be defended to the last extremity no matter if the costs
> involved are greater than their mere economic value would
> warrant. They are the true bulwarks of the race, the patrimony
> of future generations who have a right to demand of us that
> they shall be born White in a White man's land. Ill will it fare
> if ever our race should close its ears to this most elemental call
> of the blood. (226)

There is no more fitting analogy to grading by a standard than Stoddard's. Schools, colleges, and universities today are literally and figuratively White settlements (many built on land stolen from indigenous peoples), which have become tacitly, as Stoddard makes clear, a White entitlement, an inner dike to protect. While our terms may be less overtly racialized today, we still talk and think of schools and universities as "true bulwarks" for standards, or as the centers of literacy promotion, which is the White property of those settlements. In Stoddard's terms, this makes educational institutions the "race-heritage" of each generation, or the "patrimony" to be passed on to the next generation—and that generation is racially White by this logic. This makes grading by a standard the method for protecting and cleaning out the inner dike, Whitening it. In short, schools are the inner dikes of literacy as White property. Grading is the gun and bayonet, which are used against all students to cleanse them, to Whiten them or drive them out. Again, the rules for grading must change if we wish to stop trying to Whiten the dike.

When we change the rules for grading dramatically, for instance, as when one stops using a White standard to grade student performances, we realize that we must choose something else to use to determine final course grades. This makes us mindful of our assumptions about grading, mindful about what we assume a paper or written product demonstrates to us about a student, mindful of what we think we can see and what textual markers we use that makes present so-called quality in a draft. It makes us mindful that we use a standard of our own and not someone else's, or something else, like labor or effort or engagement, which arguably are much closer to the act of learning than a draft or portfolio because these dimensions (i.e., labor and effort) embody the experience of learning itself. When we are mindful that we grade in particular ways, we have a better chance to pay attention to details about our own practices and how they happen. We have a better chance not to simply Whiten the dike. Using labor-based grading contracts, I believe, requires, even encourages, this kind of mindful attention because the rules of the grading game are so dramatically different from conventional, standards-based rules. This book attempts to offer a way to change the rules of the grading game in classrooms.

ASSESSMENT ECOLOGIES AND ME

In this book, I assume some concepts that come from my theorizing of classroom writing assessment as ecology (Inoue, *Antiracist*), so allow me to summarize the theory briefly here. Any classroom writing assessment ecology can be understood to be made up of at least seven elements: power, purposes, processes, parts, people, products, and places (176). Noticing and understanding these elements can help teachers create assessment ecologies that resist White language supremacy and racism that are structurally embedded in the academy and our society. Labor-based grading contracts attempt to form an inclusive, more diverse ecological place, one that can be antiracist and anti-White supremacist by its nature. The ecology does not use a single standard of so-called quality to grade students, and focuses time, labor, and attention on other elements in the ecology, realizing that these other elements construct more of the ecology than a standard, and even provides students with a chance to critique (through comparison) conventional grading practices and their own standards.

A grading contract, like any grading system, frames and contextualizes all the activities and people that form the classroom ecology. While any ecological element can be considered and manipulated separately, all seven ecological elements are interconnected and consubstantial to each other (93), often morphing into one another at different moments in the historical unfolding of the ecology. An activity (process) becomes a rubric (part) becomes a figurative place of agreement and contention (place), etc. As complex ecological theory explains (Dobrin 144), ecologies are holistic in nature, and any given element in the system is more than what it is. The ecology itself is more than the sum of its parts (86). Understanding the writing assessment ecology of a classroom in this holistic way can help us form antiracist, anti-White supremacist, and other social justice projects through our most fundamental aspect of any course, its assessment ecology. Understanding how my classroom's assessment system is an ecology has allowed me to take advantage of what a labor-based contract offers.

I should note an initial paradox that is not lost on me, and it has significant bearing on my labor-based grading contract ecologies. I realize the oxymoronic, haunting Whiteness, as Kennedy, Middleton, and Ratcliffe would say, in my own discourse in this book. This is part of the problematic of writing assessment that led me to grading contracts, which I discuss in Chapters 1 and 2. My own brand of code-meshed English, like everyone's, is a product of my history in schools and growing up in poor and working-class areas, all culturally, linguistically, and racially mixed. I left those discourses behind, or so I thought. The discourse from the academy, the White, middle-class discourse I worked so hard to take on, seemed to give me access and opportunities that I likely wouldn't have had otherwise. But if I'm really honest, my own striving for the dominant English I currently practice started with an impulse not to be poor, not to be seen as stupid, not to be brown, not to be in the outer dikes of the US. I thought I wanted to be White. And this was the lesson that all of my writing assessment ecologies taught me in school.

You see, I was raised on Stats Street in North Las Vegas, the bad part of town, the Black part, a city created by banks' redlining practices. Everyone in my neighborhood, except for one college-aged neighbor, my brother, and me, were Black. We lived in roach-infested, government-subsidized housing. By the later years of elementary school, we'd moved to a White working-class neighborhood on the edge of several Latinx communities in the southeast part of Vegas. We moved from an outer to an inner dike, all the while following the carrot of economic success and the promise of upward mobility, an upward mobility that was easier for us than our Black neighbors on Stats. To my knowledge, we were the only ones from Stats that left. It wasn't easy. We were never accepted in the new community. Inner dikes are socially engineered to Whiten themselves automatically. Our new White working-class neighbors in Pacos Trailer Park explicitly told us on many occasions, often whenever they had the chance, that they didn't want "people like us" living there. They didn't want us brown folks in the trailer park. They used worse language. But I was determined (in all the senses that that word can mean) to stay just long enough to leave, to move in the system of dikes. What was required was school, learning, literacy, the dominant English. This meant "good grades." I didn't understand how docile this made me in school. I didn't understand the internal colonization. I didn't understand how grading by a single standard in all those classrooms of my youth were sending me one message: Be White or be gone. I loved getting good grades in school—I won't lie—but I hated how I had to get them. It was like lying every day until the lies became me, until I couldn't tell anymore what was a lie and what was me.

While I've gained much from my education, I've also given up, or forgotten, much of my own working-class, ghetto, African-American English that I began my schooling with. The aspects of my own *habitus* that I accentuate in my classrooms and scholarly work now are ones of growing up half Japanese and working poor (not working class), and of having a mom who would say she is White, but I'm not convinced she fully believes it. We have Greek, English, and Scottish ancestors on her side. My mom is not fair skinned nor fair haired, but fair enough to pass as (or to be) White in the US today. I never was. She never got a college degree, was single most of my childhood, and worked three jobs so that we could be working poor. She would say to me, "Get good grades," "do the extra credit," "no one asks how you got your A," "a B-student is an A-student who didn't apply himself." She was telling me to labor, to work. My mom is smart, detail-oriented, and beautiful in her work-ethic. She led by example. She labored every day to exhaustion without complaint, often collapsing on the couch late at night. I love my mom, and she always showed her love to me, but she was also stern about grades and school, sometimes to the point of unfairness. I know it was because she didn't want me to do what she had to do, to work and work and work and still never have enough money, or clothes, or food, or time with your family.

The lesson I took from my mom was a simple motto that I carried with me into college and my career: I may not be the smartest guy in the room, but I damn well will be the hardest working one. In college, I made sure I did more work than anyone else. I leaned heavily on the doing of things, tried hard to savor the work, focused on enjoying the labor, since I couldn't always depend on how others would judge the products of my labors. What I realize now is that I slowly over the years turned this motto into a pedagogy, then an assessment practice, which would become labor-based grading contracts. What I also realize now is that I got the first part of my motto wrong. To be judged the "smartest guy in the room" means there's a single standard to judge what smart means. That standard has always been a White racial *habitus*, a White discourse, so of course, by definition, I literally can never be the smartest guy in the room. I cannot be a White guy speaking well, to alter Quintilian's definition of an orator.

Then, there was a point in my adult life when I stopped trying to deny the language of my upbringing, the language of the streets of North Las Vegas, and I moved to retain enough of that old discourse to use as a critical optic or phonic apparatus, as a way to look and listen for the Whiteness around me and in me. I stopped resisting my body's need to move when talking. My body must move with my words, even when write. As I'm typing and reading this now, I am moving my body to feel the sentences, to feel what I need to say. I've been told I'm quite expressive and "passionate" when I speak, or teach, or just shoot the shit with others. This ability to deny a Black discourse and adopt a White discourse is a White privilege I know I have, one I must acknowledge and problematize continually, one I resist, yet know that I am allowed to take advantage of professionally.

I ain't proud of leaving the language of my nurture behind, or trying to leave it behind—a paradox in the problematic, especially when I meet students today who language the way I did back then, when my own feedback to their languaging pressures them toward a White racial *habitus*. Then again, I ain't all

15

White, middle-class *habitus*. I often draw on this in my languaging with students. Another paradox. I claim my Japanese heritage, my dad's family, despite growing up not knowing him at all. Another paradox. My mom is Scottish, English, and some Greek. Imagine that: A Japanese American, usually mistaken for Latino, who started in life speaking African-American English, living in African-American communities, yet speaking mostly Standard White, middle-class English now, and raised by a poor, working mom who sees herself as White. Paradoxes. Like everyone, I code-mesh. This thing you read now is code-meshed. My work with labor-based grading contracts is in part a coming to terms with my own intersectional, racialized educational and linguistic history through my students and their languaging. Knowing these things about me may help you understand just how many grains of salt you should take with what I offer. It should also suggest the ways I honor labor and how deeply I have felt its importance in my life, classroom, and scholarship.

It should also tell you how I might respond to critiques of my use of the term "labor." Some may have problems with the way it is often associated with childbirth, or with manual labor in economies that take advantage of the very populations of students I'm trying to help—am I making light of such activities, some of which are gendered? Some may feel that joining the terms "labor" and "contract" to then create a grading ecology is a contradiction, that the capitalist language of contracts is far from liberatory, and accentuates particular relations of power, usually understood through one's relation to labor and the means of production in capitalist economies. I use the term "labor" because it does have these associations, and I wish to flip its too-often negative connotations. It's a positive word for me, and I try to make it so in my classrooms. My discussion of labor in Chapter 3, I hope, will alleviate some concerns about an uninformed use of an important Marxian term. Finally, labor is a reference to doing things, to acting, to performing, to working in honorable, embodied ways. And it is understood tacitly as an embodied set of practices, not simply intellectual, like much academic "work" is. So I keep the term "labor." When I do my academic "work," I labor. It is generative and creative, hard and painful at times, and always embodied.

And so, labor-based grading contracts is a big part of the methods I use to enact my social justice agenda in my classroom's antiracist writing assessment ecologies. Antiracist writing assessment ecologies are, in a sentence: "a complex political system of people, environments, actions, and relations of power that produce consciously understood relationships between and among people and their environments that help students problematize their existential writing assessment situations, which in turn changes or (re)creates the ecology so that it is fairer, more livable, and sustainable for everyone" (Inoue, *Antiracist* 82). This agenda means I try to create conditions that allow for my writing classrooms to question meaningfully the White racial *habitus* that determines (in the Marxian sense, as in creates limits and boundaries, and applies pressure in a particular direction) standards for the judgment of writing and expectations teachers and others have for languaging. I want my students to have real choices in their labors of languaging. And how do I do this work knowing that my classrooms are always already situated in larger societal and institutional ecologies that determine much of how my students act in my classroom? Their languages will be graded next quarter or semester. Labor-based grading contracts is part of my answer to these questions.

SUMMARY OF CHAPTERS

In rest of this book, I offer two kinds of discussions: a theoretical discussion of grading contracts and labor, and a practical discussion of how to design and use them in literacy classrooms. I find each discussion necessary for the other, but if one is so inclined and accepts the arguments I've made and alluded to in this introduction, then you could skip the early, more theoretical chapters and read the later, more practical chapters, that is, Chapters 4, 5, and 6. This means that some readers may hear some repetition in the chapters' discussions. Part of this is so that readers can jump around, reading single chapters as cohesive and complete discussions. But I'm also resisting a dominant White, academic, linguistic disposition that defines "clarity," "grace," and "eloquence" as a lack of repetition in texts. Repetition can be rhetorically effective. Repetition can slowly reveal the important keynotes in a discussion. Repetition can help a reader feel the ideas more viscerally—feel ideas, not understand them alone. Repetition can help embody—make bodily—otherwise textual arguments. Repetition can be a compassionate, mindful rhetorical practice. And in my case, repetition also satiates my need to help broaden our academic dispositions about language in a counter-rhetorical way, as I've already mentioned above concerning my use of White language supremacy. So, I want you to return to particular ideas through my use of a counter-rhetorical repetition that invites you to be mindful of these ideas, attend to them more frequently, see something deeper in them, or feel more of your relations to them.

In Chapter 1, I offer a discussion of my own problematizing of my classroom assessment situation, which I hope offers a way to see the importance of considering alternatives to conventional, standards-based grading practices in secondary and post-secondary literacy classrooms. This chapter also discusses a way to see one central practice that I believe labor-based grading contracts provides a better ecology for, Freire's problem-posing practice. This theoretical and reflective chapter is one way I've posed problems about grading as a teacher who is trying to be reflective about his grading practices and their consequences to student learning, but it is also a practice that students should be doing in classroom grading ecologies.

In Chapter 2, I narrate my path from conventional grading to hybrid grading contracts to labor-based contracts. This chapter offers the salient research and scholarship I've used over the years to help me understand and come to my own practice. I attempt to explain the differences in various grading contract models available and offer an argument for the strengths of labor-based grading contracts. I discuss the research on grading contracts, but attempt to do so in a way that situates that research and scholarship within my own history of coming to labor-based grading contracts.

In Chapter 3, I theorize labor since it is the foundation for my contract system. Using Marxian theory, I draw an important distinction between the ways we typically value labor, and express that value, in classrooms and other economies, from labor's worth. I propose an understanding of labor as three-dimensional that may help teachers and students problematize their labor as a practice so labor's value and worth can be understood and used meaningfully in classrooms. Using Hannah Arendt's work in *The Human Condition*, mindfulness and contemplative theories, and Barbara Adam's scholarship on conceptions of time, I end the chapter by translating my theory of three-dimensional labor into practice for classrooms, which I call "mindful laboring."

In Chapter 4, I show what my labor-based grading contract looks like and the four main philosophical assumptions that I ask students to work through and respond to when negotiating the contract. This more practical chapter explains how my contract is used in my classroom and discusses a set of framing activities that help students understand and negotiate the contract, then do the reflective work that I'm arguing makes for a more critical and politically conscious ecology for students.

In Chapter 5, I discuss an increasingly important feature of my grading ecologies, our charter for compassion. I adopted the charter several years ago from Karen Armstrong's Charter for Compassion, which was originally designed for such uses among interfaith conflict. I have found that the charter is easily used in a writing class like mine, one that uses a lot of peer feedback and discussion, and directly addresses difficult discussions of race, racism, Whiteness, and White language supremacy. I provide a few ways my students and I think about compassion and negotiate each charter at the beginning of every quarter/semester. I discuss how it fits into my labor-based grading contract ecologies without it being about students' spiritual traditions or about religious proselytizing.

Chapter 6 is a kind of FAQ. The chapter contains fourteen questions concerning the use of labor-based grading contracts that I gathered from various teachers and others from across the US and on the WPA-L. In my view, this chapter does some heavy philosophical and theoretical lifting, particularly around the pedagogical assumptions I hold and that I believe make my version of labor-based grading contract ecologies effective, meaningful, and fair. This chapter's discussion is more practical and less "researchy." It is similar to the conversations I have with teachers over coffee, or dinner, or in Q&A sessions. I consider this chapter mostly practical, not a theory chapter.

In Chapter 7, I discuss the ways I've measured and found my labor-based grading contract ecologies effective. I offer the five primary goals of my own grading ecologies and how I've measured each, and what conclusions I've come to about effectiveness along each goal. These particular goals not only question conventional notions of effectiveness for writing courses and programs, but are ones a teacher might have for their labor-based grading contract ecology. They are the ways I define "effectiveness" in my labor-based grading ecologies. Mostly, the chapter is meant to offer some theoretical and practical guidance toward understanding and assessing effectiveness of a range of labor-based grading contract ecologies.

Finally, in the Coda chapter, I pull back from labor-based grading contracts and conclude the book by thinking about a larger social justice issue that many in the field of composition studies and elsewhere in the academy have become more and more compelled to consider, and see connected to their classrooms. I borrow a question from Ihab Hassan, rehearsed by Mary Rose O'Reilley, which explains the central concern of the chapter: "Is it possible to teach English so that people stop killing each other?" I suggest that perhaps one way to think about how we assess and grade in our literacy classrooms may offer a response to this kind of social justice question, one that attempts to counter the violence we see around us every day.

CHAPTER 1.

PROBLEMATIZING GRADING AND THE WHITE *HABITUS* OF THE WRITING CLASSROOM

> What school amounts to, then, for White and black kids alike, is a 12-year course in how to be slaves. What else could explain what I see in Freshman Class? They've got that slave mentality; obliging and ingratiating on the surface but hostile and resistant underneath. Like black slaves, students vary in their awareness of what's going on. Some recognize their own put-on for what it is and even let their rebellion break through to the surface now and then. Others—including most of the "good students"—have been more deeply brainwashed. They swallow the bullshit with greedy mouths. They honest-to-God believe in grades, in busy work, in general education requirements. They're pathetically eager to be pushed around. They're like those old grey-headed house-niggers you can still find in the South who don't see what all the fuss is about because Mr. Charlie "treats us real good."
>
> —Farber, "The Student as Nigger," p. 3

The problem of assessment in writing classrooms isn't simply a pedagogical one, or one about how to calculate grades, get students to learn, write, and revise their drafts, or listen to feedback. It is a personal problem and an institutional one. It is existential and structural. It is a problem about individuals engaging idiosyncratically with structured language systems that confine and pressure us in uneven power relations, relations that are mediated by our varied racialized, gendered, and linguistic embodiments. So over the years, I have found myself asking questions about my own existential writing assessment situation as a writing teacher. What am I really doing when I read students' papers? What am I doing when I place my words of judgment on them? What am I doing when I grade students' writing? What am I doing when I make present grades in my classroom? I open this chapter with Farber's now classic, and perhaps infamous, sentiment because the problem I began with in my own assessment practices that led to labor-based grading contracts is encapsulated in Farber's text. I've always wanted to unlock the chains around my students' hands and feet. Grades based on my own judgments of quality seemed to be the links in those chains. Farber's argument represents an initial way to see the problematic of judgment in writing classrooms, but it is only where I began.

I did not, however, begin my journey toward labor-based grading contracts by problematizing my judging practices. I started by problematizing grades, which led me to problematize my judgment practices, which then led to problematizing the conditions of White supremacy in my classrooms as an on-going antiracist project. But to understand the real power and critical usefulness of labor-based grading contracts, I need to work backwards a bit, starting with the problematizing of White language supremacy through judgment practices.

This chapter is a representation of my own ongoing exploration of the problematic of judgment in my writing classrooms, which is a problematizing of my own assessment practices as a writing teacher. This problematizing led me to labor-based grading contracts, but it is also a good example of the kind of reflections that I now ask students to do, and that I think are more possible and educative in labor-based grading contract ecologies. This chapter, then, is a way to see my ongoing, Freirean, problem-posing practice as a teacher who tries to continually question his own judging and grading practices, and a demonstration of problematizing judgment that I ask of my students. Its discussion dramatizes the way I came to understand the importance of what I do now, but it is not the story of my coming to labor-based grading contracts. That is Chapter 2. This chapter lays the important groundwork for that chapter, illustrating why such a grading practice builds equity and inclusion in diverse writing classrooms, illustrating why problematizing assessment in writing classrooms is always necessary if we (teachers and students) are trying to do critical work, work that leads to socially just outcomes. This means that this chapter represents various thoughts and questions that continually arise in my ongoing problematizing.

How I came to labor-based grading contracts was a journey about who I am becoming, who my students are becoming, how languaging really becomes in the world, and how that becoming implicates all of us when we judge others' languaging. Like all teachers' practices, my classroom assessment practices say a lot about me, a teacher of color, raised in a poor, single-parent home, and says something about my becoming, about my language becoming, about my teaching becoming.

PROBLEM-POSING AS PRACTICING THROUGH

When I say that in the past I problematized my existential writing assessment situation as a teacher, I do not mean to suggest that I engaged in a formal version of Freire's problem-posing approach to education. As discussed in Freire's *Pedagogy of The Oppressed*, problem-posing education moves through a process of listening to the community outside the classroom, identifying problems or issues, then dialoguing with students using codes, or what Ira Shor calls "a concrete physical representation of a particularly critical issue that has come up during the listening phase" ("Monday Morning" 38). These codes typically are cultural artifacts that embody language, such as media, newspapers, articles, TV shows, movies, plays, etc., that represent many sides of the problem or issue, that reveal the problem as paradoxes. From these codes, students again listen carefully to them in order to describe what they see, hear, and feel, offering their own experiences that relate to those codes, questioning the codes, and of course, moving to articulate things to do as a response (Brown 40–41; Shor, "Monday Morning" 39). This means that problem-posing is an ongoing process. We never leave the problems. We simply *practice through* them and from them constantly.

The natures of the problems posed then are paradoxes, which juxtapose personal choice and agency (choosing and acting in agentive and idiosyncratic ways) within larger structures that make up society, or the social that makes up our histories, context, discourses, and the boundaries within which we all act. I often think of the social structural part of problem-posing paradoxes as Marxian determination as Raymond Williams describes it, or as a "setting of limits" and an "exertion of pressures" (*Marxism* 87). Thus posing problems about my own existential writing assessment situation is articulating paradoxes that complicate how I make judgments, how I read and make meaning of the symbols my students give me and that I give back to them. Freire explains that "[i]n problem-posing education, people develop their power to perceive critically the way they exist in the world with which and in which they find themselves; they come to see the world not as a static reality, but as a reality in process, in transformation" (Freire 83). Thus problem-posing is seeing the paradoxes in the individual's relation to the social and structural. Villanueva offers another way to understand this:

> Freire juxtaposes two philosophical schools, the existentialism of a Jean-Paul Sartre and the structuralism of a Louis Althusser, to arrive at the heady term of problematizing the existential situation. Simply put, existentialism says that the essences of being human is individual freedom. Structuralism says that there are social, political, and economic systems in place that keep us from changing the way things are, systems that keep us from fully exercising our freedom, systems that we see as "natural." The way out . . . is through the problematic, by questioning the things we don't normally question, questioning just how natural the "natural" is. (Villanueva 54)

So to see problem-posing paradoxes is to see through the natural, or to see things that are natural as paradoxes, thus not natural at all, but contrived by determined systems and choices.

Over the years, I've taken this Freirian process of problem-posing and used it as a model for reflecting on how I read student writing, how I produce grades, and what I need to do differently the next semester or quarter as a teacher. I look at my comments and other grading artifacts from my class, and I ask, how natural is grading? How natural are my own judgments and ways of reading? How natural are my standards for good writing or compelling prose? How natural are the things that seem present to me in a student essay, to borrow a concept from Perelman and Olbrechts-Tyteca?[3] How natural is it for me to be the only legitimate judge of student writing in my classrooms? Where did these natural things come from? How did my history of languaging naturalize them? Problematizing my own existential writing assessment situation also helps me decide what data I continually gather from my own classes to help me understand what is happening and how it is working, or what the ecology is doing and producing. It's evidence-based reflection, which is at the heart of problem-posing.

Again, I don't claim to have engaged in a formal process of problematizing my own judgments of student writing, instead my process was informal and constant, which I believe is in the spirit of problem-posing education. I try continually to practice through the problematics of my own classrooms' assessment ecologies. The problems I posed, then, dealt exclusively with the nature of judgment and assessment more generally in my classrooms, and eventually, I called on my students to do this same problem-posing in their own judgments in my classes.

Early on, I figured out one key to problem-posing: *the centrality of articulating and coming to terms with paradox and flux.* This isn't just being comfortable with ambiguity. It is being uncomfortable with equally reasonable ideas and positions that each change over time. It is being restless in one's seat as others sit close and around you, getting up and down, moving from position to position, all the while you too move, sit restlessly, and change seats again. So what follows is one representation of my own problem-posing my own existential writing assessment situation. The codes I used, and continue to use, were my rubrics, writing assignments, grading paraphernalia, syllabi, student writing, and my own comments on students' drafts. I will not offer those codes here because this book is not a direct articulation of that twelve- to fifteen-year process, and I don't have permission to share many of those codes in this book. What I offer

---

3   Perelman and Olbrechts-Tyteca argue that orators and writers make present certain data and elements in a text by selecting them out of the universe of other data and elements possible (116). I'm suggesting that not only do writers make present particular data and elements through selection but that readers make more or less relevant the data selected by a writer. A writing teacher's White racial habitus is key to making relevant selected details of texts, and finding others less relevant or compelling.

below is a representation of that problem-posing process that attempts to keep to the spirit of my real-life, on-going process.

PROBLEMATIZING A WHITE RACIAL HABITUS

Let us return to Farber's startling words. Hearing him call students "niggers" and claim that the way we educate is brainwashing, or making our students obedient and subservient, should make us question everything we writing teachers tend to hold sacred: collaboration, feedback, our grades, and even things like the Framework for Success in Postsecondary Writing, developed jointly by NCTE, CWPA, and the NWP. Could focusing on habits of mind like curiosity, openness, and engagement be a writing course's way of making slaves of our students if we grade them by *our standards and measures* of what it means to be curious, open, and engaged? Do these habits of mind draw uncritically on White racial habits, thus potentially perpetuating White language supremacy if used as a kind of standard or set of expectations for students' work in classrooms? And how do we know what those noncognitive dimensions of students' learning look like? Might they look different in different students, different groups of students, different contexts and schools, different activities? If so, what use is it to name them as such?

Making slaves is making people do what you want them to do for your purposes. Habits of mind focus on students doing particular things, but for whose purposes? Furthermore, for Farber to call our students the n-word, he—perhaps unknowingly—calls our attention to the racialized ways language functions and marks all of us, and how a White racial *habitus* functions in our classroom assessment and grading systems as a slave-making mechanism. What he doesn't say clearly is that all the ways we judge language, even by well-intentioned teachers, are almost always racist and slave-making, almost always White supremacist.

Farber was writing in a particular historical moment of civil rights movements and Vietnam war protests, which made this consenting to systemic evil more conspicuous and perhaps exigent, although I see systemic evil no less exigent today. But Farber calls attention to racialized bodies. And while it isn't clear to me that Farber himself could see the paradox in the Black body as a metaphor for all students and their subject positions in schools, his use of it can reveal this to us. It is a rich metaphor for my own problematizing of grading and assessment in my classrooms.

Historically, the slave body is a paradoxical image. The Black slave body has been historically situated as a commodity with monetary value. It was valuable in this way because it was a source of free labor to the White body. However, this ironically meant that the Black slave body lacked value as a free and independent person, or as a citizen. And yet, the Black slave body is often represented as a valuable source of maternal love and companionship, protection, and friendship toward White slave owners. There is no better account of how such racist ideas worked themselves out in U.S. history than Ibram X. Kendi's, *Stamped from The Beginning*, in particular his sections on Cotton Mather and Thomas Jefferson. In our world, Farber's gesturing toward the Black slave body calls forth White bodies and their value. This is what Kennedy, Middleton, and Ratcliffe call "haunting Whiteness" in the discourses and logics used in contemporary popular culture, education, and social media, and it helps form part of the problematic of classroom writing assessment that I always felt uncomfortable with, even as a student myself, even when I didn't have words for this problem, or understood it as a problematic. Using the image of the Black, slave body as the normative student, because it has a haunting Whiteness behind it that reveals it in relief, is a problematic itself because it's paradoxical.

Drawing on Freud's analysis of the ego, Kennedy, Middleton, and Ratcliffe explain that Whiteness is an identification that functions "as a ghost, a haunting, that feeds on invisibility, nostalgia, and melancholy" (5). This haunting of Whiteness in discourses, then, is enthymematic, "wherein major or minor premises are omitted so that hearers may supply them" (6). Stuart Hall identified a similar kind of rhetorical dynamic, saying that race was a "floating signifier," meaning that references to race are never static or permanent. They float and can mean different things to different people, but audiences or readers must supply that meaning. In Kennedy, Middleton, and Ratcliffe's view, Whiteness is also oxymoronic, meaning it need not be situated in a binary of good and bad, White and Black. Instead, they suggest hearing Whiteness as an "oxymoron, as a rhetorical figure in which two apparently opposing terms or ideas are presented in conjunction with one another in order to generate new meanings," which then "invites us to identify multiple contradictions in discursive uses of Whiteness" (7). Thus the nature of Whiteness is to float. It can mean what people want it to mean. Most important, seeing Whiteness often means seeing paradox.

But Whiteness is not the same as a White racial *habitus* that I've argued constructs racist writing assessments (*Antiracist*). And it may be more accurate to see Farber's use of the Black body and its haunting Whiteness as a Black *habitus* that needs a White *habitus*. For Bourdieu, *habitus* are "systems of durable, transposable, dispositions, structured structures predisposed to function as structuring structures" (Bourdieu, *Logic* 53; San Juan 52). These dispositions are marked on the body as well as in ways of acting and performing. In another place (Inoue, *Antiracist*), I adapt this concept to talk about racial *habitus* more generally in judgment practices, which are structured dispositions associated with local racial formations that, in our society, are placed into hierarchies, like the hierarchy of the White free body standing above the Black slave body. Racial *habitus* function through and mark three social dimensions that affect and shape communication and thinking: linguistic/discursive, material/bodily, and performative (Inoue, *Antiracist* 42). Yet, no matter who you are or what your standards are, if you've made it to the position of writing teacher today, you have taken on a White racial *habitus*, even if only partially. You use this *habitus* to judge the language performances of students. It is *natural* to use it to grade student writing, but is it fair or educative for all students?

Now, I'm not speaking of White skin privilege when I say all teachers use a White racial *habitus* to judge writing. The racial formation one most identifies with or that others identify someone with is not primarily what I'm meaning here, yet it is also not beside the point. We language through and with our bodies, so our bodies mediate our languaging, and thus our various *habitus*, and mediate how that languaging is read, heard, and judged by others. This is why *habitus* references the linguistic, bodily, and performative, even when we only get text to read. We never just read a student's paper. We read students through their papers.

White racial *habitus*, then, are sets of durable, flexible, and often invisible (or naturalized) dispositions to language that are informed by a haunting Whiteness (Inoue, *Antiracist* 47–51). While realizing that Whiteness is not monolithic, floating, most White racial *habitus* invoke at least six traits that the literature on Whiteness identify in various ways as strong, recurring patterns. Drawing on Sara Ahmed's phenomenological approach to Whiteness and Bourdieu's notion of *habitus*, these traits may also be thought of as habits of Whiteness, which are in short:

- an unseen, naturalized, orientation to the world;
- hyperindividualism;
- a stance of neutrality, objectivity, and apoliticality;
- an individualized, rational, controlled self;
- a focus on rule-governed, contractual relationships;
- a focus on clarity, order, and control[4]

In Chapter 7, I offer a fuller discussion of these six habits of Whiteness, which I also call habits of White Discourse. I'll also say more about habits later in this chapter. For judgments or discourse to embody a White racial *habitus*, the

---

4   The literature on Whiteness that I draw on to assemble these six habits of Whiteness that can be seen and heard in White racial *habitus* is discussed most directly in Myser (6–7), Inoue (*Antiracist* 48–49; "Friday Plenary" 147), and Ahmed (153–54, 156). Other sources on Whiteness that offer insight into Whiteness as *habitus* are Barnett, Fannon, Brookhiser, Ratcliffe, and the introduction to Kennedy, Middleton, and Ratcliffe.

expression need not demonstrate all six of the above habits. And seeing White-ness in your own *habitus* does not necessarily mean that you are deploying that *habitus* toward White supremacist ends, but it likely means that White suprem-acy is an outcome in the classroom assessment ecology you participate in because of its presence if you don't explicitly do something to counter that hegemonic.

Therefore, White language supremacy is a condition and outcome, not sim-ply a trait, and is structured in assessment ecologies in such a way as to function simultaneously as an ideal and as the norm. Needless to say, White language supremacy is the structural condition that determines the standards by which literacy practices are judged in most if not all writing classrooms. As socially conscious and ethically minded writing teachers, we may care deeply about not perpetuating White supremacy, and about not being racist in our judgments and grading practices, but the paradox in educational systems is that those sys-tems that we have to work in set limits and exert pressure on us to grade, and to grade by quality, quality that is determined by White racial *habitus* that struc-ture our disciplines and social settings, which hold the most economic and cultural power.

As a problematic, Farber's student as Black slave with a haunting White *hab-itus* becomes a set of contradictions when we apply the metaphor to our class-rooms. These contradictions are generated when we remember that the Black slave body is always next to the White free body. To name a Black slave as the normative student is to invoke a haunting free, agentive, White body as the ideal student too. Farber's purpose is to jolt us into change, perhaps revolutionary change, in schools and writing classrooms. But hearing the haunting of a White body, of the ideal, free-thinking, White student who is not a Black slave, who has no agency, is equally troubling. Hearing the problematic of the free White body as the ideal student preserves tension in how we understand the material realities of diverse students and teachers in writing classrooms. We interpellate ourselves in such places and we ask students to interpellate themselves.[5] These interpellations cause the contradictions. We want our students to be free and agentive, but those concepts are soaked in a White history, and associated with White bodies. No one wants to be a slave. Everyone wants to be free. Does this mean being White is preferable to being Black?

---

5   Louis Althusser defines "interpellation" as a "hail" or a call to the individual that makes the individual a subject. He explains: "all ideology hails or interpellates concrete individuals as con-crete subjects, by the functioning of the category of the subject" (173). Furthermore, "individu-als are always-already subjects" (175–76) since we are born into a world of ideology with rituals before us that constitute the subject as a category of existence, which calls us and we recognize. Interpellation, then, is a way to see habits as always-already a part of the rituals that hail concrete subjects out of discourses and practices—or the process of hailing in assessment ecologies.

I think the trope of student as Black slave satiates many writing teachers' psychological attraction to be altruistic and helpful (including my own). To say that we should see our students as slaves in order to free them is to be the liberator, the revolutionary, the savior, the Michelle Pfeiffer who frees her students of color from their educational bondage and into a liberated life. It is to interpellate ourselves as a Christ-figure. And that's pretty White in all kinds of ways. But what are we freeing our students toward? Why must *we* free *them*? What if it is *us* who are in bondage? What if we, educators and teachers, turned around one day, the scales dropping from our eyes, and realized that we were slaves to rubrics and the giving of grades, of the need to rank ourselves and our students, slaves to disciplinary ways of reading and valuing language that kept us from seeing a wider, more colorful, deeper felt world of languages and logics? Is not this shift of paradigms possible? Are we not creative enough, generous enough, compassionate enough to try on such a paradigm? Farber is saying that students, Black, or White, or Latinx, or Asian, or indigenous, identify themselves as Black bodies, as slaves, as "niggers," and should identify themselves differently, thus they should behave and act differently in schools—they should not take on a Black slave *habitus*. They should be free. On the other hand, teachers must stop constructing classrooms that make slaves of students, and on one very real level, Farber is correct. We should stop making students into slaves.

But let's attend more carefully to the problematic, attend to its haunting Whiteness. What is so bad about being a Black body, about being a slave, about the Black slave *habitus* that we have already constructed for it? What is so natural about slaves as bad, as lacking agency and freedom? Why must the Black body be cast in such a negative way? Why can't our logics and metaphors be illogics and anti-metaphors? Why stick to the binary, a binary system that Kennedy, Middleton, and Ratcliffe ask us to avoid or put aside when making meaning out of Whiteness as a trope in society? From an historical and ethical point of view, it is the Black body, the slave, who has more ethical and admirable ground to stand on. Black slaves in the US endured the evils and unfairness of slavery, without giving up, and in fact, thrived in subtle and subversive ways. Black bodies, former slaves, accomplished many things despite the yoke of past slavery, Jim and Jane Crow, segregation, police brutality, unjust and unfair legal systems, and more. It was Black bodies that led us toward more equitable civil rights in the 1960s, even if not fully realized and rolled back in the following decades. And paradoxically, these Black agents were reacting to White supremacist systems and White racists, all of which cultivated them, provided the contexts to be agentive and ethical.

If this story of writing teachers as slaveholders and students as slaves were a Hollywood movie, the protagonist would be the Black slave (or should be), not the White teacher. This point is debatable, however, since Hollywood loves to recenter antiracist narratives and histories onto White bodies, especially White female bodies. Nevertheless, the moral center of this fictitious film would rest within the slave student. I'm not condoning or romanticizing slavery or being a slave, but I'm also not plugging my ears to the softer, haunting sounds that Farber's analogy invokes. It is not a clean binary historically, and his metaphor works from a haunting White *habitus* that also haunts all writing classrooms in our standards, rubrics, reading, and grading practices, which is part of Farber's point.

As productive as it is, I'm also uneasy with Farber's trope because I feel some things in U.S. history are sacred. Slavery and the n-word are two of them. What I mean is that White students don't get to be called slaves just because they are structurally determined in an educational system of grading. There are degrees to privilege and oppression. The real life and death consequences were and still are much worse for Black Americans. And the n-word is a part of those consequences. Invoking the Black slave body, calling all students the n-word, begins to erase the very real historical legacy of actual Black slaves and their descendants, all of whom live with the consequences of that legacy. Using the trope for all students denies this history and its legacy (ironically while calling upon it to make the point) and underplays the physical, economic, and emotional harm done to Black slaves and their descendants that simply cannot be reproduced in White or other populations.

In *PHD to Ph.D.: How Education Saved My Life*, Elaine Richardson offers her response as a student in a class in which Farber's essay was assigned.[6] She offers a cogent way to understand Farber's use of the n-word as a metaphor for students. After hearing from the class and teacher about Farber's argument, Richardson thinks to herself, *"How in the hell can the author prove that these Whitebread students have been niggered? This is a joke"* (202; emphasis in original). This comes near the end of her book that traces Richardson's own struggles with drugs and prostitution in poor, Black communities that have unique, structural antecedents that exist mainly in Black communities, and that come from White supremacist systems. What she gets at so concisely is that one cannot claim that the relatively privileged, White students at any college or university are "niggered," that the material, bodily, and structural conditions are not remotely the same. Our racial *habitus* matter. The "joke" here is that the analogy is harmful because it erases the very real structural problems of being Black in America.

Part of these problems is the way the writing of Black students like Richardson are judged and graded through their own *habitus*, which she ends this passage on. She gets a "B-" on her paper and an accusation that she plagiarized the paper (203). While she doesn't say it, I see her implying a contrast: "You want

---

6   I thank Virginia Schwarz for reminding me of this passage in Richardson's excellent book.

to see how a student can be a nigger, she's asking? Look at me (Richardson). Look how I get treated, look how my *habitus* dictates the assessment ecology I must live in. I write a great paper and get accused of a crime. That's being a nigger." So the problematic of classroom writing assessment, centered on the Black slave body that I'm discussing here is not only paradoxical in a number of ways, but dangerous to explore in particular directions, without a conscious acknowledgement of where our metaphors come from, the haunting White *habitus* informing their logics, and the very different consequences they have for different racialized bodies and languages in our classrooms.

As a way to form another oxymoronic juxtaposition to Farber, one that brings more nuance to the problematizing of judgment and grading, consider Dead Prez's "They School," a song that is critical of the school to prison pipeline in Black, urban communities, critical of what is taught in schools and how it's taught. The song embodies in African-American English a problematic through the stance and voice of the Black body speaking about Black schools in the US. The song's orientation and political agenda too are a problematic because stick. man (Khnum Muata Ibomu) and M-1 (Mutulu Olugbala) embody the voices of liberation through, even because of, oppressive, racist educational systems. The oppressive system helped make them more critical, even while oppressing them. They refuse to let the system create slaves out of them, yet they are a consequence of the system. Their reaction to it is to be revolutionary, to resist. These paradoxes are heard in the song:

> School is like a 12 step brainwash camp
> They make you think if you drop out you ain't got a chance
> To advance in life, they try to make you pull your pants up
> Students fight the teachers and get took away in handcuffs
> And if that wasn't enough, then they expel y'all
> Your peoples understand it but to them, you a failure
> Observation and participation, my favorite teachers
> When they beat us in the head with them books, it don't
>   reach us
> Whether you break dance or rock suede Adidas
> Or be in the bathroom with your clique, smokin reefer
> Then you know they math class ain't important 'less you
>   addin up cash
> In multiples, unemployment ain't rewardin
> They may as well teach us extortion

> You either get paid or locked up, the principal is like a warden
>
> In a four-year sentence, mad niggas never finish
>
> But that doesn't mean I couldn't be a doctor or a dentist

And the song ends with a direct call to its listeners:

> Cuz for real, a mind is a terrible thing to waste
>
> And all y'all high class niggas with y'all nose up
>
> Cuz we droppin this shit on this joint, fuck y'all
>
> We gon speak for ourselves
>
> Knowhatimsayin? Cuz see the schools ain't teachin us nothin
>
> They ain't teachin us nothin but how to be slaves and hard
> workers
>
> For White people to build up they shit
>
> Make they businesses successful while it's exploitin us
>
> Knowhatimsayin? And they ain't teachin us nothin related to
>
> Solvin our own problems, knowhatimsayin?
>
> Ain't teachin us how to get crack out the ghetto
>
> They ain't teachin us how to stop the police from murdering
> us
>
> And brutalizing us, they ain't teachin us how to get our rent
> paid
>
> Knowhatimsayin? They ain't teachin our families how to
> interact
>
> Better with each other, knowhatimsayin? They just teachin us
>
> How to build they shit up, knowhatimsayin? That's why my
> niggas
>
> Got a problem with this shit, that's why niggas be droppin
> out that
>
> Shit cuz it don't relate, you go to school the fuckin police
>
> Searchin you you walkin in your shit like this a military
> compound
>
> Knowhatimsayin? So school don't even relate to us
>
> Until we have some shit where we control the fuckin school
> system
>
> Where we reflect how we gon solve our own problems

Them niggas ain't gon relate to school, shit that just how it is

Knowhatimsayin? And I love education, knowhatimsayin?

But if education ain't elevatin me, then you knowhatimsayin
    it ain't

Takin me where I need to go on some bullshit, then fuck
    education

Knowhatimsayin? At least they shit, matter of fact my nigga

this whole school system can suck my dick, BEEYOTCH!!

The paradoxes of a Black body in an educational system that doesn't value that body is evident throughout the song, yet Dead Prez construct a compelling value to their own Black bodies despite this system. In the first stanza above, the first line identifies the school system as a "12 step brainwash camp," yet the speakers made it out, brains unwashed. They understand the educational system as "they schools," not "my schools," hence the line in the concluding stanza about controlling their own schools in order to "solve our own problems." By the end of the first stanza, the speaker proclaims the "four-year sentence" of "they schools" that "mad niggas never finish," "[b]ut that doesn't mean I [or mad niggas] couldn't be a doctor or a dentist." A paradox based at its core on the judgment of students: flunked out students who could be doctors or dentists. They may not have finished but they ain't dumb.

And assessment of racialized students is equally present in the song. When the Black male voice says, "Your peoples understand it but to them, you a failure," he invokes a binary: Black students struggling against the brainwashing, White system, struggling against the educational system that means to control them, control how they act and dress—control their *habitus*—but unsuccessfully. It's a system that judges, that interpellates them already as failures that Dead Prez recognize and name. The subject is the Black body embodying agency, making his own decisions despite the consequences and because of the system. Part of their agency comes from resisting the unjust educational system they grew up in. Juxtaposed to being judged as failures is "[o]bservation and participation, my favorite teachers." So despite, and even because of, the oppressive White system that determines failure for the Black body, the Black male voices of stic.man and M-1 declare their own agency and choice to learn against or in spite of it through observing and participating.

What "They School" says about the college writing classroom is directly related to the *habitus* there and not there. Consider the paradoxes of the Black, male subject position and African-American English in any writing course. Who is a "mad nigga" who don't finish in a writing classroom? What he look like? What a

33

mad nigga sound like in that classroom or in writing? Do a mad nigga's voice get graded favorably? The figure of the mad nigga begs the question: how you gonna liberate someone if you don't let em pose they own problems in they own words?

Many years ago, I realized I didn't actually have any empirical sense of whose writing I was using as examples in my classrooms on a week to week basis, or over the course of a semester. I always kept careful records of whose writing I used, so I did some research and math from my own record-keeping. What I found out was that despite my own good intentions, despite my own subject position as a teacher of color, despite my constant striving to enact antiracist pedagogies, the vast majority of examples I used in writing classrooms came from White female students—almost exclusively. Part of this problem was structurally determined in the schools I taught at, where most of the English majors and students were women. But it ain't like I didn't have students of color in my classrooms, or White men. I was simply choosing examples that best helped me teach the class, that offered the best examples of the kind of writing I wanted to see all my students emulate. What I didn't see clearly was that I was also articulating the learning of the course and the ideal student as White female *habitus*. I was an agent of the White language supremacy I was fighting against. How could my students be liberated if most of them were tacitly being told to take on a different *habitus* just to do the work of the course? How could they pose their own problems if I wasn't allowing them to use their only languages? How could my classroom be anything by "They classroom" to my students of color?

I hear another paradox in Dead Prez's song, one that connects the existential to the structural. At least in a U.S. context, but likely globally, a Black masculinity carries a haunting White subjectivity behind it, the kind that Farber assumes in his account of the preferred classroom student-agent. For Dead Prez, this haunting Whiteness is not in a student but is the educational system. And it ain't haunting at all. They name it and criticize it. Unlike Farber's slave student, these mad niggas see clearly the problem with the system. Dead Prez changes the ideal student to be Black and in the struggle for material, economic, and psychological freedom, a struggle that is the problematic of education for Black students. They reveal the structural determination in schools and how students are judged by so-called merit.

This paradox is then formed by juxtaposing the determination of White standards and systems next to the Black male body as "mad nigga," performed and referenced in the song. In the second stanza above, which is the closing to the song, it turns away from critique and toward possible systemic solutions, which calls forth the haunting White systems that Black students struggle through. The stanza is spoken like a sermon or monologue, and incorporates cues to a call and response rhetorical strategy (antiphony) that is common in African-American rhetoric (Sale

41; Smitherman, *Talking* 104) through the use of the repeated, "knowhatimsayin," which begs for an audience response, even if only private. Unlike the slave student in Farber's code, the mad nigga subjectivity embodied in this code, which is aural and textual, flips the term "nigga," or signifies on it, changing it to something more positive, another common African-American rhetorical practice (Gates; Smalls; Smitherman, *Black Talk*). Through the defiant "mad nigga" who critiques the White system, acts against it, and proposes alternative goals for schools, ones more socially-oriented and locally beneficial to Black communities, the song conjures a Black subject quite opposed to the Black slave body that Farber uses.

Mad niggas aren't slaves who don't see their own bondage, or are subservient. They are defiant Black bodies that critique and speak out against the problems in their schools and classrooms on their own terms and propose alternatives that center schools on Black communities and their needs, yet they do not succeed in the White system or society very easily. Their speech and their bodies do not have enough power to make such changes easily. And they don't wish to succeed in a White hegemonic state. In fact, it could be argued that the song sows seeds for destroying much of that White hegemonic state.

The second stanza above begins with the individual problem ("Cuz for real, a mind is a terrible thing to waste"). The existential problem is the individual mind that is wasted in a White supremacist educational system that denies the Black body, and thus denies the Black mind. The paradox is that if you succeed, if you allow yourself to be brainwashed, then you become "high class niggas with y'all nose up." You give up your Black madness for Whiteness, a Whiteness that Dead Prez knows is not fully attainable. It's more than simply selling out. It's giving up. Their response is to say, "fuck y'all/ We gon speak for ourselves." One could read this as writing off those Black students who decide to take on White racial *habitus*, to become educated in the White supremacist system. One might also see this as a juvenile language game: "fuck you, I don't care about you." But I think it is more. The "we" who Dead Prez speak for is the Black community at large, a communal we, but the problem begins with the individual mind wasted. The problematic here, as I hear and feel it, is in the way the individual Black mind and body are connected to the larger Black community. These lines acknowledge a contradiction in an individual's choice to succeed in a White supremacist educational system that tends to destroy Black communities. Succeeding in a White supremacist system becomes a purely individualistic and selfish act. And those who choose to go along ignore the consubstantial nature of their roots to their community. They just looking to get theirs, not uplift the community.[7]

---

7   This same pattern of individual education equating to uplifting the Black community can be seen in Rhea Estelle Lathan's account of African-American literacy activism in places like the Sea Islands Citizenship School in the 1950s and '60s.

Of course, this too is a paradox. In a contemporary classroom, where a standard is dictated out of necessity by a teacher, who statistically speaking is White and embodies a White racial *habitus*, mad niggas don't never succeed. They ain't gonna make no grades, and thus don't usually have the power to uplift their communities. They may not always be shamed for using the kind of African-American English that Dead Prez use, or be punished for using antiphony or signifying practices, but with these habits, with a Black racial *habitus*, comes what Smitherman calls a "Black Cultural Sensibility" ("God" 832). She is drawing on Imamu Amiri Baraka. Baraka explains the idea: "[i]t means a quality of existence, of actual physical disposition perhaps in its manifestation as a tone and rhythm by which people live, most often in response to common modes of thought best enforced by some factor of environmental emotion that is exact and specific" (Baraka 172; qtd. in Smitherman, "'God'" 833). So "fuck y'all/ We gon speak for ourselves" could be a way to express the communal Black stance of a mad nigga who isn't thinking (just) about himself, who is careless about his own safety, yet more careful about his community's well-being. Then again, mastering the dominant White code could be a way to gain some power in order to make changes in the White hegemonic system. Gotta have power and position in the system to make changes in it. Yet again, once one takes on a White racial *habitus,* it's your *habitus*, and becomes part of your values and dispositions, which makes finding fault in it harder to see and feel. Lots of shit you found fault with earlier becomes natural and good when it's our habits you're looking at. Our *habitus* are paradoxically natural to us. Thus, mad niggas be mad niggas because they were already hailed as "niggers" by White society and its haunting White racial *habitus*, but took agentive, care(ful)less action to become mad niggas.

Initially, fifteen or so years ago, I wanted to "liberate" my students from slavish ideas, attitudes, behaviors, and dispositions to language, much like Farber seems to suggest. I wanted them to be free of the narrow, White, middle-class standards that all the writing classrooms they'd experienced before mine held against them, much like those that Dead Prez might critique, but I see now that this urge to liberate my students from their assumptions about language, to liberate their bodies by liberating their languaging, is really a problematic itself, a paradox. It ain't all right, but it ain't all wrong either. It is an uncomfortable network of propositions in which I still dwell out of necessity. White language supremacy is the conditions in which we all live—it is the system of education that interpellates us as writing teachers—no matter our pedagogies. The paradoxes are in the nature and context of my own judgments of my students' writing and what I think those judgments can do for them in antiracist ecologies that work in larger racist ecologies. My judgments too often invoke a haunting White *habitus* when placed on my students' writing. I ain't White, but I embody White *habitus*. My judgments might be heard as an oxymoronic juxtaposition, as an echo chamber that offers the sounds of the world from a different location on the landscape, a location that many of my students do not share with me because we do not share the same racialized and gendered *habitus*. It ain't bad to give them that perspective, a part brown, part White male interpellated subject position.

But how can I not use the mostly hegemonic *habitus* I embody when I read anything without it turning to White language supremacy, when White supremacy is the condition in which I can even succeed as a teacher or scholar? We all need biases in order to read. We only have our biases to read from, to make meaning from. How can I not use my own racialized *habitus*, that draws on Whiteness itself, in my reading practice of students' writing, in grading? How can I share the good, powerful things that this White racial *habitus* has given me, the insights and access, without reinscribing the supremacy of a White racial *habitus*? I sit, restless, with these questions always, ready to get up and move. I know it's not just about good intentions. I want to be a mad nigga too, but I know that is not fully possible either.

Despite Dead Prez's critique of schooling, to be colonized brings with it some benefits of the colonizer, if you can struggle through the colonizing. And yet, there are losses with those gains: cultural, linguistic, emotional. The educational system has been good to me, which makes me feel at times guilty for any success I might claim. Again, more paradoxes. These same educational conditions provided for me as a teacher of color who grew up in the same kind of Black ghettos (North Las Vegas) that Dead Prez speak of, that Richardson struggled through. This is part of my problematic, contradictions in my own languaging and how it was judged in school that has placed me in the position I'm in today, a colonizing position that tries to decolonize by my own colonizing judgments, which I think is more good than bad, yet still a bit bad. There are no answers to the problematic, just more paradoxes within paradoxes, more restless sitting and moving, more practicing through.

DETERMINED PROBLEMATICS OF DOCILE BODIES

A more equivocal way to hear my problematic developed from Farber and Dead Prez may be heard through Foucault's *Discipline and Punish*. Let me start with a claim that is similar to Farber's claim and comes out of Foucault's critique of docile bodies: Our classroom assessment ecologies discipline our students in determined ways, ways that are constrained yet still have some degree of choice in them. So to say classroom assessment spaces discipline our students by constraining and pressuring them is to say that our assessment ecologies, which loosely is everything we do around student writing, is a determined docile-making ecological place.

Foucault describes several aspects of disciplining and punishing that make docile bodies. Allow me to translate Foucault's discussion from prisons, factories, and hospitals to schools, and to the typical college writing classroom's assessment ecology. To create a determined docile-making place, the teacher must employ the "art of distributions," which amounts to constructing enclosures for bodies (141), then partitioning those enclosures so that each student may have their own designated place (143). Desks, individual papers or assignments, rubrics, scoring guides, writing groups, and grades all do this enclosing and partitioning. But these enclosures and partitions also need to be useful, functional (143–44)—that is, there is a larger, organizational reason for having students write individual papers or receive individual grades, or sit in "their own desks," or have a teacher rank their drafts by so-called quality that is further partitioned by points or numbers or letters, each meaning something different. These enclosures, or spaces, are useful to the ecology, teacher, even the students. It could be to get grades for certification, or achieve a high GPA, or graduate, or know how well you are doing, or acquire a degree, or manage a large classroom, or keep track of the progress of many students, or even to learn. These enclosures categorize students and their performances out of constructed necessity, another oxymoron. Educational institutions require such enclosures and partitioning, so it is necessary to some degree for teachers and students, yet that institutional necessity is not natural but constructed, since there are other ways to teach and learn, perhaps without enclosures or partitions. Most important, these enclosures are determined by the educational system and so seem natural.

Years ago, it was critical for me to ask of my own assessment ecologies: What enclosures do I make? What enclosures does my institution make for me to use? What purposes does my school have for these enclosures? What are their purposes in my classroom's assessment ecology? How do they actually function (a much harder question to answer)? What are their effects on my students and their learning? What are their effects on me as a teacher or reader? How might my classroom do without some or all of them and still achieve our goals?

Consider grades, since that is what this book is about. Grades are a kind of enclosure. They create partitions around groups of students. A-students, B-students, C-students, etc., or types of performances, A-papers, B-papers. These grades are hierarchical in nature, and create hierarchical partitions. Because we have to grade things, because at least part of our purposes for reading student writing is to put grades on that writing or give the student a final course grade at some point, grades orient us toward students and the products of their work, papers, assignments, etc. It even orients us toward their labor, what it takes to produce that paper, even though we usually do not see or have access to much of that labor. We think in terms of grades. This is a high B-paper. That is an average C-paper. But these grades are based on judgments that we make from our own determined and naturalized *habitus*. These grade-enclosures interpellate students and teachers in subtle ways, over time, as a student acquires more and more of them on their writing. How productive is this orientation and interpellating? What other, perhaps more productive, orientations might there be for us or our students?

This enclosing and the creation of hierarchies that hurt students, particularly students of color and multilingual students, was the first thing I felt, saw, and heard in my own schooling, then in my teaching. Making and working in hierarchical partitions is what we do in writing classrooms mostly. It's all Aristotle did, partition rhetoric. At every turn, we academics and teachers are confronted with a world of partitions. It seems so natural, and the necessity of this partitioning seems reasonable. Shouldn't each student know how well they are doing, where they land in the hierarchy? Shouldn't students know what kind of writer they are, how close or far away from the passing grade they may be? I don't think these are easy questions to answer, but they are reasonable. They may only seem easy to answer because we all grew up in graded classrooms. It's all most of us know—it seems so natural to think in hierarchical terms. It comes natural to us. I'm reminded of my years practicing Kung Fu (Gung Fu) in Las Vegas as a teenager, and then later in college. There were no grades, just practicing. The evaluations that my sensei or sifu[8] gave were verbal and kinesthetic. "Watch me. Do it this way." He would demonstrate, then, "you try now." As I would try a new movement or form, my sifu would literally place his hand on my arm, waist, or leg, move it where it should go, turning my body in the proper directions. "Feel that? That is how it should feel. Try again." When I was ready to move on, there were no grades or exams, sifu simply said, "okay, you are ready. Time to move on to a new form." There were no grade-partitions, yet the system has worked for centuries to teach and learn. Half the dojos I was a part of didn't even have belt systems, a set of hierarchical enclosures that discipline students.

I'm sure it is not surprising to anyone what I am saying, that conventional classroom assessment systems are hierarchical and categorical, that students move around in the provided spaces to some degree, and each space or enclosure means something in the system, and they interpellate those who move or circulate in the system. We know this is at least unnecessary, perhaps even harmful to many students, as others before me have highlighted, particularly around grades

8   Sensei is the Japanese honorific word for teacher, and is the typical way to address one's teacher in Karate and other Japanese forms of martial arts. Sifu is the Cantonese version of the word used in Chinese forms of Kung Fu, and means master.

(Bleich; Elbow "Grading," "Ranking," "Taking," Kohn). So why do we keep doing this? We must see some benefit in this kind of ecology. In some ways, I want to believe that many of us who see this problem but do nothing about it, do so much the way Dead Prez speak of mad niggas. We are careless, or is it careful? Perhaps we feel enclosures are still more necessary than detrimental. Perhaps we think our students need them more than those enclosures hurt them. But why? What evidence do we actually have for such acquiescence in our own schools?

Foucault would say that students "may traverse [these intervals or spaces] one after the other" (145–46). He called this mobility of bodies, this disciplining through interchangeable spaces, as "an art of rank, a technique for the transformation of arrangements. It individualizes bodies by a location that does not give them a fixed position, but distributes them and circulates them in a network of relations" (146). It is a reward system that creates individuals to be rewarded through their ability to move around in the system from one partition to the next, one enclosure to the next. It encourages consent on an individual basis in the system by holding out some carrot or reward down the road, which is actualized and reinforced by mobility in the system, the moving from space to space by individuals. Moving up or around in the educational system of the classroom means you are getting somewhere, so you consent as long as you keep getting somewhere. The most used carrot is a grade. The important thing is that the big carrot is down the road. The ultimate reward is never quite now. That's what keeps folks in their place, consenting and docile. That's what allows students of color to be internally colonized. *They* may have all failed but *I* will be the exception!

This may be what fools many writing teachers into thinking it's okay to grade in their classrooms, that grading is still helping *their* students even if grading otherwise is bad. Grading is bad, but it ain't bad when I do it. My students are moving in the system, getting better, achieving higher grades, grades we invented, grades I determined. In a U.S. context, this art of rank feeds on the myth of meritocracy, the bootstraps myth. As long as we are moving from space to space in the ecology, there is a feeling of upward mobility, a feeling that we are making it on our own, a feeling of development and growth, by our own merits and talent. But of course, a student does not get a grade by themselves. It requires a grader to give them a grade, no matter how that grade is determined. Let us not fool ourselves. A grade is equal parts student *habitus*, written artifact, and grader *habitus* translated into judgment practices.

Through the use of enclosures and rewards, our classroom assessment ecologies alienate students from each other and potentially larger, more rewarding purposes for their mutual labors in schools. Partitioning turns education into a purely private enterprise, a selfish act of grade accumulation. Ain't no room for mad niggas with larger, socially conscious and communal purposes. The contradictions between the individual and the communal, between educating the individual and educating for the community, is no better seen than in the contradictions between Farber's vision and Dead Prez's, the difference between slaves as paradox and mad niggas as paradox.

But there is more to this disciplining, more to the making of a determined, docile-making assessment ecology. Foucault says that often part of disciplining is controlling bodily activities by establishing, imposing, and regulating cycles, rhythms, and processes that bodies or students do (149). This includes imposing particular gestures and bodily movements, and imposing "the best relation between a gesture and the overall position of the body" (152). The gestures that we impose on students often are linguistic, but really we are talking about movements of bodies more than we're talking about static drafts, despite the fact that it is the drafts that get graded. This is why I tend to use the noun, "language," as a verb. *Languaging* is gesturing which comes from dispositions to do particular actions, all of which are a part of our *habitus*. Our languaging is a product of our racial *habitus*, among other social dimensions. And dialectically, the racial *habitus* we share influence us.

This aspect of Foucauldian disciplining of bodies is what makes judging the Black *habitus* so fraught with problems in conventional writing assessment ecologies and classrooms. Our bodies are already integrated into larger social systems that are racialized and hierarchized. The languaging that these bodies do gets associated with those bodies. Patterns emerge. Language becomes racialized. Language becomes—is always becoming—*habitus*. And so our languaging is, of course, discursive, material or bodily, and performative in nature, and these dimensions of it are the places we draw on to judge and measure language performances in classrooms. Others have already discussed the ways language is racialized and are judged tacitly in racial terms (Greenfield; Inoue, "Friday Plenary," *Antiracist*; Lippi-Green; Villanueva, "Blind"), so I'll leave this connection between our socially constructed and historically evolving notions of race and racial formations to language at this, but emphasize the centrality of a White racial *habitus* in judgment in all writing classrooms through its use as both the norm and the ideal. Anything else begins to be mad, abnormal, less than ideal.

The discipline of Rhetoric and Composition actually already works from the assumption that writing classrooms discipline bodies, making them into our own images, our own White *habitus*. The terms now in fashion actually make this bodily assumption much more present and come from the same Old French and Latin roots that *habitus* does. Our major organizations and conferences have turned to thinking about "habits of mind," which are more flexible and transferrable for unknown, future contexts of languaging. Habits of mind share more with noncognitive domains than the cognitive ones we've come to measure in writing assessments of all types, which tend to be thought of as "direct evidence" of learning in writing classrooms, but are really only the products of that learning (I'll say more about noncognitive dimensions and assessing effectiveness of labor-based grading systems in Chapter 7). Learning is the activity, the doing, a verb. Essays and portfolios are the products of that learning, a noun.[9] We never have full access to students' learning, only to the products of that learning. This is another reason we should be skeptical of grades that purport to say something about students' learning. They aren't the learning, and they only can be an indirect measure of the products of the practices of learning, not that actual learning, which is bodily and experiential.

There is more to consider in habits of mind in writing classrooms though. All the early English references to "habit" given in the OED, which begins as early as the thirteenth century, show the word to mean clothing, apparel, and monastic attire, and the original Latin and Old French origins of the word tend to mean: to have or hold oneself, as in an outward demeanor or appearance to others ("habit"). Habits are material, marking our bodies for others to read. In its original usage, habits, imply a reader of those habits, or one who beholds those habits. Thus any description of those habits, like our evaluations of student writing, likely says more about the beholder than what is being beheld or read. Even if we think of habits as unconscious, repetitive practices, habits are still embodied. People do habits. Texts do not. And yet, people also embody their habits. Habits, like Bourdieu's *habitus*, are marked on the body, and mark the body, and they are durable, transposable dispositions, meaning they resist erasure and change or evolve with the changing ecologies in which that body circulates. Like ourselves and language itself, our *habitus* is always becoming. The paradox here is that if all languaging is becoming, then it is both evolving and beautiful.

This is not simply a play on words. I mean it in the way V. N. Volosinov describes the historical nature of language systems and utterances. He's responding to Saussure's ideas about *langue* and *parole*, that there's a distinction between a language system and various concrete, idiosyncratic utterances that deviate from that system. And this debate about whether there can be a language system that is outside of individual utterances, an ideal or even a norm, is exactly at the center of grading practices and the role of judgment in writing classrooms. Volosinov describes language as "a ceaseless flow of becoming," arguing that there is no *langue*, only *parole*, only the historically idiosyncratic that continually evolves (66). *Habitus* also are historically situated and evolve over time and in contexts.

9   It may also be useful to note that the word "essay" comes from the French word (essayer), "to try," which Michel de Montaigne helped coin.

There is no static or universal—no *langue*—no single White racial *habitus*, only historically situated, idiosyncratic instantiations. *Habitus*, including White racial *habitus*, is plural and continually evolving.

Second, I mean that *habitus* are becoming in the sense that the word also means being comely, or "fair, beautiful, nice." Becoming and comely have the same roots in the Old English *cýme / cýmlic* (come), and in Middle High German, *komlich / komenlich*, as well as early modern Dutch *komlick / komelick* ("comely") (*OED Online*). The point is, to be comely, or to become, invokes a way to appreciate all *habitus* in material ways on their own terms. Comely originally referred mostly to physical beauty or delicateness. Our writing classrooms might see and strive to understand the ways that, for instance, Dead Prez' African-American English does what it does so compactly and elegantly, on its own terms. As an historically situated, idiosyncratic Black *habitus*, mad niggas be becoming. If all *habitus* are becoming, then it is difficult to justify a preferred *habitus* in writing classrooms for any other reason than the one given in the CCCC's Statement on Students' Right to Their Own Language, which refers to a CCCC's Executive Committee resolution passed in 1972:

> Language scholars long ago denied that the myth of a stan-
> dard American dialect has any validity. The claim that any one
> dialect is unacceptable amounts to an attempt of one social
> group to exert its dominance over another. Such a claim leads
> to false advice for speakers and writers, and immoral advice
> for humans. (Committee on CCCC Language Statement 2–3)

What I am suggesting here is not just that all *habitus* are becoming, but that writing teachers' and programs' inability to value all *habitus*—and it is an *inability* to do so—because of the way their assessment ecologies are structured, amount to one social group exerting its dominance over others. It is, as the resolution states, immoral. It is racist. It is White supremacist. It is how writing teachers perpetuate White language supremacy. To put this another way, because we live in a White-dominant society, and our dominant Englishes have historical White racial roots in White racial formations in the US, coming from White racial *habitus*, not to value all *habitus*, or to punish students for not demonstrating a dominant one, is to enact racist writing assessments, White supremacist ones. Our ways of valuing and assessing must reflect how all languaging from all *habitus* are always already becoming. They are historically evolving and discursively, bodily, and performatively comely. And yet, this need to assess diverse student writing in equitable ways, socially just ways, is a paradox itself, a problematic. Shall we all go back to some past "babel" time where we speak differently, unable to communicate fully with each other? Are there no linguistic dispositions that we can agree upon to use for particular academic or professional reasons?

For good reasons, the field generally has dispensed with thinking that the products of writing processes are the most important things to focus on in writing classrooms and perhaps even in our feedback or evaluation practices; however, I'd argue we haven't addressed how to do that second part yet. The rest of this book attempts one way to do it. Nevertheless, we now focus on habits of mind, dispositions to language in particular ways that are marked on the body, in how we perform language, and in texts. But just because our field has reoriented itself to habits of mind, and perhaps our pedagogies too, it doesn't mean we've reoriented our assessment ecologies. This requires a continual problematizing of them. Our disciplinary values appear to be concerned with students' bodies, their movements, their performing, their languaging, their *habitus*. We are in the business of making *habitus*, and all *habitus* are racialized, gendered, sexed, classed, among other socially constructed dimensions, but many of us don't want to talk about these things with how we judge words.

And so, disciplining students in writing classrooms means not only that we create enclosures, allow movement between those enclosures, but by focusing on habits of mind (and body), focusing on the *habitus* of our students, we also define the best movements or articulations of the body in motion, how to write, how to read, how to engage in polite and respectful conversation in class, how to revise a draft, how to say things, even how to pronounce words. This means we assess languaging, all of it, mind, body, emotions, performance. But do we all have ways to make visible and judge fairly the movement of bodies in the practices of learning to write? Our work as writing teachers ain't never been just about words.

This leads us to Foucault's final element in the creation of docile bodies, the principle of "exhaustive use," or "non-idleness." Foucault describes it this way: "Discipline . . . arranges a positive economy; it poses the principle of a theoretically ever-growing use of time: exhaustion rather than use; it is a question of extracting, from time, ever more available moments and, from each moment, ever more useful forces" (154). This is the maximizing of bodily labor and movements, of being efficient and productive, of learning all you can, that is, learning as much as you can, getting the most of the class. Can you hear the metaphors of quantity and efficiency? We might see this disciplining through the ways teachers expect particular purposes from revisions and other labors in and outside of class, or what we expect as products of such labors, or how much change in a draft we expect from revisions because, well, we talked about that in our feedback.

Often we expect students to "use their time wisely," and "productively," which Richard Brookhiser identifies as traits of WASPness that are inherited from Benjamin Franklin.[10] Brookhiser calls them "industry" (17) and "usefulness" (19). Surely, these assumptions that build the discourses of judgment in our assessment ecologies, that can easily be heard in the habits of mind articulated in the Framework for Success in Postsecondary Writing, are not all bad, but are they all good when used to grade students? Should they be used to rank students, create partitions and enclosures, to interpellate? How natural should they be in our classrooms' assessment ecologies? Should we not problematize them with students?

But how do we create the right conditions to examine the very *habitus* and languages we use to communicate in ecologies that will produce grades and potentially use the very habits we want to investigate as expectations for quality in the class? How do we evaluate students' critiques on the very dimensions of literacy we hold them to? Do we force our movements on students and attempt to extract the most from their time and labors? Is this unfair to some students? Does it privilege others? And how do we, then, promote all students' rights to their own languages in our assessment ecologies when one standard is often demanded of our classrooms, or when others outside our classrooms do not understand the racism in such a single standard? How can a writing assessment ecology not have a standard by which we judge student writing? Does it mean that we have no standards—is this "mad nigga" thinking? Does it mean that we must return to the fall of Babel, to a world filled only with uneasy and contentious cacophonies, and not soothing, euphonious harmonies? Or is that a lie, a myth we have told ourselves too, made natural so that we can move on, do our jobs, feel good about them, and sleep at night.

STILL PRACTICING THROUGH

The trouble in much problematizing of writing assessment and judgment is that we can fool ourselves into thinking that we are so damned altruistic. That it is just about being fair. We certainly do not teach writing for the money, and we don't want to be unfair—but *being fair* and *not being unfair* ain't the same thing. In writing assessment ecologies, these two positions work from different

10   The term "WASP" has come to mean "White, Anglo-Saxon Protestant" by the middle of the twentieth century. When describing the group of people who have controlled the political, economic, and cultural centers of the US, the political scientist Andrew Hacker defined WASP this way in 1952: "they are white, they are Anglo-Saxon in origin, and they are Protestant (and disproportionately Episcopalian). To their Waspishness should be added the tendency to be located on the Eastern seaboard or around San Francisco, to be prep school and Ivy League educated, and to be possessed of inherited wealth" (1011).

assumptions about the default settings of the institution, discipline, language values, and society. If a writing teacher designs their assessment ecologies by trying to be fair to all their students, they likely will assume that treating everyone the same, judging them by the same standard, is fair. Fairness means everyone has access to the system in the same way, but everyone does not have access to the system in the same way. Everyone is not located in the system in the same place.

So the position that I find preferable is to design assessment ecologies by *trying not to be unfair*, which works from a different assumption: that the systems we circulate in, like our classrooms, departments, schools, disciplines, and society are not inherently fair to everyone. They are structured in such a way as to provide more access and opportunities to some students—in my assessment work, I focus on racialized intersectional patterns of unfairness—mostly determined by luck of birth. This is what grading schemes do that use judgments of quality, quality that is determined by a racialized group in power, a White, middle-class group, a group who often says they are establishing rules, guidelines, and standards for the good of everyone, altruistically, but turns out, those rules and standards benefit mostly people like them. Our society and schools may be pluralistic and diverse, but the systems and structures that organize them do not account well for a plurality of languages or a diversity of embodied students.

As the creators of determined docile-making assessment ecologies, we teachers can feel okay about any student who can't seem to make it, who never seems to produce drafts that meet our standards, even after our kind and generous feedback, even after multiple drafts. We constrain the ecology by creating enclosures and partitions, expecting and pressuring students to respond and revise, to move through and up categories, grades, spaces—to move their bodies in particular ways, the enticements of future carrots. So many hoops to jump through for the purposes of jumping through more hoops. We tell them they have "earned" their grades. We did not simply "give" them those grades. And yet, we hold critiques of the myth of meritocracy, a myth that supports our uses of the art of rank, movement in systems that is perhaps more circular than upward. Furthermore, we buy into theories of rhetoric and discourse that say language and meaning-making are social, while paradoxically (or is it contradictorily) tell our students, you earned that grade. You had all the means available. But the judging wasn't just about available means but about pressures and limits, about *habitus* and social formations we do not fully control, or choose, about White racial hegemony and White supremacist systems of education, which even good intentioned writing teachers are beholden to.

And even if we are not using grades on drafts most or all of the time, if we use judgments of quality at all to determine success, then there is a standard, and that standard will be used to determine students' final course grades, so the spaces and enclosures created are ones based on a haunting White *habitus*. We *de facto* stop giving students their rights to their own languages. No matter how delayed our grades are, the ghosts of White racial *habitus* are still present and felt by everyone in the ecology. We expect students to improve, to move through the system of enclosures, to be upwardly mobile. We expect their bodies to be moving outside of our classrooms for our purposes, to go to the library, to sit and read or write, maybe even in very particular ways—and these movements of the body, we know, can be good for our students. And so we punish with grades, or tacitly threaten students with them, all the while rationalizing to ourselves and them that it is all on them. It is all for their own good. They choose to do particular things in drafts and between classes. The choice to work long, or longer, or even longer, is theirs—and in one sense, it *is* theirs. It is their habits, not ours, we want them to mind, but really the ideal habits are not theirs but our habits we mind. And yet, the problematic here is that our students are in our classes to learn new things, new languaging. How else will they learn but to take on different habits, to become new *habitus*? This is the nature of becoming! Isn't being held to foreign standards how any *habitus* becomes something else? And isn't that why our students come to us?

Our students have to take responsibility, don't they? It's not our fault students fail, even though the way the ecology is set up is our fault. The system of enclosures is our fault. The disciplining and punishing is our fault. The determining of students' choice to be docile in particular ways is our fault. The way we treat mad niggas is our fault. Meanwhile, we writing teachers, can feel self-righteous about how well we treat and think of our students. And some, mostly White students, or those who have taken on a White racial *habitus* in their minds-bodies, will even say, "I don't know what all the fuss is about. Teacher treats me real good." And it may be true. And there's the paradox, the problem posed about determined, docile-making writing assessment ecologies. We aren't bad people. Our work is not evil work. We want our students to do good work. We do have some agency in the determined school systems that place limits and pressures on all of us. I sure feel like I have.

I could not write this book without some internal colonization. Then again, I ain't totally colonized. The paradox is also in the slave/docile mentality. Students don't judge for themselves or by their own measures, but depend on teachers to do so. We do know some things about language and rhetoric, and more than our students. That's why we are teaching, and why they are learning. We are in the best position to grade writing, right? Yet that seems like a natural position we should question. What is so natural about teachers grading students' writing? Why can't they do that too? Wouldn't they learn more through that process of judging, partitioning, and exercising the art of rank? But then, are we not simply shovelling the burden of the art of rank onto our students? Are they prepared to do that work ethically? Then again, are we formally prepared to do it?

We should not conflate the art of rank or our own creations of hierarchical enclosures and partitions in assessment ecologies with the methods for learning or learning itself. For many multilingual students and students of color, docile-making assessment ecologies lead to determined failure and feeling bad about oneself and one's writing, even when in a few instances, it may lead to so-called success in postsecondary writing. Enclosures create such feelings and psychologies that are wholly unnecessary for learning. The carrot of success, which is a euphemism for taking on a White racial *habitus*, keeps us from realizing just how internally colonized by grades and the hegemonic White racial *habitus* we all are. Drawing on Burke, Villanueva puts this dynamic rightly when explaining the new racism, the racism without explicitly mentioning race: "synecdoche is representation . . . synecdoche carries it all. No more talk of races; no more talk of religions, or nationalities, or languages, while talking about all of them, mixing them up in the most unsettling ways" (9). While Villanueva is speaking about writing center work, seeing the judgment of student writing in classrooms as a racialized practice that depends on White racial *habitus*, which function through the trope of synecdoche, is instructive and paradoxical. Our students are in our classrooms to learn rhetorical practices that will help them as citizens who must language in the world. They need us for this work. It is also a critical learning of a White racial *habitus*, or maybe a learning of ways to be mad against it and the institutional systems that reproduce White language privilege.

CHAPTER 2.

HOW I CAME TO LABOR-BASED GRADING CONTRACTS

> To a dyed-in-the-wool grader, the thought that grades are disturbing can come as a surprise. That grades become badges of autocratic or despotic judgments of students has not bothered them. That grades introduce a serious pedagogic fault, with a marked and often adverse influence on teaching itself, does not occur to them.
>
> A friend of mine who taught dental students favored the use of grades but was willing to weigh the question. He once lined up some large models of teeth and asked me to look at them. He pointed out the smooth contours, perfect fits, and strength of fillings in the teeth at the beginning of the row and then described carefully the progressive irregularities in teeth farther down the row. Having told me about the differences, he pointed out that I could see them clearly, though I was not a dentist. Then he asked triumphantly, "Why shouldn't I grade them from A to F?" My answer startled him. I merely said, "You just told me why you should not." He looked puzzled for a moment and then began to smile. He had been telling me specific features that he thought were right or needed correction. Not his judgment of rank but his specific observations were pertinent, whether he was teaching or just talking to me. Imagine that you are a prospective employer, and I know a student better than you do. You ask, not for my verdict, but for what I have observed, that you may judge for yourself. If I say, "I gave your applicant a '76'" and walk off, you have no observations but a perfunctory statement of my conclusions. Perhaps you are learning to drive, to paint, or to play the piano. You look to your mentors for guidance, not for their judgments. You learn to do these things because your primary interest and responsibility is with your own life and future, not just with outranking someone. If an instructor gives you a "C" every time you move, meaning commonness or mediocrity to almost everyone, you are not only not helped but you are discouraged, perhaps disgusted. Students submit to this disturbing process of labeling for years. That they survive is a tribute to their stamina, not to the teaching.
>
> —Max Marshall 25–26

In the 1950s, Max Marshall a microbiologist from the Medical Center at the University of California, offered these words after a several year experiment in his microbiology courses. The no-grading practice spread to other science departments. Over several years Marshall and his colleagues taught without giving grades in any of their courses. Marshall came to the above conclusions. Grades are "autocratic" and "despotic judgments." They "introduce a serious pedagogic fault." Students survive them out of stamina, not because of good teaching. I felt these same conclusions in my own teaching, and in part, they were the source of some of my returning to graduate school after a few years of teaching at the community college level.

In this chapter, I offer a narrative of my coming to labor-based grading contracts. I will not explain what contracts are in detail, but offer a kind of literature review that dramatizes my own problems and questions with the literature, brought on by my teaching. You might think of this chapter as a kind of background on the literature concerning grading that informed by problem-posing of grading and movement from hybrid grading contracts to labor-based ones. In another way, one can read this chapter as a fleshing out of Marshall's conclusions about grading through a look at the literature on grading contracts that led me to my current practice.

AIN'T MAKING DOCILE-STUDENTS NO MORE

My problematizing judgment and assessment in my classroom took years to articulate itself and as my last chapter and Marshall's words suggest, it began with the problematic of grades. I wish I'd found Marshall's discussion at the front end of my teaching, during the mid 1990s. His humane respect for his students still strikes me as revolutionary, even if he does not consider the ways race, class, gender, or disability might affect his conclusions, might reveal the unevenness in the pedagogic fault of grades. Then again, I wonder how diverse his 1950s University of California students were? Early on, I didn't have even Marshall's language to think about grading, and I certainly didn't have the language of Whiteness or Foucault's docile-making theory to help me make sense of what was happening in my classrooms' assessment ecologies. I just figured that thoughtful, self-conscious, rhetorically-minded pedagogy could not be White supremacist, that if I made sure to treat everyone equally in my evaluations and grading, I wouldn't be racist. But I was wrong.

During my time teaching at the community college, before going back to grad school, I also saw more obvious problems with grading writing, problems that others were discussing at the time (Tchudi; Zak and Weaver; Allison et al.). Grading seemed to get in the way of the conversations I wanted to have with students about their writing. It was a barrier when I would tell a multilingual student or a working-class White student, for instance, that her writing was interesting and moving, yet the C-grade seemed to say something else. Grades kept us from having a real exchange. Most just wanted to follow my orders, or took everything I said as an order, but I wanted them to talk through my words, think with me about their writing, and make their own decisions. Many of my students seemed resigned to low grades and following orders, and I felt it wasn't all their fault. It was in part my fault. Beyond these pedagogical problems, I found myself hating to read student writing, even though I loved talking to students about their writing.

Additionally, I could hear the resignation and past beatdowns in our opening discussion each quarter. To introduce ourselves on the first day, I always ask something like: who are you as a reader and writer? Most students characterize themselves as bad writers or simply say they don't see themselves as a writer. Yet in my experience, many students, particularly women, will identify themselves as consistent, even avid, readers. This always seems paradoxical to me, even though I know that one may love reading but not find an urge to write. However, I still find it a problematic (not a problem) to enjoy reading words, yet not enjoy using them in other ways to articulate or discover what you think or feel, or to not see your own use of words in your life as thinking or writing, as legitimate languaging. This somewhat paradoxical stance, readers who don't see themselves as writers, affected how my past students read my comments when a grade was attached. No matter how encouraging I tried to be, the grade confirmed their sense of themselves as bad or substandard writers. While I wouldn't have called my classrooms docile-making spaces back then, they were.

I'm reminded of Kenneth Burke's famous definition of humanity. I'll adjust his references to be more gender inclusive:

> [Humans are]
>
> *The symbol-using (symbol-making, symbol-misusing) animal*
>
> *Inventor of the negative (or moralized by the negative)*
>
> *Separated from [their] natural condition by instruments of [their] own making*
>
> *Goaded by the spirit of hierarchy (or moved by the sense of order)*
>
> *And rotten with perfection.* (16)

If we accept Burke's definition of humanity, a large part of being human is our languaging, our ways with words, our symbol-using-making-misusing practices. These practices create the problematic reader/non-writer stance in my students through their very modes of expression. They say, "I am NOT a writer, but I am a reader," yet there they are languaging, making and using symbols to define themselves, separated—no, alienated—from their material conditions as language users by language itself, separated by their own expression of non-writer status that they use to define themselves. How does this occur? Perhaps it is in the goading of the spirit of hierarchy enacted and symbolized through grades, in the yearning for the highest grade, in the disappointment of getting a lower mark. Why do grades have such power over us? Why are we moved by their sense of order? They suggest our imperfection, our un-success, our proximity to failure, and because we live in a society that functions from binaries, they offer us an indication, as imperfect as grades are, of how far we are from our own perfection, the ultimate motive for students.

So with this vague sense of something being wrong with my assessment practices, I went back to graduate school. I went initially to study rhetoric and racism with Victor Villanueva, but I ended up also studying writing assessment and thinking a lot about how to apply the ideas circulating in the literature on program assessment and large scale writing assessment to the writing classroom. I'd been a writing teacher for several years before returning to get my doctorate at Washington State University. I'd taught for a few years at Chemeketa Community College in Salem, Oregon, and before that I was a teaching fellow at Oregon State University, where I earned my M.A. in Rhetoric and Composition and was a Teaching Assistant. It was at OSU that I discovered my love for teaching, for helping others engage with words and create and communicate their ideas. I love pretty much everything about the writing classroom, except grading, of course. I love that it is a rare opportunity in which we pay attention to our words and the words of others. I love that the writing classroom is one of the only places we get to pay attention to how we cultivate meaning from and with the words and symbols that pass in front of us every day. When things are going well, the writing classroom is an open, engaging, and inviting place where we look at texts and artifacts and consider their ethical significance in the world and to ourselves. We sit in the presence of words. We slow our lives and minds down. We look closely. We listen carefully. We behold. We question. We ask. We sip meaning and significance from a deep well of language and culture. We care for those around us and their words. And from all this, we pose problems about our existential situations in our world of words and symbols.

But of course, my biggest problems in my teaching had always been grading writing. I didn't like doing it, and I've never met any writing teacher who liked doing it. I don't know many students who like grades either, which isn't to say that there aren't a lot of students who don't want them. My students back then at OSU, Chemeketa, and WSU didn't like getting grades either, at least not the grades I gave them on their writing. It ruined my relationship with their writing and even with them. In most cases, my grades ruined their relationship with their own writing. I found myself grudgingly reading every stack of papers because I knew that somewhere in that stack my mood and attitude would change.

I'd sour. I would have to justify each grade and that meant my stance as a reader would have to be one of looking for reasons why I didn't think the paper deserved a higher grade, or at best why I thought the paper warranted the grade I gave it—and I almost always knew the overall grade by the time I got halfway through each paper, which then turned my attention as a reader toward the markers in the paper that justified that grade, a self-fulfilling judgment practice. In short, I sensed that grading kept me from enjoying my students' writing. And as Peter Elbow argues convincingly ("Ranking" 200), I intuitively knew that I needed to like my students' writing, if not for their benefit, then my own.

Sure, I used carefully crafted and recrafted rubrics. I shared and worked through the rubrics with my students. I let them decide on their topics and kinds of writing they wanted to engage in. I demanded revision after peer workshops and my own feedback on their drafts before I put grades on papers. I tried to give them as much choice as possible, as much opportunity to know my expectations, but I still had to grade based on my expectations, even when those expectations were collaboratively crafted. The discourse of judgment and grading was based on a standard, one I translated in my judgments from our rubric. It all felt unfair to my students, not my expectations, but using them to determine progress and proficiency, course grades and GPAs, after we'd done so much collaborative work. And for my working-class, multilingual, and students of color, who often entered my courses with Englishes other than the dominant one I used as a standard, they were at a double disadvantage. They didn't have first-hand access to the standard. It is like playing a game in which you don't know all the rules until someone catches you breaking one, and you must then move back three spaces. It was a game I remember playing and somehow winning by a few lucky rolls of the dice. I was the anomaly, the fluke. It happens, but rarely. I won the game despite the rules that clearly were stacked against me. My students knew this game too. They knew the odds. I was now making them play it, telling them, if I can get lucky, so can you.

It was in Bill Condon's writing assessment course where I made my first steps toward contract grading in developing the article, "Community-Based Assessment Pedagogy." The course would literally change what I did and how I did everything from that point on, from my teaching to my research. Up to that point, I was studying rhetoric and racism. That was going to be my dissertation. But Bill's class showed me that racism is judgment, that the classroom is a site that reproduces racism and White language supremacy, that how judgments in such spaces are made have just as much to do with larger, structural forces as they do with an individual's idiosyncratic reading of a text. From the first class session, I was hooked. I saw connections to everything I did in the classroom and in my daily encounters with words. I began to see how racism is reproduced through the ways we judge language that seem to be about everything else but race. We are always judging, always assessing, from racialized bodies and discourses. If language travels with people, if it is social and historical in nature, then it is shaped by the ways groups of people who use it are shaped. Language is racialized. We language through our racialized *habitus*.

On the first day of the semester, Bill walked into class and quickly handed out a page copied from an academic journal. He said we were going to engage in a reading exercise. He wanted us to count the number of e's on the page. Because we were all good doctoral students, we dutifully counted. A few minutes later, Bill asked us to go up to the board and write our answers. How many e's were there on the page? We all went up at the same time and wrote a different number. There were as many answers as there were students in the class. How could this be? What did it mean? I was shocked. Had I messed up my counting? Didn't we all have the same page? Yes, Bill confirmed that we did. He said if we, a group of smart doctoral students in an English Department, couldn't agree on the number of e's on a single piece of paper, a simple act of assessment, how could we possibly expect to agree on much more sophisticated and complex dimensions of the same page, like effectiveness or what it says, or how proficient it is? This was my entry into writing assessment. And through that class, I came to community-based assessment pedagogy, the practice and the article.

In the article, I argue for a cycle of rubric building, using, and reflection activities that lead to the use of a rubric in peer assessment activities, which culminate in a richer, more textured set of categorical assessments of students' writing without using grades on anything. At the end of the course, instead of the teacher evaluating the student's portfolio of work, the student collects several peer evaluations using our rubric along with their own self-evaluations. The student and I would sit down together and read all of them, then I'd read my own prepared evaluation of the portfolio, none of which would have grades on them, instead we had a simple categorical decision to make for each rubric dimension: does this student's portfolio meet, not meet, or exceed the expectations of our portfolio rubric along each dimension and how does it do that? These judgments and their reasonings were recorded in each assessment document.

In final conferences, we looked at the landscape of evaluations—peers, self, mine—and came to what I called "hard agreements" about what overall assessments we could make given what folks said about the writer's portfolio and the evidence they'd provided for those assessments. The final course grade was determined by deciding how many of the rubric dimensions met, exceeded, or didn't meet basic expectations along all portfolio rubric dimensions, which we'd also collaboratively created, discussed, revised, and reflected upon over the semester. If we could argue that more than half of the rubric dimensions were exceeding expectations, then the student would receive an A, if most were meeting expectations, then a B. If there were a few not meeting, then a C. If more than half were not meeting expectations, then a D. If the writer's portfolio couldn't be argued that it met any of the class' expectations along any of the rubric dimensions, the student got an "F." This course grading system was still a quality-based grading system—that is, the final course grade depended on a discussion of the judgments of quality, albeit by several colleagues, the student-writer, and me.

In my estimation, while it didn't address the power differential between my students and myself in our assessments of portfolios (mine was always going to hold more weight in those final discussions), nor did the system account well for the ways some White and Asian female students didn't seem to resist as much the negative assessments of their writing by others, as White male students generally did, community-based assessment pedagogy was still a fairer system than conventional grading systems for three reasons. First, it offered students some added control and agency in what constitutes quality through rubric generation and reflection activities, as well as those final assessments. This leads to added agency in those discussions in the final conferences, where students get more voice in what their final grade ends up being. They get to argue, in a sense, or defend, their preferred grade, based on evidence. More importantly, they have a real and materially present voice at the table when the teacher determines course grades. Along with this, that course grade is also produced more collaboratively, not by one judge (the teacher) alone. While later I would see the intersectional, gendered, and racialized problems with various students trying to defend or argue for an assessment or a grade to an authority figure who is steeped in a masculine, White *habitus* of the university, at this early stage, this was still better than conventional power dynamics in teacher-only grading systems.

Second, community-based assessment pedagogy reduced the number of grade distinctions possible. The assessment literature is clear on this point, and it's more nuanced than what it seems at first glance. The fewer distinctions judges make, the more reliable those decisions are—that is, the more agreement there will be among various readers. Furthermore, my system asked students to think differently about these kinds of judgments. Because we weren't adding or averaging points or percentages, we could think more conceptually, closer to the way people often judge language organically in other places outside of classrooms. When we judge texts, arguments, advertisements, movies, or other discourses in the world, we rarely place them on linear, numerical scales. Instead, our judgments are more conceptual. We may not have explicit rubrics or lists of expectations, but we do work from expectations, known examples, and salient features that we read as quality or something important to make a decision from.

We say, "that commercial is so retro. I love it," or "that song is interesting in a backwards way, like the old Beatles tunes," or "I found the speech by the President baseless and unconvincing because he didn't give any reasons for any of his policy decisions beyond 'because I said so.'"

I chose to resist linear models and judgments that amounted to points because I felt that our decisions were more outcomes based. That is, we had a set of agreed-upon outcomes, our rubric, so we could simply make a categorical decision in each case, each dimension. Did the portfolio meet expectations in this area? We mostly just needed to know that. Then in some cases, we needed to know if the writer exceeded expectations. Was the writing doing something demonstrably more than most everyone else in the class?

Yes, I'm mixing assessment paradigms. The initial categorical decision could be seen as a judgment much like criterion referenced tests offer. Criterion-referenced tests purport to show how well a person does compared to a particular skill, outcome, or construct already identified, such as the expectations listed on our rubric (the criteria). Meanwhile, I was urging students to make the higher decision, whether a portfolio exceeded expectations along any given rubric dimension, using a norm referenced model of judgment. Norm-referenced tests purport to measure test takers relative to other test takers. In other words, one is exceeding expectations based on the reader's sense of what other writers in the class are doing (or not able to do).

I still think this criterion-to-normed reference judgments is a good way to help students, even faculty, make such decisions, depending on what those decisions are used for. But there is another way to see how these judgments work at the micro-level, the level of the individual reader-judge—categorization theory—and this theory likely was floating in my head at the time because we used it explicitly in the writing program at Washington State University to judge placement essays and junior rising portfolios, processes I was a part of each year. Categorization theory explains how our minds make decisions and judgments like these, and gives insight into what I was trying to lead my students through. In the context of holistic scoring, Richard Haswell, a former WPA at WSU, explains the three main types of categorization that psychologists say we make judgments by: classical, exemplar, and prototype. Classical categorization says that we judge by looking for the "non-accidental properties of a new instance and matching them with the unique set of properties that define the correct category" (245). Each category then has a set of known, ideal features and a reader attempts to match the features seen or heard in the present text with these known, ideal features. Our collaborative rubric attempted to help us articulate such categories and features, only from inductive methods, which means our process of rubric creation shared another kind of categorization, exemplar.

Exemplar categorization says that people "categorize by comparing a new instance with intact memories ('exemplars') of similar instances" (Haswell 247). Thus we read a text looking to see how closely it fits to significant features of a most representative or best example of the category. Our rubric-building process assumed a kind of reverse method for producing the categories and descriptive features. It began with actual known exemplars, texts we brought to class, ones we wanted to imitate as writers. Through a series of activities, we derived dimensions of writing from them and those dimensions' features, which we then used to help us make judgments on each other's drafts and portfolios in the assessment documents. This process was influenced by Bob Broad's dynamic criteria mapping process (see Chapter 5 of Broad). In use, the actual exemplars that our rubric was based on go away, and what remains is a bricolage of exemplar-inspired dimensions that we use to remind us of our priorities when assessing.

It is prototype categorization that I asked students to engage in during our final assessment activities on those final portfolios. Prototype categorization says that we "judg[e] how similar the yet-to-be-categorized instance is to abstract schemas [we] have of the best example or most representative member (prototype) of possible categories" (Haswell 246). The prototype for any category is, then, an "idealized construction," a "convenient grammatical fiction" (Haswell 246; Rosch 40). So we don't actually use a real example when we judge instances, instead we use convenient fictions, prototypes in our heads that are cobbled together from various examples. Our rubric, then, was heuristical in nature, reminding us of key categories and features of the prototypes in our heads that we all agreed upon to use when we built the rubric, which was a kind of classical set of categories. What complicates this is that what any individual judge can see and discuss will vary a bit, even though we are sharing the same rubric and coming to agreements about what categories mean. But since we always work from our own mental, idealized constructions of things, this paradigm of judgment seems to explain best what we were trying to do and how it would inevitably be uneven in application—there would be necessary disagreement. Each reader was reading for and explaining how close a given portfolio was to the construction of an idealized portfolio that existed in that reader's head, no matter the rubric we'd collaboratively made.

While we were using prototypes in our heads that we articulated on our rubric and agreed upon as a class, each student's (and my) expectations were still idiosyncratic by their nature. Remember, our judgments have patterns in groups because they are structurally determined, which our *habitus* help account for. Those *habitus* are a part of our language systems since our language systems are a part of our racialized and social histories in society, schools, and academic disciplines. In short, readers are constrained and pressured in particular directions to see and value particular features of texts no matter the prototypes we hold in front of us for judgment purposes. This means readers who share *habitus* will be determined to judge the same text in similar ways, but not exactly the same ways. We have agency, just not full freedom to see things in any old way. Without examining our rubric and prototypes in structural and historical ways, it will be hard to avoid reproducing blindly a White racial *habitus* in any writing classroom or rubric, thus difficult to not privilege those who already embody such a *habitus* in that classroom through our judgments of writing. This is the exact dynamic I was trying to avoid in my assessment systems. Community-based assessment pedagogy seemed to easily reproduce unfair, racialized dynamics, and this made it another structural way that writing assessment reproduced White language supremacy, despite my better intentions and my own racialized history of subordination in school. Thus as long as I had to produce grades, I couldn't account for individual variance and difference in judging language.

To summarize this second advantage, community-based assessment pedagogy asked students to think of the judgments of meets, exceeds, or not meets expectations as conceptual buckets, or categories, as discrete partitions. The writer and I decided which category each portfolio fit into after hearing all the individual assessments of the portfolio. The system resisted harmful linear, hierarchical scales, determined only by a teacher, yet there were contradictions. Our categorical method resulted in students still being placed into a hierarchical system of course grades from A-F, a system of partitions that still functioned as the art of rank, only it allowed students to control some of the movements in the enclosures created. The categories themselves were partitions in the enclosures of the rubric and portfolio. I just got my students to manage those enclosures with me. Many of these contradictions occurred because the university required grades. And of course, there are always contradictions in any assessment ecology situated in other ecologies that demand things like movement between enclosures that are already created.

The third advantage, and unexpectedly, of community-based assessment pedagogy was the way it began to change the culture of my classrooms and interactions with students. I'm sure some students saw the ecology as fairer, but many still resisted. But I began to enjoy being in the assessment ecology, just like I had remembered loving the classroom in my early days of teaching when I was so intoxicated by this new and exciting space, these new and exciting practices, that I didn't have time for the contradictions. And because I wanted the assessment of writing in my classes to be a mutual practice of students and me working through problems of judgment in language together, posing problems together, learning together, having conversations about language and how we judge it differently, I saw promise in this more student-centered assessment system, one that had fewer distinctions in assessments at the end of the course. I was getting close, but something was missing.

What was difficult to consider in this first iteration of my own assessment practices was understanding the nature of judgment and seeing other possibilities for producing course grades. I was fortunate enough to get feedback from Peter Elbow on the article. He was one of the reviewers, and he signed his review and provided his phone number, suggesting I call. He had an idea for me that he felt might help me. Of course, I called. I was deeply flattered that such an academic rock star would have much to say to me. I had cut my teeth on *Writing Without Teachers*, which had been suggested to me by Chris Anderson, my first mentor and the Director of Writing at Oregon State a decade earlier. So when Peter Elbow suggested I call him to talk about my ideas in the article, I called. He gave me his grading contract, a version of the one he and Jane Danielewicz published later (Danielewicz and Elbow), but Peter had been using and working on contracts and alternative systems of judgment in writing classrooms for at least a decade before (Elbow, "Grading Writing," "Taking Time Out," and "Ranking"). I tried the grading contract the very next semester and never turned back. Peter was right. It solved many problems around grading that I would still be having, and opened up many other possibilities. That first semester was in 2004. I've not graded a paper since the spring of that year, and my students and I are better for it.

FIRST TRY, HYBRID CONTRACTS

The grading contract I inherited from Peter Elbow judged two kinds of evidence from students' learning in the classroom to determine some course grades (those above the default B grade), which Danielewicz and Elbow refer to as a "hybrid grading contract" (250). They explain that course grades up to a B are contracted by doing particular things, by "conscientious effort and participation" (246). In early versions of my contract, this part of the method was described as "behaviors," much like Danielewicz and Elbow's contract describes things. I promised students: Behave in a particular way described in the contract, do the work asked in the spirit it is assigned, and you are guaranteed a "B" course grade, no matter what I think of your writing. I took this language from the contract Peter shared with me. But A grades required different evidence to be judged.

While most course grades were determined by effort, participation, or behaviors, grades above a B required a judgment of writing quality, usually on a portfolio at the end of the course. Again, this feature was taken from Elbow's contract given to me. In Danielewicz and Elbow's contracts, this higher course grade is determined by the teacher's judgment of those final portfolios that rose to the top upon final reading of them. They explain this in clear terms: "We need only examine the remaining final portfolios that are particularly strong to decide which students get which grade higher than B. Often there are not so many"

(253). They offer ways to make such judgments explicit, which many students will care about and want. They explain that a course grade of B "should be available to *every* student—that is, not dependent on skill or prior training"—while A grades require "specific criteria or features of 'good writing' that not every student could attain" (258; emphasis in original). In other words, A grades require judgments of writing quality that are made explicit to students, but are decisions based on a teacher's judgments of the literacy performances of those students.

Hybrid contracts' basic premise is clear: your assessment ecology will keep the most exemplary grades away from some students, regardless of their desires for those grades or the amount of work they are willing to put into their writing in order to get those grades. More often than not, these students will be students of color, working-class, and multilingual students—students with *habitus* other than the dominant White racial *habitus* embodied in the teacher, rubric, standards, and course outcomes. Thus, grades of A in Danielewicz and Elbow's hybrid contract system are determined by a teacher's judgment of the *habitus* that are embodied in students' languaging. It didn't take long for me to feel uncomfortable about this problem in hybrid contracts. And it amounts to hybrid contracts being subtly racist and White supremacist.

As community-based assessment pedagogy argues, I've never liked the idea of only the teacher grading student writing, and I've always been suspicious of any one judge deciding what is exemplary literacy performances, even if that judge is a teacher. One lesson anyone can see from academic and civic work is that fairness is a construction of the community involved, the people most affected by decisions. If you get to have a hand in the decision that affects you, no matter what it is or what it's about, you likely will feel that the consequences of that decision are fairer to you. Grades in classrooms work the same way. So my first iteration of hybrid grading contracts asked for several student colleagues, the writer, and myself to provide written assessments of the final portfolio, just like my community-based assessment pedagogy. The writer and I then got together in a final conference to read through and discuss this landscape of judgment. Up to this point, I thought the key to fairness was in collaboratively building rubrics and deciding final grades together with each student. I thought constructing fairness was about participation and method. But these things are also tied to the nature of the decisions, those decisions' consequences after the class, and the shifting, intersectional, and uneven social structures and power relations that construct my students and me.

With the hybrid contract placed inside my existing community-based assessment pedagogy, I found that the student and I didn't need to discuss or make all those distinctions at the end of the semester since all grades up to a B were already determined, and all that was left to determine was the quality of writing by those few students who may qualify for A-grades. However, in my system, the A-grades were collaboratively determined by considering carefully and with the student all the assessment documents on their final portfolio. So instead of five grade distinctions to make, students and I now only had one. It was more elegant and simpler. There was more agreement and fairness, since students helped figure the grade out.

After a few years of using hybrid grading contracts in this way, and teaching in racially and culturally diverse classrooms, the racism and White supremacist tendencies with this hybrid contract became clearer to me. It wasn't just a hybrid system. It was a fundamentally unfair system to many students of color, multilingual students, and students who came to my college classrooms with Englishes that were distant from my own and the ones I was asked to promote, that is, dominant academic discourses (or DADs).[11] As Danielewicz and Elbow say, some students will not be able to attain an excellent or superior judgment in these dominant discourses because their literacy practices are just different—they didn't grow up in White, middle-class households—and ten or fifteen weeks of instruction is just not enough time to change these linguistic realities. So many of my students of color at Fresno State didn't have a chance to get an A, even if they wanted it and were willing to work very hard for it. This didn't sit well with me. It still meant that the same students who benefit from conventional grading systems that use a White, middle-class standard discourse are privileged and placed at the top of the grading pyramid and rewarded for less labor because their White racial *habitus* is the center of all DADs. My DAD was dictating who got the highest, most coveted grades in my classrooms. Meanwhile, my students of color and multilingual students often worked harder but achieved a lower course grade.

At an experiential level, this hybrid contract was perhaps even more unfair than conventional grading. What I was telling my students from the first day is that our contract allows us to let go of grades, to focus our attention on learning and the feedback we get on our writing, and making our own informed decisions in our writing—not follow orders. My motto was, and has always been: Good writers make careful decisions; they don't follow orders. I would tell them that you don't have to worry about me not liking your writing. Listen to what I say, try to do all you can, but make your own decisions and have good reasons for why you want to do what you do in drafts. I was trying to give them a right to their own languages, but the grading system still didn't fully allow this. If a student took seriously my words, if they enacted their own right to their own language, then they only had a right to a B-grade.

---

11   I often begin talking with my students about dominant standards of English by referring to them as "DAD"—our DAD is our dominant academic discourse—but DADs are really the dominant White *habitus* that are embodied in language standards and norms.

Now, at least students who actually took my words to heart couldn't fail the class. Yet at the end of the semester, when it really counted, particularly for those who wanted an A-grade, they really did have to care about their colleagues' and my judgments of their writing—they had to follow orders—which always meant imitating a dominant White racial *habitus*. There was a contradiction, a racist problematic: All students had a right to their own languages, just not a right to an A, not a right to have their languages valued most highly, unless that language matched a White racial *habitus*. So hybrid grading contracts still participated in White language supremacy.

This core assumption in hybrid grading contracts maintains the hegemonic racial and linguistic hierarchies we see today. It does nothing to change them. It is White supremacist, since it reserves the highest categories of grades in a system that rewards students with such grades, to those demonstrating a dominant White racial *habitus*, yet it seemed to suggest that the assessment ecology was helping non-White students achieve by not failing them for their efforts, even when those efforts did not' amount to mimicking the standard. To use the metaphor of the early twentieth century, racist, separatist, and eugenicist, Lothrop Stoddard, in *The Rising Tide of Color*, hybrid grading contracts maintain the White center by managing the "inner dikes" that protect them. The White center is the A-grade partition, while the inner dike is the B-grade territory, open to all in the contract, but carefully separated from the A-grade by maintaining the dominant White racial linguistic standard. This means the "outer dikes" are the less-preferred, lower-grade-lands.

I doubt many would characterize the differential judging in hybrid contracts as White supremacist in the ways Stoddard clearly thinks of geopolitics and their connection to the preservation of the White race and White lands. And yet, by default, hybrid contracts work to produce the same inner and outer dike system, controlling movement through both. The grading philosophy, to me, sounds like this: Let the Brown and Black folks have their Bs and Cs. Let them pass writing courses. Meanwhile, the As, the real opportunities and high GPAs, will be reserved for those who can embody a dominant White racial *habitus*, which means White students get overrepresented in the A category. The world and its educational opportunities remains guarded from the rising tide of color in our schools through the system of inner and outer grade dikes.

In my own classrooms, what complicated the use of hybrid contracts further was that my good intentions to have students involved in the judgment of writing at the end of the term meant that individual student judgments would also reflect the valuing of a dominant White racial *habitus* over others. I could and did get my students—even students of color—to voice their own oppression.

This is how we internally colonized our students. We get them to enforce the partitions and dikes of grading with us.

Ultimately, I couldn't see how this hybrid contract *uncompromisingly* valued students' right to their own languages through the *judgments of writing*. What it did was allow for some affordances around language diversity, up to the B dike. A student who wrote in Black English or Spanglish could pass the class with a B, but couldn't realistically get an A. It maintained the racial hierarchies that privileged dominant White racial dispositions to language. As good as this hybrid contract was in helping many students do better in the class than they likely would have with traditional grading, it ultimately gave them the wrong lesson if they used their non-dominant and non-White discourses. The lesson was that anything other than the White DAD of the classroom was less than, was substandard, and was not excellent writing. This meant that those of us who didn't grow up with a White DAD, likely couldn't get the A—my former, student-self could not get an A, even in my own class. As a writing assessment ecology, it didn't do the kind of social justice work I envisioned for my classrooms. Social justice writing assessment projects make people's lives better, give them equitable opportunities, expand boundaries, question the authoritative and hegemonic, not simply give some students a few more opportunities, or a second-class status, even though that status is better than the third-class one they are accustomed to. I wanted my contract to do more. I wanted it to be uncompromising when it came to the racist and White supremacist system my students had to learn in.

MOVIN' TO QUANTITY OVER QUALITY

During this time, I began doing more research on grading and learning contracts. Most published work up to the early 2000s discussed learning contracts, not grading contracts, and came from education circles (e.g. Berte; Knowles; Anderson, Boud, and Sampson). Researchers tend to discuss learning contracts in terms of K-12, adult education, or nursing contexts. Often, the articles and books avoid any detailed discussion of how course grades are exactly determined. This makes sense. Learning contracts are designed to help learners achieve particular learning outcomes, not grades. They are more concerned with helping students master particular tasks or outcomes, like setting a broken leg or diagnosing a patient.

For instance, Margaret McAllister discusses learning contracts for nursing students in Australia. Each individual student's learning contract consists of "learning objectives," "resources and strategies for learning," "evidence of accomplishment," and "criteria for evaluation" (200). While the last two areas of McAllister's learning contract offers ways to understand how a student will be evaluated, she says very little about exactly how the evidence of accomplishment marshalled by the student will actually be used in an evaluation process to then calculate a course grade.

In using learning contracts in self-directed, second language learning classrooms in Singapore and Canada, Hedy McGarrell offers similar ways to structure contracts in English language learning classrooms. The main elements of McGarrell's contracts address:

1. "What will the learner learn?" (497);
2. "How will the learner accomplish an identified short-term objective?" (498);
3. "When does the learner expect to achieve a given objective?" (498);
4. "How will the learner demonstrate what he/she learned"? (498); and
5. "[H]ow will the learner's demonstration of achievement be evaluated and by whom?" (498).

While no specifics are given toward calculating grades with learning contracts, McGarrell does push for students to be a part of the evaluation process. She explains, "principles of self-directed learning require learners to evaluate not only the achievements of their learning objectives but also the quality of their learning experience" (498). She goes on to say that some teachers may find it helpful to evaluate the student's performance, but should avoid "instructor-centered techniques." Her suggestions amount to the teacher "remain[ing] a facilitator, rather than a judge, of the learning process" (499). McGarrell promotes a kind of assessment ecology that I was (and still am) looking for, one that gives students more control over the ecology and is flexible for a variety of learning paces and styles. But there is a difference between allowing students control over the evaluation of the evidence of their learning and allowing students to control how their course grades are calculated from judgments upon that evidence. As Stephen Tchudi reminds us, there are differences between response, assessment, evaluation, and grading (xv). And this is why, I'm sure, McGarrell pushes for an avoidance of instructor-centered evaluation, but it's unclear if that includes grading. Furthermore, it isn't clear at all how grades are calculated in her classroom. She remains silent on any options. Of course, learning contracts do not contract for grades. They contract for learning, so there is no reason she should explain this.

The value in learning contracts, I think, is clear. They focus on negotiated learning processes and outcomes or goals for individual projects and are individualized to each student. In *Learning Contracts: A Practical Guide*, Anderson, Boud, and Sampson define a learning contract as

> a document used to assist in the planning of a learning project
> . . . a written agreement negotiated between a learner and a

teacher, lecturer or staff adviser that a particular activity will be
undertaken in order to achieve a specific learning goal or goals
. . . a learning contract is essentially a "process plan." It is a means
of designing a learning activity with the focus on the learner
rather than the subject or the teacher. For this reason learning
contracts are particularly suitable for structuring assignments
and projects which are largely self-directed, for use in courses in
which participants come from a diversity of backgrounds and in
tailoring learning to individual needs and interests. (2–3)

Thus learning contracts promote student responsibility, agency, and control in mostly self-governed, learning processes, with an attention to what that process is meant to achieve or produce, and how that learning is evaluated for success or completion. They promote metacognition through the ways the learner must help develop the contract with the teacher, articulating what goals they wish to achieve, what evidence of success looks like, and in some cases, even assessing their own completion of the contract. But most of the literature on learning contracts do not give students any explicit control or responsibility for their course grades, which for students in most contemporary college settings is intimately linked to their learning.

While educators might agree that learning and grades are separate, we cannot just tell students this and expect that they will understand how they are separate, or be willing to act on such an understanding. Why do we think our students should trust us when we say their grade and their learning are separate while everyone and the system itself up to that point in school has acted in contrary ways? In fact, acting on this information may harm them in our classrooms or others. This makes learning contracts different than grading contracts in this key purpose. Learning contracts make agreements about learning processes, while grading contracts make agreements about grades.

The relatively few articles that were published on grading contracts in college classrooms come mostly in the 1970s, '90s, and early 2000s, sprinkled here and there. There have been some articles on grading contracts as modified, criterion-referenced systems in higher education (Hassencahl), some of which look at students' favorable reactions to them in teacher education courses (Taylor; Brubaker), college nutrition and food management courses (Blankenship), and agriculture education courses (Newcomb), while others consider their success in accounting courses (Zarzeski), larger psychology courses (Kirschenbaum and Riechmann), as well as speech communication (Stelzner; Wolvin and Wolvin), and nursing courses (Kruse and Barger; Crancer, Maury-Hess, and Dunn). Some have discussed grading contracts' uses to enhance critical pedagogies

(Shor, *Empowering Education* 159; "Critical Pedagogy") and postmodern peda-gogies (Hiller and Hietapelto), or simply as a more efficient method for calculat-ing grades that helps students write more (Leahy). Most in one way or another, make a point to discuss the democratizing elements of grading contracts, giving students more control in courses and power over their grades (Danielewicz and Elbow; Inoue, *Antiracist*), as well as authority in the classroom (Burbaker). There also have been studies about grading contract systems in college business courses that show a statistically significant increase in motivation and effort (Polczynski and Shirland), while more recent studies have shown mixed results from first-year writing students (Spidell and Thelin; Inman and Powell) and statistically significant differences in performances and attitudes about the contract in stu-dents of color in a writing program (Inoue, "Grading Contracts"). All of this scholarship on grading contracts, however, uses hybrid contracts.[12] I'll discuss in more detail Spidell and Thelin's and Inman and Powell's studies together in Chapter 7, where I discuss two criticisms of hybrid grading contracts that could be leveled against labor-based ones, so I'll avoid my critique of them here.

The central assessment issue at stake in most grading contract discussions is about the nature of judgment that produces any given grade on a written perfor-mance. Most discussions assume a binary of quantity vs. quality (Bauman 165; Shiffman 67–68; Reichert 60; Danielewicz and Elbow 250). The two competing philosophical assumptions about the practice of grading and its relation to stu-dents' learning to write might be stated like this:

> Learning to write or improving students' writing requires
> teachers to *judge writing quality*, thus course grades should be
> calculated by those judgments of quality. To be a fair assess-
> ment ecology, consistent judgments of quality are central.

versus

> Learning to write or improving students' writing requires
> students to *produce a certain quantity* of writing, thus course
> grades should be calculated by the quantity of writing a
> student produces. To be a fair assessment ecology, consistent
> judgments of quantity are central.

As mentioned already, Danielewicz and Elbow describe their contract as a hy-brid model, one that uses both kinds of judgment to produce various kinds of

---

12   The exception, as far as I can tell, is my own scholarship. While not all the grading contracts in "Grading Contracts" were purely labor-based, most were, and my own in *Antiracist* was. But of course, I didn't have this scholarship available to me when I was looking for a better contract system.

grades. Judgments of quantity are used to calculate course grades up to a B, while judgments of quality are used for those above a B. I found in my own classrooms that hybrid contracts like Danielewicz and Elbow's were unfair and White supremacist because they changed the rules of the game in the last inning, when the score was tied and there was a runner on third.

Savvy students figured this out quickly, and rightfully ignored my advice during the semester and instead tried to give me what I wanted, since clearly I was the most important judge in the room. I would be the one who needed the most convincing when final conferences came. They were negotiating with me. My students of color, those who usually found themselves at the lower end of the quality scale, were hurt more often in this schizophrenic, hybrid system of grading.

After just a few years at Fresno State, I decided to try to figure out how I might use quantity judgments only in all contract grade distinctions. There is some literature that supports this kind of assessment ecology, which I began to look at more carefully. In 1976, John V. Knapp offered a version of a quantity system to produce course grades, a grading system in which students receive a simple binary judgment on drafts, acceptable or unacceptable (Knapp 651). Once a draft is deemed acceptable, the student may move on to the next essay in the class. If they don't want to keep trying, they abandon that essay and move to a new essay. There are eight essays assigned, and over the course of the semester, students acquire as many acceptable drafts as possible, with three to four giving the student a C course grade, five to six a B, and seven to eight an A. The more writing a student accomplishes in Knapp's system, the higher their grade.

While Knapp's system avoids the teacher making too many judgments of quality on individual drafts—he only makes a single, binary one on any given piece of writing—it still uses judgments of quality by a single teacher. It is still a hybrid model. It avoids most ranking that occurs in grading and point systems, but ultimately maintains a hierarchical system of quality based on the teacher's idiosyncratic DAD, which categorizes students into acceptable and unacceptable. Any labor put forth by the student will not do. It must be labor that equates to an acceptable draft judged by the teacher. Knapp's system too easily works from an unquestioned, dominant White racial *habitus* that informs the dispositions to language that writing teachers always carry with them, no matter their intentions or who they are. The foundation of those simple binary judgments of quality that Knapp uses to make judgments of quantity is still White supremacist. His system, like the hybrid contract, protects the White center, the White literacy property, and creates unspoken inner dikes.

So I wondered: how do I avoid the White supremacy in judgments of quality on which Knapp's system still relies? Is it even possible to escape the hegemonic,

White supremacist system of judgment in schools and colleges? Knapp's system seems a fairer system, one that rewards those who do more work in the class. And those judgments of quality that he does make have a low threshold. In order to pass, a paper just has to meet minimum quality standards according to the teacher. And yet, everyone's labor is not equal in this system. A multilingual student working 10 hours on an essay may not meet the minimum standard for a passing essay, yet a White, middle-class student, who was raised in a monolingual English home, might spend five hours on the same essay, achieving a pass and moving on. Because the teacher's judgments of quality are what determines whether any draft is acceptable or not in the system, some students may still not be able to achieve a high grade, even if they desire to and are willing to work extra hard. To draw on John Rawls' idea of "justice as fairness," I wasn't convinced that a system that depended on my own judgments of minimum quality of drafts, which was by default comparisons to a dominant White racial *habitus*, gave all students a "fair equality of opportunity" (43).[13] I realized that in a hybrid contract, judgments of quality protect the White center of literacy as White property.

Beyond this problem, something else bothered me about Knapp's system. With my judgments of quality still regulating the assessment ecology, students would be too constrained, still likely to default to following my orders. In fact, the system is based on it. And I just didn't want them to do that, at least not by default. I wanted them to have good reasons to do what they did with their language and make their own decisions in writing. Perhaps unrealistically, I wanted them to be free to write, to write in a free and uninhibited place, to pursue languaging practices in ways they felt to be worth their time, which could mean learning dominant White racial habits of language. I knew that even my minimum expectations of quality, steeped in a self-conscious White racial *habitus*, would taint that ecology if used to grade, keeping many of my multilingual and students of color from more fully exercising their agency through languaging, and would likely offer more freedom to my monolingual, White, middle-class students. So I continued to search.

DISCOVERING THE PRIMACY OF LABOR

Through my research and reflection, I realized that what I value most in students is their working, their labor. This likely comes from my own poor, working-class

---

13   Rawls explains that "fair equality of opportunity" means that opportunities in a society or system are (1) formally open to all, and (2) "that all should have a fair chance to attain them" (43). I realize the critiques of Rawls' theory of social justice by scholars such as Iris Young who argue for more structural understandings of fairness, but I think taken on its own, this bit of Rawlsian theory holds up as structural.

background, as well as my own particular *habitus* in school. As a student, I knew I'd never be the smartest kid in the class. My grades seemed to prove that to me. How White people in and out of school talked down to me and treated me also suggested this to me. I can remember just showing up to neighborhood events, Halloween parties, block parties, and seeing the disgusted looks on the adults' faces by my mere presence. They were all working-class Whites. I was a Brown kid, Japanese, to them Mexican. I was 13, 14. I lived in an explicitly racist world. The racism was very present to me. Most of the time, it wasn't even veiled. I felt this same tension in school. During my Freshman year of high school, I got an A in honors French and every other class I took, yet received a B (not a B+) in English, not honors English, regular English. How was this possible? What was I doing wrong? Apparently, nothing. It was me, my *habitus*. I knew this but didn't want to admit it, admit that my language and body were being judged together. This sense of me against the world helped cultivate a stubbornness in me. I wasn't gonna let those White folks get the best of me. They can't stop me from working hard. At least, I have my labor.

The summer before my Freshman year of high school, I figured I may not be rewarded with all A-grades in school, but I sure as hell could be the hardest working motherfucker in the room. And so, that is what I did. I wrote lists and schedules. I was diligent and careful in my planning of my time. I started things early and worked longer on everything. I did not—and to this day, still do not—procrastinate. Now, to have this as your philosophy for achievement and success in school and to not always be rewarded for it meant that I needed some other motivation beyond grades, more motivation than sticking it to the man with my As. My motivation was the work itself. I figured, shit, I'm spending most of my free time on school work and studying, I should try to enjoy the doing of it. I won't lie and tell you that I was an enlightened soul at 14. I wasn't. But looking back, I was cultivating a privileging of labor over quality from age 14 to graduate school, in part out of necessity. So it really is no wonder that by the time I was a writing teacher, I saw problems with the clear and present contradictions in my own classrooms between my students' labors and the grades I was giving their products of those labors. It was unfair. I knew this, felt it—had felt it for years! It just took several more years to figure out the problematic.

To put it bluntly, to produce course grades, I trust my judgments of the quantity of writing more than I do of the quality of writing. But I realize that mere quantity doesn't necessarily equate equally to time spent laboring over a draft. Some people are faster at producing a lot of text, some are slow typists, some pine over every sentence, some just throw every word in their head down on paper, piling up pages quickly. There is lots to unpack here: we aren't simply talking about quantity or quality, but my judgments of such things. What makes more work better than so-called quality of work in a classroom where the goal is learning to write in English? Isn't it true that often less is more? How does quantity as a primary value in an assessment ecology address social inequalities in the nature of various students' languages or discourses? What's the relationship between focusing on quantity and the quality of literacy performances, or better yet, student future success? If using judgments of quality is White supremacist and racist, what makes using judgments of quantity of writing any fairer or antiracist? What about students who have other demands on their time, intersections of class and economics, intersections that surely played a role in my own background? Aren't there students who likely don't have to work and go to school at the same time? Won't they be just as privileged in a purely labor-based grading system where arguably time is the key factor for success as in typical quality-based systems of grading? Aren't those more time-privileged students also more likely to come from more economically well-off families, and aren't those families statistically more likely to be White families? These were, and still are, my concerns and questions. I don't have clear answers, even today. I do have some answers that have worked, but not fully. These questions continue to be a problematic.

So in my rethinking of grading contracts, I saw Knapp's binary judgments, which may never be avoided, as both an innovation and a problematic: judging quantity by judging minimum quality is better than having judgments of quality only, but this still ignores the work put into drafts. It ignores the labor. Nancy Reichart attempts to address this issue in her contract system, embracing both kinds of judgment. Her version of hybrid grading contracts articulates both quantity and quality criteria for students to meet in order to get the assigned grade (63). Unlike Danielewicz and Elbow's hybrid contract, which uses only quality judgments for grades above the default B grade, Reichart's uses quality judgments together for all grade distinctions. Her system is similar to Knapp's, only more explicit about what counts as minimum quality. Reichart's contract attempts to be clear about the fact that in order for a draft to be complete and count, even if a student is just trying to do the minimum, it must meet a particular set of quality standards. These standards though are still based on dominant White racial *habitus* and standards of "good writing" determined and judged by the teacher. How can these kinds of binary judgments be done in such a way that check my own version of a White racial *habitus* and discursive biases, while still using them because they're the main ones I have to judge language?

One early discussion that was particularly helpful in solving this quality vs quantity problem was Barrett John Mandel's "Teaching Without Judging," which was published in *College English* in 1973. Essentially, Mandel's system is one based on quantity of work completed by students. If a student wants a C in the class, they attend class regularly and turn in a complete C-level essay. The designation "C-level" refers to the requirements of the essay, not Mandel's judgment of quality. For Mandel, C-level work was a collaboratively written draft that students wrote and submitted. If an individual student wanted a B in the course, then they turned in B-level work. The range of B-level work Mandel listed were things such as "an intellectual journal covering the course readings and the class itself. Due twice: mid-term and end of the term," or "close analysis of one play (if the analysis differs from that which evolve in class discussion). Due any time" (Mandel 629). So to get a higher grade, Mandel's contract asked students simply to do more work in the class. What I took from Mandel's system was the idea of a contract that used only judgments of quantity, not quality, to determine all course grades. The more work or labor a student does for the class, the higher their grade should be.

Now, one might think that Mandel, like Knapp and Reichart, still had some minimum threshold for quality of any writing that meets the requirements for A- or B- or C-level work. According to Mandel, this is not the case. He accepts whatever the student hands in, but of course, offers his feedback on it for improvement on the next assignment. He explains,

> I will, theoretically, *accept* trash submitted for an "A". But I
> *believe* that in a non-judgmental, unpunitive, encouraging
> context, students will want to work toward achieving self-
> styled and often very challenging goals. While nothing in the
> format of the course coerces a student to do anything which
> reason, energetic teaching, and the student's native curios-
> ity do not inspire, I, needless to say, constantly encourage
> self-discipline and self-respecting work. (629; emphasis in
> original)

Mandel calls this having "faith in students," which he admits is easier for him than many other teachers (629). On occasion, he says, he gets the "rushed or careless junk. But [his] approach to teaching is geared to those who can and want to learn, no[t] to those who, for reasons they are entitled to, cannot avail themselves to the opportunities to learn" (629–30). In short, Mandel designed his assessment ecology around students who are willing to have faith in the ecology and in themselves to learn. He feels no need to keep his students in line, to force them to turn in writing of quality that he determines is acceptable, instead Mandel's ecology assumes that students will want to form lines in the ways they know how, that they won't need to be held accountable since they can be responsible on their own. They want to learn and want to work.

When I first read Mandel's article, one published when I was only three years old, I couldn't help but find a deep affinity to his ethical stand concerning his teaching and students. It struck me then and now that my students are entitled to give me whatever they want—or rather, whatever they *can*. And I'm equally entitled to tell them what I think of it and how it may not be helping them toward their goals in the course. They may be ready to listen or not, but their learning and labor should be their choice. I cannot coerce them into learning or enlightenment. I agree with Mandel still. This is how we all should be able to work with students, to labor together. I realize that all teachers may not be able or willing to try "energetic teaching" that inspires students to do "self-disciplined and self-respecting work," or that if we do attempt this kind of teaching, we could recognize such efforts by all students, or even that such energetic teaching will always lead to students responding in these ways. I also realize the problematic in notions of teaching that promote unquestioned ideas about students that just need freedom and encouragement to do what they want in order to really learn, yet classrooms require environments that encourage risks and learning through failure, doing what we can, not what others tell us to. While I think Mandel's system is not overly-idealistic about his students, I do realize that to many, it seems like pie-in-the-sky, dreamy pedagogy.

I also know that Mandel's system sounds a bit like hippie-free-love-anti-teaching, and this may discredit it in some teachers' eyes. But I ask why? What is so wrong with a "non-judgmental, unpunitive, encouraging" classroom assessment ecologies? Who says that judgmental, punitive, and discouraging assessment ecologies work better? I know, I'm creating a false binary, but I'm also trying to reveal what our real assumptions are about the kinds of judgments we make on student writing, how we use them, and why we think those uses are the best ones to employ for mostly institutionally demanded elements of our courses (i.e., the need for grades). I'm trying to show our assumptions about our students when we create assessment ecologies that grade student writing and think this is good for them in some way. Do grades motivate students? No, but they do force students, coerce them into doing things, which we usually read as motivation. Coercion is not motivation. Real motivation is doing something even when—and usually when—there is no extrinsic reward, when no one is watching.

And those who say they are motivated by grades I'm guessing have been fooled by the system, integrated into it, thoroughly disciplined, made docile by grades, made to think that their yearning for grades is motivation, because they know no other kind. The yearning for grades, the yearning to be graded, has become so habitual to many students, especially those who have been rewarded by them, that it feels natural. It feels fair and right, but as Freire and Villanueva remind us, part of literacy education is questioning how natural the natural is. Why do I yearn to be graded? How is it fair and helpful to me exactly? What assurances do I actually have that the grades I'm getting will help me in the future?

Grading contracts can offer this questioning because they raise these questions precisely. When grades are absent, many students must ask: What am I motivated by? What do I really care about in the learning, in this work in front of me? At a deeper ethical level, forcing someone to do something because we just know it's better for them by dangling grades in front of them, places ends over means, beyond being a habit of White discourse. I think, both ends and means need to match. Our methods for assessment should match our good ends or goals. It seems deeply disrespectful of others—no matter who they are—for me as a teacher to coerce students into doing things they are unwilling to do, but I can make them because I know what they want. While one can never quite escape a certain level of coercion in classrooms, one can reduce it dramatically. And call it what it is.

Invoking his "liberal role" in "the liberal arts" to justify his pedagogy, Mandel cites a student author from *Change* magazine, who "lambasted her left-wing professors for shooting off their mouths about liberal, human values, and teaching in an atmosphere of stuffy, conservative self-deception." Mandel continues by quoting the student: "Don't speak of the liberation of the subjugated and then lower my grade because I hand in a paper late" (630). This is at the heart of the problematic I kept seeing in grades in writing classrooms that attempted to be critical ones or self-conscious and reflective ones. Our pedagogies and writing philosophies are warm, soft, social, and inviting, but our assessment ecologies are cold, hard, individualistic (even selfish), and discouraging. Conventional assessment ecologies are too often uncritical of where their standards for quality and methods come from, who benefits most from them, who has more or less access to them, who uses them to judge, and what the patterned, racialized consequences are because of those judgments and methods, and who controls them.

This blindness or silence in conventional assessment ecologies is a product of Whiteness. It is White blindness, or silence, that writing teachers too often have. It is an inability to recognize that we are controlling the rules of a racialized language game that allow us to win, asking (racialized) others to play, knowing that many cannot follow very easily the rules we've made that help us win, and by default make sure they lose, because as long as others keep losing, we win. Keep the barbarians in the outer dikes, or better yet, keep them out of all the dikes, goes the tacit logic of the system.

Mandel's article was the key to convincing me that how much labor students were willing and able to do in my classes was a fairer, more socially just, more antiracist, way to calculate grades. I also noticed at the time that in my classes at

Fresno State, an historically Hispanic Serving Institution, most of my students came from working-class Latinx families, many of whom labored in fields in the San Joaquin Valley's farms, or they themselves worked in the labor economies in and around Fresno. Bodily labor was important, understood, and I think, respected as honorable work. I became more and more aware of my own body at work and in work, which affected several dimensions of my own writing. Thus it wasn't just the quantity of writing that I wanted to account for in my grading system, but quantity of labor. But this isn't quite true either. What I finally settled on is labor power, a Marxian concept, which I'll discuss in Chapter 3. For now, quantity of writing and time might roughly be equated to quantity of labor, even though this isn't completely true. At this stage, one in which I moved to a labor-based grading contract, I was thinking almost solely in terms of quantity.

Now, one might think that a grading contract system that rewards the amount of work or writing done in a writing class instead of any judgments of quality on the teacher's part would not be very effective at helping the institutionally vulnerable students that I have spend most of my career teaching. I'm speaking of students of color, multilingual students, and working-class students. I'm speaking of students who tend to come to writing classrooms with less contact with the dominant White racial *habitus* that informs the standards in all courses that ask for writing, and that outside contexts and audiences value as most communicative. But in fact, these are the very populations that benefit most from grading contracts. I conducted program-wide assessments of mostly labor-based grading contracts at Fresno State, which showed that most students of color actually do better in many dimensions of quality in final portfolios, and are happier with their writing experiences, feeling that the absence of grades helped them in their learning (Inoue, "Grading Contracts"). Blackstock and Exton also found similar conclusions about hybrid grading contracts in community college and tribal college writing courses, where most of their "nontraditional students also largely fit the profile of 'basic writers' elaborated by David Bartholomae's book *Writing on the Margins*" (279). In their surveying of students, they found that hybrid contracts helped their students because "[b]asic writers perceive that they do not have control over their writing skills, but they can usually control their ability to attend class, engage in academic activities, and complete assignments" (284).

Blackstock and Exton use a similar contract as Danielewicz and Elbow's and say that its shift from focusing on quality of products to the writing process was instrumental in helping their students find the contract helpful in their courses (284). Like all hybrid grading contracts, Blackstock and Exton also found some difficulties with the hybrid aspect of the contract. When discussing motivation, which often goes hand-in-hand with discussions about grades (e.g., if there are no grades, how will students be motivated to revise or turn in a polished draft?), they admit that students who were motivated by such things as grades and percentages will not be satisfied with a hybrid grading contract system. Even still, they point out that it is important to identify in some way the conditions for an A, the only final course grades in which quality of writing in a final portfolio is considered (288). Still, they see problems and contradictions with so-called clearly articulated criteria for A-quality work in contracts and rubrics, saying that the "language is admittedly subjective and tends to raise more questions than it answers." So they "are moving toward adopting simple behavior criteria: students may earn an A by submitting additional drafts of the assigned essays" (289). In effect, Blackstock and Exton appear to move toward a purely labor-based grading contract.

And so, this is where my story about how I came to labor-based grading contracts moves to what I use today, a purely labor-based system that only uses quantity of labor, no matter its products, as a way to calculate final course grades. I'll describe the details of this contract in the Chapter 4, but now I end with Max Marshall, the professor of Microbiology with whom I began this chapter. While he isn't speaking about grading contracts but of getting rid of grades completely in college courses, Marshall articulates one problem of grades and learning in 1960 (reprinted from an article in 1958) that I think labor-based grading contracts easily solves:

> Suppose that, instead of a grade, words are used, perhaps a comment like this: "Slow on the uptake, earnest, reasonably industrious." This could be equivalent to a "C," but that student is entitled to his place in the world. He goes to school not to get a teacher's judgment but because the teacher has more experience than he has. In some situations his talents and efforts may have to be discussed, but this is a sort of indecent gossip and should be restricted whenever possible. To describe his work is bad enough. To use a mere symbol, a "C," is an unhelpful imposition. The student asks what to do with his sick horse and is told that his horse is sick. A healthy attitude calls for concern with the student's talents and efforts and what to do with them. A teacher can be friendly with and can respect any honest student. A barrier is erected between the two when the teacher merely bestows the highhanded "C" mediocrity. (Marshall 26)

Words instead of grades. Yes. Learning instead of measuring. Yes. Students finding motivation in and through their own languaging instead of grades. Yes.

David Bleich called these things, "descriptive evaluation" (29), and even cites Max Marshall's 1968 book, *Teaching Without Grades*. Brian Huot called it "instructive evaluation" (69). I think, particularly given the values and understandings about literacies of our field and their connections to writers' subjectivities, we should demand these kinds of assessment ecologies, or least work consciously in ways against the prevailing ecologies of grades.

CHAPTER 3.

WHAT IS LABOR IN LABOR-BASED GRADING CONTRACTS?

Part of problematizing my own grading practices and moving to labor-based grading contracts was coming to a fuller understanding of labor in a classroom writing assessment ecology. This chapter theorizes labor as it pertains to writing classroom assessment ecologies.

Labor is the engine that runs all learning. You can't learn without laboring. Labor requires a body in motion, even if the motions are small or slight. We speak through our bodies. Our lungs inhale air, chest and belly expand and relax, mouth opens and closes, lips and tongue dance together. Each time we speak, our bodies move in amazingly elaborate and coordinated ways, like a synchronized dance group, each dancer moving their part, forming a larger organism that produces something more than the sum of the individuals dancing. Our brains also expend a lot of energy doing the work of thinking and processing. In fact, many magnetic resonance spectroscopy (MRS) studies have confirmed the heavy energy demands of the brain. The human brain uses 20% of the body's total energy expenditure, with two thirds of that energy going to cognitive processes of thinking, the electrical impulses that activate neurons (Swaminathan).

If labor is energy used, calories burned, then thinking is hard labor. When we write, a similar coordinated dance occurs, whether we put pen to paper, or fingers to keyboard, or dictate into a smartphone, our bodies move and our brains work to make and process language. When we read text or make sense of images or symbols, we similarly expend bodily energy, even if in subtle ways. When we manipulate a computer keyboard or mouse to scroll through pages on a screen, or lick our fingers to turn a page, our eyes move back and forth, our brains activate neurons. We sit in a chair, move our hips and adjust our position to get more comfortable, shifting ourselves every now and then. Perhaps we drink tea as we read, or walk around the room. Some of us may even move our lips, mouthing the words our eyes scan across the page, or speak those words in whispers to ourselves. These bodily movements, combined with our brain's firing and burning of energy, make the acts of languaging bodily labor, work, energy expended. Bodily labor is fundamental to all learning. No one learns without laboring, without doing in some way, without moving their body, even if only slightly.[14] This is what my labor-based grading contract assumes at its most basic level: to learn is to labor.

If this is true, if labor is the most fundamental thing we are asking of students, then we should understand its dimensions theoretically, particularly if we are using it to calculate final course grades, as labor-based grading contracts do. Understanding labor in a variety of ways can help us design and use it more thoughtfully and carefully. Furthermore, as I hope much of my discussion in this chapter illustrates, theorizing labor more precisely can also reveal the problems and limitations of conventional classroom assessment ecologies that ignore or do not account explicitly for labor in grading. That is, understanding what exactly labor is and how it functions in ecologies reveals how conventional ecologies that do not use labor as a way to calculate grades may be harming students or treating them unfairly.

Up to this point, I've used the term "labor" to mean roughly the work done in and for a course, that is, the bodily work of reading, writing, and other activities associated with what it takes to engage in a writing course. I reference this work in the labor-based grading contract and the course's labor instructions for all assignments in a couple of ways, by time spent on a task or activity, and by the amount of words produced when writing (if the activity is a writing task) or the number of pages or words read (if the task is a reading one). In this chapter, I pause to think carefully about the concept of labor, define it from two different directions, first from a Marxian theoretical perspective, and second from the theories of labor offered by Hannah Arendt. I also rearticulate these theories of value and labor into a simpler theory that may help students better understand labor in contract grading economies, which I call three-dimensional labor. Finally, I end the chapter on a short discussion of one consistent theme, seeing labor as a mindful practice that is important to students' learning. My central questions in this chapter are simple: What is labor exactly? How might we understand it in order to better design and use labor-based grading contracts?

ASSESSMENT ECOLOGIES ARE ALSO POLITICAL ECONOMIES

Marxian theory seems the most obvious place to begin theorizing and understanding labor. The concept of labor is important to Marxian theory, and it isn't hard to see how all assessment ecologies are also political economies since not

---

14   I realize that I am neglecting those who are paralyzed or disabled in ways that keep them from moving their bodies, and I cannot account for this, except that even those disabled in these ways still have brains that expend enormous amounts of energy, hearts and lungs that beat and move, all in order to labor with language, or process language.

only is one main element of assessment ecologies power relations but they are also complex systems similar to political economies. In many ways "ecology" and "economy" are interchangeable, at least in the way I refer to them in this chapter. Assessment ecologies, even ones that avoid giving grades, still are systems of exchange. In them, texts, ideas, judgments, and labor are exchanged. Riddell, Shackelford, Stamos, and Schneider offer a good definition of political economy that seems easily applicable to any classroom assessment ecology if we replace "economic events" and "economic systems" with classroom assessment events and systems:

> Political economy . . . is more concerned with the relation-
> ships of the economic system and its institutions to the rest of
> society and social development. It is sensitive to the influence
> of non-economic factors such as political and social institu-
> tions, morality, and ideology in determining economic events.
> It thus has a much broader focus than economics. (quot. in
> Sackrey et al. 3–4)

In writing classroom economies, the above "non-economic factors" also apply to the value and functioning of grades and what we might loosely call writing quality of drafts, or some judgment of a draft's quality based on a comparison to some dominant standard used by the reader-grader, who is typically a teacher. This means that classroom assessment economies are sensitive to influences by these non-draft-quality factors that circulate around a text. While these factors can be broad in scope and reach, they can also be understood in some unified sense as *habitus*, which I discussed in Chapter 1. In a general way, *habitus* identifies the sociocultural and structural elements that become internalized as individual habits and dispositions that readers bring to texts, see in them, and use to make meaning. Thus, reader's judgments of a text say more about their own biases and values than they do about so-called quality of the text in question. This is one way to account for how the same text can be judged by the same person very differently at different times, when the ecology has changed or the influences in the system have changed. This also reveals the unevenness in classroom assessment economies.

To talk about a political economy of the classroom, then, is to talk about relationships of things in the ecology, of *habitus* embodied in texts and embodied in readers judging, of grades or judgments themselves, and of writing and reading labors. These relationships are also between ecological elements across the entire ecology (i.e., grading practices and processes, material conditions and places, people, documents and assessment parts, values, expectations, learning products, etc.), which include outside influences (e.g. other classes, students' working conditions and family lives, their relations to certain kinds of labor and commodities, etc.). Tony Scott has discussed this second aspect in the political economy of writing classrooms, looking closely at the way students' lives in fast-capitalism intersect with their lives in the classroom. Scott's pedagogy attempts to account better for the way working-class students tend to experience learning and college by focusing on the curricular theme of "work," giving students a chance to examine and interrogate work, labor, and their lives in relation to these things.

While outside-the-classroom capitalist structures' effects on students' labor in writing classrooms is important, it is not the focus of this chapter. My focus is on understanding the concept of labor in the classroom, considering how theories of political economy, among others, offer an explanation of the labor students do for our courses, which then tell us more about what happens when labor-based grading ecologies are functioning and perhaps how to design them better in the future. Additionally, in this chapter, I use political economy synonymously with assessment ecology. They refer to the same system, only political economy foregrounds the ecological element of power relationships among elements and in exchanges, while assessment ecology highlights the system's holistic and complex nature.

In his own defining of political economy, Scott emphasizes the way the concept calls attention to "the systemic/ideological and the particular/material" (15). His summing up of the concept is worth repeating:

> Broad trends and political policies— systems that organize
> and value human labor— have profound effects on individu-
> als; in turn, individual decisions and actions are what embody
> and enact those broad trends, policies, and systems. "Econ-
> omy" isn't the sum total of a set of formulas or quantified
> indicators: those are only attempts to understand and describe
> a dynamic, codependent, evolving material entity. (16)

While he's speaking of a political economy that is the fast-capitalist one often thought of as outside the writing classroom, it's easy to see how this could apply to a classroom's assessment ecology as a political economy. All assessment systems use student labor in exchanges with other things of value, such as grades, essays, feedback, or learning products or outcomes, but typically labor is not a commodity, not the thing exchanged directly. Below I'll say more about how this works and why it's important to make clear. In labor-based grading contract ecologies, however, labor is an explicit commodity that is exchanged, making it more valuable and present (not ignored) in the system—thus, making it more valuable and valued in the economy.

Scott's definition focuses attention on the consubstantial nature of the structural to the existential, the systemic to the material, the system to the labor that constitutes much of it. And the value of labor is central to understanding the system and one's place in it, as well as the power relations that define one's movement and learning in the system. In fact, labor as a unit of exchange and value is the foundation of all classroom assessment economies, whether we pay attention to it or not. Thus, as I'll discuss later in this chapter, a labor-based assessment economy provides particularly fruitful ways to ask students to problematize their labor practices in order to understand the nature of their labor and its value, or what they learn from their labor.

If assessment ecologies are political economies, then it is not hard to see that one primary unit of exchange, one commodity, is grades, even when we construct assessment ecologies that may work against handing out a lot of them, as with portfolio pedagogies (Hamp-Lyons and Condon) and grading contracts. While as writing teachers we are interested primarily in what students learn and how they learn, we usually have to give grades, at least a course grade. And students cannot NOT care about their grades. The course grade will live on after the course is over, even long after the events and details blur from clear memory. Many outside our classrooms care about grades. Grades are valuable to these others, and are often exchanged for scholarships, degrees, certifications, awards, admission into graduate schools, jobs, etc. So much of the political economy of the writing classroom depends on and affects how grades are produced, distributed, exchanged, and consumed by students and those outside the classroom.

To say that the writing classroom is a political economy is not a new position. John Trimbur offers a compelling argument for writing teachers to pay closer attention to the circulation of writing as a kind of commodity in classroom economies, although he's speaking more about the production of readings of cultural texts, like books, ads, etc., that are often discussed in writing classrooms. Trimbur draws heavily on Marx's formulation of the process of production, distribution, exchange, and consumption found in *Grundrisse*. He concludes on two points. The first is that Marx's evaluation helps writing teachers see that in a classroom where student writing and readings of texts are circulated, "the question to begin with is not so much where the commodity goes as what it carries in its internal workings as it circulates." He continues, "the distribution of commodities [like cultural texts and student essays] cannot be understood apart from the distribution of the means of production" (209).

Let me put this in different terms. In labor-based grading contract economies, the labor of reading, drafting, feedback from peers and teacher, and all the activities that go into producing and reading a draft, are circulated in a cycle of production and can be considered part of the process of production as well as distribution, exchange, and consumption. What gets circulated in this recursive cycle are various activities and abilities of different agents in the classroom, what I've referred to as *habitus*, all of which determine how the student essay is read and judged. When no grades are circulating in these cycles, only documents and judgments, then labor and its value become more prominent and important, and more obvious, assuming that everyone is willing to agree to give up having those grades on everything. Attention by people in the economy returns to the labor and what it produces. Trimbur concludes, "we cannot understand what is entailed when people encounter written texts without taking into account how the labor power embodied in the commodity form [like a commercial being analyzed by a class or peer feedback on an essay] articulates a mode of production and its prevailing social relations" (210).

To understand fully this conclusion, it's important to understand the distinction that Marx makes between labor and labor power that Trimbur invokes. As Marx explains in volume one of *Capital*, "[l]abour is, in the first place, a process in which both man and Nature participate, and in which man of his own accord starts, regulates, and controls the material re-actions between himself and Nature" (n. pag.).[15] In other words, everyone owns their own labor, the work they can do. However, in capitalist markets, one might sell one's labor for a time because one may only own their labor and not other commodities for exchange. One's own labor may be all one has to exchange in the marketplace. In chapter six of *Capital*, Marx explains that one's labor, when offered and exchanged in the market, becomes a commodity itself, which he calls, "labor power": "[b]y labour-power or capacity for labour is to be understood the aggregate of those mental and physical capabilities existing in a human being, which he exercises whenever he produces a use-value of any description" (n. pag.). I'll say more about use-value below, but for now, it's important to see in Marx's words that one can exchange one's labor power for a time, but not one's labor, since the latter is connected to one's biological body and life. One may labor, but one has labor power to exchange in the marketplace. Hannah Arendt agrees with this notion of labor in her theorizing of labor as mainly biological, which I'll discuss later in this chapter.

At this point, according to classical Marxian theory, if you sell your labor, you sell yourself as a slave, which means you would cease to own your capacity to do labor for your own living. You become a commodity.[16] In labor-based

15   I retain the sexist pronoun used in the original material quoted in this chapter for accuracy reasons, realizing its exclusionary nature. When I reference a generic plural, I use the plural pronoun that is more gender inclusive.

16   This definition of labor and its connection to the slave offers an interesting critique of Farber's analogy to the normalize student as Black slave I discussed in Chapter 1. Essentially, according to this Marxian reading of labor and labor power, students cannot be slaves, since all still control their own labor.

assessment ecologies, then, it is your labor power that you exchange, not your labor. Labor power is an abstract concept used to describe the commodity that people exchange in a political economic system who have no capital or material commodities. When all you have is your labor, you still have your labor power as a commodity for exchange in the marketplace. In *The Principles of Communism*, Engels too makes the point that in markets where commodities are exchanged labor power is exchanged as a commodity.

Trimbur's conclusion, then, speaks to the ways that labor power circulates in something like an essay and its associated feedback in a classroom by peers and the teacher. Thus, what is entailed in what students can learn or a reader can provide to a writer must be a result of the way the labor power embodied in the essay and its feedback articulate the mode of production of the essay and feedback, and of the prevailing social relations of the classroom. Our labors are never lost, because their residue, labor power, circulates. Put even more simply, a student's feedback on a colleague's draft accumulates value through the ways it is circulated in the assessment economy, through the labor done and encapsulated in the draft, its feedback, and other exchanges around the draft. Value is created and accumulated by that circulation. The engine of that circulation is the labor that students do. What is carried forward or exchanged in the system is labor power accumulated.

Thus when feedback is used in various ways, ways beyond the draft it discusses, say in problem-posing activities with the writer about the nature of judgment in feedback, that circulation creates more value because of the labor power accumulated in the system. Labor by people is the biological engine, the kinetic energy used in the system, that creates and circulates this value. Labor power, then, is the stockpile of materials that each person in the system offers in exchanges and that accumulates in the system. It is the potential energy to be used and exchanged, collected and accumulated.

The second conclusion Trimbur draws in his article is equally important to my present discussion. The "unity of opposites in the commodity form— exchange value and use value—enables not only tangential and impertinent readings. Its unity is a contradictory one" (210). I'll come back to the contradictions of use- and exchange-value below. They are important to learning in any assessment economy, but labor-based grading contract economies offer explicit ways to take advantage of these contradictions. For now, note that Trimbur has broken ground on thinking about the Marxian articulations of labor and value in cycles of production, distribution, exchange, and consumption in writing classrooms.[17]

---

17   I wish to thank John Trimbur for his gracious time and good feedback on an earlier version of this chapter, in which he helped me think about labor power and nuance the concept of "worth" that I discuss later.

We also should keep in mind that the term "economy" has an etymology that helps us see classroom writing assessment cycles of production, distribution, exchange, and consumption as ones that cultivate private practices and social customs, which helps make sense of where those "tangential and impertinent" judgments of texts originate and why contradictions exist in the first place. The etymology of the terms also reveals another reason why writing classrooms blur the lines between public and private, the social and the individual.

The Oxford English Dictionary shows the etymology of the word "economy" coming from the ancient Greek οἰκονομικά (*oikonomia*), which derives from two familiar words to those who study rhetoric: *oikos* (household) and *nomos* (law). Several of OED's definitions (2a, 2b, 3, and 4) reveal this etymology by focusing on the management of the household or the body, while others focus on the management of society and community ("economy, n." n. pag.). In *The Political Economy of Communication*, Vincent Mosco also explains this etymology, concluding that "political economy therefore originated in the management of the family and political households" (23). So a classroom writing assessment economy calls attention to the various, diverse *habitus* of the people in the economy, and how we all are always situated in larger social systems, communities of diverse individuals who also fit into groups of people. The diverse *habitus* in the classroom are vital to the way the system functions to create and circulate value in labors. The value and nature of our labor as individuals is a function of our *habitus* in context, of who we are, where we come from, what dispositions we carry, where and how we work for the class, and so on. In some sense, this etymology reminds us of the interconnected domestic (personal) and social spheres that are managed simultaneously, that work together symbiotically, always by everyone.

This blurring of public and private, market and home, agrees with Bradley A. Ault's discussion of *oikos* and the larger market economies in ancient Hellenic societies, which he describes as "coexistive" with each other (262). Ault argues that "notions of domestic self-sufficiency" of archaic and Hellenic households are likely inaccurate. Household management wasn't based on providing for one's own family alone, rather "the orientation of the household would tend . . . towards market exchange, and hence local and regional economic development" (259). In various ways, Ault shows how the private household was a center of commercial exchange, or at least interconnected to the larger commercial exchanges in the *agora*. For instance, archeological findings in Megara Hyblaia reveal how houses contained more and more storage space from the eighth to the sixth century, likely for storing surplus commodities that the household produced for the market (Ault 260).

Labor-based grading contract economies highlight in a number of ways the interconnectedness of private and social practices (e.g., private labor and publicly circulated labor power) of students and teacher, of the private home and public market, of commodities' movement between these spheres, and of these spheres' relations to cycles of production, distribution, exchange, and consumption. Furthermore, reading generously the ancient Hellenic society, we might see their conception of economy as one that not only blurs the line between home and market, but the personal and the social. In the political economy of a labor-based grading contract classroom, one's personal learning is consubstantial, interconnected to, everyone else's. Learning is only social. There is no private learning, no private judgments. This gives extra reason to consider compassion and something like the Charter for Compassion (discussed in Chapter 5) as central to understanding the meaning and significance of labor and labor power in classrooms since it asks students to labor for one another in communal ways.

Finally, Mosco offers an equally compelling definition for political economy that reminds us of a needed emphasis when using it to understand the concept of labor. That emphasis is "the study of *the social relations, particularly the power relations, that mutually constitute the production, distribution, and consumption of resources*" (24; emphasis in original). Two things that Mosco's definition highlights may not be clear in Riddell, Shackelford, Stamos, and Schneider's. The first is the political economy's focus on relationships that make up an assessment ecology. These relationships affect labor and how it is valued and circulated. The second is that those relationships develop power relations (and may be such relations) that "mutually constitute" cycles of production, distribution, exchange, and consumption. As Mosco explains later in the chapter, power can be understood as relations that organize the "ability to control other people, processes, and things, even in the face of resistance" (24).

In labor-based grading contract economies, the cycles of production, distribution, exchange, and consumption that constitute writing assessments are inextricably threaded with power, which makes labor and its value threaded with power relations as well. One important aspect of these power relations are the *habitus* of the people involved and where those *habitus* are in relation to a dominant standard or to others in the classroom. When used as the standard, dominant White racial *habitus* determine the power relations in classroom assessment economies. But in labor-based economies, attention is called to these power relations (and *habitus*), allowing them to be more easily seen and interrogated. Additionally, one *habitus* is not privileged as the standard, instead amount or quantity of labor determines grades—labor power becomes more important. This means that much like Marx's critique of capitalist systems, the point in more liberatory political systems is to give as many people as possible control over the means of production. In this case, I'm referring to the means to produce value in and around writing and reading practices, or around students' labors of learning, which amount to the production of course grades. Liberation, then, comes from the ways students' labor power is circulated as a commodity. To do this, we must understand better how value is produced through student labor and exchanged through labor power in labor-based assessment economies, and how those economies provide for more critical learning than conventional assessment economies.

LABOR IS AT THE CENTER OF ALL THEORIES OF VALUE

The value of labor has been a central concern for economists, even before Marx. The eighteenth-century economist Adam Smith placed labor at the center of his economic theories that focused on alleviating poverty and reducing infant mortality rates, which he saw as connected to poverty (Sackrey et al. 30). Labor, Smith says in the introduction to *The Wealth of Nations*, is the "fund which originally supplies" a nation "with all the necessaries and conveniences of life" (Smith n. pag.; Sackrey et al. 43). Thus, labor is important to Smith's theorizing of value in economies, keeping in mind that his point of reference was a mercantile economy, not a capitalist one, and perhaps one closer to those of ancient Hellenic economies.[18] Still, we can see how Marx's ideas of labor follow in Smith's steps, and both theorize value of labor in markets.

Smith explains that value has two categories that help explain why things cost what they do and why those prices rise and fall. He says:

> The word value, it is to be observed, has two different meanings, and sometimes expresses the utility of some particular object, and sometimes the power of purchasing other goods which the possession of that object conveys. The one may be called "value in use"; the other, "value in exchange." The things which have the greatest value in use have frequently little or no value in exchange; and, on the contrary, those which have the greatest value in exchange have frequently little or no value in use. Nothing is more useful than water: but it will purchase scarce anything; scarce anything can be had in exchange for it. A diamond, on the contrary, has scarce any value in use; but a very great quantity of other goods may frequently be had in exchange for it. (Smith n. pag.)

18   Laura LaHaye in the *Concise Encyclopedia of Economics* provides this definition of mercantilism: "Mercantilism is economic nationalism for the purpose of building a wealthy and powerful state. Adam Smith coined the term 'mercantile system' to describe the system of political economy that sought to enrich the country by restraining imports and encouraging exports." Book IV of Adam Smith's *Wealth of Nations* offers an extensive treatment of his notion of the mercantile system.

So political economies work with and generate use-value and exchange-value, the former is determined by the uses the producer or others might make of the commodity in question, while the latter is the value that is produced through exchange by others desiring the commodity, or what someone can trade the commodity for on the market. Use- and exchange-values are easy to understand, and while distinct, are also related and create a contradiction that Trimbur, and Smith, have already mentioned. Later, political economists like Jean-Baptiste Say and David Ricardo will elaborate on what they saw is a linear causal relationship between use- and exchange-value.

In simple terms, we don't buy things we don't have a use for, most of the time. One can see the link between use- and exchange-value in the value of a theoretical home purchased in 2005 for $250,000 before the housing market collapsed in the US, which in 2008 reduced dramatically the prices of homes in most areas. This theoretical home in 2009, let's say, is valued at only $150K, or rather its exchange-value on the real estate market is valued at that price. However, to the family who lives in the home, cares for it, has meaningful familial experiences in it, and can afford their mortgage without hardship in 2009, the home has a use-value that is hard to put a price tag on. It's their home. It gives them more than what their money can buy. It is in this *more than* quality that we might see the contradiction in use- and exchange-values. One might see a similar gap in a student's hard work on a draft that receives a lower than expected grade. To the student, the labor and draft may have accumulated more value than the grade suggests.

This gap is not simply one created by equivocation in the term value. This would dislodge use-value from exchange-value, suggesting that they are not intimately connected to one another. Smith, Marx, Say, and Ricardo keep them wedded together, as do I. Grades, for instance, would not be very exchangeable if they were not indicators of use, of learning, and thus of what the student offers future employers or graduate programs, or is some predictor of future success. Grades, theoretically, are useful in these ways. However, in theory, GPAs have only as much exchange-value as they have use-value, in theory. Even in labor-based grading contract economies, where there are no grades on drafts, it is the judgments and feedback that have exchange- and use-value. Grades have no exchange-value because they are not used in a labor-based system. Theoretically, the use of my feedback on a draft to a student might be measured in the degree or extent that the student can use that feedback in future work on the draft or for the class. Its exchange-value is linked to those uses. If there are several other assignments in which the student must use my feedback in some way, say discuss them with me, create a revision plan, or pose problems about the judgments I make on their draft, then my feedback is highly exchangeable because it is highly useful, but not necessarily outside of the classroom, at least not directly.

However, in all economies, use- and exchange-value for a commodity rarely match up perfectly. Commodities often have different use- and exchange-values simultaneously. This simple distinction between use- and exchange-value in a classroom assessment economy helps us see why students might find a teacher's feedback or grade mostly useless (having little use-value) in the class, which might lead them to do nothing with that feedback, or see the grade as simply the only thing that is important. However, they may also know that they need to accumulate high grades in the class because of the higher exchange-value those grades purchase after the course is over, through their translation into a higher course grade. The classroom's assessment economy sets up these different use- and exchange-values. My guess is that ideally most writing teachers would like to think that their feedback, and maybe even the grades they give students on their writing, have equally high use- and exchange-values. This begs the question: How exactly is the classroom's assessment economy constructing high use-values for all the commodities it circulates? The bottom line is that the two kinds of value are interconnected, so the gap is not an equivocation but a paradox created by the political economy in which that commodity and value circulate.

Part of the reason Smith can conceive of two categories of value in economies is because of the need to exchange commodities and a common unit of exchange, money. In capitalist markets such as today, the gap between use- and exchange-value appears more evident because value is usually measured in monetary ways, which is one level removed from the measurements of use, and more importantly from desire and aesthetic, emotional, and ethical considerations from which people actually operate, which I'll call a commodity's actual *worth*. Worth varies by person, and is measured in a multitude of ways, not just by possible use but also by aesthetic appreciation, how a commodity makes one feel, by our desire for the commodity, and by our moral or ethical associations around the commodity, all of which are not the same as need or use. This unaccounted for aspect of value, what I'm naming worth, helps name the contradiction that Trimbur points out in his discussion of use- and exchange-value.

Trimbur identifies the contradiction's source in the way that the capitalist mode of production "reproduces the prevailing and contradictory social and economic relations . . . where socialized production, with its promise of overcoming material scarcity, is at odds with the goal of private profit" (208). He offers a systematic way of understanding the gap, the contradiction. I argue that part of this contradiction in the capitalist mode of production is that it doesn't account for worth (or value produced by desire that is linked to ethical, emotional, and aesthetic dimensions), yet worth is a part of the judgments we make that lead to production, distribution, exchange, and consumption of all commodities. Note that worth accounts for embodied ways we encounter commodities in all systems that Marxian explanations of use- and exchange-value neglect. The bodily emotional responses we have to commodities, including the value we place on our labor power, affect our desires for them, or our feelings about them. This is an individualistic way to understand how these contradictions or gaps are created that is also systemic or structural. If worth involves the categories of aesthetic, emotion, ethics, and desire, then worth is key to the circulation of commodities in the writing classroom. This suggests that worth may help us articulate the contradictions in the valuing of commodities and the place of labor power in such valuing.

Now, arguably desire is the larger category within those I've used to define worth. It often encompasses ethical, aesthetic, and emotional dimensions. To understand desire as systemic, one might look to how it is manufactured, or socially structured, in a number of ways that many, such as Lacan (i.e., the imaginary), Althusser (i.e., interpellation), and Freud (i.e., overdetermination) have discussed. The undervalued home above is a good example of this. Another example is the worth a luxury car gives someone who wants others to see them as successful and happy, attributes that some associate with the luxury car. The car owner could have bought a reasonably priced economy car, but the luxury car has more worth in particular social circles, which may make one feel good about oneself. The owner may also desire the luxury car for other private reasons that stem from what Lacan described as "the imaginary," a coherent system that congeals into an internal, whole, ideal image of the self that mediates the world and one's self (Lacan). The luxury car's use-value is the same as the economy car, but one's desire will regulate an individual's sense of its worth, which may lead to a decision to purchase regardless of its exchange-value. In this case, worth is not the same as exchange-value, since worth is measured in desire, not in money like exchange-value. And use-value is beside the point. Any car will be useful, but that is not the main criterion by which the buyer is making the decision to buy. In fact, such decisions in capitalist economies may tell us about the class-related *habitus* of individuals. The less money you have the more likely your purchases must be regulated by a commodity's exchange- and use-values. The more money you have, the more luxury and privilege you have to make buying decisions based on a commodity's worth to you, regardless of exchange- or use-values.

In some instances, the differences between use- and exchange-values may help create worth, or may contradict it. In some cases still, it could be argued that worth operates outside of both use- and exchange-value. No matter the worth an individual places on the luxury car, for example, that worth is determined in the Marxian sense that is both an individual set of decisions that are constrained by larger, social structures that pressure people to make particular kinds of decisions, or to have particular kinds of desires. Here we see at the

micro level, the level of personal desire, the consubstantial nature of the circulation of value in economies that Scott identifies, the way individual desires reflect
or react to broader trends.

The gaps between use- and exchange-value are also produced because of a
common unit of measurement, money, which didn't exist uniformly in pre-
capitalist economies where bartering was more common. If one is a pig farmer
today, one doesn't exchange their pigs for produce or clothing. This would be an
exchange based on a more direct measurement (e.g., one pig equals six bushels
of corn or two pairs of wool trousers), and this measure would be contingent on
many local factors— it's rhetorically and socially constructed (if you like), constructed in the physical exchange between farmer and merchant and the agreements they make or assume about the labor power encapsulated in what they
offer and the degree of worth each sees in the commodities exchanged. Value in
a barter system is out of contingency and necessity. Value is very idiosyncratic
and uneven. It may depend on what one party needs, making the use-value more
important. In other cases, it may be that one party wishes to exchange yet again
to a third party for other goods or services, which makes the exchange-value
more important in that particular exchange. This is a system that is messy and
inconsistent, but very human.

In capitalist economies, we sell pigs for money, then we buy our produce and
pants with that money. While this kind of exchange is unspoken today, it isn't
natural, and needed explicit mention by Plutarch in his historical recording. In
Chapter 16 of *Life of Perikles*, Plutarch writes of Pericles:

> As to his paternal estate, he was loth to lose it, and still more
> to be troubled with the management of it; consequently, he
> adopted what seemed to him the simplest and most exact
> method of dealing with it. Every year's produce was sold all
> together, and with the money thus obtained, he would buy
> what was necessary for his household in the market, and thus
> regulate his expenditure. (n. pag.)

Apparently, Plutarch reports that Pericles' family was not very happy about
his practice of exchanging the surplus commodities of his household into money every year. As Plutarch explains in the same passage, the women and sons of
his family found Pericles a poor manager of the household, and "blamed his
exact regulation of his daily expenses, which allowed none of the superfluities
common in great and wealthy households, but which made the debit and credit
exactly balance each other." The tension in Pericles' household economy occurred because of his practice of translating the household's commodities into
monetary exchange-value and managing only that value. Without making too

much of this brief passage, could it have been that Pericles' family saw some of the worth of those commodities disappear once they were only understood in terms of their exchange-value? Did they wish to live with some contradictions, "superfluities," in the valuing of their commodities, which included their labor power captured in their surplus?

In conventional economic theory, the regulation of prices falls under the scarcity principle, in which the monetary price of a scarce commodity is said to be determined by the supply of that commodity and its demand in the market. The price will go up until an equilibrium is found, meaning until demand drops enough that there are just enough buyers for the supply of the commodity that exists in the market. What this explanation avoids is how even when prices go up, and often because they do, desire goes up, which can suggest worth. Scarcity does not fully account for the gap between use- and exchange-value because it doesn't account fully for demand, which can be a product of contingent and rhetorically influenced judgments. We trade in exchange-value. We live and experience use-value, but we are motivated by desire, by the worth of things, which is often communicated rhetorically.

This is why advertising is so important in capitalism. Fast-capitalism isn't that interested in communicating commodities' use-value, or even exchange-value, but it is very interested in manufacturing desire. Desire, the advertising industry knows, creates worth, which can operate outside of or in contradiction to use- or exchange-values. In fact, advertising is most successful when worth is more than exchange-value, and exchange-value is more than use-value—in other words, when it can produce lots of desire for a commodity, and charge inflated prices for the commodity, despite its much lower use-value. This illustrates the central importance of worth in all political economies, including assessment economies.

DESIRES CONFUSE WORTH IN ECONOMIES

In *The Theory of the Leisure Class*, Thorstein Veblen offers a way to understand how worth is generated in political economies in his famous theory of conspicuous consumption. He argues that those classes of people who can afford to will buy the most expensive clothing, accoutrements, houses, food, etc., they can because "the consumption of these more excellent goods is an evidence to wealth, it becomes honorific . . . the failure to consume in due quantity and quality becomes a mark of inferiority and demerit" (64). So rich people buy expensive items conspicuously to show them off, not because they can but because doing so shows their wealth, their success, and so their merit. A person's conspicuous consumption is meant to equate to the quality of their person in some way, or their worth in society. By default, those who do not conspicuously consume such items with high exchange-value automatically reveal their inferiority, their lack of worth. Veblen's theory suggests one important aspect most applicable to the writing classroom. The commodities of value we exchange, like papers and feedback, which encapsulate our labor power, are associated with our own value and worth as individuals. Criticize my paper and you criticize me to some extent, or it feels like that.

But one might argue that grades are meant to equate to merit, and a student doesn't wear their grade on their body. Or do they?[19] Grades on writing equate to one judge's comparison to a White racial *habitus* embodied in a local dominant set of discursive standards understood by that judge. Haswell's categorization theory explains this well, which I discussed in Chapter 2. So grades have a difficult time being a reliable measure of quality or value, especially if the student in question comes to the classroom with a different *habitus* than the one embodied in the standard. This is often the case with working-class students, students of color, multilingual students, among others. Often times, grades do not equate to merit, or worth, at all, or merit and worth are equated falsely to only a dominant White racial *habitus*. In reality and experience, any valuing of student writing, then is a problematic, a set of problems that could (and likely should) be posed by and with the student, in order to understand the contradictions in how their writing is valued.

One could see conspicuous consumption as a necessary element in thriving capitalist economies, manufactured through advertisement, because without the desire for more consumption and lots of monetary exchange, the system doesn't work very well for those who stand to gain the most, i.e., those who control the most in the system. The urge is always to produce more, to buy more, to make more profit. But why do we work from a principle of more consumption, and consumption at the highest exchange-value? One possible reason is offered by Max Weber in *The Protestant Ethic and the "Spirit" of Capitalism*, written just a few years after Veblen's theory (1905). Weber argues that the Protestant work ethic was influential in the rise and dominance of capitalism in the US. Values like labor or work as a "calling" or as an "end in itself" came from Calvinist doctrine that then encouraged or agreed with capitalist modes of production (19). What happens, according to Weber, is that such a Protestant ethic turns into a "spirit" of capitalism that favors profit for profit's sake (21). The best calling for one's life is to labor in order to make money— or rather, one shows one's hard work, merit, and worth through the money one has made—but the focus is on the signs of election, of merit, the conspicuousness of making money. And this

---

19   Bourdieu's theory of *habitus* suggests that students might very well display dispositions that are read in determined ways. I've made a similar argument for "racial *habitus*" in assessment ecologies in Chapter 1 of *Antiracist Writing Assessment Ecologies*.

economic system favors those who control the means of production, capitalists, not the people laboring.

Again, we can see analogues to students who simply want high grades, the signs of merit, worth, and good labor, but who care little for what they learn or whether they learn. But even if we believe that most of our students do not simply want grades but want to learn to be critical citizens (as I do), they are still circulating in assessment economies that determine desire in particular directions, that is, determine desire for accumulating high grades. These desires benefit those who control the means of academic production more than they benefit students (the academic laborers), like achieving high GPAs, or blindly reproducing the dominant White *habitus* despite the *habitus* of the students themselves.

You might ask, "how could these good students who desire to learn what I'm asking them to in my writing classroom, who do the work I'm asking them to do, be benefiting me (the teacher) or others in the institution more than themselves?" First, I'm not speaking of intentions, which have little to do with the circulation of value in political economies. Value is generated despite our intentions. I'm speaking of the value circulated in the assessment economy, which usually is linked to desires for high grades and desires to please the teacher (or receive favorable judgments of their writing by teachers). These desires raise the worth students place on grades as commodities. This conflates exchange-value of those grades with worth (learning and meaning), and this conflation of exchange-value and worth is central to how conspicuous consumption and the spirit of capitalism work.

These desires are manufactured in the system, likely before our students even entered our classrooms, but how do our classrooms call attention to these desires as manufactured? How do we call attention to the differences between use-value, exchange-value, and worth in the commodities that circulate in our assessment economies? How do our assessment economies allow for alternative desires to construct value and worth in labor power in drafts circulated? These questions become more problematic (in the Freirean meaning) when we consider the contradiction they present to many students of color, multilingual students, or students whose *habitus* do not easily fit into those *habitus* expected in the writing classroom, namely White, middle-class *habitus*. These dominant White racial *habitus* become what is desired because the assessment economies, who are controlled by teachers and school administrators, set them up as most exchangeable through curricula and learning outcomes. Dominant White racial *habitus* have a high use-value in the academy and other markets, but again, people often confuse exchange-value with worth. And forget that use-value is constantly evolving and only a product of the labors and exchanges of people in the economy. You

93

cannot change what is useful until you introduce something else useful. The system doesn't change without actual differences, contradictions, disturbances, without circulating what was previously undesirable or unknown.

Veblen's conspicuous consumption theory fits well with Weber's ideas around the Protestant work ethic and its fueling of the spirit of capitalism in the US. One is not worthy unless one can show one's worth. And what signs of value and worth are offered in a capitalist society? Signs of the consumption of commodities, particularly ones with high exchange-values, like high grades. But this is only the story told to laborers and students in their respective political economies. Acquiring such signs of value and worth benefit most those with the most control and power in the economic system, capitalists and teachers, not those laboring for a wage or a grade.

Labor-based grading contract economies are set up and primarily controlled not by the teacher, but by students and teacher. In conventional grading economies, students are asked to labor in order to acquire, perhaps conspicuously, grades as signs of merit, worth, and election. Even if their intentions are altruistic, teachers benefit most in this system because they maintain their power to control students in most ways, such as the standard to be used, or the ways one should speak or write, or the power to determine a grade based on their sense of quality. They get what they want from students, whether that means the kind of writing they deem most helpful or educative for students or the kind of labor they want from them. Students' labor then is not for students but for the consumption of signs of merit that is supplied by the teacher. Yet not so ironically, the signs of merit and worth are mostly out of reach for many of our students whose *habitus* do not agree with the dominant White *habitus* of the academy. In these ways, teachers control students by controlling the signs of worth and value, which control students' labor without much regard for how much labor is expended in any individual case. This is because the signs of worth are controlled by the labor power perceived by the teacher that are encapsulated in documents and drafts and judged by comparing them to a single White, middle-class standard.

One might argue that teachers know more than students. They know what is good for students. This is why they are the teachers. Fair enough. We know more. But knowing more and even knowing what labors and things might be good for students, does not mean that control over students' labors and drafts is the best way for students to learn, whether that control comes from a teacher controlling what counts as quality or the labor directly. As I discussed in Chapter 5 under the question, "How can a teacher respond to students who put in minimal engagement in the labor, or try to game the system?" people learn exactly what they are able to at that moment in their lives. Forcing students to do otherwise is often futile, and may cause them to resist even more, turning them away from the very practices and ideas that we want for our students.

Beyond this good reason, political economies that control the desires of the many usually mostly benefit the few, which do not make for ethical or fair economies. No matter the alleged benefit of some kind of labor, the laborer-student must understand and accept that labor as beneficial. If they do not, then it will not matter what a teacher thinks is most beneficial to a student. Labor-based grading contract assessment economies account directly for students' desires and their understandings of labor in the economy. This is vital to fairness and socially just classroom economies. Students and teacher are continually asked: Who does the labor power circulating in our assessment economy benefit most? How might that labor power be circulated in compassionate and fair ways? Students' participation and sharing in power is crucial. The labor they do may still be quite uneven, but because it is valued in negotiated ways and its worth is continually investigated, as I'll explain below (and in Chapter 7), it can be fairer and lead to critical understandings of reading and writing practices.

LABOR-BASED ECONOMIES CIRCULATE BOTH VALUE AND WORTH

If we really are motivated by worth—and I argue we are and should be— then even a utilitarian view of grades as high in use-value is not enough to circulate them in the political economy of the writing classroom if learning is our first priority. Grades do not account for worth. They do not account for contradictions in use- and exchange-value of labor. They do not account for the embodied ways humans learn. They do not account for the multiple dimensions in which we experience learning and being human. Like the sentiments of Pericles' family, if we focus on exchange-values, values that are incomplete translations of use-value, values that may hide embodied aspects of labor, we focus too much on exchange and lose the nuanced, contingent senses of worth in the commodities we circulate. Especially for learning environments like schools and classrooms, labor's worth is most vital, since it is how we might best capture what, why, how, and that we learn.

When a labor-based assessment economy distinguishes and articulates different values and worth of the labor power encapsulated in textual commodities, when it investigates the different exchange- and use-values to various people in the system, labor power can be uniformly measurable (by an agreed upon standard) and fairly, in at least three ways. That is, because we can separate use- and exchange-value from worth, it is easier to not attach a teacher's perceptions of labor's use-value or its worth to exchange-value (a student's course grade), yet still articulate and circulate all three in the economy.

The labor-based grading economy I'm arguing for defines and circulates exchange-value as the ways it determines when a student has done what they were asked to do. Did the student complete all the words asked of them and submitted in the manner asked? Simultaneously, use-value would be articulated and circulated through the material labor done in the present moment, and articulated in reflective documents and practices (e.g., journals, reflection practices, labor tweets, and labor logs). Worth would be felt and understood through reflections and metacognitive work that articulates the meaning and significance of the labor power encapsulated in classroom commodities. It is realized and understood in periodic and focused reflective practices. In this way, a labor-based assessment economy can circulate use-value, exchange-value, and worth separately to students' advantages, while still maintaining their interconnection or relationships to one another. Figure 3.1 illustrates the various ways labor's values and worth can be understood and measured in labor-based grading contract economies.

experience of labor over time →→→	
exchange-value, measured in labor power uniformly by a single, agreed-upon, standard, is past-oriented, and represented by a numerical value What and how much labor power is accumulated or circulated?	**worth**, measured in metacognitive labor in diverse ways that reflect on exchange- and use-value of labor done, is future-oriented, and represented discursively in metacognitive and reflective documents What is the meaning or significance of the labor or labor power already circulated or accumulated in the present document or activity?
use-value, measured in material labor done in diverse ways, is present-oriented, and represented discursively in metacognitive and reflective documents How useful is the labor and what is its nature?	

Figure 3.1. The three measurements of labor in labor-based grading contract economies.

While I'll discuss more precisely the ways that labor value can be measured in the next section, Figure 3.1 represents graphically the way worth is attached to both exchange- and use-value. It is derived from a close examination of and reflection on the exchange- and use-value of the labor power accumulated in a document or activity. The figure represents exchange- and use-value on the left side, activities that would happen chronologically first. Meanwhile worth is represented on the right side of the figure and produced after exchange- and use-values are circulated and understood by the student in numerical and discursive ways. Exchange- and use-value must first be measured before worth can be understood. Each are separate and measured in distinct ways. Each have an orientation in time. That is, exchange-value focuses students' and teacher's attention on past labor power accumulated in a document or activity and represented numerically. It can be understood by asking, what and how much labor power (in time or number of words) is accumulated or circulated?

Use-value focuses attention on the present labor in the moment. It is primarily measured discursively in reflective documents. It focuses attention on the work that is being done, and can be reflected upon either as one does it or immediately afterwards. It can be understood by asking, how useful is this labor and what is its nature? Finally, worth focuses attention on the value of past labor in order to consider future labor practices. It is measured discursively in reflective documents and activities, and can be understood by asking, what is the meaning or significance of the labor or labor power already circulated or accumulated in the present document or activity? Later in this chapter, I map these ideas to my concept of three-dimensional labor, showing how this three-part framework for measuring labor may also be a way to frame all labor and assessment activities, and can help teachers assess the effectiveness of their own labor-based assessment ecologies (discussed in detail in Chapter 7).

It should be obvious at this point that labor-based contract grading economies do not get rid of use- and exchange-values of commodities in and outside of the classroom. They make them more obvious and distinct, while revealing contradictions. At their core, labor-based grading contract economies provide for ways to value and measure labor and labor power, involve students in negotiating how labor is measured and valued, and offer ways to measure labor in nuanced ways. Understanding labor in the above ways keeps separate the ways a course grade is calculated (exchange-value) from how a student accomplishes labor and uses it to further their immediate needs in the classroom (use-value), from the lessons and practices learned through reflections on their labor (worth). Figuring out how to measure labor in such economies is therefore important to determine.

MEASURE THE VALUES OF LABOR SEPARATELY FROM ITS WORTH

If you cannot tell already, central to my conceiving of the political economy of the writing classroom is how texts, languages, and judgments themselves are valued. If as Trimbur argues about Marx's notions of capitalist modes of distribution are accurate, then value and worth are carried forth, accumulated, and transformed in the full cycle of production, distribution, exchange, and consumption. And the fundamental thing carried forth in this cycle is labor power. In *The Wealth of Nations*, while not making the distinction between labor and labor power, Smith is thinking about labor in markets. This is why he says, "[l]abor, therefore, is the real measure of the exchangeable value of all commodities." It is, in a sense, universal. Smith goes on:

> The real price of everything, what everything really costs to the man who wants to acquire it, is the toil and trouble of acquiring it. What everything is really worth to the man who has acquired it, and who wants to dispose of it or exchange it for something else, is the toil and trouble which it can save to himself, and which it can impose upon other people. What is bought with money or with goods is purchased by labour as much as what we acquire by the toil of our own body. That money or those goods indeed save us this toil. They contain the value of a certain quantity of labour which we exchange for what is supposed at the time to contain the value of an equal quantity. Labour was the first price, the original purchase-money that was paid for all things. It was not by gold or by silver, but by labour, that all the wealth of the world was originally purchased; and its value, to those who possess it, and who want to exchange it for some new productions, is precisely equal to the quantity of labour which it can enable them to purchase or command. (n. pag.)

So, according to Smith, labor is the common denominator of all value, no matter the kind. And value is determined in large part by the "quantity of labor" encapsulated in a commodity. This, I think, is intuitively true for learning in the writing classroom at all levels. But what does Smith mean by quantity? How do we measure the exchange-value of labor? It wasn't hours of labor put into the production of a commodity. Smith saw this as too abstract, since things like skill of laborers or the fertility of land vary too greatly. We can see this problem in the writing classroom, where one student's writing practices may produce more or a different quality of writing than another student's labor given the same constraints of time and information.

Thus measuring labor by time didn't make sense to Smith because in one instance one hour of labor may produce two units of something, while in another place it may produce four units, and in yet another place it may produce four units of a commodity that is of a different quality. Labor measured by time didn't consistently equate to the same amount or quality of a commodity. It is the units, the commodity, that is measurable, according to Smith. He says: "though equal quantities of labour are always of equal value *to the labourer*, yet *to the person* who employs him they appear sometimes to be of greater and sometimes of smaller value . . . In reality, however, it is the *goods* which are cheap in the one case, and dear in the other" (n. pag.; my emphasis). Thus, according to Smith's theory of value, measuring labor by time encapsulated in a commodity is difficult because it is always relative to the laborer's skill or other material conditions that may constrain or aid the laborer in their tasks. In other words, the amount of labor time put into any given commodity of a particular quality is separate from its exchange-value in the market. Labor's exchange-value is felt and used by the laborer, but the exchange-value of the commodity produced by that laborer is felt and used by the employer who contracted for the labor.

We have the same problem in writing classrooms. Time spent on literacy tasks, like reading a text or writing a draft, as a way to measure quality of those tasks' outcomes, is difficult to use as a consistent method for determining grades. Students are not the same, and given the same time parameters will not produce writing of the same quality, meaning their literacies produce drafts that are judged by readers to be different. They will also not produce the same amount of text. Furthermore, they each likely will explain what they learned through the activities of writing differently. These differences across various students and between the quality, quantity, and learning within a single student's experience are the gaps between use-value, exchange-value, and worth.

Often what many teachers say is that we cannot grade on effort because it is unfair.[20] If I grade based on whether all students produce a 2,500-word draft, I've set up a system in which not everyone has an equal or fair chance to achieve the same passing grade because some may need quite a bit more time to produce such a draft, or may produce a draft of that length in a reasonable amount of time but may not be able to do the kind of intellectual work asked for in the assignment. If I grade based on asking students to spend six hours only on their drafts, then again I've set up a system in which some students' six hours do a lot more toward the goals of the class than others, or a system in which I'm asking everyone to find the same amount of time in their week, regardless of the other demands in their lives, such as family, jobs, other classes, etc. These factors in students' lives often intersect with gender, race, and other social dimensions not in the students' full control. If the products of labor are relative to mostly unknown factors in students' lives, then it appears unfair to use quantified labor to produce grades (exchange-value) in a course. This kind of assessment ecology, however, assumes as its central purpose to produce and circulate grade-

---

20   I am using the term "effort" as synonymous with labor here because I think many would articulate this problem in this way, but as my discussion in this chapter should make clear, effort is not a precise term. I prefer "labor" since it is has these Marxian associations, and "effort" often refers in lay terms to the nature and quality of labor.

commodities. How has the economy accounted for use-value and worth of labor? Without an attention to value and worth distinctly, the primary purpose of the writing classroom might too easily be to circulate external exchange-values.

Note that Smith and even Marx assumed that the purpose of capitalist economies was to produce excess exchange value so that capital could be accumulated. This means it was important to figure out how to value commodities uniformly if the system was to be fair, or at least consistent. While labor was necessary to produce commodities, and labor power was a commodity itself, its measurement was not uniform. Each person's labor was valued differently, so some would do better than others in the economy. As a measure of value, labor-time was difficult to use as a consistent measure of any commodity's value. This unfairness in the economy, that one person's labor-time can produce more value than another's, is only unfair if the purpose of the economy is to accumulate and circulate exchange-value, such as money or grades, and if there is an agreed-upon standard by which to judge the products of labor. This is the case in capitalist economies and conventional, quality-based grading economies.

However, in the writing classroom, where our purposes are to accumulate learning, knowledge, practices, ideas, and literacy, it is reasonable to say that our primary purpose for our classroom assessment economies is the circulation and accumulation of labor's worth. And worth of student labors cannot have a uniform standard by which to measure it, even though we can have a uniform standard for measuring exchange-value (labor time or quantity), which is what Marx and Smith understood. This means that the value of labor measured by time on task or amount of text read or written, can be a fair measure of exchange-value, since exchange-value of labor is not connected to the circulation of worth, and worth is circulated more so in the economy. In short, the measures of exchange-value (i.e., grades) are circulated separately from the measures of worth (e.g., learning, focused reflections, feelings about the work, etc.). In the pursuit of accumulating worth in/through labor, students produce exchange-value by default, which is measured in uniform ways and separated from use-value and worth in the economy.

In an assessment economy that doesn't account for worth, but only for exchange- and use-value, and does not address the contradictions that are produced when these things are measured, the final grade, the exchange-value of the commodities circulated, is emphasized. This is especially true for writing assessment economies in which the commodities' used to determine the course grade are only valued by their so-called quality, i.e., grades on drafts that are used both to indicate a student's progress (exchange-value) and provide some measure of quality to the student (use-value). Quality of literacy practices should not be measured in such ways. It can too easily conflate use-value, exchange-value, and worth. It does not do a good enough job at addressing the gaps and contradictions that inevitably are produced among these measures of literacy labors.

David Ricardo, writing some thirty years later and responding to Smith's theories of value, offers a labor cost theory that centers on quantity of labor to determine relative prices of commodities, not wages paid to labor (as Smith had proposed). In his chapter "On Value" after summarizing Smith's ideas of use-value and exchange-value, Ricardo explains, "commodities derive their exchangeable value from two sources: from their scarcity, and from the quantity of labour required to obtain them." But he didn't mean all commodities. Much like Smith, he qualifies use-and exchange-value. There are some commodities that have exchange-value based on "scarcity alone," such as art, "scarce books and coins, wines of a particular quality, which can be made only from grapes grown on a particular soil" (n. pag.). While these kinds of commodities aren't prevalent, they do exist and "are procured by labour," meaning to buy them, one must have money, which means one must have captured labor in money to exchange for the commodity. However, because Ricardo is still trapped in a use- vs. exchange-value binary for commodities, and does not account for the dynamic, contingent, and unevenness of worth, he cannot escape a theory of value that doesn't ultimately equate to money. For the writing classroom, this is the same as saying that we need quality-based grades to measure the value of student labor. Any exchange is still one level removed from the labor power that is the foundation of political economies, and the contradictions of exchange- and use-value in the system.

Marx comments that Smith "sometimes confuses, and at other times substitutes, the determination of the value of *commodities* by the quantity of labour required for their production," making the exchange-value of labor the ultimate measure of value of a commodity. According to Marx, wages is the measure of the quantity of commodities (Marx, *Theories of Surplus-Value*; n. pag.; emphasis in original). The equation that one might form from Marx's reading of Smith is thus:

Quantity of labor (labor-time) = quantity of commodities = wages

This equation, says Marx, is circular. Quantity of labor or labor-time is measured in wages. But the equation doesn't cause problems with Smith's theorizing of the nature of surplus-value since it "keeps firmly to the correct determination of the exchange-value of commodities—that is, its determination by the quantity of labour or the labour-time expended on them."

And so, Marx identifies Smith's theory of exchange-value as one based on the quantity of labor exchanged in the market and contained in a commodity.

Value is labor-time. He illustrates it this way, which can easily be read as describing labor-based writing assessment economies, where workers are students and commodities are the things, labor power, drafts, and judgments they circulate:

> Let us assume that all workers are producers of commodities, and not only produce their commodities but also sell them. The value of these commodities is determined by the necessary labour-time contained in them. If therefore the commodities are sold at their value, the labourer buys with one commodity, which is the product of twelve hours' labour-time, another twelve hours' labour-time in the form of another commodity, that is to say, twelve hours' labour-time which is embodied in another use-value. The value of his labour is therefore equal to the value of his commodity; that is, it is equal to the product of twelve hours' labour-time. The selling and buying again, in a word, the whole process of exchange, the metamorphosis of the commodity, alters nothing in this. It alters only the form of the use-value in which this twelve hours' labour-time appears. The value of labour is therefore equal to the value of the product of labour. In the first place, equal quantities of materialised labour are exchanged in the commodities—in so far as they are exchanged at their value. Secondly, however, a certain quantity of living labour is exchanged for an equal quantity of materialised labour, because, firstly, the living labour is materialised in a product, a commodity, which belongs to the labourer, and secondly, this commodity is in turn exchanged for another commodity which contains an equally large quantity of labour. In fact, therefore, a certain quantity of living labour is exchanged for an equal amount of materialised labour. Thus it is not only commodity exchanging for commodity in the proportion in which they represent an equal quantity of materialised labour-time, but a quantity of living labour exchanging for a commodity which represents the same quantity of labour materialised. (Marx, *Theories of Surplus-Value*, n. pag.)

In the above description, the value of a commodity equates to the labor-time materialized in it. If we're talking about the exchange-value of an essay, then I'm sure we'll find uneven amounts of labor in one classroom for the same essay produced by different students in that class. So quite literally, this theory of value based on labor-time is not a consistent system for exchange-values if the purpose of the economy is to exchange commodities fairly and acquire more labor power fairly. Of course, those in capitalist systems of market exchange do not necessarily operate from an assumption that all labor will be measured fairly. It's about getting an advantage, getting labor cheaper and cheaper.

For capitalist markets, the purpose is to accumulate capital, but this purpose does not equate well to any writing assessment economy. Our purposes are to learn how to read and write in particular ways, or to do them more critically. What we accumulate, then, in labor-based grading contract economies is individual worth, since it embodies what one has learned and what one can transfer after the course is over. Since exchange-value is separated from worth, using labor-time as a measure of labor can be a fair method, if we don't place judgments of quality on that labor-time—that is, if we keep the exchange-value separated from use-value and worth. In short, for the purposes of course grading, everyone's time is of equal exchange-value in the assessment economy, even though that same labor's use-value or worth may not be measured the same.

But for Marx, there was a different problem with the above formulation of value. In a capitalist mode of production, says Marx about Smith's theory, where the "material conditions of labour belong to one or several classes" and "nothing but labour-power belongs to another class, the working class," labor-time no longer determines the measure of exchange-value of commodities. The equation above no longer works to explain the value of commodities because of the division of labor inherent in capitalist modes of production. In short, some only have their labor power to exchange as a commodity, but do not get to control the exchange-value of that labor power. Power relations, who controls more of the conditions of labor, matters and places an entire group of labors in a weaker position, thus they are more often taken advantage of or exploited. And commodities' exchange-values are based on the materialized labor embodied in them, no matter their use or worth. This is part of the contradiction that Trimbur discusses (208), one that promises profits and the distribution of commodities and contradictorily reproduces an uneven (unfair) relation of power between the laboring classes and the valuing of their own labor, which is to say that laborers don't completely dictate their wages.

The same kind of division of labor exists in classroom writing assessment economies, where students labor and teachers assign labor, where some students have more immediate access to the dominant English that is measured as more valuable than others. These uneven labor conditions create unfair, racist, and White supremacist outcomes. Students have varying degrees of limited to no control over the exchange-values (grades) of the commodities they produce by their labor, such as drafts they write, except to put more and more labor-time into documents, which may not amount to a better grade. For many multilingual and students of color, or students who come with different *habitus* than those that inform the dominant discourse of the classroom, more time does not always equal more exchange-value in a draft. This unfairness in judgment is tied to a single agent's power to dictate value in the economy—that is, to dictate the value of students' labor. Agreeing with Ricardo, Marx explains this problem, "the expressions 'quantity of labour' and 'value of labour' are now no longer identical, and that therefore the relative value of commodities, although determined by the labour-time contained in them, is not determined by the value of labour, since that was only correct so long as the latter expression remained identical with the former" (Marx, *Theories of Surplus-Value* n. pag.). Marx understood that the value of labor, how one agent might judge it, is not the same as the quantity of labor, or labor-time.

Thus, one ethical problem with capitalist political economic systems is that laborers do not control the value of their labor, capitalists do, and this creates unfair gaps among exchange- and use-value of one's labor power accumulated in commodities, increases capital accumulation for capitalists and decreases them for laborers. These gaps are unfair and racist, given who typically controls the assessment economies of classrooms and the dominance of a White racial *habitus* in the standards of writing quality in most or all classrooms.

However, the gaps among worth, exchange-value, and use-value do not make an assessment economy unfair. They simply are. They reveal social difference and diversity, and individual significance and worth. The gaps are the problematizing of labor, judgment, and language that is the center of what is learned and accumulated. Yet Marx's criticism of capitalist economies reveals an important insight for us. If any labor-based grading contract economy is going to be fair and equitable, student-laborers must participate in determining the exchange-value of their labor.

To emphasize, Smith's confusion between labor's time and value that Marx identifies doesn't account for divisions of labor and the fact that laboring classes don't control exchange rates of commodities, just like our students. It would seem that a fairer economy would share this power with student-laborers equally. Near the end of the chapter, Marx comes to his critique. He says that Smith "confuses *the labour of other people* with *the produce of this labour*" (emphasis in original). Thus the exchange-value of a commodity is equal to the quantity of other people's labor materialized in that commodity, according to Marx. He explains:

> It [*sic*] emphasis here is on the change brought about by
> the *division of labour:* that is to say, that wealth no longer
> consists in the product of one's own labour, but in the quan-

tity of the labour of others which this product commands, the social labour which it can buy, the quantity of which is determined by the quantity of labour it itself contains. In fact, only the concept of exchange-value is here involved —that my labour now counts only as social labour, and consequently its product determines my wealth by its command over an equal quantity of social labour . . . The emphasis here lies on the equalisation, brought about through the division of labour and exchange-value, of *my* labour with the labour of *others*, in other words, with social labour (the fact that *my* labour too, or the labour contained in my commodities, is already *socially* determined, and has fundamentally changed its character, escapes Adam), and not at all on the difference between *materialised* labour and *living* labour, and the specific laws of their exchange. (Marx, *Theories of Surplus-Value* n. pag.; emphasis in original)

Thus the exchange-value of commodities in a capitalist mode of production is socially determined by the labor materialized in any given commodity, not the living labor, the labor that it might take any give person to produce a commodity, the actual labor of human bodies. This means that actual, living labor, as Marx puts it, and the labor materialized in a particular commodity for exchange, or the product of labor, are rarely the same. Additionally, labor power is different from materialized and living labor, since labor power is what is accumulated and exchanged through a commodity in the market. It is accumulated through circulation. Consider the way a house gains in value between each sale.

This provides for a way to define how an assessment economy might measure the exchange-value of labor. It can be time on task and/or amount of text read or written. It is the textual document, say a letter that offers feedback to a peer on a draft, that circulates, and one way to measure the labor materialized in that document is the time the writer spent drafting it, another is the number of words that make up the letter. These values will never be the same or consistent in any collection of letters in a class. Yet it is a useful contradiction to investigate, which would reveal additional contradictions around the worth accumulated in the economy at that point.

So, living labor is what people do to live and produce, to learn and be human, which I associate to use-value of labor in Figure 3.1. While one might measure it numerically, such as engagement ratings of labor sessions (see Chapter 7), it should also be measured in discursive ways, such as reflections on one's laboring, since the uses we make or understand of our labors are not strictly empirical measures of quantity or number. Worth, then, becomes an intersection and outgrowth of exchange-value, use-value, and the embodied ways labor is experienced in and outside a classroom.

To sum up, measuring labor in a labor-based grading economy can be done in three separate ways, three different measures that are dictated by why we are measuring labor in those three ways. In other words, how and why we measure labor are determined by the purposes that the economy sets for that measuring. These three ways of measuring can intersect with one another, yet stay distinct and separate in how they operate and circulate in the economy. First, we measure to produce an institutionally demanded course grade, which requires a numerical number that is fair and whose standard of measurement is agreed upon by everyone in the classroom. This is the exchange-value of students' labor. Second, we measure labor by its usefulness to students in their learning and development in the course in order to know what we've done and what that labor offers us as learners. This can be done by some quantitative measures like engagement ratings on individual labor sessions, but primarily is done through frequent, even daily, personal reflections on labor. These reflections determine the use-value of labor and are separated or disconnected from determinations of exchange-value. Finally, we measure worth of labor by articulating the significance and meaning that we find in our present and past labors of the class. This is done by reflections on labor patterns and labor data that we keep throughout the quarter or semester. These reflections, which are done at crucial times in the quarter or semester (e.g., midpoint and final), determine or articulate worth of labor to the individual student.

Each value of labor can be measured separately, while maintaining their interconnected natures through articulations of worth. But to do this work, the standards of the measurement of exchange- and use-value must be negotiated and agreed upon with students, so that those who labor and have the most stake in the economy, those who are meant to benefit most from the purposes of the assessment economy, can have more control over the value of their labor, and the meaning of their labor's worth. These power relations make labor-based grading contract economies fairer and more socially just. They allow any classroom assessment economy to respond directly to the local diversity and contexts in any classroom.

LABOR CAN BE UNDERSTOOD AS THREE-DIMENSIONAL

I realize that the previous Marxian theory may be too much for many writing teachers, and certainly not a good way to explain to students how labor will be used to grade and understand their learning in a course. I offer it because central to my understanding of labor-based grading contracts is a Marxian critique of the culture of classroom assessment, its relations to the labors involved in learning and to larger capitalist modes of production.

Now, allow me to recast the above into a form that may be more useful for writing teachers and students in classrooms. This section offers a way to explain the exchange- and use-value of labor and its worth to students. Labor-based grading contracts as I have described them in this book assume three dimensions of labor, each of which are measured differently for different purposes. Each dimension is enacted by students, meaning there are moments in the labor of the course that ask students to pay attention to particular dimensions of their working in order to have more control over the nature and products of their labor practices by being more self-aware and critical of their laboring as practices. In short, paying attention to these three dimensions of labor offer students direct ways to quantify and articulate their labor. This is also to say, these three dimensions provide direct ways to gather data on their labor in order to understand the exchange-value, use-value, and worth of those labors to the student and perhaps the class as a whole.

These dimensions of labor are a framework that takes care of grades (determines the exchange-value of labor), circulates separately frequent reflections on their labor (generates use-value of labor), and ends with more formalized reflections that problematize their existential labor situations at key moments in the term or semester, which aid in articulating what their labor means and how it is significant to them (articulates worth of labor). The three dimensions of labor are:

- *How students labor*, measured by explaining the step-by-step process of labor involved in any practice or assignment through labor instructions and student reflections on labor. It is most associated to the use-value of labor. This dimension answers the question: How am I laboring and what does it offer me?

- *That students labor*, measured by the quantity of student labor in time on tasks, number of words or pages, or duration of practices and activities most often recorded in labor logs and labor journals. It is most associated with the exchange-value of labor. This dimension answers: How much am I laboring?

- *What the labor means*, measured by reflections on noncognitive and metacognitive domains through engagement ratings and mindful practices that help students pay attention to their labor in order to make sense and meaning of it, done often in labor logs, labor journals, labor tweets, and midterm and final reflections on their labor as a practice. It is most associated to labor's worth. This dimension answers: What is the nature of my labor and what do I learn from it?

The above aspects of labor that my contract requires also illustrate the order in which I ask students to pay attention to their labor, which offers a slow, deepening, and cumulative sense of their labors in the process of any assignment and through the course of the semester or quarter. We begin with discussing and running through the process of the labor instructions (the *how* of labor) for an assignment. Each set of labor instructions emphasizes clearly what they are supposed to do, step by step, helping students see exactly how they might labor. As they do the actual labor, they keep track of the amount of time in the labor, with cues from me at each step that explain how much approximate time each step should take or how many words are expected of them to produce (if writing is the labor) or read (if reading is the labor) (the *that* of labor).

Breaking up an assignment into labor steps, even the most mundane of activities, focuses students' attention on the material and time dimensions of learning in a writing course. It is about the doing, the labor commodity (labor power), not about that labor's products, or the completed commodity, even though we care about that and spend time doing other labors with those documents. We are attempting to measure labor in our assessment economy, not its products. This means we understand how we should do something, then pay attention to how we do it in the acts of laboring. One doesn't learn to write by turning in a finished paper. One learns *in the labors* of researching, drafting, and revising—in the doing—and learns best if one pays attention to how one is doing those labors.

Finally, after they've completed a session of labor, or in the middle of a longer labor process, students pause and reflect briefly on their engagement, recording an engagement rating in their labor logs (the *what* of labor). Additionally, labor instructions often ask students to tweet a snapshot of something significant in their labor, such as an annotated page they read or a pre-writing document done before drafting.[21] These brief moments of assessing what they've done and recording either an engagement rating or a tweet about something they've learned offer ways to be mindful of what they are learning in their labors. It offers ways to pay attention to one's labor as they do it.

Once a week, we complete this reflecting on what their labor means by making entries into their labor journals. Finally, during midpoint and final times, students reflect upon all the data they've gathered up to that point, looking for patterns and other things they are learning about their labor as a set of practices. I prompt students with questions about patterns and the contradictions between apparent use- and exchange-values. This moves them toward problema-

---

21   Recently, I've moved to using private tweet-like technologies, such as Slack, which allow my students' messages to be accessible only to our class.

tizing their labor and learning. In this three-dimensional way, labor is more fully articulated and experienced. Labor becomes more than a means to complete a reading or a writing assignment. It is also the ends that we savor or try to understand better. Thus, through the processes of assigning, articulating, doing, and reflecting on our labors, students' learning is continually articulated and experienced as bodily labor in three dimensions.

Beyond these somewhat practical reasons for thinking of labor in three dimensions, labor is also a vital part of the material conditions of all life, making it important to pay attention to in educational processes, especially literacy education, which often is understood as learning to be a citizen or becoming critically aware of one's self and one's world.[22] The labors of learning languaging is the human condition. If we accept that languaging is labor, then labor as a fundamental part of the human condition agrees with Kenneth Burke's definition of humanity that I discussed in Chapter 2.

In her influential book, *The Human Condition*, Hannah Arendt discusses extensively the concept of labor as part of the human condition, along with two other related concepts, work and action. While I've been using these three concepts synonymously, these three terms form a hierarchy for Arendt. She explains that "[l]abor is the activity which corresponds to the biological process of the human body, whose spontaneous growth, metabolism, and eventual decay are bound to the vital necessities produced and fed into the life process by labor. The human condition of labor is life itself" (7). Work, then, is activity that is "unnatural" yet "provides an 'artificial' world of things, distinctly different from all natural surroundings . . . The human condition of work is worldliness" (7). Finally, action "goes on directly between men without the intermediary of things or matter, corresponds to the human condition of plurality, to the fact that men, not Man, live on earth and inhabit the world" (7).[23] For Arendt, these three kinds of practices are connected and create ongoing, historical cycles, forming the human condition and history. Arendt explains further,

> Labor assures not only individual survival, but the life of the
> species. Work and its product, the human artifact, bestow a
> measure of permanence and durability upon the futility of
> mortal life and the fleeting character of human time. Action,
> in so far as it engages in founding and preserving political

22 James Berlin identifies the purpose for writing instruction in the twentieth century as preparing citizens (189), while ancient Hellenic education was explicitly about preparing citizens for their duties as citizens (Marrou), something George Kennedy's history of classical rhetoric shows as well.

23 Arendt does not use an inclusive pronoun to identify humanity, but the archaic "man."

bodies, creates the condition of remembrance, that is, for
history. (8–9)

So in Arendt's conception of the human condition, labor is biological and
preserves life at its most fundamental level. Work identifies the material, the
artifacts we produce, and provides some permanence and durability to our
temporary and limited life, while action pertains to the political and historical
trends and movements that are bigger than the individual, allowing societies
to have memory and a sense of history by allowing what individuals do to
continue on, contribute to larger things, and extend beyond their limited time
on earth.

I will not engage in a critique of Arendt's theory of the human condition, but
I will voice my resistance to her hierarchy, which sets up an elitist, linear set of
practices that devalue the biological (labor) and favor intellectual and political
practices (action). It is reminiscent of Plato's hierarchy of souls or human types
in *Phaedrus*, in which the very acts that Plato and Arendt are engaged in are the
definition of the highest level in their respective hierarchies. Regardless of what
one thinks of her hierarchy, Arendt offers some useful ways to consider labor, if
we assume that labor references the biological and is always connected to both
work and action. I do not want to separate the three concepts, but place them
all under one category, labor.

When placed inside a writing assessment ecology, labor is the enactment
of ecological processes that produce artifacts and other things, or ecological
parts, what Arendt's identifies as "work." These parts and processes offer longer-
standing lessons and take-aways, or ecological products, to the people in the
ecology (Arendt's "action"). But as I've discussed elsewhere (*Antiracist* 93), writing assessment ecologies are complex systems in which these elements are consubstantial to each other. They inter-are. So the processes of labor are the parts
of work are the products of action are the processes of labor, etc. It seems clear
to me that Arendt understands the necessity of all three practices in the human
condition, even if she holds them as a hierarchy. I do not. We cannot have history (action) without the biological necessity of laboring bodies (labor), or the
tools and artifacts that make our world and action possible (work).

All these elements, which I call three-dimensional labor, are equally important and necessary for coming to critical consciousness about ourselves and our
world, about meaningful and ethical language practices. Thus, I wish to use
Arendt in a corrupted way. Instead of seeing labor-work-action as a hierarchical
set of elements to the human condition, one can use Arendt's concepts as useful
ways to flesh out three-dimensional labor, and understand a mindful, recursive
cycle of articulation and reflection that students can participate in so that they

take more control over their labor as a set of practices and find more meaning and purpose in those practices.

In a lengthy footnote, Arendt provides a useful etymology for the term labor. She explains:

> All the European words for "labor," the Latin and English *labor*, the Greek *ponos*, the French *travail*, the German *Arbeit*, signify pain and effort and are also used for the pangs of birth. *Labor* has the same etymological root as *labore* ("to stumble under a burden"); *ponos* and *Arbeit* have the same etymological roots as "poverty" (*penia* in Greek and *Armut* in German). Even Hesiod, currently counted among the few defenders of labor in antiquity, put *ponon alginoenta* ("painful labor") as first of the evils plaguing man (*Theogany* 226). (48)

What is immediately useful here is to notice that labor is an embodied process, which suggests that if we can keep the embodied aspects of labor in the ways we explain and measure labor in the writing classroom it offers us a fuller explanation of student labor and its value and worth. Arendt uses this etymology to move toward seeing labor as always about the biological, the body in pain and misery, which results in "deformation of the human body" (48). For Arendt, not only does she find historical evidence that labor is associated with pain and suffering, but with bodily disfigurement. However, as Arendt does frequently in her discussion, I suggest we take a page from ancient Hellenic society. The ancient Hellenes saw life and the material world always in flux. This was part of the way they saw the biological and seasonal changes in people and the world around them. People and the world are always in cycles of change, which can be seen in Plato's ideas about the soul and reincarnation in his *Phaedrus*. It is also a good way to characterize our students in their educational processes. They are always changing, fluxing, becoming.

The Pre-Socratic philosopher Heraclitus of Ephesus may be the most known for his ideas of life as constant flux. In two fragments misquoted by Plato (*Cratylus*, 402a),[24] Heraclitus says: "[t]hose who step into the same river have different waters flowing ever upon them" (Freeman 25); and "[i]n the same river, we both step and do not step, we are and we are not" (Freeman 28). Daniel Graham explains the first fragment: "[t]he sentence says that *different* waters flow in rivers *staying the same*. In other words, though the waters are always changing, the rivers stay the same" (emphasis in original). The river is changing, and its changing

---

24   In the dialogue, Plato has Socrates say: "Heracleitus is supposed to say that all things are in motion and nothing at rest; he compares them to the stream of a river, and says that you cannot go into the same water twice."

is part of its essence, so rivers-as-change is constant. The river is and is not the same. Perhaps more precisely, the river as a human construct that we can refer to can always be the same, but the river as an experienced phenomenon in the world is never the same.

This doctrine of flux and unity of opposites should sound familiar. The Sophist Protagoras of Abdera's famous Humanity-measure uses it too. Protagoras' fragment says, "Of all things the measure is Man, of the things that are, that they are, and of the things that are not, that they are not" (Freeman 125).[25] If we accept the idea that life is flux, that change is essential to life, and that as Arendt says labor is a necessary part of the biological human condition, then labor does not deform bodies, it changes them in inevitable and necessary ways. Laboring is life. Suffering is part of laboring. And as the first of Buddhism's Four Noble Truths reminds us, life is suffering. Laboring is part of how change and flux happen. We cannot avoid the fact that what we do affects our bodies, marks them in visible ways. Like Heraclitus' rivers, we are change. We are flux. And yet, we have a sense of stability in who we are.

In Chapter 1, I reiterate my theorizing of the way our labors, languages, and material conditions mark our bodies in ways that become racialized, calling it racial *habitus*, drawing on Bourdieu's term. Thus there are historicized and racialized implications to particular kinds of labor and their effects on our bodies. These effects have intersectional implications to socioeconomic position and gender performance in classrooms as well. We might then say that we are always becoming gendered, raced, aged, and disabled bodies. If we accept the ancient Hellenic doctrine of flux and unity of opposites, then one's status as an abled, woman, man, Asian, Black, or White person, for instance, is always in flux, just as those categories themselves are constantly and historically changing, as Omi and Winant explain about racial formations. Seeing the biological aspects of laboring as pain and misery is not cause to avoid it or devalue it, as Arendt appears to do, it is simply recognizing a natural part of the flux of life that inter-is our bodies.

Now, if we take Arendt's theory of the human condition, her hierarchy of labor-work-action, and transform it into an interconnected and ever-recursive process—that is, if we do not favor one element but see them all as simultaneous and equally important—we get the three-dimensional articulation of labor that I began with, only now it is set as a framework for labor in the classroom. Figure 3.2 illustrates how Arendt's terms sync up with three-dimensional labor.

---

25   I reference Protagoras' fragment as "Humanity-measure" and not "Man-measure" for reasons of inclusion, since Protagoras doubtfully would exclude everyone but men in his theory of knowing and judgment. I retain the language of the fragment because it is the language of the original translation that Freeman inherits from the Diels translation.

Three-dimensional Labor	Arendt's Theory
1st—*How students labor*, measured by articulating the process of labor involved in any practice or assignment through labor instructions (i.e., by step-by-step, process instructions) and student reflections on labor. It is most associated to the use-value of labor. This dimension answers the question: How am I laboring and what does it offer me?	**Labor**—Necessary, bodily actions (the bodily processes of reading and writing)
2nd—*That students labor*, measured by the quantity of student labor in time on tasks, number of words or pages, or duration of practices and activities (i.e., through labor logs and labor journals). It is most associated with the exchange-value of labor. This dimension answers: How much am I laboring?	**Work**—Products and artifacts used purposefully (texts produced and time spent on tasks)
3rd—*What the labor means*, measured by reflections on noncognitive and metacognitive domains through engagement ratings and mindful practices that help students pay attention to their labor in order to make sense and meaning of it (e.g., in labor logs, labor journals, labor tweets, and midterm and final reflections on their labor as a practice). It is most associated to labor's worth. This dimension answers: What is the nature of my labor and what do I learn from it?	**Action**—Articulation and acts of agency and distinction (noncognitive and metacognitive awareness)

Figure 3.2. The three dimensions of labor and Arendt's three aspects of the human condition.

What may not be clear to this point is how the second and third dimensions of labor align with Arendt's terms (work and action), and what all three terms contribute to the three dimensions of labor in a writing classroom's assessment economy. What I hope to explain below is that if we can map Arendt's theory to the three dimensions of labor used in labor-based grading economies, the economy can help students engage more meaningfully in problematizing their own existential situations. Doing this offers students more potent and critical ways to language and approach future rhetorical situations. It also allows them to explore the ways their personal labor is connected to larger structures of labor in our class, the school, their own educational histories, and even larger social structures that contribute to *habitus*, such as gender, class, and race, among others.

Arendt describes labor as biological, unending, and cyclical (105). It is the way people reproduce themselves and things in the world (106). It is the physical doing of things. This is the *how* of labor's first dimension. When teacher and students articulate this dimension in economies, we point out what literally will be done, in what order, and what quantities or amount of work is expected. Doing this in labor instructions can reveal how language is biological, how learning to read and write is never-ending and requires us to take time to move, to do things. A reading "assignment" is not simply a task to check off a list, not something done, a chapter swallowed or consumed, but it also designates a period of chronological time in which one's body is in laboring processes in particular material places. It is energy expended and time experienced that results in change. Reading a chapter, like writing a draft, is movement and flux. It is verbing, not a noun.

Conceiving and designing an assignment initially in this first dimension of labor can help teachers consider what they are actually asking students to do, how much time they are expecting students to spend, and how that doing leads to learning in some way. It should also prompt us to work with our students on labor processes, collaboratively work out with students what fair labor processes are, and continually check on students' abilities to do the ideal labor set forth in labor instructions. For instance, what do we expect students actually to do when we ask them to read a chapter of a book? Do we expect them to find a quiet location with no distractions or people working in the background? Do we expect them to read all thirty-five pages in one sitting? Do we expect them to be sitting in a hard chair, back erect and at a table, or lying on their bed in their room, or sitting in their car waiting to go to class? Do we expect them to spend two or three hours reading, or as much time as it takes to finish the entire chapter? Do we expect that they will be doing this reading after a long day of working a job? Do we expect them to have satisfied their bodily needs for food, water, and rest first, before they begin reading? Do we expect them to be mindful, to pause every so often and take an assessment of what they've just read, ask themselves a question about it, maybe take some notes somewhere? Do we want them to annotate the text in some specific way?

The point is, understanding and articulating the how of labor can help students not just do the kinds of labors that we (teacher and students) agree will most help them succeed, but pay attention to, and be mindful of, their bodies and the places those bodies are in when they do reading or writing for our courses. Our students may realize in the process that when such biological, chronological, and material processes of labor are made explicit, some of their habitual practices many not be very conducive to the ideal laboring envisioned for their learning. This doesn't address material, economic, and other constraints that are very real for many students, but avoiding what a teacher understands as ideal labor is just as detrimental to students' problematizing and learning as ignoring their material constraints and conditions. In other words, just because it is unrealistic to ask everyone to perform the same ideal labor in the same ways doesn't mean we cannot articulate what we understand at the moment to be ideal labor as a kind of shore marker or buoy to help give reference to those in the ecology. Doing this also allows the class to self-consciously change what it expects as ideal labor over time. This can help us better understand and respond to the material constraints and bodily differences in students' varying labor practices.

Arendt makes an important distinction that often comes up in my classes when students begin paying closer attention to the first dimension of their labor. Because it is connected to the body, according to Arendt, labor is also private (111). Thus "every activity which is not necessary either for the life of the individual or for the life process of society is subsumed under playfulness" (127). Play is private. Occasionally in my classrooms, students wonder about whether certain stretches of time count as labor, since they must record their labor in labor logs. For example, does pausing in one's reading in order to "take a break" and just relax for an hour, while still thinking about the reading, count as reading labor? Does one's drive home after class in which one is brainstorming a draft or thinking through ideas from the book a part of the labor of the class to be recorded? Or would these times be in the realm of play and not recorded? What does that chill break or drive home produce for the student or their colleagues in the course? Must one's time always produce something measurable? Our bodies have needs, and some of those needs are rest and downtime from strenuous tasks. Can taking a break from intense reading be necessary for a student, just as necessary as getting home? Can we account for that labor-time too?

I've always left these questions up to the student to decide and reflect upon in labor journals. My sense is that if that student feels that the break from the labor somehow contributes to the labor, or helps them, then it may be counted. However, the larger question about the role of play in labor is important to have. Should we not strive to transform our "work" for the class into "play"? Shouldn't we find joy or playfulness in our labors? Is play really a private matter only? Why is play often seen as private while work is easily seen as public or even for others' benefit? Ultimately, while I realize that many people separate work and play, I'm not sure that this separation is always useful or meaningful in an educational context, since as I've suggested above, learning languaging is part of the lifelong human condition. I do not deny that there are many grey areas in how we labor and play. And I think most would agree that oftentimes, labors that begin as work or for school, end up being fun and play, and vise versa. The distinctions between work, rest, and play seem fuzzy at best and mostly contrived, likely for the purposes of controlling people. If you can devalue play and make work more important in a society, then you can get a lot of people to define themselves by their work, by their laboring for an elite group, or a corporation. They will sacrifice themselves for their work. This, in effect, gets people to consent to modes of living that mostly benefit large corporations and their relatively few shareholders and CEOs. No matter how one feels about such idea(l)s, the distinctions between rest, work, and play seem good places to reflect upon together and problematize.

The second dimension of labor, *that* we labor, which calls attention to how much labor we produce, is mapped to Arendt's notion of "work." She explains that work "fabricates the sheer unending variety of things whose sum total constitutes the human artifice . . . objects for use" (136). Thus work is connected to material artifacts and instruments and so quantifiable. They have a definite beginning and end (143), are durable but wear out with use (137), and have usefulness for human ends. In fact, they are defined as means to human ends, making their usefulness the primary standard by which to measure them (154). Arendt, however, does not confine work to mere objects. Work, like labor, is connected to people and their uses or purposes. A tree in and of itself has no purpose for humans until we conceive of it as something to use for particular purposes, like fire wood or the materials for a house. Once a tree is lumber it has been transformed through labor into an instrument of human work.

Arendt connects work and its instrumentality to Protagoras' Humanity-measure doctrine through people's judgment and purposes for the things being judged. She does this by identifying a corruption in the way the fragment has been typically translated. According to Arendt, Protagoras' fragment does not say "man is the measure of all things." The phrase uses the Greek word, *chrēmata*, which does not mean "all things," instead it means "specifically things used or needed or possessed by men" (158). Therefore, Arendt explains,

> He [*homo faber* or working human] will judge every thing as
> though it belonged to the class of *chrēmata*, of use objects,
> so that, to follow Plato's own example, the wind will no lon-
> ger be understood in its own right as a natural force but will
> be considered exclusively in accordance with human needs
> for warmth or refreshment (158)

The implication of this to the second dimension of labor is that the work in the second dimension of labor articulates and makes judgments on the products of our laboring, the artifacts students produce and the time spent in labor. Thus, part of our laboring is to make purposeful judgments on and about that laboring itself. When students pay attention to the fact that they labor in particular ways, then record measurements on those sessions of labor, they transform that labor into countable or quantifiable labor power that is exchangeable in our economy for a final course grade. Of course, the second dimension of labor offers more than just the calculation of course grades. Arendt's notion of work articulates the beginning and end of periods of labor and what those periods of laboring produce, and like Arendt's rendition of Protagoras' Humanity-measure fragment, as a dimension of labor they include judgments of usefulness and purpose, which can be accounted for quantitatively in engagement ratings in labor logs and number of words or pages produced or read, and in more qualitative measures in weekly reflections in labor journals. Thus students purposefully keep track of the fact that they labor and how much they produce or work through.

While there may be other small judgments that measure labor which we might ask students to do as they labor, it is the quantitative, instrumental, and purposeful aspects of the second dimension of labor that Arendt's concept of work reveals that I think is most useful to students. That is, finding small ways to judge and measure labor in quantifiable ways is vital to seeing instrumentality and purpose. Furthermore, if we are using labor as a way to calculate final course grades, and if our learning in the class is articulated as labor (through labor instructions), then quantifying our actual labor in some way is important to help students know their progress and determine final grades, even if many of us find quantifying things in humanities-based classes problematic. But the problem of quantifying things in literacy classrooms is mostly a problem when we try to quantify learning or quality of students' learning, reading, or writing practices, then use those measures to grade how good students are or how well they've done something. This is not what the second dimension of labor calls for. And because it is more easily separated from the other two dimensions of labor, it is less confusing to students as some judgment of quality. It is more easily seen as unconnected to judgments of quality.

In fact, it is not as problematic to quantify how much time a student spends writing a draft, or how many words they produced, or how much time they spent reading a book if that quantifying is only used to understand their practices, learn something from that quantifying, and make a simple binary judgment of fact (not value): did the student complete the labor task asked of them? Did they write five hundred words? How many words did they write? Did they read for two hours? How many hours did they read exactly? Did they tweet a picture of an annotated page from their reading? In these ways, the second dimension of labor can help students conceive of time on task and the amount of words produced or read in a given labor session as instrumental to their learning and to understanding what that learning actually consists of. Time and amount of words, for instance, become measurements for the purpose of understanding their learning as labor. This is how I try to explain those quantifiable things in labor instructions to students, and how we try to articulate them in each assignment's statement of goals. But as one might expect, it often requires students to have some initial faith in the labor-based system and experience it for a while before they realize and feel what benefits there are for them.

The third dimension of labor is *what* the labor means, which I connect to Arendt's notion of action (as seen in Figure 3.2). She associates closely action with human diversity, individual distinctiveness and distinction. Action, according to Arendt, defines being human. She explains:

> With word and deed we insert ourselves into the human world, and this insertion is like a second birth, in which we confirm and take upon ourselves the naked fact of our original physical appearance. This insertion is not forced upon us by necessity, like labor, and it is not prompted by utility, like work. It may be stimulated by the presence of others whose company we may wish to join, but it is never conditioned by them; its impulse springs from the beginning which came into the world when we were born and to which we respond by beginning something new on our own initiative. To act, in its most general sense, means to take an initiative, to begin (as the Greek word *archein*, "to begin," "to lead," and eventually "to rule," indicates), to set something into motion (which is the original meaning of the Latin *agere*) . . . it is not the beginning of something but of somebody, who is a beginner himself . . . another way of saying that the principle of freedom was created when man was created but not before. (176–77)

Thus Arendt sees action as the way human plurality is inherent in the human condition (175), and to be an agent means to both act and speak, to engage in both words and deeds (178). We begin as single agents speaking and doing (189), and this feeds into a community who continues those actions after we leave or die (198). In a broad sense, Arendt sees action as the way to understand how humans make history, science, politics, and the most durable elements of society, ideas, by making themselves. She eventually moves her discussion to forgiveness, which is our unique power to undo or alleviate the problems of not knowing fully the consequences of previous acts (236–37).

Arendtian action offers several ways to elaborate the third dimension of labor, the reflective dimension that provides students with ways to make sense and meaning out of how and that they labor. While the habitual and iterative process of small acts of reflection condition students to pause and reflect upon how they are working or that they are, I still offer more formal moments in the semester or quarter to think more carefully about their labor. The weekly reflections offer a series of low-stakes moments, as do our midterm and final reflections on our labor log data and labor journal entries. One move Arendt's action asks us to consider in such reflections is how the student is an agent acting in their labor. *How does their labor make them? In what ways is that labor beginning some practice or bit of learning for them? Who are they just now beginning to become? What bit of meaning in their labor practices is worth sharing with their colleagues in class? What can be carried on, made larger than just some private insight for one student?* These are hard, and arguably, abstract questions to pose to students, but asking students to think about themselves not only as individual students completing work for a class or teacher but as agents acting in purposeful ways that then begin the production of something else through their practices, something larger than themselves, can be a bit less abstract.

Such reflective activities or prompts might begin in the early weeks of a semester to focus on the student as an agent acting, deciding and doing things, in their labor, then gently push them to think about their words as deeds, and their deeds as words, push them to pose their own questions about what their labor means to their own development, to their own growth as a writer or reader. This making meaning of their labor may start with understanding the first dimension of labor: How did you do what you did? What happened first, second, etc.? Where were you? What was physically happening in your surroundings? It can then move to the second dimension: How long did you take to do key steps in the labor instructions? How much did you produce? At midpoint and final times, I ask them to reflect not on a single session of labor, but all their labor as a set of practices that stretch over the semester or quarter. To help them see patterns and their labor as practice, I ask them to fill in a table that I provide them (Table 3.1) from their information collected in their labor logs.[26]

---

26   In recent versions of the labor logs, which are Google Sheets that I give to my students, most of the data in the table, along with some graphs, are automatically filled in through formulas in the spreadsheet.

Table 3.1. Sample reflection table that helps students see their labor as a set of practices that produce worth.

Average duration of most engaged sessions/ average Duration of all sessions (min)	No. of sessions/total no. of all sessions	Average Engagement Rating (1–5)	Total duration of most engagement sessions/all sessions (min)	Main Location of Labor
60/70	4/29	3.5	240/2030	Home
Average duration of W sessions	Average duration of R sessions	Average engagement of W sessions	Average engagement of R sessions	Average minutes of labor per week
62	45	4.5	3	600

This table allows students to see their labor as practice in a few quantifiable ways. There are other ways to quantify and represent the labor data we gather, but this gives them some places to begin reflecting. They might compare key sessions. Are labor sessions from week 8 or 9 faster or slower than sessions done in weeks 1–2? Are they doing more or less labor? What slowed the student down or sped them up in the later weeks? How engaged was the student and what contributed to that engagement or lack of it? How much time did they spend drafting for class? Does this amount seem enough to get the learning the student was looking for? What keeps the student from spending more time? Finally, what lessons did they learn from seeing their labor in this way? What did they think might be worth sharing with their colleagues in class?

These final questions about sharing connects simple reflections to the larger, more communal properties of Arendtian action that make it more than an individual insight. Action participates and contributes to the larger community of people, so reflections that move students in that direction are shared with colleagues and fulfill the complete cycle of labor-work-action that Arendt articulates. In labor-based grading contract economies that use compassion as a key element in constructing the cultural space of judgment, sharing personal insights, making them communal theory about reading and writing, is compassionate behavior (I'll say more about this in Chapter 5), and opens up meaning and deeper learning by dramatizing the ways various students labor in diverse ways and share their theorizing from the dramas of their labors. It makes one's private reading labor, for example, also about helping others learn and do language acts too.

MINDFUL LABORING IS THE LARGER THEME

A fundamental aspect of labor-based grading contract economies is slowing down, experiencing labor and time differently, or mindfully. I believe students usually learn best when they can just be in the labor, when they can stop thinking so centrally about the end product or goal and center all of their energies and attention on the labor they are engaged in right now. What we do now is all we really have, so I remind them continually in my labor instructions and through our mindfulness practices each class session, to be mindful of the fact that they are laboring in particular ways, to savor that laboring. It is all you have. We are lucky to be able to do this work for each other. One might think of mindful laboring as the act of self-consciously laboring at something, doing something while simultaneously noticing that you are doing that work, that you are doing it in a particular way, that you feel a certain way as you do it, that that laboring makes you feel, see, hear, understand, and experience other things that are wrapped up in the labor.

The institutional, historical, and pragmatic reasons for the fixation on the end-product are clear, and it's more than just about the writing classroom's heritage of product-based pedagogies, such as Berlin's Current-Traditional pedagogy. The focus on end-products in classrooms stems from the ways that classroom assessment economies function, how most are set up to produce a grade, an exchange-value, and pay little formal attention to the nuanced and contradictory meanings of the use-value and worth of labor. When most of the value and worth of students' labor is neglected, students themselves neglect it and are not in the practice of seeing it, or noticing that they labor, especially while they are in the act of laboring. Labor is usually something to get through, to be done with, not to savor. We try to do as little laboring as possible and produce the most product from that laboring. This is exactly the wrong way to learn literacies.

So getting to a place in which most students are mindfully laboring, that is, being in their labors for the class with less concern for what it produces and more concern for savoring the laboring experience, feeling and experiencing as fully as possible the doing of writing or reading, paying attention to what happens when they labor, can take all quarter or semester. Labor logs, labor journals, and labor tweets help make labor more present, more obvious, more there, so that students can begin to investigate it, and this allows the class to also use it as a fairer way to calculate course grades than judgments of so-called quality on products of their labors, commodities that inherently are valued in contradictory ways.

Labor-based grading contracts focus everyone's attention on time and tempo of practices and work, which automatically reconnects our intellectual labor to our bodies. Thus it is important to remember that labor-based grading contracts ask students and teacher to pay attention to the doing of things, to what and how we do our work, then articulate that labor as learning. This means that we pay attention to our bodies, what they are doing, how they feel as they move (or remain still), where they are in time and space, and what the experience of that timing and spacing is like. This is tapping into ourselves as whole humans doing language in self-consciously embodied ways, ways that are situated in our lives.

When discussing how to meditate and form contemplative practices, Arthur Zajoc, a physicist, argues that one cannot meditate fast. It always happens at the speed of breath and heartbeat. It cannot be rushed. He explains:

> Whether beholding a painting or listening to music, whether reading poetry or viewing a play, time must slow down in order for us to enter into the object of our attention with our heart as well as our head. If our thinking runs along with the worries of the day, or presses too forcefully, we remain outside the art of the painting, poetry, or performance. (51)

Zajoc is drawing on a set of contemplative practices, which have been used to help students learn in various disciplines (Barbezat and Bush). Contemplative practices help practitioners slow time down, or experience it as slower, enter objects of contemplation, such as our own breath, our bodies, an orange slice, a peanut, a picture or painting, a musical composition, the sensation of our feet in shoes or walking. Once entered, the practitioner explores the object of contemplation, feels as much as they can without judging themselves for not doing enough or experiencing something they think they should have.

I posit that our grading economies in classrooms should be more like the beholding activities Zajoc references. The OED's entries for "behold" all focus on spending time to view something in its beauty: "to hold or keep in view, to watch; to regard or contemplate with the eyes; to look upon, look at" ("behold"). Many of the early references to the word in English, which begins with Old English (*bihaldan*) refer to Biblical passages or God, thus it often is associated with looking upon or contemplating beauty or the divine, which takes time to do. One must pause and spend time to behold. It is respectful and reverent. Daniel Barbezat and Mirabai Bush tell us in their discussion of the practice for college classrooms that beholding has a recent tradition in art history (149). Beauty, as in art, requires that we keep that which is beautiful in our view, to hold it there. And if beauty can be found in everything, then writing assessment as a classroom practice, as an economy made up in part of people and their words, might incorporate practices of beholding, mindful practices that purposefully pause and pay attention to what is in front of us, what we are reading and how we are experiencing that reading, how we make judgments of the text and its author, what pressures those judgments place on others in the economy, and how those judgments circulate in the economy before, during, and after our reading.

Thus, one key aspect of all labor is time. As the contemplative practice of beholding illustrates, the most fundamental aspect of what I'm calling mindful laboring is taking the right amount of time and noticing that you are doing something in a particular way, in a particular place, under particular conditions. Mindful labor is experienced as labor while one is laboring. One notices that they are laboring, which opens up ways to notice the context, conditions, and nature of that laboring, and then what meanings might be understood. But it requires time.

I don't find that most students are practiced at paying close attention to the various dimensions of time in their laboring. Beyond understanding what time it is on a clock, we often do not pay attention to the multiple ways that we experience and frame time in our lives. Doing so can help students collect data on their labor time and make sense of that data in reflections, producing a fuller, richer sense of their three-dimensional labor. Barbara Adam, a Sociologist who has done copious research on the concept of time, offers a theory of timescapes that may help explain time as a component or measure of labor. In turn, her work may help teachers consider various kinds of labor data to collect, and language and activities that move students toward mindful laboring. Adam's research on timescapes (*Timescapes of Modernity*; *Time*) theorizes that time is complex and multidimensional. Her purpose for such theorizing has been to develop better ways for sociological research to be conducted, but her conception of timescapes reveals how time is not a simple construct, and we conceive and manage it in a number of ways. She offers seven ways by which time is experienced, understood, and/or framed:

- *Time frame*—bounded, beginning and end of day, year, life time, generation, historical/geological epoch;
- *Temporality*—process world, internal to system, ageing, growing, irreversibility, directionality;
- *Timing*—synchronisation, co-ordination, right/wrong time;
- *Tempo*—speed, pace, rate of change, velocity, intensity: how much activity in given timeframe;
- *Duration*—extent, temporal distance, horizon: no duration = instantaneity, time point/moment;
- *Sequence*—order, succession, priority: no sequence = simultaneity, at same time;
- *Temporal modalities*—past, present and future—memory, perception/experience and anticipation. (*Timescapes Challenge* 7–8)

Each way of framing time offers very different observations and conclusions about time and people, about what might be recorded in labor logs, or what might be considered in labor journals. Adam's seven ways of time, as I'll call them, offer ways to consider time in labor-based assessment economies. I'll discuss just three that I find most useful.

Time as *duration*, *sequence*, and *temporal modalities* have been touched on already in my earlier discussions of labor logs, through the data I currently ask students to keep track of. For example, through labor logs, students know the amount of minutes they have spent on either reading or writing labors, when those labors took place, and the sequence or order in which they did any given labor assignment or the order they did various assignments in the quarter or semester. In labor journals, we consider past and future labor sessions, often comparing two past sessions, and always projecting forward toward future practices. However, Adam's *time frame*, *timing*, and *tempo* offer additional possible data and reflective prompting.

Adam explains that time frame is constructed by the researcher, and is a choice that creates boundaries and determines findings by determining where you "place subjects" (*Timescapes Challenge* 8). The time frame of clocks and calendars are stable, "externally located, [and] socially constructed," while "personal frames of life time and family time, or times of illness and stress" are more fluid, contingent, and relative. Thus the units of measure for more personal frames of time "expan[d] and contrac[t] as people move along in their life course" (8). For labor-based assessment economies, thinking about our labor from our own personal time frames generates a host of interesting and educative questions. What kind of time frame is the student working from? What are the boundaries in which labor for the class is forced to adhere to? Does the student work full time and go to school? Does she have family obligations each day? Does she take other courses? Let's say she works, goes to school full time, and is a mother who must share childcare duties with a partner. This might segment her typical weekday into three or four units of time in any day with boundaries like: time that she attends class; time that she takes care of her children and family; time that she has to do school work; and time that she works at a job. These will likely not be equal segments of time, but may be how she conceives of her time in a day. Meanwhile, her week may be broken up into two or three larger segments of time: school time and work time during the weekdays; and school-work time, family time, family care time, and sleep and relaxing time on the weekends. These are the boundaries that form the time frames in which the student might consider the labor required of her for the class.

Seeing one's labor in a personal time frame requires a student to first notice what time frame they work in or might work in. Then they might begin to see how much time (in minutes or hours) they actually have to do the labors of the course. This can help students notice particular kinds of data to be logged or reflected upon. For example, a class might keep track of the kinds of segments of time in their personal time frames they have, how much time each segment gets in any given day and during each week, and when those segments occur in the day or week. What time frames are students trying to fit the course's labor into? How many segments are there in their personal time frames? What is the biggest segment: work, school work, family obligations, something else? What should it be at this moment in their life? How many minutes or hours are they giving to each segment of their life's time frame? At what point in the day or week does the segment of time dedicated to the course's labor occur? Where did a particular labor session fall during that week and how productive or meaningful was that labor? How might its position in their daily or weekly time frame help create that labor, make it productive, engaging, or meaningful (or not)? Are they consistent each week in where they fit the course labor in their life's time frame? What are the consequences of its position in the day or week? Is it at the end of other taxing or strenuous labors? Is it first in any given day or week? What segments in their personal time frames are being sacrificed each week?

Obviously, part of reflecting and learning from one's labor as situated in one's personal time frame is not just about reading and writing in more engaging and meaningful ways, but also about learning how one learns, managing one's time best, and understanding the boundaries and limits one has in one's life. Knowing one's labor in this way can alleviate some guilt and the sense that one is not good enough for college when one realizes that their life's personal time frame is not ideal or works against them in subtle ways, and other things are either more important at this time or can be reprioritized temporarily. Further, sharing these insights with colleagues in class can help students see that they are not alone in their struggles, that often personal time frames coalesce into patterns for reasons that are outside of the students in the room. Many students may be oppressed by larger societal structures that unfairly place boundaries and limits on their lives, making it nearly impossible to accomplish what is expected of them in college. But understanding this insight from their own labor data may offer ways to problematize their own existential situations.

Adam explains that timing, the third way of experiencing time in the list above, offers other kinds of measures and observations. This element concerns itself with synchronizing and "achieving good time" and it is relative to other events, contexts, that happen around or in conjunction with the events in question. For students, again, this provides different useful labor data, often comparative data. When are the good and bad times of each day or week for the labor of the class? That is, when during each day or week is the student most equipped, ready, and able to do the kinds of labor the course asks of them? Why are these times best? Could they change these timings during the semester or quarter? Does a student typically do the labor of the class during a good period, a bad one? Why? Was a particular labor session done at a good time in the day or week, one conducive to their learning or engagement? How many labor sessions in the semester or quarter fell into good time periods and how many into bad ones? Why? What kept all labor sessions from being done in only good periods? How did the timing affect the student's engagement and interest in the activity? What other activities or obligations synced up in the student's day or week that made it easier or harder to complete this labor session? Were multiple tasks or obligations coming at the student during certain periods in the labor? At what points? Why? How did the student respond? How did this syncing or timing affect what the student learned or how they engaged in the labor?

Finally, Adam says that tempo is about speed and pace, who must adapt to whose timing. How fast is an activity going? When must it begin or end? These factors make tempo a function of power arrangements (9). In other words, who or what dictates pace and speed of labor indicates who has more power in the arrangement. In labor-based assessment economies, students might use the concept of tempo to keep data on tempo of assignments in order to understand some of how power moves in the class, and perhaps to change it when that movement of power is not helpful to students' learning. How much time is given for an assignment of labor and who determined this? When does that labor begin and when must it end, and who decided these tempo limits? How well does the tempo of the labor match what the student feels they need before and after completing the work? Does this tempo fit within most students' personal time frames? Did the student adjust the tempo of the labor (e.g., exclude or skip steps) from what was given in the labor instructions? How often does the student adjust the tempo of the labor instructions over the course of the term or semester? What effect did this have on the total amount of time spent on reading and/or writing labors in the course?

The important thing to remember when attempting to make labor more mindful in an assessment ecology, one that uses labor to determine course grades, is to honor whatever labor is offered by students, while still pushing students to ask hard questions about that labor. What happened in your labor? How did you experience it? Did you do enough? What shortcuts did you take? Could you change some things in your habits or weekly routines that would allow you to do more or labor differently? Thus, mindful laboring is practicing reading and writing self-consciously by noticing and articulating where and how our labor fits into our own personal time frames, how it and other things sync with good and bad moments in our life, and what the speed, intensity, and engagement that labor is.

There are no bad ways to labor if laboring is done in a compassionate spirit and with an attempt to learn and help others learn. We can only labor at the paces we can, the only pace anyone can learn, which always takes time, time not so ironically we should pay attention to itself. As Zajonc reminds us of meditation, I believe the labors of reading and writing too cannot be done fast, especially if it is connected to people, to their beauty, to their languaging, to their bodies, to their agency, to their becoming. Mindful laboring allows for such praxis, and connects it to the grading of a course, which makes grading not a method to measure students' writing competencies or development but a process of paying attention on purpose, a process of learning about one's whole self and the structures of language and judgment that make up and affect each of us.

Contracts?

CHAPTER 4.

WHAT LABOR-BASED GRADING CONTRACTS LOOK LIKE

As I theorized in Chapter 3, labor is work the body does over time. Labor in the writing classroom is the experience of languaging. No matter what our pedagogical assumptions are about learning or literacy, about grades or how to evaluate student writing, we all take for granted that our students must labor in order to learn. They must read or write, take notes or discuss. All pedagogies ask students to labor, to do something in order to gain something else. However, typical grading systems rarely account for students' labor in any way. They usually ignore the actual labor of learning in favor of systems that judge the so-called quality of the outcomes of student labor, favoring a single judge's (the teacher's) decisions about the quality of the products of labor. Because labor is neglected in such conventional grading systems, they often are unfair to diverse groups of students. As I've discussed in the previous chapters, labor-based grading contracts attempt to correct this problem.

In this chapter, I explain my own labor-based grading contract and its grounding philosophy (see Appendix A for one version of my contract). This discussion is meant to be practical and useful to a teacher in designing their own contract, planning its use, and discussing it with students in a writing, literature, or literacy course. While it is not necessary to have read the previous chapters, I reference those ideas in this one. I start by offering an explanation of the core system that produces the final course grade for everyone, move to explaining how to assign higher grades than the default contract grade, and briefly explain how this system offers a more socially just way to produce grades in writing courses that are situated in a diverse and inherently unfair society. In the second half of the chapter, I discuss four key statements that make up the main aspects of the philosophy of my labor-based grading contract, which inform my contract's preamble (its first two pages) that students read and discuss. Working through these statements, I feel, gives a teacher enough information to build and use their own labor-based grading contract system in their own course and talk to students about it, so I discuss each statement in detail, sometimes explaining how I have such discussions with students, and offering some data from my own classrooms to help illustrate the philosophical statements.

HOW LABOR-BASED GRADES ARE DETERMINED

A labor-based grading contract is essentially a set of social agreements with the entire class about how final course grades will be determined for everyone. These agreements are articulated in a contract, a document, that is negotiated at the beginning of the term or semester, then reexamined at midpoint to make sure it is still fair enough for everyone. It is a social, corporate agreement, which means it may not be a product of full consensus, but instead hard agreements. What can we agree upon now that seems fair enough, at least until the midpoint of the quarter or semester? Everyone promises to meet the contract's stipulations, and the teacher promises to administer the contract in the spirit it has been negotiated. Like Danielewicz and Elbow's contract, my corporate contract has a default grade of B (3.1).[27] If a student meets the basic guidelines of the contract, which means they do the labor asked of everyone in the spirit it is asked, and submit all work in the manner asked, then they will get a B (3.1) final grade no matter what I or anyone else thinks of any of their work.

My contract boils down to the matrix or table on the final page (Table 4.1) that delineates the labor required for each final course grade. This table identifies the key ways labor is marked and accounted for when calculating course grades. The calculus is simple: the more labor you do, the better your grade in the course will be, with no attention to quality of writing turned in (on the part of the teacher). While the substance of all discussions, feedback, activities, and the like are always about quality, or rather about how readers make meaning of texts, how they see quality, what quality means to each reader, what various expectations different readers have, all those judgments of writing are separated from the calculation of course grades. Thus, how anyone judges writing quality is divorced from how final course grades are determined. In effect, the labor-based grading contract works from a key assumption: *It's better to separate the course grade from how and what students learn in the course.* This is how I enact in the assessment ecology the distinction between exchange-value and worth, as discussed in Chapter 3.

On a day to day basis as the teacher-administrator of the contract, I assume that all students are doing all the labor required of them, which is articulated carefully in labor instructions for every reading and writing assignment, discussed as the first dimension of three-dimensional labor in Chapter 3 (Figure 3.2). All labor is quantified in words read or written, and in estimated time a student is expected to spend on the activity, which is also broken up into steps with duration per step also listed, discussed as the second dimension of labor in

---

27   The University of Washington requires that instructors provide a numerical course grade only, one between 0.0 to 4.0 for each student. 3.1 is in the middle of the "B" category.

Chapter 3 (Figure 3.2). If I've marked nothing in my gradebook, the student is meeting the contract's requirements. I only mark when a student doesn't turn something in, turns it in late, or turns it in incomplete, otherwise the full labor requirements are met. Let me repeat: I only need to mark something in my gradebook when a student doesn't complete appropriately or on time any bit of labor for the course. This means there are only two ways for me to record a lack of labor fulfillment by a student: non-participation (usually absence from class) and late, incomplete, or absent assignments.

Table 4.1. The final grade breakdown in the grading contract

	# Non-Partic Days	# of Late Assigns.	# of Missed Assigns.	# of Ignored Assigns.
A (4.0)	3	3	1	0
B (3.1)	3	3	1	0
C (2.1)	4	4	2	0
D (1.1)	5	5	3	1
E (0.0)	6	6	4	2

Labor expectations then are described to students and measured along the first two dimensions of three-dimensional labor, as can be seen in Table 4.1's breakdown table, which is located on the last page of my contract for a 10-week, FYW course. While the details may change, depending on how often the class meets or how many assignments there are expected to be in the class, or whether the course is in a ten-week quarter or a fifteen-week semester system, I have found these are the only categories of labor I need to determine fair enough course grades. They are not the only ways we keep track of our labor, but they are the ways that we can quantify our labor practices and use that quantification to determine a final course grade. As discussed in Chapter 3, since a course grade in a labor-based grading ecology only signifies *that* the student labored (the second dimension of labor), then course grades need only be determined by such quantifiable measures. This part of the contract often gets the most attention when negotiating its terms, because it means the most to students' final course grade

This also means that all assignments are labor, so they are all treated equally when calculating grades. A late formal essay draft or a late informal reflection of a paragraph each count as one late assignment. They both have the same impact on the student's grading contract. This keeps the system more elegant and simple, but it also reinforces the idea that all labor in the class, at least for calculating grades, is of equal value. One hour of labor is worth one hour of labor, regardless of the kind of labor you are engaged in during that hour and even though not all labor is equal when understood in terms of other domains, such as learning or engagement. While this aspect of the grade can make some students more anxious during the quarter or semester, it reinforces the idea that all of the labor of the course is important to do, and should be done with an equal amount of care. It also makes the course generally more rigorous, if by rigorous we mean that it typically requires students to do more work on a specified pace or tempo during the term, and attempt more engaged and intense work, although this does not mean more high stakes work.

Since grades do not equate neatly to learning or even quality of writing, there is no sense in trying to make them equate. Grades have never equated to students' performances in courses. All we have to do is look at the pervasive use of "extra credit" assignments in courses. If all students had a fair shot at getting the highest grades possible, why is there extra credit? The impulse for teachers to give extra credit is understandable. We want all of our students to do well, and to do as well as they would like to do. But in quality-based systems of grading, teachers know that some students in their midst simply do not have enough time or fluency in the dominant White discourse of the classroom (at least according to their own judgment of things) to get a high grade. This feels unfair, so conscientious teachers offer extra credit, which amounts to more labor. Do this extra thing, and I'll raise your grade, goes the logic. So grading systems that accommodate extra credit assignments are working from a labor-based model, but usually just in terms of the extra credit stuff. Extra credit assignments would not be needed if everyone in the class could achieve high grades by doing the assigned work. Extra credit is a way to satisfy students' desires for better grades, and allow teachers to feel generous and fair. Real fairness in assessment ecologies is constructed with students and does not need extra things to make up for the fairness that the ecology already lacks. What labor-based contracts assume is that all labor counts and all labor is equal when it comes to calculating course grades. This in and of itself builds equity among diverse students with diverse linguistic competencies since it is a grading system that does not depend on a particular set of linguistic competencies to acquire grades.

I try very hard not to give students busy work, and explain carefully why they are doing each bit of labor. When students understand why they are doing something, how it helps them, and have had a hand in how that work is assessed, then there is a higher chance that their work is not going to be experienced as "busy work," or as work that does not help them toward their goals for the course. So the categories above in the breakdown table do not suggest amount of labor time spent on an activity, amount of text read, or amount of text produced, three ways one might quantify labor in a writing classroom; however, these things are provided in each set of labor instructions given for everything we do in the class. If I'm going to grade based on labor, then I should make clear how much labor is expected and how it is counted. In the past, I'd simply ask students to read Chapter Two, but in a labor-based grading ecology, I provide multiple ways to understand the labor expectations for that same reading in labor instructions. Completing the instructions means a student has completed the labor expectations.

All labor instructions have three parts: a brief description of the assignment, a statement of the purpose and goals of the labor, and a step-by-step process for completing the labor.[28] I de-emphasize product in the description by documenting carefully the labor process—that is, labor instructions are mostly a step-by-step process of what students should do, how much time they should take in each step, and what that step should produce (if it does) in words written or read (see Appendix D). In these instructions, I provide my expectations for their labor along several dimensions:

- The process of the assignment (what chronological steps are involved in the labor?)
- Time on tasks/steps (how many minutes does each step in the process take?)
- Quantity (how many words need to be produced or read in the step?)
- Due date/time and method of submission for the products of the labor (when, how, and where is the product of the labor submitted for use in the course?)

The first two items above are difficult to know if students have done them. I feel I must trust my students when they say they've completed the process and spend enough time on tasks. The other two items above can be checked and quantified easily. These are the main markers for me as the administrator of the contract. If those two aspects of the labor instructions are met, then I do nothing. I do not need to record anything in my grade book. The student is meeting the contract. If an assignment is incomplete or late, then I record that in my gradebook and let the student know what I've recorded.

At my current institution, all final course grades are recorded as a numerical value from 0.0 to 4.0 in the system. Students know this and so they need to know exactly what a C or a B means in this matrix. There are lots of problems with using such a fine-grained grading system as this, but I'll avoid that discussion. I will say that the more distinctions that are made in a grading system, the less consistent grades can be, even when there is only one grader, and the harder and longer it will take for a grader to determine any given grade. In short, the

---

28   Gin Schwarz, who graciously read an early draft of this book, and a former grad student of mine who has used grading contracts for some time, inheriting them from her old professor, Jerry Farber, called my labor instructions "like following recipes with labor ingredients."

more distinctions one must make, the longer it will take to grade and the less reliable one's grades will be. Furthermore, as you might already guess, the difference in a final course grade of 3.1 and 3.2 or 3.0 is so small and difficult to discern that it is arguable that the distinctions are meaningless. For these reasons, I only use the five distinctions listed above, which amount to the middle grade in each traditional category. At previous institutions that recorded grades using the letter system with a plus/minus, I simply used the letters with all the grades as full grades, no minuses or pluses.

The categories of labor that affect final course grades listed in the far-left column are typical kinds of records kept by most teachers. The first category, "# Non-Partic Days," is essentially the number of absences from class. In this contract, a student may miss up to three classes and still meet the default B (3.1) grade described in the contract. It is labelled as "non-participation" because technically at my institution, I cannot base a course grade on absences, but I can base it on participation, which in my classes always amounts to being there. This isn't the place for me to argue my disagreement with my institution's regulations on absences either. I only wish to highlight the importance of bodily presence to learning. One cannot learn a fundamentally social and contextual practice like language if one isn't physically present in the room with other bodies that are practicing language too. So participation, group work, discussion, reading, and writing are always a part of every class session. The contract makes more obvious that students' progress and learning in the class demand that they be there physically to experience that social laboring.

The other three columns distinguish the three categories of assignments turned in. Items 4–6 of the contract (See Appendix A) explain each distinction. Below is the language of those items from this version of the contract. I've dispensed with the numbering, but each item is numbered for convenience and referencing with students in classes.[29] Note that the language is in terms of what students agree to do in the course.

> **Late/Incomplete Work**. You agree to turn in properly and on time all work and assignments expected of you in the spirit they are assigned, which means you'll complete all of the labor instructions for each assignment. During the semester, you may, however, turn in a few assignments late. The exact number of those late assignments is stipulated in the table on the last page of this contract, which we negotiate. **Late or incomplete work is defined as any work or document due**

---

29   Because I inherited my contract from Peter Elbow, the numbering of these items and its format, I take from his contract. Again, I'm grateful to Peter for his gift.

134

that is turned in AFTER the due date/time BUT within 48 hours of the deadline. For example, if some work (say a written reflective piece) was due on Thursday, February 15 at 11:59 pm, that piece must be turned in by 11:59 pm on Saturday the 17th.

Missed Work. If you turn in late work **AFTER the 48 hours** stipulated in #4 above (Late/Incomplete Work), then it will be considered "missed work," which is a more serious mark against your grading contract. This is due to the fact that all assignments are used in class when they are due, so turning in something beyond 48 hours after it is due means it is assured to be less useful, and its absence has hurt your colleagues in class (since they depended on you to turn in your work for their use).

Ignored Work. You agree not to ignore any work expected of you. Ignored work is any work unaccounted for in the quarter—that is, I have no record of you doing it or turning it in. My sense is that ignoring the work so crucial to one's development as a learner in our community is bad and unacceptable, so accumulating any "ignored work" will keep you from meeting our contract expectations [see Main Components Table, Appendix A].

At negotiation times, the breakdown table is the part of the contract most often discussed and altered. I have found though that there are long periods, a couple of years even, in which the contract rarely changes. The breakdown table settles, likely because it has gone through so many rounds of negotiation with students at the same institution, students who often work under similar conditions. So I don't get too worried if a class finds the contract mostly or completely okay during the first week of classes. I'm more interested in them explaining to me what they hear the contract saying, what its philosophy is, and how they think it can help them achieve their goals for the class.

HIGHER LABOR-BASED COURSE GRADES

To get a higher grade than the default one (3.1), students simply do more labor. This is why the A (4.0) and the B (3.1) grades look the same on the breakdown table above. In order to get a higher grade than the default grade, you have to meet the labor conditions for a B, then do additional labor. I have two sections in the contract that explain how to get higher grades. These sections explain possible ways to do more labor that benefit the class in some way and what that labor means for their final course grade. For instance, I might offer four choices, of which a student must choose two or three to complete in order to get an A (4.0). There is, however, a problem with this all-or-nothing labor choice.

You see, I want the labor to be meaningful enough to warrant the highest grade possible, the "exceptional" or "superior" grade. So my reasoning has been that to get the A (4.0) grade, you must do all the listed extra labor assignments—remember, I only make the distinctions listed on the table. Now, this worked better in a system that only asked teachers to designate letter grades (meaning fewer distinctions possible), but in a system like UW's, in which students know there are eight possible grades between 3.1 and 4.0, it feels unfair to many students in my classes. What if during the busy quarter, a student begins to do the extra labor, does two of the items, but can't quite finish the third? Shouldn't they get credit for the additional labor they did? It was still additional labor. Thus a few years ago my students and I came up with a graduated system that works with the UW's overly complex grading system. Now each labor option is worth .3 on the grading scale. Here's how I explain this in the contract, which is for a writing course whose topic is "investigating language":

"A" or Higher Grades

The grade of B (3.1) depends primarily on *behavior* and *labor*. Have you shown responsible effort and consistency in our class? Have you done what was asked of you in the spirit it was asked? Higher grades than the default, the **grades of 3.4, 3.7, or 4.0**, however, require *more labor that helps or supports the class* in its mutual discussions and examinations of language. In order to raise your grade, you may complete as many of the following items of labor as you like (doing three gets you a 4.0). Each item completed fully and in the appropriate manner will raise your final course grade by .3.

- A **substantive revision of two (2) mini-projects** that meaningfully takes into account all feedback and conversation had over both previous mini-projects (described in labor #6 on the syllabus).

- A **20–30 minute, individual class presentation**, with a lesson outline, handout for the class, and a post-activity reflection letter (addressed to Asao), on the material we've agreed upon (described in labor #8 on the syllabus). These presentations may be on chapters from Lippi-Green's text that are not officially assigned.

- **Three (3) additional mini-project responses** (#7 on the syllabus) for colleagues NOT in your writing group, so extra responses for others. Each response should follow exactly the same labor instructions as those provided for the mandatory ones. These must be done in three different weeks (i.e., for three different mini-projects).
- A **more in-depth final project** (described in labor #9 on the syllabus).

Improving Your Contracted Grade

The above means that you can improve your grade between the numerical distinctions in the grid below [the Breakdown table] by accomplishing additional labor. For every item you complete on the above list, your contracted grade will improve by .3 grade points. So if you meet the conditions for a B-contract (3.1), then your grade can improve in the following ways:

- **1 item** completed = course grade of **3.4**
- **2 items** completed = course grade of **3.7**
- **3 items** completed = course grade of **4.0**

If you are working toward a C-contract (2.1) or lower, the same .3 movement up the grade ladder applies by completing 1–3 items on the list above. Your course grade, then, equates to a 2.4, 2.7, and 3.0, respectively.

Note that most of the suggested additional labor attempts to help their colleagues in class. It also demands typically that they work with me to accomplish that labor. This allows me to help students manage their goals for such labors and shape their efforts in ways most helpful to the class in general.

What this system might look like is a version of extra credit, which I've already said is a flaw in conventionally graded ecologies, because its presence admits that some students will not be able to achieve the highest grades possible, so they need extra credit to achieve those grades. The difference in my labor-based system is in the premise we start from about the original contract. We are contracting for this extra labor too, meaning it's not really extra. It's labor I'm not going to ask all students to do if they don't want to, but still want a reasonably high grade (3.1).

In conventionally graded ecologies, because each assignment's worth towards the course grade is determined by a teacher's judgment of the quality of that assignment and not the labor that went into it, it is highly likely that many students cannot achieve the highest grades without extra help, without circumventing the original agreement assumed in the course's grading system and its assignments. In effect, some of each quality-based grade is off limits to some students, and more accessible to others, and these groups of students tend to fall into racialized and class formations in the US (see Inoue, *Antiracist*; Lippi-Green). This accessibility in writing assessment ecologies is White language privilege. White language privilege in writing classrooms is due to the uneven and diverse linguistic legacies that everyone inherits, and the White racial *habitus* that are used as standards, which give privilege to those students who embody them already. The difference in labor-based contracts is in the reasonable chances of all students—not some of them, not the "most prepared" among them, but all of them—to get any grade possible, including the highest.[30] Doing this in one's grading system enacts both John Rawls' theory of social justice as fairness and Iris Young's structural approach to social justice, which I discuss briefly in Chapter 1 and more extensively in Chapter 7 (see goal 5).

There is another way to achieve a higher grade than the default, and this clause was added a few years ago. It came out of a discussion in one FYW course that had an unusually high number of students doing all the labor as asked. By our midpoint renegotiation, they wondered if there could be some reward for those students who ended the quarter with a clean contract, meaning they'd turned every assignment in on time, and participated fully in all classes. In truth, I was already thinking about this option, but it was good to hear them ask for it. So we came up with a clause that we included underneath the contract's final breakdown table. This clause defined "exemplary labor" and offered an extra .3 final course grade points:

> **Exemplary labor.** If by our final meeting conference (end of quarter), you miss no classes (participate in all activities), have no late, missed, or ignored assignments, and do not use a gimme, then you will earn an extra .3 (equal to one item in the "Improving Your Contracted Grade" section) to your final course grade. This rule is meant to reward those students who engage in all the labor of the course in the fullest spirit asked of them and demonstrate themselves to be exemplary class citizens.

I've kept this on my contract, since it rewards those students who are diligent and hardworking. It also acknowledges that I do ask a lot of my students. I've

---

30   I should note that when I say "most prepared," I really mean the *most prepared to use the dominant, White discourse* that the classroom in question rewards. Many students who come to us with other Englishes have been *prepared*, only prepared in linguistically other ways.

also debated about including another way to achieve a similar grade bump (.3), which I've tested out in recent courses, but have not formally included it in the contract.

Since we keep track of our labor during the quarter in labor logs, I know the amount of estimated labor I've assigned, the average total labor for all students, and the actual total labor in minutes of each student. Those students who achieve the most labor in the class are given an extra .3 grade, as if they had done one of the additional labors for a higher grade. This rewards those students that do a lot more labor than their colleagues but may not have done any of the extra labors for a higher grade. I have determined the "most labor" by how much labor is logged in their labor logs. I take the top two or three students in the class, determined by total labor in minutes from their labor logs, and in our final conference I tell them that since they are one of the top performers in the class, I'm giving them an extra .3 grade hike, even if they already got a .3 bump for exemplary labor. Who seems to get this extra labor-based grade bump? At UW Tacoma, in my FYW courses, it has gone to a similar group as those who get the exemplary labor, immigrant students. In my last FYW class, a male Vietnamese student, a female Filipino student, and a male Russian student, all born in other countries and immigrating with parents to the US during their public schooling.[31]

The problem I have with making this an official way to do extra labor in class is that it uses the labor logs to determine grades, something I've said I will not do because I want those logs to be an honest reflective tool for students, not an accountability measure. By leaving it as informal, I can compare the student in question to their performance in class and to how they reflect upon their labor in our final portfolio reflection letters (a required part of that letter). Do these numbers match up with my sense of the student? Does their discussion of their labor as a practice in their portfolio letter match those high numbers? If things square up, then I feel good about applying this rule. But by making this an official part of the contract, it would entice students to fudge their labor logs, I worry. It could also disadvantage students with less time in their lives to work, or who read or write really fast. What I want it to do is reward those students who put in more time, who work long but do not have to. I realize that like other *habitus*, the dispositions and competencies that allow some students, like my immigrant students, to do noticeably more labor than their peers, advantages them. But I'm okay with this advantage, since it is not one that typically is rewarded, is less of a privilege as our languages that we come to college with, and is a disposition that should be rewarded in school. I value labor. And that is

---

31   In my current courses, this trend has continued.

not hidden or obfuscated in my courses.[32] So using this informal rule as I have feels right.

Labor-based grading contract ecologies attempt to make accessible all grades to all students. It is clear and apparent what one must do in order to get an A-grade, and those requirements are reasonably accessible to everyone and negotiated with students—that is, they get a say in the labor requirements for each grade possible. An hour of labor or one hundred more words on an assignment is clear and unambiguous to all students. But asking students to meet a teacher's standards for an "A" on a paper is not so clear, even when rubrics and examples are given—nor are such standards always attainable by anyone in the classroom. Since labor for higher grades is clearer and more accessible than quality-based criteria, since we live in conditions of White language Supremacy in schools and society, labor-based grading contracts make for fairer writing classrooms.

Now, I'm putting aside for now the criticism that labor-based models may privilege those students who do not have to work or take care of family members and go to school at the same time. I'll address these and other criticisms in the Chapter 6, but they are real concerns not easily overcome. The point is, this key difference makes labor-based grading contract ecologies more racially equitable by making all final course grades more accessible to every student in the room, regardless of the languages they practice, their linguistic backgrounds, or most other social dimensions.

WORKING OUT THE UNEXPECTED

There are always unforeseen problems and situations that come up in students' lives. The contract should account for these unplanned and unknowable issues that may keep a student from meeting the contract obligations, despite their willingness to. Under the breakdown table, I offer a plea or gimme clause to address these unexpected issues that affect their abilities to do the labor in the manner expected in the class. So this clause allows anyone to escape the penalty for such things, but only once in the quarter or semester. Here's the clause from this contract:

> **Gimme**. I (Asao), as the administrator of our contract, will decide in consultation with the student whether a gimme is warranted in any case. The student must come to me (Asao

---

32   I should note that in the class I refer to here, the labor numbers for the three immigrant students who achieved the most labor in the course clumped together—and that is what I look for when I review the class' numbers before those final conferences. The average amount of labor in the class was 5,641 minutes. These top performers achieved: 8,385 minutes, 7,410 minutes, and 6,113 minutes. The next closest student logged 4,630 minutes (a Filipino immigrant).

Inoue) as soon as possible, usually before the student is unable to meet the contract (before breaching the contract), in order that he/she and I can make fair and equitable arrangements, ones that will be fair and equitable to all in the class and still meet the university's regulations on attendance, conduct, and workload in classes. **You may use a gimme for any reason, but only once in the semester.** Please keep in mind that the contract is a public, social contract, one agreed upon through group discussion and negotiation, so my job is to make sure that whatever agreement we come to about a gimme will not be unfair to others in class. A gimmie does not allow you to ignore any work expected of everyone in the class. A gimme is NOT an "out clause" for anyone who happens to not fulfill the contract in some way; it is for rare and unusual circumstances out of the control of the student.

While the language in the contract dictates that students come to me immediately upon breaking some contractual terms, in practice the use of the gimme is easier. During our final conferences at finals week, when we sit down and go over what I have recorded on their contracts, the student and I decide the best way to use the gimme, if needed. I tell them that I'm not going to push anyone for evidence of anything. If they wish to use a gimme, they can, and I don't need to know the exact circumstances of things. In fact, I'll try to help them use the gimme in the way that will most benefit them. It turns out that only about one to three students ever need to use this part of our contract in any give class of twenty-five. The way I work this gimme is simple. I can move a category of delinquent labor over one category to the left on our breakdown table. So an ignored becomes a missed, a missed assignment becomes a late assignment, and a late becomes an on-time or complete one. I also allow the gimme to take one non-participation day away.

FORMING AN AGREEABLE CONTEXT FOR SOCIALLY JUST LEARNING

Practically speaking, by forming a larger ecological place free of quality-based grading judgments, labor-based grading contracts provide an agreeable context in which antiracist or social justice-oriented language work can occur. That is, beyond creating a more socially just grading system by not calculating grades based on standards that reproduce White language supremacy, labor-based grading contracts also open up the classroom to do other social justice language work. For instance, these conditions allow my classrooms to investigate White

141

language supremacy and racism in typical ways students' writing is judged in schools and society (see Inoue, *Antiracist* and "Classroom Writing Assessment"). These kinds of discussions and explorations with students offer them flexible strategies to make more informed decisions about the way people communicate in and out of school, because their strategies are informed by not just rhetorical theory but understandings of the politics of language and its judgment. There are at least three reasons for how labor-based grading contracts help encourage such social justice work through classroom conditions:

- They eliminate so-called quality-based hierarchies within student formations based on grades by not using a single standard by which to judge or compare students' performances. This means they use only measures of labor to determine final course grades and eliminate the contradiction of critiquing White language supremacy in a course that also uses a White language standard to grade writing, which is the norm in other classes.
- They allow students and teacher to address the ways some discourses and other *habitus* are privileged in the judging of language in the world yet avoid using such privileging to determine grades and future opportunities for students. They offer real, tangible ways to allow students and teacher the right to their own languages and *habitus* in the class.
- They open a space for practices that can fail or miss the mark, allowing students the freedom to take risks, and try new things in their writing without the fear of losing points or failing the course. They allow students and teacher chances to redefine failure more productively (see also Inoue, "Theorizing Failure"), since failure is just a situated judge's assessment of a performance that assumes a single standard, without acknowledging other differently situated judges and standards.

While our grading mechanisms and systems are hardly the most important part of the learning in a class, they determine the outcomes of pedagogies and curricula intended to help students learn. In other words, grades ain't important, but they are to how courses' ecologies afford learning opportunities. Grades exert immense pressure on students when made more present in the course. Labor-based grading contracts attempt to make them less present and exert less pressure, by ironically paying attention to how grades are constructed.

THE PHILOSOPHY AND CORE ASSUMPTIONS

Now that you have a sense of what the basic elements of a labor-based grading contact are, I turn to where my students and I actually begin on the first day of class. I frame our contract by using the preamble to have discussions that lead to a negotiation of the terms of the contract. The first page or so of the contract is a preamble that explains the philosophy of the contract and why I choose to use it for grading in the course. I ask students to read it several times in various ways during the first week of the course. We reflect upon the contract, particularly the first two pages, rearticulate what they mean, and consider how the contract may change how we all behave and what we expect from each other.

Peter Elbow gave me my first contract, including the preamble, so my preamble is based on his, which he discusses in "Taking Time Out from Grading and Evaluating While Working in a Conventional System" (20). This means some of my language and the contract's general structure, come directly from his contract and his language, but I have changed significantly much of the wording (remember, his contract is a hybrid contract), but there are a few statements that I have kept of his. I am deeply indebted to Peter for his generosity and original wording of his contract. Because the preamble is so important to our opening discussions, I offer it below in full. I should note that the two underlined references are links to online resources (a video and an article).

> Imagine that this wasn't an official course for credit at UWT, but instead that you had seen my advertisement in the newspaper or on the Internet, and were freely coming to my home studio for a class in cooking or yoga. We would have classes, workshops, or lessons, but there would be no official grading of omelets or yoga poses, since letters and numbers would be meaningless in those scenarios. But we all would learn, and perhaps in an encouraging, fun, and creative environment. In considering this course and that home studio scenario, we might ask ourselves three questions: Why are grades meaningless in that home studio setup? How do grades affect learning in classrooms? What social dynamics do the presence of grades create? In both situations, instructors provide students or participants with evaluative feedback from time to time, pointing out where, say, you've done well and where I, as the instructor, could suggest improvement. In the home studio situation, many of you would help each other, even rely on each other during and outside of our scheduled meetings. In fact, you'd likely get more feedback from peers on your work and practices than in a conventional classroom where only the teacher is expected to evaluate and grade.
>
> Consider two issues around grades. First, using conventional classroom grading of essays and other work to compute course

grades often leads students to think more about acquiring grades than about their writing or learning; to worry more about pleasing a teacher or fooling one than about figuring out what they really want to learn, or how they want to communicate something to someone for some purpose. Lots of research in education, writing studies, and psychology over the last thirty or so years have shown overwhelmingly how the presence of grades in classrooms negatively affect the learning and motivation of students. Alfie Kohn (2011), a well-known education researcher and teacher of teachers, makes this argument succinctly. To put it another way, if learning is what we are here for, then grades just get in the way since they are the wrong goals to strive for. An "A" doesn't build a good bridge for an engineer, nor does it help a reporter write a good story, or an urban planner make good decisions for her city. It's the learning that their grades in school allegedly represent that provides the knowledge to do all that they need to. And so, how do we make sure that our goals aren't about grades in this class, but about learning to write?

Second, conventional grading may cause you to be reluctant to take risks with your writing or ideas. It doesn't allow you to fail at writing, which many suggest is a primary way in which people learn from their practices. Sometimes grades even lead to the feeling that you are working *against* your teacher, or that you cannot make a mistake, or that you have to hide part of yourself from your teacher and peers. The bottom line is, failure at writing is vital to learning how to write better. And we have to embrace our failures, because they show us the places we can improve, learn, get better—and these are the reasons we are in college! Grades on our work and writing do not allow us to productively fail. They create conditions that mostly punish failure, not reward it for the learning opportunity it can and should be.

As you might already notice, what I'm arguing for here is a different kind of classroom, and even education. Sir Ken Robinson (2010), a well-known education researcher, makes the argument in a TED talk that typical schooling, with grades and particular standards, is an old and mostly harmful system that we've inherited, but now needs to change. One harmful aspect of this old system is that it assumes everyone is the same, that every student develops at the same pace and in the same ways, that variation in skills and literacies in a classroom is bad. It is clear the opposites of these things are more true. For all these reasons, I am incorporating a labor-based grading contract to calculate course grades in our class.

I offer this first draft of a contract that focuses on the responsibilities we'll assume, not the things to which someone else (usually the teacher) will hold you accountable. The pedagogical shift I'm suggesting is in part a cultural one, one that I would like you to control. Therefore, we will try to *approximate* the evaluative conditions of a home studio course. That is, we will try to create a culture of support, or rather a *community of compassion*, a group of people who genuinely care about the wellbeing of each other—and part of that caring, that compassion, is doing things for each other. It turns out, this also helps you learn. The best way to learn is to teach others, to help, to serve. So we will function as collaborators, allies, as fellow-travelers with various skills, abilities, experiences, and talents that we offer the group, rather than adversaries working against each other for grades or a teacher's approval.

Do not worry. You will get lots of assessments on your writing and other work during the semester from your colleagues and me. Use these assessments (written and verbal) to rethink ideas and improve your writing and practices, to take risks, in short to fail and learn from that failing. Always know that I will read everything and shape our classroom assessment activities and discussions around your work, but you will not receive grades from me. Sometimes, I will not even comment directly on your work, except in class when we use it or discuss it. I want you not only to rely on your colleagues and yourself for assessment and revision advice, but to build strategies of self-assessment that function apart from a teacher's approval.

- **Therefore the default grade for the course is a "B" (3.1).** In a nutshell, if you do all that is asked of you in the manner and spirit it is asked, if you work through the processes we establish and the work we assign ourselves in the labor instructions during the quarter, if you do all the labor asked of you, then you'll get a "B" (3.1) course grade.

It will not matter what I or your colleagues think of your writing, only that you are listening to our feedback compassionately. We may disagree or misunderstand your writing, but if you put in the labor, you are guaranteed a B (3.1) course grade. If you miss class (do not participate fully), turn in assignments late, forget to do assignments, or do not follow the labor instructions precisely, you will get a lower course grade (see the final breakdown grade table on the last page of this contract).

In other places, I discuss the way I organize ongoing discussions around labor-based grading contracts along three key questions ("A Grade-less" 72) and illustrate how these discussions play out in one course of mine that attempts an antiracist writing assessment ecology (*Antiracist* 184–94). The three questions are: "What does labor mean in our writing class?" "how do we know how well we are doing if there are no grades?" and "what does assessing mean in our class?" (*Antiracist* 186). These are good questions to open with, and I stand by them as a way to open initial discussions of the preamble, but I find these days that they are more often than not quickly answered. So in the first week, I offer a number of propositions for my students to respond to that are either assumed or stated in other ways in the preamble.

These statements form some of the key ideas that make up the contract's philosophy that I find helpful to pose to students. I'm not looking for them to agree with me, but I am asking students to consider these statements, consider their resistances, confusions, or concerns, respond to them, and find ways to have enough faith in the system for a few weeks, which will give them experiences and data to decide if the contract is still fair enough for them at that time (I'm referring to the midpoint renegotiation). I have also shown in detail how students often change their orientations toward labor by the midpoint renegotiation, moving from a stance of laboring to earn grades to laboring to learn (*Antiracist* 194–213). Articulating these statements, and asking students to respond to them, as well as discussing them in light of the course, can help students form productive orientations toward their labor. To get to these changed orientations, I offer these four statements for reflection and discussion:

- Our purposes for our labors in a class affect our learning-products, motivations, and engagement in those labors.
- The most important thing that we control and that affects our learning is how much time we give to our labors.
- The presence of grades in a course is detrimental to our learning because they keep us from paying attention to our labor and learning through failure and risk-taking.

- Grading literacy performances by a single standard of so-called quality is racist and promotes White language supremacy.

The remainder of this chapter explains these four statements, which suggests how my discussions in class go. I do not go into this kind of detail with each class, but I do hit the highlights. I offer the following discussion as a way to help you prepare for discussions and activities with students, to think more fully about the philosophy of the contract in a practical way, and to see some limited evidence of the statements from my courses. These discussions about the contract are meant to show students that this system of grading is not arbitrary, nor blindly designed, but one carefully crafted to help them learn and grow without harming them in the process of determining course grades, while also being as fair as possible to everyone.

STATEMENT 1: OUR PURPOSES FOR OUR LABORS IN A CLASS AFFECT OUR LEARNING-PRODUCTS, MOTIVATIONS, AND ENGAGEMENT IN THOSE LABORS.

One of the primary things I'm offering students in this preamble is to rethink the purposes for the grading ecology of the classroom, which in our terms means rethinking our purposes for the labor we do. I'm asking students to consider some research on grades in the preamble (Kohn), and reconsider the purposes doing things in our course. Students often just try to get the highest grade possible by doing the least amount of work. This isn't a negative commentary on students. I don't think my students are lazy. Quite the opposite. I think they are savvy and smart, hardworking and diligent most of the time. But if your labor isn't considered at all in the grade of a course, and one's progress and learning is measured by grades in a course, then a smart and savvy student, one who is busy with many other things in their life, will try to do only what they have to in order to receive the highest grade possible, nothing more. It doesn't make much sense to do more, when labor is not valued in any visible way.

If you know from experience, like many of my students of color, multilingual, and working-class students do, that no matter how much work you put into a paper, you are not likely to get a high grade, then you put in the minimum you can, and make the best of things. That's just being smart with your time since more time on the task doesn't equate to a higher grade, and it often seems like wasted effort despite the contradictory fact that getting high grades, by necessity, is your primary purpose. This psychologically protects you. If you do poorly on the paper, it's less of a judgment on your abilities. Hell, you really didn't spend much time on it anyway. What often gets lost in this practical and protective approach to coursework is what is best for one's own learning and development. So purposes for laboring in a course, even courses that ignore labor, matter.

As discussed in Chapter 1, grades determine (as in creates boundaries and exerts pressures) much of the purposes for labor and work in a course. These purposes to get higher grades kill authentic learning by deemphasizing labor and time, and emphasizing the grade on the final product. What I mean by authentic is simple. Grades represent one judge's ranking of a written document, but they say little to nothing about the substance of the performance of writing, the actual labor of writing that produced the document. Grades say little about how or what learning actually took place around the making of the document, which I'm arguing is the actual learning, and only offer a hierarchical ranking of the student, which is deceptive, unfair most of the time, and harmful to the student—and it offers very little to the student in the way of feedback for improvement, which is usually a teacher's goal. So, grades highjack much of the purposes of any feedback that may be associated with it. This means they deny labor's value to students and teacher.

Teachers complain about this all the time: "My students only care about the grade. They don't read my comments," etc. This is because reading and doing something meaningful with your comments is not their purpose when grades are a part of the assessment ecology, when they are present. Their purpose is to get a grade, and you gave them that. Their purpose in the grading ecology is met, even if unsatisfactorily. But I cannot help wonder if we as teachers are also equally disappointed with our students because they seem to devalue our labor. We spend a lot of time reading and writing feedback to students, and when they do nothing with it, it hurts. But it hurts because our labor has not been acknowledged or valued either—that is, we want them to use our labor in our feedback, see the value in it. When grades are present, they hijack the students' purposes for their labors and how they understand teachers' labors. Their purpose becomes to get a grade, ours to give one.

Furthermore, the document being evaluated does not say much more about a student's actual labor of learning—a document is not the actual learning, but we often treat is as such. It is an outcome of learning. It only represents indirectly learning to write. While writing programs usually consider the written products of students to be direct evidence of learning in assessments, they are not exactly that. They are not a direct measure of learning to write. They may be the most direct measure a program uses in an assessment, but they are not the *actual learning to write*. Student written products may be the most direct evidence of some outcome that the program uses, but typical writing outcomes are not learning (the verb). They are the products (the noun) of learning.

Getting students in a program or classroom to produce a certain kind of written product does not mean that anyone has learned anything in particular. It means they've been able to reproduce a certain kind of document in those circumstances. That's all we really know. Did they learn something by making those documents? Probably. But while we might reasonably say *that* our students learned something because they produced a certain kind of document, we certainly cannot know the nature of that learning for sure. And this isn't even considering whether students can or will be able to transfer what they learned to future contexts. Understanding the nature of learning (the verb) requires that students have purposes in the assessment ecology that allow them to gather such information on their learning (their verbing).

So, as I see it, the performance, the practice of writing itself, learning as a verb, is what we care most about in writing classes. This is not to say that those practices shouldn't lead to some product worth judging or evaluating, only that if we care about learning itself, if that is what we are trying to encourage in students, then the actual doing is the authentic learning worth measuring in the assessment ecology. When grades are placed into an assessment ecology and used to rank literacy performances, they become a surrogate for actual learning-products because they substitute for quality by virtue of being the symbolic representation of the evaluation of their performances. Grades *represent* the evaluation, but are not *the* evaluation of language—that can only be more language. Thus, grades are a floating signifier, appearing to be specific, but meaning whatever the beholder of the grade wishes them to mean.[33] This tends to mean that students' purposes for taking any class is first to get a good grade when it should be to learn, to practice, to understand, to grow, in short, to work, to labor at something and cultivate ways to understand and be in that labor. Taking grades out of the assessment ecology allows students room to cultivate other purposes for their learning labors.

Go ahead and test my claims above, if you think I exaggerate. On the first day of the next semester or quarter, ask your students to write for a few minutes in response to questions like these: Why did you take this class? What do you hope to accomplish in this course? How will you know if and when you accomplish your goals? I've done this kind of activity in various ways in every quarter

---

33   In *Introduction to the Work of Marcel Mauss*, Claude Lévi-Strauss coined the term "floating signifier" to explain symbolic thinking brought on by symbols that have no referents, which was like Mauss' "mana." Lévi-Strauss explains, "it would just be a zero symbolic value, that is, a sign marking the necessity of a supplementary symbolic content over and above that which the signified already contains, which can be any value at all, provided it is still part of the available reserve" (64). Stuart Hall has argued that race is also a floating signifier, saying, "what racial difference signifies is never static or the same" (2) and this means that "race is more like a language, than it is like the way in which we are biologically constituted" (8).

or semester for the last ten or so years, I have found a pattern in most students' purposes for taking a writing course, especially first-year writing students. Often half or more of the class will say something to the effect of: I hope to get an A in this class, or my goal is to do well in the class. While they may provide examples of actual learning they are striving for, these things are always framed by an explicit or tacit articulation of grades as the ways they know that they have achieved their goals. What does it mean to do well in a class for most students, and how do they know when they have? Do you think a student can get a D or an F in a course and still say that they did well in the same course? Students are not dumb when it comes to grades and how they affect them. Once presented as connected to the purposes of their work in a class, they can draw the connections, make the critique of grades, even though in most cases paradoxically they still must get a final grade, and acquire grades in other classes.

Statement 2: The most important thing that we control and that affects our learning is how much time we give to our labors.

From one angle, Statement 1 says that we can control our learning by controlling our purposes for our labors in classrooms. This second statement says that we also control our learning by controlling how much labor we do each week. Both of these philosophical statements are meant to provide students with agency and control over their progress and learning in a course, showing how the grading contract helps them with this.

On one level, this second statement is obvious: the more time one spends laboring, the more one will learn or the better one gets at the task they are doing. Deep and meaningful learning isn't usually about getting the most in the least amount of time. It's about getting the most out of the most amount of time. In his famous book, *Outliers*, Malcolm Gladwell popularized the 10,000 hour rule, which says that it takes on average at least 10,000 hours of practice to master a skill or art (40). Gladwell draws on research in psychology (e.g., Levitin; Ericsson, Krampe, and Tesch-Romer), which as others have mentioned after Gladwell's book came out, actually offers more complicated findings. Mastery, they say, doesn't always come by doing something for 10,000 hours. It can come earlier, sometimes much earlier. In particular, Brooke N. Macnamara, David Z. Hambrick, Frederick L. Oswald's meta analysis of studies on expertise found that it really depends upon what kind of skill or practice one is trying to master, and that other things matter just as much, and sometimes more when getting better at them.

This finding can be seen in Ericsson et al.'s work that Gladwell bases his 10,000 hour rule on, in which they observe that structured practice and "better training methods," such as those that include feedback loops, and what I read as reflective or metacognitive training (365), provide for expertise through practicing. The idea that the best labor required is connected to metacognitive aspects, what I call mindful laboring or three-dimensional labor in Chapter 3, can be read in Ericsson and Poole's more recent discussion of expertise building in their concept of "deliberate practice." Regardless of whether one finds Gladwell's 10,000 hour rule accurate or not, what is not questioned is that it requires time and labor to get better at practices, and structured laboring, with feedback, is preferable. Additionally whether or not there is a magic number to attain "mastery" at something, like writing, the number is high—in other words, getting better at something like writing takes labor and time, and that labor is best when it is mindfully done and when one's labors are reflected upon in order to understand them and do them better next time. Finally, even if we can consider many other factors in any individual attaining expertise in writing, what we cannot disregard is that the most important factor is how much time the student spends on the labors of learning to write, because the student has the most control over these aspects of learning to write.

Now, we know this intuitively as writing teachers and students. But when the systems of assessment, when one assessment ecology after another, reinforce the opposite idea, that one should be efficient with one's time in order to produce something worth a grade, then the temptation is to simply go for the grade and put aside the messiness and inefficiency of learning for another time. Doing this, makes students have to see their labor as only a means to an end, not the end itself. Ultimately, what is put aside is time, time in practices, time on drafts, time in texts, time with language, time to talk with others about one's learning. Time is lost, and time is to a large extent labor. And losing time and labor really means losing the learning-products of the ecology because as I discuss in Chapter 3, time and labor construct value in assessment economies, which means they accumulate worth for students. We may not control how any reader judges our writing, but like our purposes, we do control the amount of time we spend on an assignment or practice in a course, and that means we always control the value and worth of our labors.

It's easy to lose sight of this important, even central, reason for taking any course—to spend time laboring at something in order to change oneself. Grading by quality and the conditions for learning over time are always at cross-purposes in writing courses. In short, the grading ecology determines students' behaviors in writing courses, how they approach labors and what value they place on them. Thus, students are *determined* to do what they *must*, not what they *should*. So this statement helps students confront this dilemma, revealing what we really value and asks students: how much do you really value your learning and your labor? It reveals exactly what our ecology will value by saying our labor equates to our course grade.

The data I collect in my own classes each quarter and use in our labor logs suggest both Statement 1's and 2's strengths. As a way to illustrate labor's effects on engagement, motivation, and learning, I offer some limited data from a recent first-year writing course of mine, conducted in the Autumn quarter of 2016. For purposes of anonymity, I used an online random number generator (random.org) to generate five roster numbers (one quarter of the total course enrollment), and those students' labor log data for this illustration. I've replaced the roster numbers with letters for further anonymity and reference here. This method offers some assurance that I have not hand-picked students to make my point and preserves students' anonymity. I ask students in their labor logs to rate each labor session they record with a simple 1–5 engagement rating, 1 being completely unengaging, 3 neutral, and 5 a most engaging session overall. Considering just their most engaged labor sessions, these five students' labor practices might be represented this way:

Table 4.2. A sample of five students' most engaged labor practices

Student	Avg. duration per session/all sessions (min)	No. of sessions/ total no. of all sessions	Highest Engage- ment rating (1–5)	Total duration of most engag. sessions/all sessions (min)	Main Location of Labor
A (WF)	127.89/113.29	35/49	5	4476/5551	Home
B (LF)	270/141.63	6/45	5 and 4	1620/5665	Home
C (WF)	109.75/83.74	8/38	5	878/3182	Home
D (WM)	187.85/110.29	13/35	5	2325/3860	Library
E (LF)	68.43/71.49	16/74	5	1095/5290	Home

Table 4.2 shows only the data from the labor sessions recorded by each student in which they recorded their highest engagement rating, which usually was a 5. The only exception was student B. Since she had recorded only one session at a 5 engagement, I included sessions that she rated at 4 and 5. I also included a brief description of each student by gender and race. For instance, student A was a White female (WF), student B a Latina, etc. This gender and racial information I received from our interactions and their own identifications of themselves in introductory narratives in the course. I offer them only as references to the

level of diversity in my classrooms. They are not meant to represent any group of students. My classrooms are rarely ones that have a lot of students who embody White language privilege, but it does still exist.

The first column of data shows a ratio: the average duration of the most engaged sessions over the average duration of all sessions recorded during our ten-week course in their logs. For reference, you can see in the next column the number of sessions each of these averages refers to (also a ratio) over the total number of sessions recorded for the ten-week quarter. Note in the first column that the most engaged labor sessions for all students except student E were on average longer sessions than their average session overall. While not definitive, it appears that there is a strong association with the length of time students spent laboring and higher engagement in that labor. The more engaged the students were the longer their labor sessions were, except for student E. Additionally, this length of time seems to be relative. Student A spent 4,476 minutes in her most engaged sessions, which amounts to 80.63% of her total labor time recorded. While on the other end of the spectrum, student C spent only 878 minutes out of a total of 3,182 minutes recorded, which is only 27.59% of her total labor time. Lots of things can account for the dramatic differences in labor time that have little to do with motivation or engagement, which I'll discuss in Chapter 6. For instance, students are different in how they work, or how fast they can do particular activities. Some students have work and family obligations that put other pressures on their available labor time for the course.

It is worth noting too that the one seeming outlier in this data set is still typical in most ways. Student E, whose ratio was flipped, has less average time spent in her most engaged sessions, yet represents the median (the middle value in the data set) for total duration of all sessions. Being the median of duration for all sessions in the set means that she didn't spent less time in her labors for the class than most others, nor did she spend more time than most. She was exactly in the middle. She also had a large number of sessions rated as 4s on engagement, and her labor sessions rated at 3 and lower averaged 57.65 minutes per session, a shorter amount of time per session than her most engaged sessions (68.43 minutes). If one calculates her most engaged sessions as those rated at 4 and 5, then her ratio in the first column would be 83.25/71.49 minutes, which fits the pattern of all the other students' ratios, with longer highly engaged sessions than all other sessions. This makes sense to do, given that her total number of labor sessions is higher than all others in the data set.

Additionally, student E's sessions rated at 3 average to 58.81 minutes per session, which are lower than both her average session length for both those rated at 5 and 4 engagement. Like everyone else in the data set, relative to her own labor practices, the more she labored in any given session, the more engaged she was. She illustrates how difficult it is to have a standard by which one measures most engaged or effective laboring, at least in terms of duration of individual labor sessions. Likely, student E's difference in this column may be a product of her own life circumstances that didn't easily allow for long sessions of labor, or she may have purposefully broken up her labor into smaller increments of time, or she may have been more stingy with her rating scale. Regardless, the patterns are clear for all students. Relative to their own labor practices, the more each student labored, the more engaged they said they were. This ascending pattern of labor time associated with engagement ratings for sessions is consistent across all students in the set and suggests that their labors affect their motivation and engagement.

Could this kind of labor data be recorded in a class that grades conventionally? Perhaps. But I think it would be more difficult to argue that traditionally graded students chose to labor longer for something other than a grade. However, because it can be argued reasonably that the above students labored longer in their highest engaged sessions for some other reason than a grade, since there were no grades on any of the products of their labors, we might say that our labor-based grading contract helped them to labor to learn, not labor to earn a grade. My previous discussion of another set of students in a different university moving their learning stances from laboring to earn grades toward laboring to learn (Inoue, *Antiracist* 194–213) also affirms the conclusion I'm making here. That discussion was based on written reflections and other documents produced by students.

I should make clear that I do not use labor logs to grade students on their labor, which I tell them up front. I explain that they likely would be too tempted to fudge their numbers if I did, and this would make the logs busy work, less accurate, and less effective as true reflective devices. I want them to use the logs honestly and as a way to reflect upon their labor as practices. Since I do not use the labor logs as a way to keep track of students' labor, I think these labor logs are more accurate than if I did. As the above data show, it can be unfair since the amount of labor time can vary. Some students need more time than others to do the same practices and produce products that we can use in the class together. Some need more time to read texts, while others can read much quicker with similar results. Some students work and take care of families, and simply do not have the same amount of time available in their lives. So labor time is not the only way engagement, motivation, and learning can be manufactured in a course's assessment ecology, but perhaps it is a good internally relative indicator.

There is also another consistency in the above data that may offer some evidence of the strength of the first two statements. The location of the most engaged labor was home. Even at a most superficial level, one might postulate that these students may have found that home, perhaps a safe place, a place of love and security, a place where they may be encouraged to labor at their school work, is a highly engaging place, or it could be that home is a necessary place in which they do labor for the course. In our labor instructions, the first two steps of labor ask the same things every time. Find a quiet place to do the labor in peace. Do some mindful breathing for two to three minutes as we have done in class together. These steps remind students that where they do their labor and what mindset they have are vital to their labor's success and to their own learning.

This message is reinforced each week in our labor journals, where I ask them to choose one labor session from that week to reflect upon, and discuss three things: (1) where and under what conditions did they do the labor; (2) what intrinsic and extrinsic aspects of the labor session made it most meaningful or engaging; and (3) what did they learn about their labor from reflecting on the session? Labor journal entries are designed to move students, in a small way, through the three dimensions of labor. Could these labor practices, the attention in our labor instructions on place, and what our labor means in our weekly journals have affected these students purposes for laboring and how much labor they subsequently did in the course? Perhaps.

Certainly another possible indicator, although a quite imperfect one, of learning is the final course grade. In typically graded classrooms, where course grades are produced from grades on writing and activities, what the final grade indicates is less clear than in labor-based grading contract ecologies. Why? Conventional grades tend to be measures of how different a student is from their teacher, according to the teacher's judgment. This is not always a good indicator of learning. On the other hand, final grades produced in labor-based grading contract ecologies equate quite directly to the amount and nature of labor expended in the course. If we accept that labor is the act of learning to write, that in order to learn to write one must write, and the more one writes the better one can get at it, then a final course grade based on labor is a more accurate reflection of *learning to write* (the verb) than other grading ecologies, even if it says little about the nature of that learning. While I can't say what the nature of each student's learning in Table 4.2 was without looking at their final portfolios and self-assessment letters written to me in the final week of the course, I can say that their learning to write likely varied as much as their numbers on the table do. This is a testament to this labor-based contract ecology's abilities to allow for diverse learners and diverse learning, to reward a broad range of laboring to learn, since all these students met the contract's guidelines.

A note: I do not provide these data to my students when discussing this statement. I do, however, have these data in my head when I make such statements to students. And I tell them that while this is a philosophical statement, it is one I test every quarter, so it is more of a conclusion from research on labor in writing classrooms. I could not be as definitive with my students if I didn't have such data. Because I do have it, I can tell them confidently: the more labor you put into this class, the more learning you will get, the higher your final grade will be, but only if you set the right kind of purposes for your labors, and labor mindfully.

STATEMENT 3: THE PRESENCE OF GRADES IN A COURSE IS DETRIMENTAL TO OUR LEARNING BECAUSE THEY KEEP US FROM PAYING ATTENTION TO OUR LABOR AND LEARNING THROUGH FAILURE AND RISK-TAKING.

Typically, the quality of the product of a student's performance and the learning that that product is meant to represent are summed up in a letter or number. The grade is determined by a teacher's judgment of the product's quality, which is a personal, idiosyncratic comparison to a standard informed by White racial *habitus*. Despite this obvious situation to everyone, we want students to strive for better and deeper learning, to take risks in their writing, and to focus on (be conscious of) their writing processes and the ways their audiences react to decisions they've made in texts. We do not want them focused on the grades assigned to the products they turn in, yet many of us give those grades when we do not have to. So our assessment ecologies send mixed messages to students. We want them to care and strive for the learning, not the grade, but the grade is present and so seems significant, and it does matter down the road.

The whole scenario is like telling a starving man that he can have a sandwich if he just does this one important thing as you direct him that will save his life, but he must do it exactly as you say, then you put the sandwich on the table next to you as you begin to explain things. He can't help but stare or glance at the sandwich. It is right there. He is starving. He needs that sandwich. And you keep telling him: "stop looking at the sandwich on the table. What I'm telling you is more important. What I'm telling you will save your life. Focus on what I'm saying."

The paradox is that the starving man needs both the sandwich and your life-saving instructions, but one of those things is an ecological condition that is artificial, the condition of starvation. The man did not starve himself. The ecology he is in has created his condition of starvation, kept food from him. In similar fashion, we have artificially starved our students by making grades important and necessary in the system, using them as "carrots" (note the metaphor) to get students to do things, then making the highest ones scarce, all the while we tell them to stop thinking about the grade, focus on what you're doing. These artificial conditions of starvation do our students harm and keep them from focusing on the labor of learning. And when yoked to standards that are informed by White racial *habitus*, these artificial conditions become doubly unfair, racist, and White supremacist. Just like actual starvation and food scarcity on the planet, in classrooms, higher-grade starvation happens in non-White regions more often than White ones, making both problems racial in nature.[34]

So the presence of grades and what they mean in terms of exchange value— exchanged for future opportunities—tends to short circuit students' capacities to see and take advantage of failure, to be mindful and reflective of what they have learned, since failure is defined mostly as punishment because it has little to no exchange value. The result of such ecological conditions is that most students do not take risks, and see failure at doing something as bad and perhaps psychologically harmful. In most classrooms, I've found that when a teacher hasn't thought carefully about how their assessment ecology constructs and circulates failure, failure is not seen so clearly as a construction of the ecology itself, rather it's a personal deficit in students. In another place (Inoue, "Theorizing Failure"), I define the nature and production of failure in writing programs, showing how complicated the concept is, at least when trying to understand its presence and distributions in writing programs. For my present purposes, let me boil down some of that discussion and apply it more directly to this third statement, which is about the classroom and students' dispositions toward labor, learning, and grades.

There are, as I see it, at least three kinds of failure an assessment ecology might construct and circulate: quality-, labor-, and productive failure. Quality-failure is defined by any deviation from a dominant, written standard, which is universally characterized by a White racial *habitus* (Inoue, "Theorizing Failure" 338; *Antiracist* 47–51). The production of this kind of failure in writing programs and classrooms is predictable. It produces more failure in students of color than White students, which I have shown using data from Fresno State's writing program ("Theorizing Failure" 339). Labor-failure is "not achieving or demonstrating a defined degree of effort, quantity of written products, and/or amount of time spent on an activity" (339). In the same program, labor-failure produces fewer instances of grade failure and happier students (341). It also allows for what I call "productive failure," which is a positive kind of failure, a necessary kind. Productive failure "opens new ways of seeing and languaging," and centers on students and teacher investigating, researching, and negotiating expectations and ways of judging texts, and it "pushes schools, colleges, and universities to expand, to become more inclusive of more kinds of students and their linguistic worlds" (346).

---

34   A 2017 report by several global organizations found that "chronic food deprivation" is estimated to be the condition of 815 billion people, with 98% of that global number coming from Africa, Asia, Latin America and the Caribbean (FAO, IFAD, UNICEF, WFP, and WHO 6).

Now, let's think more deeply about productive failure. The OED offers several common place definitions for failure: "To be absent or wanting" and "[t]o be inadequate or insufficient." These definitions often reference quality in writing classrooms. When we talk about an essay or a student failing, we often mean the writing (or writer) does not meet a certain standard as judged by the teacher. I want to encourage students to play with this kind of failure, not be afraid of it, but to dwell on and use it in some fashion. In other words, I don't want them to think that any evaluation of their writing in our class that says the draft didn't meet the reader's expectations is a bad or abnormal thing. In fact, if our purposes are to learn, then we need this kind of failure to help us, and it's quite typical. We have to produce failure, or find ways to see it more clearly, if we are going to grow. It is productive because failure shows us at least two things: (1) that we have places to grow, and (2) that failure itself is determined by larger structures in schools, language, and society, all of which individuals have little to no control over. So while writers can control much of what they do as writers and learners, the nature of failure in ecologies is equally produced by those ecologies themselves, and failure can have value and worth to the writer in those ecologies.

A student can still fail at an assignment in a labor-based grading contract ecology. As already discussed, labor-failure is not doing the labor required in the spirit asked, and according to a few basic requirements (e.g., due dates and times, and word counts). This use of the term is actually more in line with the word's origins. The word failure comes from the French, *faillir*, "to be wanting" or more accurately to almost do something. In the French, *faillir* is a kind of auxiliary verb that is never used by itself. One does not *faillir*, one *faillir*'s at doing something else. For example, I can say, "*je faillis lire le livre*." (I almost read the book). The lesson we might take from this etymology is that failure in a classroom can be defined structurally in the ecology as *almost or not doing something*. Thus, in labor-based grading contract ecologies, failure as a mark in a teacher's grade book can be a reference to almost or not doing something apart from how any given reader might judge the nature of that something or its products.

Again, let me illustrate how this plays out in a classroom with data. In the same course as the students represented in Table 4.2, there were three students who did not meet all the grading contract's terms for the default B-grade (3.1). These students each received a 1.6, or a C- according to the school's official grading scale. These students represent the three lowest course grades given. Two didn't complete their labor logs, with only three or four entries in each. One of those students was a White male, the other was a Black male. But one, a Latino completed his labor log into the final week of the quarter. I'll use him as an example of failure in the course, even though he technically completed the course with a marginally passing grade, making failure in our ecology a C-. His labor log data look like this.

Table 4.3. Failing student data from labor log

Student	Avg. duration per session/ all sessions (min)	No. of sessions/total no. of all sessions	Highest Engagement rating (1–5)	Total duration of most engag. sessions/all sessions (min)	Main Location of Labor
X (LM)	60/70	4/29	4	240/2030	Home

As one can see in Table 4.3, across the board, student X had less labor time than his colleagues in Table 4.2 in every dimension recorded. And internally, his data is consistently opposite of all the students in Table 4.2. Student X's average duration per highly engaged session was *lower* than the average duration of all his labor sessions, the opposite phenomenon noted in students represented in Table 4.2. His highest engagement rating of any session was a 4 (he had no 5s). His highest engaged sessions were also shorter than all those in Table 4.2, even higher than student E's average session duration. His total number of all sessions recorded in the quarter was also fewer than all students in Table 4.2. And while his total duration of all sessions in the quarter was lower than all the other students, it isn't so low as to suggest he wasn't doing work in the course. He was just not spending enough time to learn as much as we had contracted for, with a number of missed and late assignments, and non-participation days recorded in the gradebook. His lack of enough labor time is clear, I think, in the low number of highly engaged sessions (total of 4), and the low duration of all sessions (average of 60 minutes).

It isn't self-evident why student X wasn't able to labor in ways that would allow him to meet our contract, but it is consistent. His labor practices are markedly different in frequency, duration, and engagement ratings than those recorded in Table 4.2. Both tables amount to this: *the less one labors, the less one learns, and the less one learns, the less one is engaged and the lower one's final course grade is.* But, student X, because he completed all the labor of the course, even if minimally, still passed—and I'd argue, still learned more than he would have in a graded classroom. Thus the absence of failing grades on assignments in the class likely helped this student persist and pass the course, even if only marginally. My argument here is that if I had been grading his work along the way, he surely would have gotten many low marks, and this likely would have resulted in him either failing the course through quality-failure or failing due to him just giving up, since failure in quality-failure graded systems means punishment. And few are willing to keep taking punishment when they do not have to.

Failure in our labor-based grading contract ecology was constructed differently. In this case, failing to meet all the labor requirements didn't have to mean failing the course, but it clearly meant a much lower grade than the default contract B-grade (3.1). Complete failure to do labor was, of course, not learning enough and failing the course, but no one did that. One student, a Black male, did drop the course in the first few weeks of the class, and he seemed clearly to have other priorities in his life that kept him from doing the labor of the class and attending the class regularly. The other Black male in the classroom mentioned above who finished the course with a 2.1, but did not complete a labor log, also had other priorities or issues in his life that kept him from doing more labor in the course.

I cannot help but be concerned about the pattern in these two Black males, something our labor-based contract ecology clearly wasn't able to change, although one technically passed the course. We (his colleagues in class, who knew him, and I) did reach out to the student who stayed in the course on several occasions, which may have helped him finish the course, but it was not enough to help the first student. I do not wish to make any judgments on either student's situations, not knowing the details, nor knowing other pressures or issues in their lives. I am reminded of Pegeen Reichert Powell's good book on retention in which she argues through several case studies and looking closely at the rhetoric of retention that there are many good reasons why students fail or drop out of school. Retention is not always, or perhaps even mostly, a pedagogical issue, but an administrative problem that originates from the constraints and pressures of the complex lives that our students lead. As teachers, we should be diligent in our efforts to help our students persist in our courses, if that is their wish, but these efforts should be tempered with an understanding that sometimes other things determine students' abilities or willingness to do the labors we ask of them. Thus my student who withdrew from our class may not be considered a failure, but a student who may have made a productive decision in his life. It is hard to say. What is more reasonable to assume in each situation is that an absence of grades on work, changing the nature and distribution of failure in the course's assessment ecology, and a focus on paying attention to one's labor (as Table 4.3 illustrates) may have helped each student pass the course and learn more than in a typical graded classroom, leaving the course with a better experience.

While I don't know what life factors affected my two Black male students' labor practices, I do know that Black student graduation and success rates in universities is low nationally. A recent Education Trust report shows that of 232 institutions of higher education in the US that improved their graduation rates over the last decade, the gap between White and Black student graduation rates has widened (Nichols et al. 1). Black students graduated at a rate of 42.4% in 2003 and 46.8% in 2013, meanwhile White students at the same institutions graduated at rates of 59.1% and 64.7%, respectively (2). On top of this, almost a third of the institutions reporting saw graduation rates for Black students decrease or stay the same, and over half saw their graduation rate gaps remain the same or increase (2). There are lots of additional factors that keep Black males, such as these two students, from laboring in the ways I know they can in any writing classroom, but grades on their writing, one's based on a single, White racial *habitus*, was not one of them in my class. Perhaps Claude Steele's work on "stereotype threat" (Steele; Steele et al.) may tell us something about the pressures that Black students face despite the assessment ecology they may be participating in. Or maybe it was other social pressures and microaggressions in and outside of our classroom that I just couldn't see or hear affected these two Black males more than other students of color. Sometimes our assessment ecologies are not enough.

STATEMENT 4: GRADING LITERACY PERFORMANCES BY A SINGLE STANDARD OF SO-CALLED QUALITY IS RACIST AND PROMOTES WHITE LANGUAGE SUPREMACY.

The first two statements above are about individual control, what students themselves control: Their purposes for laboring and how much they labor. The second two (the previous one and this one) are about systems and structures that we do not always control, but can manipulate to make fairer, more equitable, and more inclusive conditions regardless of students' backgrounds, linguistic competencies, or cultural logics used, thus Statements 3 and 4 are about grading and failure, and how those structures are tied to racism and White language supremacy. Given what I've already said, this fourth statement may not need saying, but I offer it nonetheless. It is an idea that I want my students to consider explicitly. As already mentioned, failure is a construction in the ecology linked historically to particular bodies who have and do circulate in classrooms and schools. This is because both the norm and the ideal for writing and writers in writing classrooms at all levels are based on White racial *habitus*.

It is clear that even my example classroom above is no exception to this racializing of failure. All three of the lowest grades in the course were given to students of color, the two Black students and a Latino.[35] I tried hard to avoid this. It wasn't in my mind beforehand, and I do not mean to suggest that most teachers have prejudices about the capabilities of any student before they get a chance to see what a student can do, although the research on implicit bias (e.g., Banaji and Greenwald) and stereotype threat (e.g. Steele; Steele et al.suggest that all of us, no matter who we are or what political or ideological positions we hold, have racial and gendered biases. What I mean is that the assessment ecologies we

---

35   This fact may be deceptive, as most in the class were students of color, with 12 of the 20 students identifying themselves as students of color.

create have biases in them already, ones we create but cannot see easily. Grading and ranking systems used in conventional assessment ecologies work from biases about failure as much as they do from racialized linguistic biases that come from our *habitus*. White language supremacy, or a privileging of White racial *habitus* in standards that then get used to grade, in writing classrooms is structured in the systems, disciplines, and society in which we already circulate and live in.

So when I say grading by a single standard is racist and White supremacist, I'm not saying that writing teachers are racists or White supremacists. It is the standard and how that standard is used, that structures the racism and White language supremacy in classrooms. It is the systems and assessment ecologies we inherit, that seem natural and right, that are racist and White supremacist. And too often, we cannot even see this fact—our own *habitus*, our dispositions, are too naturalized as preferable in the system, and are often all we have to make language and judgments in the system. When we get rewarded for our own *habitus* in school and society and we see others rewarded in similar ways, it reinforces the naturalness, the rightness, of that *habitus*, and makes it more invisible to us. So, teachers enact their own ecological biases, which align in writing classrooms with race, gender, heteronormative, and able-bodied *habitus*. This is to say, while we may not explicitly be trying to punish habits of writing that Black or Latinx students use, for instance, we are trying to reward those who meet our senses of a standard discourse, which align more with White, middle-class *habitus*, *habitus* acquired in social spaces that many students of color do not grow up in. The system is set up to reproduce itself as a White system and a White ecological place.

You, the teacher, are a product of the system. In the end, the use of quality-based grades on writing makes discursive difference (from a dominant White standard) into deficit and failure. But language difference in an assessment ecology is necessary if students are to gain true critical perspective on dominant ways with words, and thus have informed ways of making decisions as writers themselves. This means that one vital way to see the White language supremacy of the system, to understand how most or all judgments on texts in the classroom participate in circulating White racial *habitus* to some degree, is to have other racialized ways of languaging at play in an ecology. Because we are a part of the system, it is less likely that teachers of English are the primary source of such critical distancing from our own norms and ideals, our own *habitus* and language standards in our classrooms. We naturalize our own ways of thinking and languaging. And this is why I want my students to confront this statement: their diverse ways with words are the key to criticality in our ecology, even if some may wish (for good reasons) to take on a dominant White racial *habitus*.

To help with these conversations, I often provide students with Rosina Lippi-Green's "linguistic facts of life" (6–7) that boil down to five things the linguistics community have come to take as givens through decades of research. Sometimes, I ask students to see how our contract works with these assumptions to create conditions that allow for learning to write and practicing writing in a variety of ways without harming writers for inheriting the habits of language they already practice. Lippi-Green's linguistic facts of life help us discuss why we need productive ways to fail and see failure as something other than a bad thing. More importantly, they help us see how racist and White supremacist typical grading practices are that use one standard, since that standard must come from somewhere, from some group of speakers and writers, who have a gendered, classed, and racialized history. The facts of life are these:

- All spoken language changes over time.
- All spoken languages are equal in linguistic terms.
- Grammaticality and communicative effectiveness are distinct and interdependent issues.
- Written language and spoken language are historically, structurally, and functionally fundamentally different creatures.
- Variation is intrinsic to all spoken language at every level. (Lippi-Green 6–7)

What these boil down to is that language in real life communities is not an abstract thing on its own, a set of rules or practices that are outside of groups of people using language. In fact, when we teach language practices and conventions in classrooms, we are really teaching reifications, convenient fictions that allow us to nail down what is unnailable, which the first and fifth facts of life assume. These facts of life also provide us with reason to be critical of a single, dominant standard, not to avoid learning it, but to understand more fully what it really is at this historical moment, what it does to us, where it comes from historically, who used it, why, and who benefits now in the classroom when it is used as a standard for everyone.

As the first fact of life states, any language is constantly changing because it is a set of habitual practices that people do among other people. It is always moving and transforming, always becoming. A dominant set of language conventions, then, is a convenient way to talk about preferable language practices, preferable habits of doing language with others, but not about how language actually exists in the real world with real people. So any standard of academic English is a myth, a reification, an abstraction that is not real, yet many act and make decisions about people and language as if there is a standard that we can point to and explain in the same ways, then use to judge language consistently. In different (non-racial) terms, this is a set of fallacies that Pat Belanoff revealed to us in 1991 in her four "myths of assessment," which are: (1) "We know what we're testing for"; (2) "We know what we're testing"; (3) "Once we've agreed on criteria, we can agree on whether individual papers meet those criteria"; and (4) "it's possible to have an absolute standard and apply it uniformly" (55). It is the fourth myth of assessment I'm focusing on when presenting Lippi-Green's linguistic facts of life, since judging and grading writing by a single standard produces failure by definition and out of necessity.

Now, we could also look to some of the work on error and grammar to confirm these facts of life about language in our classrooms and their connection to White language supremacy. Joseph Williams' article, "The Phenomenology of Error," argues that readers' linguistic expectations around seeing error in student writing help create that error when reading and judging. We see error because we are looking for it. But what counts as error for most writing teachers? What *habitus* construct error? Error is connected to Standardized Edited American English (SEAE), so it too is a racialized phenomenon because SEAE is constructed by a dominant White *habitus*. Chris Anson's work on the social construction of error also offers further proof that our *habitus* determine how we judge students', and that determination is affected by students' own *habitus* that teachers construct from their knowledge of the student and the writing in front of them. We cannot avoid our biases, not just about language, but our racialized, gendered, and other ideological biases that are embodied in the world among flesh and blood people.

Combine this question about judgment with what we know about implicit racial and gendered biases, and grading becomes a dangerously racist and White supremacist practice in literacy classrooms when we use so-called quality as the basis for grades. In brief, researchers who study how our brains make decisions have concluded after decades of study that people make decisions in two ways: one is mostly unconscious and a fast way, prone to error, and the other is a slower, more conscious way, less prone to error (Kahnmann; Jolls and Sunstein; Greenwald and Krieger). The first way is linked to implicit racial bias. With writing teachers' busy schedules and heavy workloads, how likely is it that we make fast judgments on student writing? Quit likely.

If there is time in class, I also offer students the results of a recent study that show these racial implicit biases in language practices that are not simply about what is on the page. The study is situated in a profession that depends on impartiality and a careful regulation of biases in judgments, the field of law. There is lots of evidence that implicit racial and gender bias exists even in this field (Negowetti), but this study demonstrates just how unconscious racial implicit biases are in the way attorneys read and judge writing that they perceived as being from a White attorney in training and a Black one (Reeves). The empirical results come to this conclusion, which the report offers:

> There are commonly held racially-based perceptions about
> writing ability that unconsciously impact our ability to ob-
> jectively evaluate a lawyer's writing. Most of the perceptions
> uncovered in research thus far indicate that commonly held
> perceptions are biased against African Americans and in favor
> of Caucasians.
>
> These commonly held perceptions translate into confirmation
> bias in ways that impact what we see as we evaluate legal writ-
> ing. We see more errors when we expect to see errors, and we
> see fewer errors when we do not expect to see errors. (6)

The findings they are referring to indicate that the same memo judged by 60
partners in various law firms was judged to have on average more errors when
the memo was attributed to an African-American author (4.1/5.0 errors) rather
than a White author (3.2/5.0 errors).[36] When grading, these kinds of implicit
racial biases in our judgments have racist consequences, and even when they
don't, they favor White racial habits of language, which promotes White language supremacy. Remember, these findings come from professional partners
in law firms who are reading the exact same brief in each case, and yet they see
more error in writing attributed to African-American writers. Are we, writing
teachers, really any less racially biased than experienced, professional lawyers?

One important nuance to consider that affects the way implicit racial biases
can create—and likely do create—White language supremacist conditions in
writing classrooms can be heard in the report's discussion of their findings. After
reiterating Williams' point that we find error when we look for it (although they
do not cite him), the authors explain:

> Our evaluators unconsciously found more of the errors in
> the "African-American" Thomas Meyer's memo, but the final
> rating process was a conscious and unbiased analysis based on
> the number of errors found. When partners say that they are
> evaluating assignments without bias, they are probably right
> in believing that there is no bias in the assessment of the er-
> rors found; however, *if there is bias in the finding of the errors,*
> even a fair final analysis [of those errors] cannot, and will not,
> result in a fair result. (5; my emphasis)

---

36   The findings were separated in three kinds of errors, which the report shows the following
averages as: "spelling grammar errors," 2.9/7.0 (Caucasian) and 5.8/7.0 (African American);
"technical writing errors," 4.1/6.0 (Caucasian) and 4.9/6.0 (African American); and "errors of
facts," 3.2/5.0 (Caucasian) and 3.9/5.0 (African American).

What this amounts to is an unfair system—an unfair assessment ecology—working consistently the way it was designed. When the authors of the report say it is the "bias in the finding of the errors" what they mean is that these readers, partners in law firms, see and count more error in a text when the author is perceived to be Black, compared to when the same text is perceived to be written by a White author, and that the assessment ecology, the system that structures the way those lawyers make judgments on those texts, is set up to find more error in this exact way. The assessment ecology is White language supremacist.

How is the assessment ecology structured as White language supremacy? There are two systems at work. The first is a fast system of judgment that often works from implicit racial, gendered, and other biases. This judgment system contains predetermined judgments about things, instances, and people. According to Daniel Kahneman, two common fast thinking processes that our brains use are WYSIATI (or "what you see is all there is") and the availability heuristic.[37] These systems not only allow us to make quick decisions about lots of things in our lives, things that would otherwise bog us down too much, but they are also mostly unconscious mental processes that are themselves products of racialized places in society, places where we get the limited information our brains store to make fast decisions, places that are overwhelmingly populated by White people. Our brains associate White people with certain legitimized, language practices, certain preferred *habitus* that we encounter in such places. So when race is connected to an instance of language, our brains are already conditioned to hear or see certain things through mostly unconscious, fast judgments. We see or hear what we are prepared to see or hear.[38] This creates the racial implicit bias against Black writers, or what the authors of the above report call confirmation bias. In their recent collection on raciolinguistics, Samy Alim, John R. Rickford, and Arnetha F. Ball offer several chapters from various contributors that illustrate and explore just how language practices influence and construct people as racialized, as well as reproduce our ideas about race.

The second system I mentioned above that creates the racism in the lawyer study is a set of systems in schools and society that help determine language use by groups of people who are racialized in society. The effect is to move racial formations toward particular linguistic practices, and these practices are reaffirmed through conspicuous instances of racialized individuals using language

37   I explain both of these ways of thinking in the next chapter under the question, "Don't some students want or need grades so that they know how well they are doing or so they can be motivated to do the work?"

38   In *Thinking, Fast and Slow*, Daniel Kahneman illustrates over and over in numerous studies that memory and recall are not so clear cut. Eye witnesses are not very reliable. We can be primed to recall almost anything about a past instance, even things that have been confirmed in recordings to never have happened.

in patterned ways (e.g., in Hollywood and news media). These together create the effect that Black people talk that way and White people talk this way, etc. What these two consistent systems produce is White language supremacy in the judgments of language. This is what the study finds. And it's all done by people who likely are trying not to be racist, by trying to be fair—that is, trying to use a standard against everyone equally, a standard that is by design not equal because it favors the language habits of one racial group, and punishes any deviation from those habits as error. Meanwhile, no one is mentioning the connection that the standard has to dominant White racial formations in society, nor are they noticing that the habits of judging—the ways our brains make fast judgments—tend to privilege Whites and punish everyone else.

This is a lot to offer in a class session that is meant to discuss the grading mechanism in a writing classroom. I realize this. However, part of the discussions and practice of labor-based grading contracts is to critique the larger systems of grading in schools and help students more fully understand the ways systems of judgment are determined systems that easily reproduce racism and White language supremacy. They are made to do so. This is an important lesson in writing and literacy, one that begins our work in posing problems about the nature of judgment and language use in our classroom, schools, and society. Thus I do not see it as wasted time, rather it is our first steps into the subject of the course.

Accent is perhaps an easier and more accessible first example for students that a class can link to this fourth statement. Perceived accents, either in oral language practices or written, can be one marker that triggers fast judgments by teachers and students. Lippi-Green explains the real issue around accent and suggests implicitly how students might inquire or pose problems around it:

> in the serious study of accent, the object is not what comes
> out of one person's mouth, but what the listeners hear and
> understand. Derwing and Monro put it very simply: "From
> our perspective, listeners' judgments are the only meaningful
> window into accentedness and comprehensibility" (2009:
> 478). (45)

What she means is that accents are only accents if we assume one version of pronunciation is the standard, then everything else that doesn't sound exactly like that is a deviation from that standard, making those instances of the language accented. Accent is speech's version of error or failure in writing. And of course, if, as her fifth linguistic fact of life states, variation in language is an inherent part of language use, then the idea of ranking accents, or using them to make judgments about other people's language ability or intellectual capacities, is wrong and potentially racist. It is, as the CCCC Statement on Students Right to Their Own Language states, simply one social group attempting to oppress or dominate another through judgments of language (Committee on CCCC 2–3). And as Kahneman and others who study judgment have noted, we are not always aware of our biases, therefore we cannot always be aware that we have biases against accents we perceive in our students.

No one is immune to such linguistic biases. Just hearing an accent in any instance of speech proves that you have a linguistic standard by which you make sense of instances of language. And if you cannot describe that linguistic standard, then it's probably naturalized to you. Your linguistic standard is that English that doesn't sound accented to you. We don't have to think about this judgment of accent. It is an automatic judgment we make, usually unconsciously, fast. We all have these accent biases because we live in a society that reproduces such biases. We may not draw exactly the same conclusions or make harder decisions based on accent, such as, "is this candidate qualified for this job?" but our brains have such biases, even writing teachers. Thus, I point out to students that our concern isn't whether we all have such standards or biases in our heads, but how do we use them against others and how are our judgments used in the assessment ecology in which we circulate them? And most important, if all this is true, then how shall we grade writing in this course?

CHAPTER 5.

WHY I USE A CHARTER FOR COMPASSION WITH MY CONTRACT

In Chapter 4, I discussed what labor-based grading contracts are and how to initiate them in one's classroom. Part of that negotiation process could be discussing key statements that come from the contract's preamble or its philosophy, but there is another possible aspect of the contract that can be incorporated into those discussions: the ways in which a critical, gradeless writing classroom can cultivate a place of compassion so that the class can do the critical, brave, and difficult work involved in discussing the politics of language and its judgment.

Understanding compassion and cultivating an ethic of care, which as Nel Noddings has discussed is an ethic in which we act on behalf of others from a feeling of "I must" (95–96) that often comes with feelings of joy that stem from feelings of relatedness (144), has been a parallel study of mine alongside understanding labor-based grading contracts. This has led me to using Karen Armstrong's Charter for Compassion, which began as a request in a TED talk she made on February 28, 2008. But my use of a Charter for Compassion in my classrooms began with my personal study of compassion. I had no plans to offer it to my students, no plans to use compassion as a key philosophical element in my labor-based grading contract ecologies. I simply felt a growing need to understand compassion in my own life as more than an emotion or feeling, as doing, as action.

What I realized was that the tough discussions my students and I were often having around Whiteness, race, and racism in our judgment practices needed a more cogent and explicit ethical foundation in our assessment ecology. We needed a way to discuss and negotiate a set of agreements that could be ground rules, which we could then use to help us understand each other's motives, contributions, feedback, and actions in the course. I was asking my students to do this hard work without helping them understand how anti-racism and anti-White supremacist work in our writing classrooms can fulfill a basic, human ethical need, the need to be compassionate to others, to relate to others, to care for one another. I felt that a gradeless course environment made the topic of compassion more possible than graded classrooms, since we were already in the habit of understanding our labors together for other purposes than grade chasing.

Additionally, peer feedback practices in all writing classrooms already lend themselves to thinking about compassion as part of our work. We trust each other to read and offer meaningful feedback, so consciously discussing and creating a compassionate atmosphere seemed appropriate. What I found almost immediately upon incorporating the Charter for Compassion was that when we see socially just writing assessment ecologies as places of caring, compassionate labor that meets the needs of others around us, when we see our discussions of the racial politics of language or the White language supremacy in judging practices in schools as compassionate labor for others, we can enter into and sustain that work in productive ways because we can see better how it is part of our need to form connection, even through understanding our differences.

Knowing that everyone is trying to be compassionate in our mutual labors makes it easier to be brave, rather than comfortable, as Arao and Clemens put it. Creating a "brave" culture in the classroom means that we all are uncomfortable yet safe. When we are uncomfortable, it often means we are in an unknown place. We are confronting things we do not fully understand. But this doesn't mean we are not safe from harm. Being safe in a classroom can be hard to discern since it refers not just to physical harm, or harm to one's future opportunities, but psychological harm.

Arao and Clemens' work on cultivating "brave spaces" as opposed to safe ones in order to do social justice work on college campuses argues that safety and comfort often get conflated by students when doing the hard work of social justice (135). Furthermore, they suggest that participants should spend significant time together defining the space of their dialogue on social justice issues as "brave" and establishing brave ground rules that are conscious of the dominant ideological structures and ideas that produce those structures in order to not reproduce dominance and other social justice problems, the problems in the classroom and society that the dialogue is meant to critique and change. They argue that this opening set of discussions is a necessary beginning to any social justice work (142). Arao and Clemens offer some comparisons between common ideas that tend to define safe spaces and how they might be transformed to be guidelines for brave spaces in classrooms. Table 5.1[39] offers one way to visualize these:

---

39   I want to thank Virginia Schwarz for her roundtable on race talk in classrooms that she conducted at the 2018 CCCC annual convention in Kansas City. At the roundtable, Schwarz shared her version of the charter for compassion, in which she includes a discussion of Arao and Clemens' article and a table similar to Table 5.1. Schwarz' charter was based on Lucia Pawlowski's version, who was also at the roundtable.

Table 5.1. Common safe space guidelines transformed by Arao and Clemens into brave space guidelines

Safe Space Guideline	Brave Space Guideline
Agree to disagree (143).	Engage in controversy with civility (144).
Don't take things personally (144).	Own your own intentions and your impact (145).
Challenge by choice (146).	Challenge by choice, but question your reasons for choosing (be aware) (147).
Respect (147).	Respect (but articulate what respect looks like in the classroom) (147–48).
No attacks (148).	No attacks (but articulate the difference between personal attack and a challenge) (148).

In many ways, as you'll see below, because labor-based grading contracts provide for an opening dialogue about the course's grading mechanisms (the contract negotiations), it also conveniently allows for the setting of ground rules that help students and teacher craft a brave ecological place for brave social justice assessment work. The Charter for Compassion is one vehicle I have found that easily and quickly does this work with students, and like Schwarz' class, I find it an important document to negotiate with my students as we also negotiate our labor-based grading contract.

OUR CHARTER FOR COMPASSION

In the version of the contract I discuss in Chapter 4, the preamble mentions cultivating a culture of compassion in the classroom. This is a reference to the charter. During the first week of class, along with negotiating the grading contract, we work through a short set of activities to build our Charter for Compassion alongside the contract. I use a version of the charter that Karen Armstrong started in order to address interfaith conflict worldwide, with a few slight modifications for our classroom setting. Armstrong is an author and documentarian on comparative religion, and her non-profit organization that now helps individuals and organizations all over the world promote the ideals in the charter explain their mission this way on the website:

> Charter for Compassion International provides an umbrella
> for people to engage in collaborative partnerships worldwide.
> Our mission is to bring to life the principles articulated in the
> Charter for Compassion through concrete, practical action in
> a myriad of sectors. (Charter for Compassion International)

The charter itself was drafted in Geneva, Switzerland in 2008 by a collection of forty-two religious, spiritual, and secular leaders from a number of diverse areas, religions, and locations in the world. The website explains their backgrounds as coming from "government, business, education, philanthropy, religion & spirituality, health care, the environment, peace, and social justice." It is a simple document that centers on what Harry Gensler, an ethics scholar, has called the universal tenet of all human religions and spiritual traditions, the Golden Rule (Gensler 1). In Christian traditions, it is often spoken as: Do unto others as you would have them do unto you. The Charter for Compassion International website offers a list of other spiritual traditions that have similar tenets, all provided by Gensler, suggesting the Golden Rule's universality, which I list below as stated on the website:

- Baha'i Faith: Lay not on any soul a load that you would not wish to be laid upon you, and desire not for someone that things you would not desire for yourself. (Baha'u'llah Gleanings)
- Buddhism: Treat not others in ways that you yourself would find hurtful. (Udana-Varga 5.18)
- Christianity: In everything, do to others as you would have them do to you; for this is the law and the prophets. (Jesus, Matthew 7:12)
- Confucianism: One word which sums up the basis of all good conduct . . . loving kindness. Do not do to others what you do not want done to yourself. (Confucius, Analects 15.23)
- Hinduism: This is the sum of duty: do not do to others what would cause pain if done to you. (Mahabharata 5:1517)
- Islam: Not one of you truly believes until you wish for others what you wish for yourself. (The Prophet Muhammad, Hadith)
- Jainism: One should treat all creatures in the world as one would like to be treated. (Mahavira, Sutrakritanga)
- Judaism: What is hateful to you, do not do to your neighbour. This is the whole Torah; all the rest is commentary. (Hillel, Talmud, Shabbat 31a)
- Native Spirituality: We are as much alive as we keep the earth alive. (Chief Dan George)
- Sikhism: I am a stranger to no one; and no one is a stranger to me. Indeed, I am a friend to all. (Guru Granth Sahib, p. 1299)
- Taoism: Regard your neighbour's gain as your own gain, and your neighbour's loss as your own loss. (T'ai Shang Kan Ying P'ien, 213–218)
- Unitarianism: We affirm and promote respect for the interdependent web of all existence of which we are a part. (Unitarian principle)

- Zoroastrianism: Do not do unto others whatever is injurious to your-self. (Shayast-na-Shayast 13.29)

When I first offer it to my class, I emphasize that our use of the Charter for Compassion is not my way of proselytizing or turning my writing course into one about spirituality. But because writing is a social activity, it requires that we interact and read one another—in all the ways one might read another person. It requires that we discuss and come to some ethical agreements about how we'll conduct ourselves in all of our practices. The study of rhetoric and writing has always been closely tied to ethical practice. Ethics was a central concern of Plato's in *Phaedrus*. It was an important consideration of Isocrates' good student of rhetoric. Ethics' role in the study of rhetoric has been long debated in Aristotle's *Nicomachean Ethics*, *Politics*, and *Rhetoric* (Rowland and Womack). Richard Weaver's important book, *The Ethics of Rhetoric*, draws on Plato's *Phaedrus* to discuss the ethical dimensions of rhetoric. John Duffy more recently argues that the teaching of writing and rhetoric is always already a teaching of ethical rhetoric, that is, rhetoric is always connected to ethical questions and practices (230).

Compassion is my entry and overarching framework for ethical conduct in and through writing in my classrooms. We must have some assurances that those around us are trying to treat us well, to treat us as we would like to be treated if our positions were reversed. Now, the golden rule, as I'll discuss below, is more complex than this, but I try to keep it as simple as possible for my students since our class is not a philosophy class on the Golden Rule. Our charter fleshes out the foundations of our rhetorical ethics by defining through action what compassion will mean.

The template charter, which is adopted from Armstrong's charter, that we read together and discuss, offers a simple promise that all in the class agree to. It states:

> The principle of compassion lies at the heart of all religious, ethical, and spiritual traditions, calling us always to treat all others as we wish to be treated ourselves. Compassion impels us to work tirelessly to alleviate the suffering of our fellow creatures, to dethrone ourselves from the center of our world and put another there, and to honor the inviolable sanctity of every single human being, treating everybody, without exception, with absolute justice, equity, and respect.
>
> It is also necessary in both public and private life to refrain consistently and empathically from inflicting pain. To act or speak violently out of spite, chauvinism, or self-interest, to

impoverish, exploit or deny basic rights to anybody, and to incite hatred by denigrating others—even our enemies—is a denial of our common humanity. We in this class acknowledge that we have failed to live compassionately to some degree.

We therefore pledge to do all that we can, knowing we'll fail on occasion, to restore compassion to the center of our lives (at least in this course and during this quarter) and attempt to engage with our colleagues in this course with compassion. This means we will work to think first of others, their benefit, their well-being, and their learning, knowing that others are compassionately working for our benefit. We will strive to see our interdependence and interconnectedness, and labor for one another.

The following specific actions and behaviors we pledge to do in order to encourage and adopt a compassionate stance toward our colleagues in this class:

As we read together the above charter, I ask us to pause after each paragraph and consider the key ideas. We gather observations about each paragraph, without trying to come to any conclusions. I emphasize two important assumptions that I make from my reading of the charter. First, one cannot be accidentally compassionate. Compassion requires intention. Second, compassion is not simply a feeling or emotion. It is action. We can only *do* compassion, and often we fail at it, so it is a *practice* we develop over time but never perfect.

There are at least five key values that the charter highlights for our initial discussions. I try to make sure that we discuss each by asking questions about the key ideas we identify in the charter's words. I push the class to discuss these values in some way:

- Compassion is a universal human practice.
- Central to compassion is the act of treating others as we wish to be treated if we were them in their situation.
- Compassion is action that alleviates suffering in others, and assumes one's presence with those who suffer.
- Compassion is not selective—every human being deserves justice, equity, and respect, and we should not act or speak in ways that deny others these basic human rights, regardless of who they are or what they express to us.
- Compassion places others' needs and learning first, knowing that we are all interdependent and connected.

I've never had a student disagree with any of these key values. In fact, all of my students have agreed with all of them. To me, this is a testament to both the universality of the values and the generosity of my students. They recognize the goodness in these values and want to be compassionate. They want to care for their colleagues next to them, even though in many cases, they do not know their colleagues yet. In a humanistic way, I want to say that my students have shown me that they recognize the warmth, beauty, and goodness that a person feels when they care for others, when they attend to others' learning and suffering, even when that suffering is not life or death.

I realize there is a big difference in the kind of suffering that is referenced in the Charter for Compassion and the "suffering" that one might endure in a writing course, particularly from the labors of that course. The suffering in a writing course by U.S. college students, like mine, might be best characterized as struggles, not suffering. It is important to acknowledge this in class, since the literature and charter use the term suffering to refer to more serious problems than lack of sleep, or struggling with understanding a text, or even the pain of getting critical feedback on one's draft.

Today, with all that is going on in many parts of the world, with millions of refugees fleeing war-ravaged homelands, with the systemic problems of racism and sexism and Islamophobia and xenophobia in the US, calling the struggles of relatively privileged U.S. college students suffering could be problematic, if it isn't continually recognized that suffering comes in many degrees of severity, that our suffering is the suffering of the relatively privileged—what some call, "first world problems." To avoid confusing students, I keep the term suffering, knowing that we should remind ourselves that suffering is never universally experienced in the same ways or degrees, nor does it have the same consequences to individuals, even in our classroom.

To set the context for our work together, and build reasons for why it is important to a class like ours, I briefly offer some of the scientific research on compassion. This is usually one slide in class or a handout that we quickly go over. Sometimes it is a series of short readings and a reflection done before class. Sometimes we look at all the material in class together. There is a lot of neuroscientific and biological research that asks questions like, is compassion biological, does it have any biological basis or benefits to people, or is it a culturally constructed concept and set of practices? It turns out that there is growing research showing how the human brain is hardwired for compassion. It's biological, with many tangible benefits, and one key to activating compassion is through mindfulness practices.

Psychological researchers, such as Dacher Keltner, who has an eighteen-minute TED Talk on this subject, offers the neurological and psychological research on compassion, revealing ways that it can be measured in the brain and body, and activated through key biologically-driven bodily practices around facial expressions, voice and vocal sounds, and touch (Keltner, "TEDxBerkeley"). If there isn't time to watch the video in class sessions, his short essay, "The Compassion Instinct" or his condensed video ("Dacher Keltner on the Evolutionary") covers much of the same ground, which can be assigned outside of class or read in class. The article and videos point students to various studies that reveal the biological aspects and necessity of compassion. I've also found it useful to use some of Keltner's and his colleagues' articles, podcasts, and other materials on the Greater Good Science Center at the University of California, Berkeley's website.

Additionally, there have been several notable studies and meta-analyses of such studies on the effects of mindfulness practices on compassion centers in the brain, such as the inferior parietal cortex and dorsolateral prefrontal cortex (DLPFC), and the frequency of compassionate (or pro-social) acts by study participants (Goleman; Weng et al.). The Association for Psychological Sciences offers a short news release of Weng et al.'s 2013 study that is written for lay audiences, which shows that compassion can be taught through mindfulness practices. This online article is a good way to discuss this research with students. Emiliana R. Simon-Thomas summarizes some of these research findings discussed at the 2012 conference, "The Science of Compassion: Origins, Measures and Interventions" (Simon-Thomas). Her short article offers several videos of presentations on the science of compassion. Daniel Goleman's short *Washington Post* article on the research of compassion covers similar areas, and Richard Davidson's short video in which he presents his and his colleagues' research (the Weng et al. study) on how compassion is trainable is useful in illustrating to students how biological compassion is, and how it can be consciously cultivated. Davidson's video is particularly useful because he provides an easy method for a loving-kindness meditation that his study participants used as a compassion intervention, which can be easily translated for classroom use, particularly in preparation for reading and providing feedback to colleagues' drafts.

Often, I incorporate loving-kindness practices in my classes to reinforce our culture of compassion. Loving-kindness meditation has a long history in Buddhist traditions, and is called *metta bhavana*, or just *metta*, in the Pali language. Steven Smith, a teacher at the Insight Meditation Society in Burma and an advisor for the Center for Contemplative Mind in Society, explains that *metta* meditation is:

> care, concern, tenderness, loving kindness, friendship—a
> feeling of warmth for oneself and others. The practice is the

softening of the mind and heart, an opening to deeper and
deeper levels of the feeling of kindness, of pure love. Loving
kindness is without any desire to possess another. It is not
a sentimental feeling of goodwill, not an obligation, but
comes from a selfless place. It does not depend on relationships, on how the other person feels about us. The process
is first one of softening, breaking down barriers that we
feel inwardly toward ourselves, and then those that we feel
toward others. (Smith)

Smith's *metta* meditation offered in the short online article is essentially the
same method that Davidson's study participants used as a compassion intervention. Often, the first time I offer such a meditation to my students, I provide
a guided meditation, such as Emma Seppala's fifteen-minute, guided loving-
kindness meditation that includes a sound recording that guides practitioners
(Seppala). While both Smith's and Seppala's are essentially the same practice and
method, I like Seppala's because she guides the practitioner with her voice. At
the earlier stages of the course, such as the initial discussions that build our charter, I do always ask students to do *metta* meditations. Sometimes, I simply show
them these resources as a way to reveal the ways various disciplines and people
have come to the same conclusions about the human need to be compassionate, showing that there are ways to cultivate compassion and loving-kindness
and that these practices have been around a long time. Often I incorporate a
simplified version of *metta* meditation in our labor instructions for reading and
providing feedback on colleagues' drafts.

In our early discussions over our charter, which culminate in making lists
of behaviors and actions that will encourage a culture of compassion in our
class, this contextualizing with the biological and psychological research often
can prompt students when making their lists to be very practical and concrete,
to focus on the bodily and physical, not just abstract ideals. For instance, some
classes have offered items like, "look at others who are speaking in class" next
to more abstract actions like, "when someone is speaking, give them your full
attention." These may lead to the same set of practices, but each item focuses
our compassion work differently. The first, focuses our attention on cultivating
compassion through bodily comportment and eye contact. The second is more
abstract and may be seen as encompassing the first but often can be translated
as simply a state of mind through the key word, "attention." I find practices that
are more practical and concrete, ones that focus on moving or positioning our
bodies to be more effective in the long run than ones that are abstract. But I
think it is okay to record both.

So in the blank space at the bottom of our charter, we build a list of actions or behaviors that can be done in all of our course activities that encourage a culture of compassion. This is the list we build together. After our short discussion on the words of the charter itself and my brief contextualizing of compassion as a bona fide, researched thing, we build our list of compassionate actions that we promise to do in all our labors of the course. To do this list-building, I give students a short list of excerpts from various scholars and others who talk about compassion, which I initially found on Stanford's Center for Compassion and Altruism Research and Education website (Center for Compassion and Altruism in Research and Education).

Since I teach within ten-week quarters, we don't have a lot of time to read in full even one of the articles or chapters that these excerpts draw on, which would be preferable. What I'm trying to offer them in the excerpts is a way to see the academic conversation around compassion, and see it as something other than a touchy-feely, English-teachery thing that might be disregarded as impractical fluff, or too sentimental to be rigorous enough for a college classroom. I'm sure that my own *habitus* is an important part of how well these activities go off in my classrooms, just as it is important to the success of other aspects of my labor-based contract graded classrooms. I always play to my strengths, while also trying hard to call attention to the privileges I have to my students, which is a rhetorical way to be mindful with my students. For instance, my male, athletic stature, and masculine voice likely aids me when trying to convince students that compassion is not simply a touchy-feely thing. I'm also trying to direct them in particular ways, so that their list of actions and behaviors will be meaningful and helpful to us. All of these discussions and activities, which stretch over two class sessions, but take only twenty to thirty minutes in each session, help us understand compassion and come up with practices that cultivate compassion.

The actual work of building the list of such actions and behaviors is really an intellectual discussion that asks students to develop a list of behaviors we can commit to by first considering some of the literature and ideas on compassion. I start us with individual freewriting on the subject, move to group discussions, then a large class discussion. Once each group has discussed and come up with their lists of compassionate actions, I collect them and organize them in our charter. We read together the final version, and each week we vote on two or three compassionate actions we'll most focus on in our work that week. Each day in class, we read the two practices voted on that week. The building of the charter may be stretched over two class sessions. My prompting for our list of behaviors and actions is simple: What behaviors and actions can we do in all our activities that will encourage a compassionate culture in our class?

DISCUSSING THE CONCEPT OF COMPASSION

While each class comes up with their own list of practices and insights into compassion, I now turn to what I see as some of the important ideas in the literature on compassion that my excerpts draw on, which I believe make for an informed discussion of compassion that leads to the kind of classroom assessment culture I'm aiming for. I do not intend the following to be a full discussion of the concept of compassion, instead it is a summary of the key ideas I tend to discuss with my students about compassion.

It is often stated that Charles Darwin himself saw sympathy and what might be considered compassion to be an important evolutionary trait in all animal communities (Ekman; Goetz et al. 4). The more compassion that exists in a community, argues Darwin, the more numerous the community is. In part, compassion is how we help each other, how those who need it get comfort and aid in communities, and it helps form relationships between individuals in communities. Jacoba M. Lilius, Jane E. Dutton, Monica C. Worline, and Sally Maitlis offer this definition of compassion, and it suggests an etymological and philosophical way to consider Darwin's hypothesis:

> Compassion comes into the English language by way of the
> Latin root "passio," which means to suffer, paired with the Latin
> prefix "com," meaning together—to suffer together. The concept
> of compassion and its link to suffering has deep philosophical
> and religious roots. For instance, Christian theologian Thomas
> Aquinas noted the interdependence of suffering and compassion
> when he wrote: "No one becomes compassionate unless he suf-
> fers" (cited in Barasch, 2005, p. 13). Ancient Chinese traditions
> acknowledge the interrelationship of suffering and human con-
> cern in the figure of Kwan Yin, often referred to as the goddess
> of compassion. Hindu imagery depicts compassion through a
> half-ape half-human deity, Hanuman, whose chest is cleaved
> open to reveal his heart to others undefended. Some Buddhist
> traditions induct individuals seeking to cultivate their compas-
> sion into the vow of the Boddhisattva, whose life is dedicated
> to being present with and relieving the suffering of all beings
> (Barasch, 2005; Chodron, 1997). A recurring theme is thus the
> relationship between one's own suffering and self-oriented com-
> passion, and compassion for others (Neff, 2003, 2009). (274)

When reading this excerpt with students, I ask them, how does the Latin etymology help us understand the word compassion? What would it mean to "suffer with" another in our classroom, say, during feedback activities or when we have discussions? I point out the various traditions that these authors use to illustrate how universal the idea is. We might also look at the list of golden rules from various spiritual traditions from Gensler (listed earlier in this chapter) to further illustrate this point. I ask about the universality of suffering itself, something the passage above assumes. What do they consider "suffering" and how should we regard the idea in our class? Is struggling with a dense text for our class suffering? How might sharing one's draft with colleagues for their feedback be a kind of suffering, or revising a draft that you really like and feel is a part of you also suffering? Might stress and anxiety from outside the course be suffering too?

Sometimes I'll offer Buddhism's Four Noble Truths, which is understood by many to be the foundation of the tradition. Tradition says that these "truths" were articulated by the Buddha after he struggled for enlightenment. They might be stated as: (1) suffering exists in life; (2) craving, desire, and ignorance are the causes of suffering, in short, attachment causes suffering; (3) suffering ceases when one detaches from cravings, desires, and the unknown; and (4) freedom from suffering can be achieved by practicing the Eightfold Path. I offer these ideas not to proselytize but to show the assumptions about the existence and universality of suffering assumed in these discussions of compassion, and how they suggest compassion and suffering go together. I focus only on the first three ideas, not the forth.

I also emphasize that these "truths" likely should not be thought of as static or "truths" at all. They are practices, actions that help us see that compassion, which includes self-compassion, is not simply a state of mind or a feeling, but a set of practices we do every day. They are labor. Stephen Batchelor, Christina Feldman, and Akincano M. Weber, three long-time Buddhist teachers, explain this very idea about the four noble truths, saying that the term "truth" is not what the Buddha had in mind at all, if one reads them in context of the Buddhist canon, instead, they are practices, or as Feldman says, "liberating investigations." Stephen Batchelor agrees and offers this understanding of them:

> as long as you're using the word "truth," you're going to be
> just a whisker away from having a dogmatic view. If we take,
> for example, the second noble truth as it is usually translat-
> ed—that "craving is the origin of suffering"—to me that is
> a metaphysical statement. You're making a very generalized
> claim about the nature of reality, and so immediately people
> get drawn into the discussion: Well, is that really true? What
> about this? What about that? And down you go into the
> rabbit hole of theology. Whereas if you frame it as a task, the

challenge is: how do I let go of craving? Then you are setting
up a whole different doorway to the thoughts and the discussions that follow. Your discussion inevitably will be pragmatic.
It won't be, "Is this true? Is this false? Is this right? Is this
wrong?" but, "How do you get it done?" (Batchelor et al.)

In short, Batchelor suggests that the Four Noble Truths might be most productively articulated as questions whose stasis is policy (what do we do?), and not
a stasis question of fact (what is the case?). So to understand the Four Noble
Truths in the way the Buddha offered them, according to Feldman and Bachelor,
is to see them as inquiries and action that come to personal insight, which leads
to social changes in the community, since they make a point to remind their
readers that the Buddha was a social activist who was interested in making the
social world a better place.

Finally, in the same dialogue, Akincano Weber offers his version of how to
understand the Four Noble Truths as actions. He is inspired by the English
monk Nanavira Thera, who offered an analogy between the Four Noble Truths
and a scene in *Alice in Wonderland*:

Alice doesn't have a bottle that describes its contents. She
finds a bottle that tells her what she should do with the contents—"Drink me"—and then things happen: she shrinks and
grows and so on. In the Buddhist application of the analogy,
the label on the first truth says, "Understand me." On the second of the truths, the label says, "Give me up." On the third
bottle, it says, "Realize me," and on the fourth bottle it says,
"Develop me." So if we boil down the teaching of these four
truths, they are four different calls to action. (Batchelor et al.)

I like to think of our charter for compassion as a call to action. What are we
going to do to make our classroom a more compassionate, and thus a more
educative, place for all of us? How are we going to liberate ourselves through
our own investigations? How will our labor make us more compassionate, more
equal, more free to learn in the ways we can?

Furthermore, if everyone suffers in some way (the first Noble Truth), then
compassion is important to helping everyone learn and grow. Compassion may
help us notice others' and our own cravings, desires, and ignorance and how
they cause us anxiety, stress, and pain (second Noble Truth). We then might be
more able to detach from those cravings and desires (third Noble Truth), not to
have no desires, but to allow for other ideas, voices, and judgments in the classroom to exist and be valued. Since our context for this discussion is writing and

reading texts, I move us to think mostly about the ways we are attached to our judgments and ideas of things, and why we must hold so tightly to them. Why does having a firm belief in something mean we must deny others' rights to hold firmly to their contrary beliefs? If we wish to listen to, interact with each other compassionately, and grow or learn—i.e., change ourselves—then how does detachment help us do this? How do we, like Hanuman, open our unprotected hearts to others in our class? It is not easy practicing.

I also ask students to consider the last sentence, one that is about people's interconnection, suggesting how someone else's suffering in the world may be connected to their own. I might ask, can you think of some ways that your own success in this class may be dependent on other students' success around you? There are lots of ways this occurs directly. Writing group members who read and provide feedback help writers with their drafts and writing practices. Class discussions of texts and readings are communal ways of sharing insights and readings of texts. In such discussions, we learn how others read a text and learn from their reading labors. The better those around you are at reading a text, the fuller your own understanding of the text is after hearing about others' reading experiences if you are open to them. And the opposite is true. If colleagues do not read carefully or offer thoughtful discussion on a text in class, you will have a more impoverished sense of the text after those discussions, which is a kind of suffering—albeit a suffering you may not be fully aware of. The same is true concerning feedback sessions. So being diligent in our homework and other labors and sharing our understandings together are labors of compassion toward our colleagues, and if we don't do them in the fullest ways possible, we can cause suffering to others.

In their historical treatment of the concept, Getz, Keltner, and Simon-Thomas offer this definition of compassion:

> We define compassion as the feeling that arises in witnessing another's suffering and that motivates a subsequent desire to help (for similar definitions, see Lazarus, 1991; Nussbaum, 1996, 2001; Table 1). This definition conceptualizes compassion as an affective state defined by a specific subjective feeling, and differs from treatments of compassion as an attitude (Blum, 1980; Sprecher & Fehr, 2005), or as a general benevolent response to others regardless of suffering or blame (Post, 2002; Wispé, 1986). This definition also clearly differentiates compassion from *empathy*, which refers to the vicarious experience of another's emotions (Lazarus, 1991). (2; emphasis in original)

These authors point out how compassion is often seen as distinct from empathy, or the "vicarious experience of another's emotions." Compassion is its own emotional response to others' suffering, but it is not just a feeling. It is a feeling mixed with a desire to help alleviate suffering seen in others. Our class discussion might ask: is it preferable that people act on their ethical feelings toward others? Is it better to help someone through their suffering, than just to notice it and do nothing? What keeps people from turning their empathy into compassionate action in our classroom, in your past classrooms? How do we notice others' suffering or struggles in our class if we do not always have direct access to that suffering, say in the drafting or revising of a paper, or a reading of a text? Is it preferable to tell those around us when we suffer in silent or invisible ways? If we think we see a colleague suffering, are we obligated to ask about it or call attention to it in some public but respectful way, or maybe a private way?

Often, I bring up the idea that much suffering in classrooms, especially writing classrooms, is created by grading and the institutional requirement of grades. This is one benefit of labor-based grading contracts. Thus in conventional classrooms, one thing that may stop many students from turning their empathy into compassionate action for others is the detrimental effect that such actions may have on their grades, particularly if that grading ecology is set up around a teacher's judgment of so-called quality of drafts. The ecology is one of competition and scarcity of the higher grades. By helping others achieve higher grades, you risk losing your chance at the few higher grades given out. It feels like an unfair choice. And this suffering from grades is not even, particularly if we consider which groups of students are most privileged by White language supremacy that shape standards for grading. Yes, in literacy classrooms, the intensity or degree of suffering by grading can be racialized and classed.

Some students will occasionally say that compassion does not require seeing others suffer. That it is an act that we can do because we know others will appreciate it and benefit from it, even though they are not suffering. There is an element of truth to this, but it is not technically what most scholars understand as compassion since it is intimately linked to suffering of others. As the above discussions show, compassion arises from seeing, hearing, or knowing of others' suffering or struggles. It is action directed at alleviating suffering of those whom we come to understand as less fortunate than us, those who cannot help themselves as we can. It isn't simply doing nice things for just anyone.

What some students are referring to here (compassion that doesn't require suffering in others) might be akin to giving money to those who have plenty of money, without looking for those who are needy elsewhere. It is still nice to do, but does not solve a problem that someone else has. Of course, in our U.S.-based class context, where the kinds and degree of suffering may be minimal, and often not in need of others' assistance, and where we are concerned only with learning, I hear this altering of compassion as a way to fit a third-world definition of compassion into a first-world context. It asks indirectly: what if there is no suffering? What is our responsibility to those around us then? But suffering need not be about imminent life-and-death situations. As suggested above, it can be about anxiety and undue struggling. So this can be a useful expansion of compassion for the writing classroom setting, a way of considering loving-kindness as part of our version of compassion, but we should continue to be mindful of the ways compassion have been understood to help those who suffer in dire ways and are in need.

Another response to this question, a more ambitious one, might be to ask how can we find those in need nearest to us, so that we might exercise compassion toward them in the process of accomplishing our course goals? This is not an easy question to answer, and many students will not be prepared to answer it or follow up on whatever the class comes to (ideally). Furthermore, the dangers of searching out needy recipients of compassion can end up being a paternalistic enterprise that does more harm than good. I have found that it is better to be vigilant for those needing our compassion, but not try to turn a writing class into a training ground for humanitarian work. But having the discussion about what our individual and collective responsibilities are as people who live among so much suffering and inequality can be beneficial to students.

What it can reveal is that we are all interconnected and our individual learning in school does not have to be—even should not be—an individual affair. What gives us the right to exercise the privilege of learning in this classroom when so many around us are denied this privilege, and suffer in poverty, or sickness, or mental illness? One's education in school may indeed be at the expense of those outside the school, those in the community who suffer without help or compassion from anyone, and do so mostly because of luck of birth. There may be more learning, joy, and engagement when we expand our circle of responsibility and care. Again, it is not easy work, but brave and hard work, work that many might see as far from the work of a writing classroom. But is it? Is the compassion imperative a part of the ethical in learning rhetoric and writing? This is a question each group of students should wrestle a bit with, and I'll return to it in a way in the final Coda chapter of this book.

Obviously, there are no firm answers to any of these questions. I merely offer them as ways to get students to think more deeply about a seemingly simple idea like compassion, which could look only like treating others nicely, or thinking nicely about others, and connecting it to the learning and labors in the writing course. This discussion also allows me to talk about some of the structures in the course that help us be more compassionate. For example, I ask several students each week to read to the class their labor journal entries, and we talk about our similar struggles. I often ask the class questions like, "did anyone else have a similar struggle or issue with their labor this week?" It is rare for several students not to raise their hands. By commiserating in this way, students develop an eye and ear for the struggles others endure in our course, seeing them as similar to their own, or noticing those who seem to struggle more or differently. My hope is that once the struggles of others are made present, students will be poised to be compassionate to their colleagues, to see their responsibilities in the class as more than simply to get their own grade or take care of their own individual learning, but to expand their sense of care and tend to the needs of others.

CONNECTING EMPATHY TO COMPASSION

Noticing the struggles of others as interconnected to one's own learning in a class and cultivating a desire to care for those who suffer requires empathy. Most definitions of compassion, including all those the charter works from in my courses, depend on understanding empathy and feeling empathy for others. While we cannot force students to feel something for others, we can understand the feeling and articulate some intentions for our actions. While seemingly contrary to the passages on compassion discussed above, I believe that *actions come first and feelings of empathy follow actions*, not that other way around. Doing leads to feeling. Bodily position, eye contact, touch, the movements we make, all contribute to how we feel in a conversation or situation. Try arguing intensely with someone while lying down on a couch. Try shouting and being angry at someone while smiling at them. Try studying a picture or page of text really closely, very carefully, while slouched in a chair and your head resting on its back. Now, try studying that picture or text sitting straight up, head slightly leaning forward, breathing a bit shallower than usual and faster. Which position is more conducive to focusing hard and carefully on the object?

What we do and how we orient our bodies in places matters to our feelings and attitudes. Our feelings of empathy toward others, even toward those we don't know very well, is no different. Our bodies must first be in a place and oriented in particular ways, only then can we act compassionately for others. For our class purposes, I urge students to consider that it is unwise to wait to feel empathy if we know we need it to cultivate compassion and interconnectedness. We cannot wait to feel empathy for others. We can consciously construct empathy by positioning our bodies in ways that mimic empathetic responses in the presence of others.

To test this idea of empathy as spatial and embodied, that it can be cultivated by orienting our bodies in the presence of others, we might do a thought

185

experiment. Think of a non-romantic, loving relationship you have with another who is not a family member, maybe a long-time, best friend, one you'd say you have lots of empathy for. How did you gain that empathy over the years? When you first met this person, did you have the same degree of empathy that you do now? Did you care as much about them initially, were you as deeply affected by their problems and troubles, as you are now? Of course not. So how did your feelings of empathy change? Could your increase in empathy have occurred through being in the presence of your friend and practicing such bodily orientations that lead to increased feelings of empathy? Could you have been cultivating dispositions, a *habitus* marked in bodily ways, by how you lean closer and listen carefully with furrowed eyebrows as your friend speaks, or just being in their presence as they suffer or have troubles. Being with someone else as they experience trouble often makes us more sympathetic to their plight. When we say, "we've been there with you," or "we've gone through a lot together," it draws on this intrinsic quality of being in the presence of others who suffer. I think, empathy is a human response to being in the presence of others' suffering or struggling, and it becomes a disposition through the way our bodies are habitually oriented in space. Doing this over and over, perhaps out of politeness at first, but later out of a growing sense of empathy, creates empathy, and so cultivates compassion.

If there is time, perhaps an activity that demonstrates the connections between spatial and bodily orientation and how we feel toward others and their ideas can help develop discussions about empathy. One measure of empathy is how well we listen and retain the stories and ideas that someone else offers us. When we are more empathetic, we want to listen more carefully because we understand that the other person who needs or asks for our empathy is soothed by or appreciates our empathetic listening. Their suffering is noticed or listened to. So one empathy activity might place students in pairs and ask one student (student A) to either lie down on the floor, if it is comfortable to do and student A is able and willing, or turn their chair away from the other student (student B) and recline as much as possible, so that they are in a relaxed position. Student B will then read or tell a story to student A. The story can be one about a time that student B struggled, failed at something, or was sad about something, or something that they are genuinely excited about at the moment. It should be a story they are willing to share. It should have specific details, and be written down first, likely prepared before class. Student A listens to the story, and student B reads their story to student A. Once they've finished, they switch positions and Student A reads while B listens. Finally, they sit down and freewrite for five minutes: What was your colleague's story about? What details do you remember? This takes fifteen minutes.

You then repeat this process with new pairs, only this time, change the orientation. Have the listening student sit straight up and alert in their chair, facing the other student, looking into their eyes or face the entire time. Once you have two freewritten summaries, ask students, perhaps in groups of four (the two pairs), to compare the summaries. Which one did you remember in more detail? Which one were you more interested in? How did your bodily orientation affect your ability to listen? How did your orientation affect your feelings of focus or attention to the story? How did your partner's bodily orientation affect your reading of your story?

The discussions together about what they observed might make observations about the ways our attention and care for others is not simply an inner thing. Our bodies and others' bodies' orientations and spatial proximity to our own matters to what and how we perceive things, what we remember, and our abilities to focus, remember, concentrate, and engage. This same activity can be done with reading too by asking students to read similar short passages in various bodily positions, standing, sitting, lying down, slouched in a chair, with one's face close to the passage and farther away, etc.

Martin L. Hoffman, a clinical psychological researcher, who has done extensive work on empathy, explains that

> Compassion . . . is not a sharing of another person's emotional
> state, which will vary depending on what the other person's
> emotional experience seems to be, but an emotion of its own
> . . . In compassion, the emotion is felt and shaped in the
> person feeling it not by whatever the other person is believed
> to be feeling, but by feeling personal distress at the suffering
> of another and wanting to ameliorate it. The core relational
> theme for compassion, therefore, is being moved by another's
> suffering and wanting to help. (289)

So empathy is important to compassion and is mixed with the action to alleviate the suffering of others. It's a feeling of distress over another's suffering. It urges us to do something. It is a pathway to action. But if we don't always feel empathy in strong enough ways that move us to action, then we cannot be compassionate. So can we be compassionate without, at least initially, being empathetic toward another? I think so, at least as a method to begin, to cultivate empathy in ourselves. I've never met anyone who has disagreed with the idea that being compassionate, doing actions to alleviate others' suffering, is not preferable and ideal for everyone, so building empathy as a bridge to more compassionate action in the future seems safe to me as a set of practices for the writing classroom.

So we can cultivate empathy and compassionate acts simply by orienting our bodies in the material places we make in the classroom and doing particular things for others, first out of duty or respect, then out of caring and compassion. Rick Hanson and Richard Mendius, a neuropsychologist and neurologist (respectively), argue that our brains can be programmed to be more empathetic and compassionate. Empathy can be practiced so that it is habitual. Doing this, they argue, leads to neurochemical responses in the brain that make us happy.

Hanson and Mendius offer several strategies for cultivating empathy that come from research on the brain. They define empathy as a connection with another that completes a thou-I relationship, one in which you know that the empathetic one feels your feelings. Empathy is a reassuring stance and understanding between individuals that makes clear each is understood. They explain, "[w]e are social animals, who, as Dan Siegel puts it, need to feel *felt*" (138; emphasis in original). Listen to that. We need to *feel felt*. Can you deny this? Hanson and Mendius call empathy "respectful and soothing" and is generous because one is willing "to be moved by another person" (139). They offer this explanation: "empathy is neither agreement nor approval. You can empathize with someone you wish would act differently. Empathy *doesn't* mean waiving your rights; knowing this can help you feel it's alright to be empathic" (138). From this understanding of empathy, they offer six practices that will sound familiar, given what I've said above, but are nevertheless helpful in building the compassionate practices in a classroom charter for compassion or just talking about how a class will understand the ways we can be empathetic and compassionate toward one another. Here are the six practices, with a paraphrasing of Hanson and Mendius' suggestions about each one:

- **Set the stage**: Remind yourself to be empathetic and that it feels good to be so. Relax your body and mind so as to be open to others, keeping in mind that your thoughts and feelings are here and others' are over there. They are separate but you are present with the other person's thoughts and feelings. "Keep paying attention to the other person; be *with* him [her/them]" (140).
- **Notice the actions of others**: Take careful note of how the other person moves, positions their body, makes facial expressions, etc. Imagine yourself doing those same bodily expressions and movements so that you can feel what they are feeling (140).
- **Sense the feelings of others**: First "tune in to yourself . . . your breathing, body, and emotions," then "watch the other person's face and eyes closely . . . Relax. Let your body open to resonating with the other person's emotions" (140–41).

- **Track the thoughts of others**: "Actively imagine what the other person could be thinking or wanting" (141).
- **Check back**: When it is appropriate, "check with the other person to see if you're on the right track" (141). This is similar to Peter Elbow and Pat Belanoff's response strategy of "say back" (Elbow and Belanoff 8).
- **Receive empathy yourself**: "Be open, present, and honest. You could also ask for empathy directly" (142).

Once we finish our initial discussions of compassion and build our Charter for Compassion, I reference the above practices and the full charter in all labor instructions, reminding us of our commitments to be compassionate. I have found this use of compassion as a companion to labor-based grading contracts to be very useful and successful, particularly because my writing classrooms focus on understanding the ways Standardized Edited American English (SEAE) and dominant discourses expected of students in school are historically associated with a White, middle-class racial *habitus*, and those discussions require compassion and empathy. I also make explicit the ways that using such a White racial *habitus* in the judgment of writing perpetuates White language supremacy. These two focuses are ways I offer critical language practices for students, ways to be critical about language, how we judge it, and its consequences on others. They also tend to be a hard pill to swallow for many students. It makes many White students feel uncomfortable. So in order to be brave, we must find ways to support a safe environment that may also be uncomfortable for some. A culture of compassion that everyone actively defines, builds, and maintains is the way I've helped do this important work. While I've not done any explicitly empirical or quantitative study of how the Charter for Compassion has affected my classrooms, students mention it positively in end of quarter course evaluations and in their final reflective documents at the end of each quarter. Ultimately, each teacher must decide what is agreeable with their own pedagogies and teacherly stance in the classroom. I find compassion agreeable and helpful.

CHAPTER 6.

WHAT CONCERNS ARE THERE OF LABOR-BASED GRADING CONTRACTS?

Some may have reservations about using a labor-based system of grading in a writing or English course, or have questions about some of the details, differences, logistics, and consequences. In this chapter, I address the most popular concerns and questions that I've not directly addressed in my discussion already (although I have briefly covered some of this territory in previous chapters). Many of these questions come from several sources: a query to colleagues on the WPA-L listserv on May 03, 2017; numerous faculty members at various colleges and universities where I've given workshops and talks over the past three or four years; and a wonderful group of engaged teachers and graduate students in the CUNY Graduate Center's Composition and Rhetoric Community group.[40]

I have designed this chapter as a kind of modified FAQ that mostly stands on its own. I try to address each question comprehensively from both a theoretical and practical level, so I consider this chapter an important part of theorizing labor-based grading contracts and the ecologies they help cultivate. One should keep in mind that the grading ecologies I speak of in this chapter are based on primarily my own labor-based grading contract ecologies, ones mostly situated in universities that serve primarily students of color and first-generation, working-class students (i.e., Southern Illinois University Edwardsville, California State University, Fresno, and the University of Washington Tacoma). Not all contracts are the same, not all labor-based grading ecologies are the same, nor are all teachers and students embodied in ecologies in the same ways, so some of my

---

40   I wish to thank the CUNY Graduate Center's Composition and Rhetoric Community group for their good questions and concerns about contracts in a lively discussion via Google Hangouts one evening on April 20, 2017. Those good graduate students and teachers are: Jason Myers, Robert Greco, Sean Molloy, Alexis Larsson, Erin Andersen, Seth Graves, Lindsey Albracht, and Anna Zeemont. Also, I am grateful to all the good folks on the WPA-L who provided me with questions to include and address in this chapter in a threaded discussion on May 03, 2017. Some of those folks are E. Shelley Reid, Abby Knoblauch, Courtney Wooten, Cynthia Baer, Dayna Goldstein, Arun Raman, Dan Sharkovitz, Clancy Ratliff, Nick Carbone, Traci Gardner, Julie Dugger, Bethany Davila, Jarron Slater, Donna Qualley, John Whicker, Dirk Remley, Misty Beck, Michael Pemberton, Maja Wilson, Matt Dowell, Janet Lively, Jacob Martens, Thomas Wright, and Jonathan Hunt. I have included many of these colleagues' questions in some form in this chapter.

responses should be understood as coming from a writing teacher of color, who also exercises male privilege in the classroom, and whose students are mostly first-generation, and often at least 50% students of color and working class. I try hard, however, to be conscious of my privilege, and humble enough to see my shortcomings so that I might learn from them.

WHY DOES YOUR LABOR-BASED GRADING CONTRACT USE A DEFAULT B-GRADE (3.1) AND NOT A C-GRADE (2.1)?

The default grade that any contract offers is up to the teacher and their sense of what works best with their students, as well as what works with the nature of the course and work involved. I have always begun with a default grade of B (3.1) in my courses. I do this because I know that I tend to ask for a lot of labor of students, so getting an "above average" grade seems appropriate to me if all the contract terms are met. The labor I'm asking of students is worth an above average grade in my opinion. I want my students to do more than an average amount of work (or my notions of an average amount). I realize that if everyone is doing what is asked of them, then the notion "above average" becomes what is average. So be it. I do not hold tightly to conceptions of things like average. I prefer to think of it as a "typical" grade. In all courses and grading systems, concepts like "average" performance are convenient reifications for grading purposes. More important, I know that Bs matter to most of my students and are worth attaining. Most students just aren't satisfied with grades lower than B (3.1), so that's the benchmark we hold.

This makes sense from a consequences standpoint too, which is one way to gauge the fairness of an assessment ecology. The consequences of students receiving a B (3.1) instead of an A (4.0) on their transcript in their FYW course is insignificant, while getting a C (2.1), I think, has a perceived heavier negative consequence, although still insignificant in the long run. So less harm is done to students should they not meet the contract, but meet most of its terms, or get a C (2.1). Students may not always see this, since every grade counts and every class should be taken seriously. Thus the psychological effect of working toward a default B-grade (3.1) is more satisfying than a C-grade. It feels better to work toward a B-grade than a C-grade, even though the contract attempts to help us problematize these feelings about grades. Feeling good with what you get for your labor, regardless of what that labor consists of, is part of what makes systems fair for individuals.

So there are pragmatic reasons I use a default B-grade. But, there are also deeper philosophical reasons too. Many students come into my class still assuming a point-acquisition philosophy. This philosophy says that a course grade equates to how much you learned of the total amount offered or expected in a course. One's course grade, then, is like a gas tank gauge, registering how full the student got in the course. The more information the student learned, the higher their grade. The more points one acquires, the more one has gotten from the class, the higher that student's grade is, so goes the logic. But this logic is one engineered into most assessment ecologies by the use of points and the methods designed by teachers for students to get those points (or keep them away from some students). If there is 1,000 points possible in the quarter, and you acquire 850 of those points, you got an 85%, a B course grade because you allegedly learned 85% of the course material. But the points are artificial and arbitrary.

So this point-acquisition philosophy isn't a universal logic for all assessment ecologies, and this logic determines what course grades mean to students. When my students translate this logic to our labor-based course, they can mistakenly assume that doing all the labor means you've done everything possible in the course, so like the full tank in the point-acquisition philosophy, you should get the highest grade possible, an A-grade (4.0). Of course, this point-acquisition philosophy is not what I assume. It's not the logic of labor-based grading contracts. Labor-based contracts assume an if-then-agreement logic. If the student accomplishes the labor terms we negotiated, then they will receive the course grade we agreed upon for that labor. The grade doesn't signify how much of the total course material you've learned, or even how much you've done of the total labor possible. It means you've met the labor terms in the contract for the grade that we agreed to. A B-grade (3.1) means the student met the contract terms for a B-grade. An A-grade (4.0) means the student has met those negotiated and defined terms (more labor).

Like all contracts, the terms that define the default grade, and even the default grade itself, should be negotiated with students. I do this every quarter. Occasionally, we modify the default grade of the contract from a B (3.1) to a B+/A- (3.4). This sometimes is offered by one of the students at our midpoint renegotiation time in reflections on the contract, which would then require a discussion and anonymous vote.[41] Sometimes, I offer it myself because I can see that they are too timid to ask for it. This only happens when it is clear that while most students can complete the terms of labor we agree upon, they are finding it difficult to complete any of the extra labor required to get a higher grade, yet they want to try. They feel that most of that extra labor is unrealistic for most or all of the students in the class. This makes the contract unfair, since fairness is partly defined by the amount of access to all grades that all students have in the class. This is consistent with John Rawls' theory of justice as fairness

41   For all negotiations of any contract details, either in the first week of the class or at midpoint, a super-majority (2/3) affirmative vote is required for my classes.

that I discuss in Chapter 2, in which the two general conditions of fairness in a society are (1) that all opportunities be formally open to all, and (2) "that all should have a fair chance to attain them" (43). Not so incidentally, the other main part of fairness is that all people in the ecology have as equal say as possible in the important decisions of the ecology, that is, that all get to participate in decision-making (see Inoue, "Articulating Sophistic" 41, 44), which makes the negotiation process vital to the fairness of the contract.

TO WHAT EXTENT CAN LABOR-BASED GRADING CONTRACTS ADDRESS LEARNING OR COURSE OBJECTIVES OR OUTCOMES?

If you are worried about measuring or showing evidence of students learning course outcomes, then I respectfully suggest that you rethink the assumptions that make this question possible. I'm not saying that teachers should not be concerned about learning outcomes, only that grading mechanisms have little to do with students acquiring them, or demonstrating them. We just think they do. Strictly speaking, no system that produces a course grade or that ranks individual performances in some way can assure that students are meeting or developing along course goals, objectives, or outcomes. We like to believe that giving grades helps students achieve outcomes, but really all they do is assure us that *we (teachers) think* that our students have achieved them by assigning a symbol to performances, symbols that have the appearance of precise measurement. While this may often be a necessary assumption, grades are not teaching, nor are they learning. The presence of grades does not mean the presence of learning, and only suggests that we have measured something in some precise way.

And like the SAT and other large scale tests that produce similar numbers that appear to measure students in some way, our grades cannot do this evenly or reliably. Yes, grades appear to measure outcomes—at least in one judge's eyes—but do our grades really measure outcomes that students have learned? Numbers and rankings in our society, especially when they are elaborate, give the appearance of precision—often because of their complexity—but precision of measurement is not in the scale alone. It is in how accurate and consistent the scale can be used. Pat Belanoff's four "myths of assessment" suggest why using any scale based on our own judgments of writing is suspect in terms of its validity to make judgments on students and their writing, and the reliability of our judgments themselves. Grades on writing and points seem precise, but we have no indication that they are or can be.

The assumption in questions like this one, which seek to understand labor-based contracts in terms of conventional grading ecologies, is flawed in that it tries to compare labor-based contracts by a standard set by conventional grading or point acquisition systems, using conventional systems as a kind of criterion by which to establish contracts' level of validity in teaching outcomes. But I question the criterion's (i.e., grades that measure outcomes) validity itself to be a criterion. This question implies that conventional grading systems already do this, hence the use of them as a criterion by which to judge contracts, but it is a dubious assumption to say that any conventional system of grading by quality helps students learn or achieve outcomes, just as it is equally dubious to say that the same system measures students' written performances in a reliable way. Grades may measure outcomes in some way, but we do not have any guarantees that those grades are accurate, consistent, or measure what we say they are measuring, unless a department or program has elaborate, costly, and frequent norming sessions that move teachers toward such practices. And even if this is happening, which I doubt, there is still the problem of racist and White language supremacist standards that will be inevitable when a program chooses the standards by which to norm its teachers to. So it is ironically also good that we do not have reliable or internally similar standards for the same classes in a program or department.

Another way to see the problem with this question is to see grades as a reification of measurement in the same fashion that Stephen J. Gould speaks of reification in science and its measurement. Gould explains that when it came to the biological sciences, particularly those that sought to understand human variation and race, scientists made two fallacies historically: reification and ranking. The fallacy of reification, he says, is "our tendency to convert abstract concepts into entities" (24). Gould illustrates reification through IQ tests and the reification of the IQ score, which doesn't exist outside the IQ test that came out of Alfred Binet's work at the Sorbonne. One's IQ is not real. It says nothing actual about one's ability to think, or analyze, or problem solve, or get along in the world, but like grades, its presence suggests its reality. If we forget that we've made up this number for intelligence called IQ, we may forget that the idea of a unified concept of "intelligence" is also a fabrication and not real. This calls into question the validity of such numbers and grades for making decisions about people's abilities or future opportunities because grades are the same kind of reification, a fabrication we made up, a fictitious, unified symbol for an uneven, complex network of practices, and competencies.

In our case, we see that writing effectively is important for students and citizens, so we seek to characterize it and students in order to make divisions and categories. But these divisions are not universal to people or their writing. We make them up in order to grade student writing. We create the construct of "good writing" or the ideal essay, then reify it by pretending (or forgetting) that the construct we use to grade is not real and does not exist. We then grade actual writing, and use those grades as if they are real indicators of something that exists outside of our construction of it. As I discussed in Chapter 2, Haswell explains how judgment from exemplars and prototypes work, and that in fact, we need some exemplars and prototypes to make judgments on texts. This sounds similar to reification, and it is. But the fictions we use in prototype, exemplar, and classical categorical judging, according to Haswell, are constructs that are understood *to be constructed* (hence the name), thus they might be reconstructed in other ways, for other purposes or students. We know that constructs are not real, but when we forget this fact, then they become reifications, fictions that we treat as real and that manipulate us, instead of the other way around.

As I've mentioned in Chapter 4, and as I'll discuss below in the question on grades and motivation ("Don't some students want or need grades . . ."), Daniel Kahneman shows through numerous studies conducted over several decades how our brains make judgments through two systems, one fast and one slow. Among the heuristics of the fast system, which is the more problematic one, are ones that need reifications, or categories that help us make quick decisions about things and people. Thus we all can and often do fall into the mind-trap of reification. It's how our brains make important quick judgments, whether we think of that process as using exemplars, prototypes, or categories of dimensions, all these processes of judgment work from constructs that often become reifications out of necessity that we must be mindful of, and continue to question. Labor-based grading contract ecologies avoids grades as reifications of some kind of measurement of an outcome or of "good writing," and allows students and teacher to use our necessary systems of judgment without letting them harm students through the application of grades as reifications.

Furthermore, Gould explains that reification goes hand and hand with the second fallacy. The fallacy of ranking, which is "our propensity for ordering complex variation as a gradual ascending scale" (24). Thus if grades are reifications that rank writing, but those grades are just constructions, then what are we ranking? Why is any particular order a good order? Why not some other order if there is nothing essential about what "good discourse" means or is? More importantly, as Gould illustrates in his discussion and David Goldberg argues about racist discourse in Western traditions, ranking is a part of a much longer racist, and White supremacist, tradition in Western intellectual history. The impulse to rank is too often naturalized itself.

Aristotle based a career on categorizing and ranking plants and animals, then on rhetoric. Later on, the West generally ranked people in terms of race (Hannaford; Goldberg; Gould). Ranking has been deeply embedded in racist thinking, discourses, and logics, mainly because it has been deployed as a way to justify a number of racist, empirical, and colonial projects over the last four hundred years. Education at all levels has been and still is a part of these racist projects because it is deeply enmeshed in the hegemonic structures that keep our societies and cultures going, even though there is always the counter hegemonic in the hegemonic.

In schools and universities, the fallacy of ranking is wrapped so tightly into the reifications of grades, it is difficult to separate them. We must be extra cautious when our purposes for grading are to measure things like outcomes in students, particularly diverse students. Outcomes are predetermined constructs themselves, and we could end up treating them as reifications (unquestioned, naturalized constructions), then rank people based on those reifications without considering seriously who we are ranking and what literacies they bring with them, or the legitimacy, usefulness, or consequences of the outcomes themselves that we promote. It may be better, as Chris Gallagher has argued, to think in terms of consequences, not outcomes. Consequences are open-ended, so can embrace and encourage a multitude of unexpected outcomes in students' labors. Labor-based grading contracts provide an ecology easily amenable to noticing, understanding, analyzing, and exploring the unexpected consequences of students' reading and writing labors, without forcing a particular standard.

No one in any school or university is immune to the fallacies of reification or ranking. As Edwardo Bonilla-Silva reveals about how White people talk about race in the US, we may be perpetuating racism without being racist ourselves. We're just judging good writing, which may be a reification, but which ends up excluding and oppressing some students because of who they are or where they grew up. Our reifications of measurement that we enact through grades on writing cannot help but be reflections of the White middle-class *habitus* that all teachers to some degree embody. In short, my first answer to this question is that addressing writing course outcomes may not be the best ecological purpose for any grading ecology because of the way grades tend to be dubious reifications of measurement and rank students unfairly by privileging a White middle-class *habitus*.

Now, let's assume that the constructs we wish to measure in students is appropriate, that we—teachers, students, and other stakeholders—have agreed in a particular site or school that we value a writing construct and it is not a real thing, but one we've consciously chosen and will present that way to students. This construct is articulated in our outcomes for a writing course. Let's call our construct "using evidence appropriately to prove a thesis for an academic audience." Now, how do labor-based contracts address these kinds of outcomes, ones perhaps more critically maintained in a classroom and writing program? Because we do not need to rank performances in a labor-based grading contracted course, any deviations

197

from what might be expected, from a standard that the teacher holds and promotes, can be more educative for students because they set up learning questions
that pose problems about the nature of judgment and the politics of language:
Why is *that way* of using evidence better than this way for academic audiences?
Where did that academic audience get these ideas? Why do some of us already do
this in our writing, while others use evidence differently to back up a thesis? Why
is this kind of information called evidence for this claim and this other kind not?
Who made those rules up? Who do those rules benefit in our classroom?

The point in feedback cycles and discussions of revisions is not to adhere to
one way of doing language, although most students may be trying to emulate
the standard, but equally to understand where the standard comes from, who
automatically benefits from it, why that group benefits, and what other reasonable possibilities there are to achieve the same rhetorical practices and goals, even
though many academic readers, who embody White racial *habitus* do not accept
those ways with words. Furthermore, this grading ecology honors the actual
learning happening, the laboring, the working, that students do, regardless of
what they can produce at that moment. The ecology has addressed the outcome
in a more critical way, and not harmed students who do not already come embodying a White racial *habitus* in the process.

Having said that no grading system can guarantee that students will learn or
develop literacy competencies, I do think that labor-based grading contracts offer conditions that help students learn and develop along explicitly stated course
goals better than conventional grading ecologies. I need to note my vocabulary
here. I have ethical problems with course outcomes. They are too narrowing
and White supremacist. I prefer to frame all my courses and programs around
course *goals*, which are broader and can accommodate a wide and diverse range
of discourses, logics, and practices. Goals are what Chris Gallagher calls "aims"
(or consequences) in his good critique of outcomes. Gallagher explains that
outcomes tend to articulate the end point of learning. In deductive fashion,
"outcomes are determined before the educational experience commences, even
as they describe its end" (44). Outcomes ignore the students in front of us in
favor of an idea of them and an idea of what that fictional group should learn,
which of course may be based on teachers' senses of their past students. Thus,
outcomes are a reification of learning that are created in part from a reification
of future students. Furthermore, outcomes depend on those who create them to
use another reification, one about what their fictitious future students need to
learn from their writing classroom in order to succeed in their fictitious futures,
all of which no one can really know. What ends or outcomes do we tend to articulate in writing programs? Dominant academic English that is informed mostly
by White, middle-class *habitus*, which ends up privileging students who come

embodying White racial *habitus*. This is deeply unfair to the students I've taught at SIUE, Fresno State (an HHSI), and UW Tacoma, where most of my students have been working, first generation, multilingual, and students of color. Thus the use of outcomes to grade in writing courses is typically unfair for many students, and usually White supremacist.

Gallagher promotes "consequences" or "aims," because they "are always emergent within educational experiences; they cannot be fixed beyond or outside those experiences" (47). Labor-based grading contracts work very well with course aims or what I call goals, which are broader and open to what we end up getting through our labors. Goals are articulated usually as labor or practices themselves, and seek the emergent, defining the consequences of labor as learning, making anything produced by students potential learning. Thus the students' and my job as teacher is to understand what learning is happening in the labors of the course and make order out of it, make meaning from practices. This is why there are lots of recursive ongoing reflective activities in my classrooms and an attention to mindfulness through labor logs, journals, and labor tweeting. Thus a course goal may sound like: "practice multiple, meaningful and self-conscious ways of reading texts for various purposes." The labors that make up the terms of the contract would need to make sure that students practice multiple ways to read for different purposes.

Notice that the goal is to practice something purposefully, and it doesn't define in any fine way what the outcome or product of those practices will be. It doesn't even define what the practice will look like or be experienced as. These things are too difficult to determine beforehand. In many ways, having to delineate carefully the labor processes in each set of labor instructions (discussed in Chapters 3 and 4; also see Appendix D for example labor instructions) helps me as the teacher make sure that students meet such course goals, which are always reiterated in each set of instructions.

The ethical point in using labor-based grading to meet course goals instead of outcomes, however, is more than avoiding White language supremacy. Using labor as the way to calculate course grades is also ethical on the grounds of fairness in what is graded, or what counts toward grades, and so what counts as course goals. What we can ask from students and what we can expect from everyone in the room regardless of where they come from or what *habitus* they embody should be the same or commensurate. And yet we know we cannot expect the same ecological products from every student. We never get the same things from students, even when the instructions or prompts are the same. This is common knowledge, yet this is often what we assume in conventional point-based systems because we typically only grade the end products of student labors. And yet still, we don't really want to read the same essay twenty-five times. We want variety, surprises, difference. We inherently value diversity. So we like the fact that literacy is varied and inherently chaotic, that our students never produce the same things in the same assignments. But our grading systems' assumptions don't match these literacy values. Our assumptions about literacy production and how grades are calculated should match. When they do, the ecology better addresses course goals and is fairer to all.

Thus, labor-based grading contract ecologies directly address course goals, because course goals are labor-based (about practices), not product- or outcome-based. This means that course grades directly reflect how well students meet course goals. But no system of grading can reliably or fairly address narrow, pre-determined course outcomes, unless you have a perfectly homogenous student population that matches your teachers' *habitus*.

HOW DOES A TEACHER DETERMINE WHEN A STUDENT HAS DONE ENOUGH LABOR TO GET CREDIT FOR ANY GIVEN LABOR/ASSIGNMENT?

One might also ask what is the absolute minimum effort expected in order for an assignment of labor to be okay or count? In Chapter 2, I discussed Mandel's classroom in which he accepts pretty much whatever students turn in, even if it is rushed and slap-dashed. He explains that some students may not be ready to learn and that he encourages his students to turn in "self-discipline and self-respecting work" (629). I tend to use this default position when checking students' labor. In my classes, there is always some product that their labor results in or produces, even reading a chapter for the next class session. These products may be a short piece of writing posted on our CMS or a brainstorming document. Additionally, I incorporate a labor tweet/Slack[42] in most labor instructions. This typically means checking labor is a fairly quick job, unless my job is to respond in some way. I don't work very hard at making distinctions in labor products between good or bad labor, or whether enough time was spent. Instead, I use a simple rubric to make my determination of whether a particular product of labor is done adequately and reflects the expectations of labor in the activity. Each labor assignment is complete and counts if it meets in the affirmative the following questions:

- Is the labor product(s) posted on time and in the correct place?
- Does the labor product(s) include everything I asked for and meet the minimum word count?
- Is there a labor tweet/Slack(s) posted as instructed (if applicable)?

---

42   As mentioned earlier, I have moved recently to a closed message system (Slack) that only students in the course see, but is similar in use as Twitter.

This is easy and fast to do. If all three criteria above are a "yes," then I don't record anything in my gradebook. I only record something in my gradebook when they don't meet the labor requirements. Usually, I record late/incomplete assignments or when a student does not participate in class. For a number of reasons, I assume that if a student is present, then they are participating. Some may have concerns about "on time" labor, or exact due dates that seem inflexible; however, part of what we negotiate in our contract is the number of late (assignments turned in within forty-eight hours of the due date and time) and missed assignments (those turned in after the forty-eight hour rule). So I feel students have at least two opportunities (week one and midpoint renegotiation) to set the rules of the grading ecology such that they all can be successful. And of course, I'm paying attention as well.

Perhaps the most contentious item above is the second one. It technically may appear to be judging quality, and as I've said already, the labor-based grading contract prohibits using quality judgments as a basis for grades. I try to keep "everything I ask for" in any given assignment to quantifiable items, such as having a response for two questions I might provide. However, there is a big difference in using quality to determine a grade on a performance and using minimum notions of quality (i.e., did the student respond to all three questions, and thus what do I consider to be a response to each question?) to determine labor done, which is not a grade. The second way of judging is more generous and does not use distinctions of quality, except for bare minimum notions of quality or of content to determine the presence of what is asked for in the labor, and most important, it does not rank performances by quality. Is there the presence of language that addresses in some way the question I asked students to respond to?

Let me show you how this typically looks. Let's say the labor assignment was to read a chapter from a book, tweet/Slack an annotated page about something interesting the student read, and write a 150-word paragraph that reflects upon that interesting idea found in the chapter so that we can discuss them in class the following day. And let's also say that in those labor instructions, I asked students to spend between forty-five to sixty minutes reading and annotating, then ten minutes brainstorming the idea found in the text, and a final fifteen minutes writing the paragraph, which amounts to a total labor time of around seventy to eighty-five minutes. So the expectations of labor are about seventy to eighty-five minutes of reading and writing, a tweet, and a 150-word paragraph. After the appropriate due time, I check the posts and tweets. A student, let's call him Liang, tweets and posts a paragraph that is exactly 150 words but doesn't include the one thing I asked for in the paragraph, a discussion of the interesting idea from his annotated page. This labor is therefore incomplete. So I don't count it, but I don't ask him to do it again. Now, if he doesn't post his paragraph, then I do ask that he complete that.

In the drafting step of the labor instructions, I usually put a bullet list of the elements I ask them to include, making clear that they are not an outline, unless I want them to use it as such. For labor like this, I might say: "Be sure to include in some way in your paragraph of at least 150 words the following elements," then offer a list, such as:

- A short one to two sentence summary of the chapter section that you are responding to;
- A quote from the section that helps us understand the words and ideas you wish to talk specifically about; and
- Your discussion of or response to the idea or quote that helps us think about it more deeply.

As you can see, I'm doing a number of things in these instructions. I'm implicitly leading them through a rhetorical set of moves that many academic texts do. I'm making sure that they talk about something in the text specifically. And I'm preparing them for our class discussion on the text. I'm not concerned about what exactly they say, or that they get everything accurate to my standards. Those details are for our discussion in class, or for a response I may make to them, but they are not a part of my deciding if their labor is adequate. As long as they have these three parts in the paragraph in some form, the paragraph is complete labor done.

Now, let's say Liang's paragraph was 150 words, had all three elements above, but seemed slapped together, hasty, and just repeated the same idea in the quote over and over. So it isn't very deep, and I can see it won't help him much. I might even say that he isn't trying very hard. His labor is still complete and counted, but I would reply to him privately and tell him what I'm confused about in his paragraph and labor, how I don't think this kind of work will help him in meeting our goals. What happened? How are you finding the quote and how are you trying to think about it? Were you confused by the instructions or the chapter? Can you try harder next time or use the labor more mindfully to meet the goals of the course? I would point him to the third bullet, and ask him how his discussion helps us think more deeply about the quoted idea. Depending on the activity and the product, I might even suggest alternative timings for such labor steps or other practices. Often I'm telling students something like, "if the instructions say that you should spend twenty-five to thirty minutes, factor a bit more time for yourself, maybe forty-five minutes. It appears you may need some extra time to produce the kind of material that will help you in the class." Most important, I leave Liang's learning up to him, and so I must leave much of his labor to him.

Now, some might say, well, you're leaving the time spent on labor a mystery. You may ask for a certain amount, but you don't know how much actual time is spent. Correct. This is not something I can measure with any accuracy or consistency across students, even if all students dutifully record everything in their labor logs. Many students tell me during each quarter that they don't log everything, small bits of labor here and there, which may amount to significant differences in actual labor time over a quarter. This is the nature of time and trying to keep track of it. It's elusive. But putting aside these problems of accuracy and consistency, if I used the labor logs to account for the time spent on the assignment, I believe it would be too enticing for students to fudge those numbers. That is, it is too tempting for even good students in the heat of the quarter, when much is happening and lots of unexpected things press them for time, to simply input more time in their labor logs, which makes the logs inaccurate, useless in our reflective activities on them because they are not actual representations of their labor practices, and now busywork. I tell my students this, because they may think that I'm going to use them to keep track of their labor for their grades. I do not. I want the logs to be true mindful and reflective devices that help them pay attention to their labor as practice and understand their material conditions in the quarter, which may help them do things differently. In the end, much of what I count as complete labor is done by trusting my students and done in as quantifiable way as possible, always trying to give the student the benefit of any doubts I may have, even if I may still ask that student about their labor if it seems to be less productive that I hoped for.

HOW CAN A TEACHER RESPOND TO STUDENTS WHO PUT IN MINIMAL ENGAGEMENT IN THE LABOR, OR TRY TO GAME THE SYSTEM?

Other ways of voicing this line of questioning are: Do labor-based grading contracts allow teachers to avoid engaging with the quality of students' writing, or the substance of it? What do you do about writing that is poor or substandard? If we grade what we value, does grading on labor suggest that we do not value quality? If we grade what we teach, and we grade on labor, are we valuing labor at the exclusion of writing quality? I've suggested responses to several of these questions in the above discussions already, so I'll address the gaps mostly in this section.

Conventional quality-based grading ecologies often teach students to game the system because the object is to get the highest grade in the most efficient way possible. And products are all that matter when it comes to acquiring those grades. In those ecologies, since labor is hidden and not rewarded—in fact, more labor on an assignment may often feel like it is punished (and certainly not rewarded)—many students' responses will be to find ways to game the system, to do the least amount of work while getting the best grade possible. There are also some students who, no matter what, simply are not motivated to be in college or in the course. They don't see the value of learning to write in the ways the course is designed to offer. While these are two different groups of students, I believe labor-based ecology's priorities help both groups and address this question.

And yet, no system can stop a student from plagiarizing or doing the minimum work, or just inching by with just enough labor to meet the contracted terms. But many systems can punish students even more. As can be taken from my example above of the fictitious student Liang, I do not try to stop students from doing the minimum, but I do let students know when I see signs of it, and encourage them to do more. Each student has the right to do what they wish and accept the consequences of those decisions. Conversely, I do not have the right to force them to do otherwise. I try to be compassionate and honest with all my students, without beating around the bush or being permissive. If I think a student is doing the bare minimum and could work harder or longer on their labor, I tell them. If I see signs that a student is uninterested in the course's labors, I ask them about it. But I try to get them to articulate the problem first, usually in the labor journal entries or reflective work we do each week in and out of class. Often it's an email or two, or a conversation after class privately.

I don't think it's a good idea to coerce students into doing more work than they are willing or able to do simply because I feel they should. There are consequences for a student not meeting the terms of labor delineated in the contract, so I let them know this, but I don't force more labor on a student who isn't willing to initiate that labor, and I don't think badly of students who for whatever reason are not ready to do the work we ask of everyone in the class. Even if I'm right about how much more labor they should be doing, making a student do more work or redo work they've done because it was shoddy or hasty, likely will result in the student grudging me and feeling negative toward the class or the work. I'm not convinced this leads to effective, long-lasting learning. I'm more convinced it leads to students not liking the class and the work we do together. Many times, I've come to find out that I'd read the signs wrong. They were engaged in the class, and other things were happening in their life. Usually, just me asking if they are okay and showing them that I noticed their lack of labor or engagement in the class helps them. Some of the time, they thank me for noticing.

Developing quality and learning are labors that the people in the ecology must be responsible for on their own, not made accounted by the grading system in the ecology. Labor-based grading contract ecologies separate grades from two competing elements in any assessment ecology: (1) the labor and work that students do, or the ecological processes; and (2) the quality of writing judged by someone and the learning through dialogues and reflections on languaging, or the ecological parts (such as, feedback, responses, assessments, etc.), learning products, and people. Grades are then applied to the first and not the second. Figure 6.1 shows graphically how one might represent these elements of the ecology.

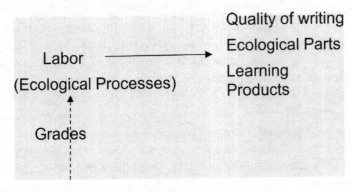

Figure 6.1. Grades are applied to labor, not to so-called quality or judgments of learning.

Normally, grades would be on the other side of the figure, applied to the learning products, thus completely ignoring the labor that produced those products. While this system does leave room for students to game it by not doing the expected labor or doing the minimum, this is no different than any other system of grading. All grading systems can be gamed. The game in conventional systems is simply different.

There are five philosophical assumptions that inform my labor-based assessment ecologies, and explain why I don't force students to do more labor than they are willing, even if that labor is technically asked of them by the contract.

Philosophical assumption #1: *Every student can learn exactly what they can at that moment, and no more, no less.* This sounds circular, but it's really a way for me to express the simple idea that all of us have our own lives and learning journeys, that people do not always neatly fit into the same educational boxes, that our learning is always deeply contextual and contingent—that is, we learn in our complex lives that are always in process. Sometimes we are not ready for a course or lesson or idea, and it doesn't mean we are incapable or dumb or lack ability. It means that at that moment in our lives, other things take up our time, mental space, and attention. We are not ready. It is not our time for that idea, lesson, or course. Because of this, I try hard to never make moral or value judgments on what I see my students doing (or not doing), because I am only seeing what I can, not all there is (this how I try to avoid the WYSIATI heuristic explained in the next question, "Don't some students need . . ."). Sometimes I ask them: "I notice that you haven't been spending a lot of time on the course's labors. Do you think you are ready to do this work with us at this moment in your life? Would you like to talk about what has been keeping you from doing the labors?" I don't try to solve problems for them, only be a compassionate listener who reflects back to them what I hear them saying, and help them hear what that means for their progress and learning in our course. If they ask, I offer practices and ideas. This, I feel, is a responsible way to acknowledge and respect each student's unique learning moment on their terms, while still keeping my promises around administering the contract.

Philosophical assumption #2: *Learning literacy practices is better done in non-coercive ecologies of compassion, encouragement, and risk taking.* Too often we try to coerce our students, or force them to do what we know is good for them. We are the experts. We know. But we are not simply teaching subjects (as in ideas and topics) *to* students. We teach *with* students about themselves and others *as subjects*, helping them get all they can at that moment.[43] The first assumption above explains part of the reason for this assumption. Being non-coercive means I accept where my students are as they come to me, which may be uncomfortable for me initially. To teach in this way, I must consider the learning place we make together, the ecology. Doing this means the class as a whole must try hard to be compassionate to each other.

Learning the very private yet social labors of languaging requires trust and care. Writers must trust readers, particularly ones who will make judgments of their literacy practices. And everyone must engage in practices that reveal their ways of caring for the wellbeing and learning of others. We must labor for others first, then we learn. While it seems a cliché, I believe when we give, we receive, but we do not receive just to get. It is a kind of paradox in learning and compassion. In fact, I think we learn the most important things in community with others, giving and tending to others. Learning is not meant for the individual alone, but is meant for the individual among others. We often learn for the sake of others. Cultivating this principle in the ecology creates a kind of space that encourages students to take risks, to fail, to do more, to want to learn because learning becomes something more than a selfish activity of achievement. The labors of learning become compassionate communal activities that are larger than oneself. And I think, this philosophy helps convince more students to not simply do the minimum labor possible, but more.

Philosophical assumption #3: *One is all and all is one.* This principle sounds quite abstract but it really is not. I mean it quite literally, and it is associated with the previous principle. When one of us needs help, we all need help. When one

---

43   I am thankful to my former colleague, Rick Hansen, at Fresno State, for this articulation. Rick used to say that we teach students not writing.

of us fails, we all do. When our colleague next to us is struggling, we all struggle. Everyone's learning in our ecology is connected. If José is having trouble with a reading we are doing, and Kayla sees José but does not help him, then both José and Kayla end up being hurt. José may not be able to discuss very well the text in the group activity later, or offer much feedback on Kayla's or their other colleagues' papers. All students in the ecology are interconnected, and this is especially true in learning environments that involve developing literacies.

The historical practice of grading has fooled us into believing that learning in school is an individual endeavor because grades are doled out to individuals. Your grade is yours. You earned it. We then forget that grades are not learning. They symbolize it incompletely. We forget that we learn in communities with others. We learn through dialogue, through exchange, through interaction, through sharing, through doing with others—and this is most true for learning language. Language only exists through acts of exchange and sharing with others. To extend the cliché I opened with in the last point, *we not only give to receive but receive in proportion that we give.* Thus the vast majority of anyone's learning amounts to a series of gifts that others have given, that we each humbly accept in cycles of giving and receiving. I know this sounds pie-in-the-sky and hokey to some, but I'm convinced that if a class believes it and acts on it, it always changes that ecology for the better. It allows us to trust that what someone is doing is all they can at that moment, even as we encourage and push them to do more in the next moment.

Philosophical assumption #4: *It's better to design grading ecologies that encourage learning, since teachers cannot actually teach anything.* Of course, we know that teaching isn't the same thing as learning. But I think one possible outcome of this premise is that one cannot consciously teach anyone anything, if teaching means that we distribute or bank (to use Freire's metaphor) information or practices in students. What we do is create conditions, ecologies, that encourage learning, stunt it, or do some combination of the two. Understanding the nature of learning in a particular group of students can be the focus of the assessment ecology, and one can do this by paying attention to the labors that embody learning and practices.

In some form, I am often asking my students, "what did you learn?" or "how did you learn that?" This isn't just creating a process and condition for them to pay attention in a mindful way to the fact that they are learning something, or even how they did it. It is also a way for me to gather important information on this particular class and what elements in the ecology they respond to the best. In some classes, it has been the group responses and assessments to each other's work that has engaged and energized my students the most. In other classes, it has been the particular ways I ask them to read and think about the ideas as they read. In still other courses, students seemed most moved to learning by the way we frame all activities as compassionate activities, ones that help their colleagues first before themselves. Using the multiple kinds of labor data produced in my classes to investigate how learning is happening helps me understand each ecology as a unique one, learning about it as we go. What I often find is that the best responses as a teacher are to step aside while still tending the ecology at the macro level, and let learning happen in the ecology without feeling the Whitely impulse to step in, take over, and be the benevolent savior in charge (see Chapter 1's discussion on Whiteness as a set of habits).

Philosophical assumption #5: *Good assessment assumes that students want to learn, and does not stop those who will try to game the system.* I prefer to think the best of my students. I believe that people generally will respond in kind to ecologies that not only encourage them but think highly of them. We often live up or down to the expectations of us by others. How much would you do for someone you know really, deeply respects you and trusts you with important things? When a writing assessment ecology sets lots of boundaries and gate-keeping mechanisms, when it doesn't trust students to be responsible on their own for their own learning and the course, when it tries at most turns to make students accountable for assignments and other work of the course, it sends messages to students that say, "you are not to be trusted," "you must be held accountable or you'll get away with doing nothing." These kinds of ecologies tell students that they have little goodwill and are not mature enough to want to learn. I don't believe this.

Time and again, my students respond in responsible ways. They show me how dedicated they are to learning; how much labor they will do even though they work and have family obligations; how wonderfully generous and optimistic they are about what our class offers them, what knowing about language might give to them. Most do not try to game the system. Some likely have and do. I won't design an assessment ecology around the few who wish to game the system. That is a futile cause. I will admit that I prefer to see most things half full, rather than half empty, but I'm okay with that, and okay with some gaming the system, knowing that they still got from the ecology exactly what they could. Me forcing them to do more would not have changed that. And the cost-to-benefit ratio of further eroding our relationship and souring the student's attitude toward writing and school by forcing their feet to the labor fire of our course is too out of balance. The ways that the ecology must change would harm everyone else. It is the TSA mentality. Because there is one shoe-bomber on one flight, everyone is now suspect and must take their shoes off to be checked. I'd rather spend my time engaging those who are willing to engage, while encouraging those who don't initially. I'd rather the student leave the course and quarter thinking about what they were willing to get and didn't get, and why, instead of what I made them do against their will.

DON'T SOME STUDENTS WANT OR NEED GRADES SO THAT THEY KNOW HOW WELL THEY ARE DOING OR SO THEY CAN BE MOTIVATED TO DO THE WORK?

This question is really about how rewards and motivation work in classrooms. Often when teachers try to address this problem in writing classrooms, we neglect the nature of the grade-reward and how that kind of reward is situated and circulates in our assessment ecologies. Sometimes, this question stems from our own feelings that most students who fail to meet our standards in our classrooms do so because those students are lazy or simply don't apply themselves. Sometimes it stems from our sense that grading by so-called quality of writing helps students see their progress—that grades can show progress of learning to write on a linear scale, which can appear helpful to students. But these senses of the benefits of grades come mostly from our own unique histories of learning and subject positions in our own writing or English classrooms that we took as students. They come from our own histories with grades on writing, which usually are not the norm for students in the classrooms we teach.

In most cases, grades simply cannot motivate students to learn or help them know how they're doing in the course, even though they may appear to do so. The scholarship on grading writing supports this conclusion. In fact, it is unanimous about the unreliability or inconsistency and the idiosyncratic nature of grades (Bowman; Charnley; Diederich; Dulek and Shelby; Elbow; Starch and Elliott; Tchudi). Just as much research shows how grades and other kinds of rewards and punishments actually de-motivate and harm students and their abilities to learn anything (Elbow, "Ranking"; Kohn; Pulfrey, Butera, and Buchs). Furthermore, when grades are generated by comparing students' writing to a single standard, then language diversity and difference in *habitus* is squelched, and a dominant, White racial *habitus* is reinforced as the norm for discourse. This doubly harms many students of color and other students who come to our classrooms with non-White and non-middle-class *habitus*.

Of course, there's also the pedagogical argument that most of us know against grades as helpful feedback. In Stephen Tchudi's hierarchy of assessment practices, grading is on the opposite end from feedback (xii–xiii). Grading is closed, summative,[44] has a high degree of institutional pressure on it, and is very limited in what it can say to a student about their draft. It is not very helpful

---

44   In the literature on response and classroom assessment, there is often a distinction between summative and formative feedback on writing. Summative feedback typically happens at the end of a cycle of drafting and explains what is present in the draft, usually in evaluative terms, answering questions like: how good is the draft or how does it compare to a standard? Formative assessment is future directed and attempts to offer ways to improve or revise the draft, asking questions like: What potential is in this draft and what might be done next?

in showing a student anything about what they've done or what they should work on in their writing. The second practice, feedback, is open and formative in nature (Elbow, "Ranking" 188), and has little institutional pressure placed on it to say or do anything in particular. Unlike feedback, grading mostly punishes those who do not meet an idiosyncratic judge's notion of what counts, which is no better illustrated than in the way we read error (Williams, "Phenomenology"; Anson), as discussed in the fourth statement in Chapter 4 about grading being an inherently racist and White supremacist act. If there is no pedagogical value to grading, then the only function it has left is to uphold linguistic hierarchies in student formations. In fact, grading is one primary way that teachers and schools maintain what Lippi-Green reminds us is "Standard Language Ideology" (SLI), a set of beliefs about a dominant English that James and Leslie Milroy first articulated. Lippi-Green defines SLI as:

> a bias toward an abstracted, idealized, homogenous spoken
> language which is imposed and maintained by dominant
> bloc institutions and which names as its model the written
> language, but which is drawn primarily from the spoken lan-
> guage of the [White] upper middle class. (67)

I've added a racial qualifier to Lippi-Green's statement, but given the rest of her discussion in the book, it's easy to see why this is appropriate. Even if you don't agree, then I offer my own arguments about the dominant White racial *habitus* in writing standards here and in other places (*Antiracist*; "Classroom Writing Assessment"; "Friday Plenary Address"), or perhaps philosophical arguments (Goldberg) or those from writing center work (Greenfield; Grimm) provide more evidence for referring to SLI in racialized terms. I tend to refer to SLI as White language supremacy or White language privilege.[45] So on multiple fronts, grades on writing only appear to help students know how well they are doing, and in fact, do other more harmful things.

Our own brains and idiosyncratic histories work against us when understanding grades' function in classrooms. If you've always been rewarded by the system of conventional grades, it is difficult to really understand how grades hurt most students in most writing courses, how they can be an inhibiting factor to learning. You may be able to sympathize with this concern, but if you're still putting quality-based grades on writing, then you likely cannot empathize.

---

45   The distinction I make between White language supremacy and privilege is in the focus of my statement. White language supremacy highlights the systemic, the way in which systems and structures make White *habitus* central in language assessment ecologies, while White language privilege focuses attention on the preferred habits that give benefits to racially White individuals or groups.

This is typical for most writing and English teachers, and the research on judgment suggests answers. As I've discussed briefly in several places already, Daniel Kahneman explains a heuristic that our brains use to make judgments, in this case about what our students need to be motivated and to do well in our classes, which may not be the same as what *we* needed or were motivated by in *our* pasts as students, which often is our models for good pedagogy and assessment practice. The heuristic is called, "what you see is all there is" or WYSIATI. He says about the heuristic:

> It explains why we can think fast, and how we are able to
> make sense of partial information in a complex world. Much
> of the time, the coherent story we put together is close
> enough to reality to support reasonable action . . . [but]
> neither the quantity nor the quality of the evidence counts for
> much in subjective confidence. The confidence that individ-
> uals have in their beliefs depends mostly on the quality of the
> story they can tell about what they see, even if they see little.
> We often fail to allow for the possibility that evidence that
> should be critical to our judgment is missing—what we see is
> all there is. Furthermore, our associative system tends to settle
> on a coherent pattern of activation and suppresses doubt and
> ambiguity. (87–88)

This means that if we aren't slowing our thinking down; gathering enough data about our real students in front of us; looking carefully at that data; posing rival hypotheses from those we start with; being more self-conscious and mindful about how we decide to construct our classroom grading ecologies; asking questions to students about what the effects of grades and particular kinds of failure are on them in our classrooms, particularly students who are *not like us*; we will use only the information that is most apparent to us and suppress doubt and ambiguity that may arise from those data alone.

What are those data? When it comes to the usefulness of grades, it's often our own experiences with grades. Were you explicitly trained in graduate school on the history, philosophies, psychology, study, or effects of grades? Were you ever shown alternative ways to grade or produce grades in classrooms in grad school? If not, and I'm guessing most readers of this book were not, then you rely on what you inherited from your own educational past. If your own narrative of success in writing happens to have in it grades, and grades helped, rewarded, and motivated you in school, then they may appear to be helpful, rewarding, and motivating in your own classrooms. That is all the data we see about what motivates students in writing classrooms, and our brains suppress any doubts or ambiguity about this conclusion. So, how do you really know that your grading of writing helps students know how well they are doing, or motivates them to write? What data or evidence do you actually have for your answer? The brain's WYSIATI heuristic suggests that you need very little to be confident in whatever answer you have.

Another brain heuristic, the availability heuristic, also works against us in these matters. This heuristic explains the "process of judging frequency by 'the ease with which instances come to mind'" (Kahneman 129). This heuristic typically substitutes one question or problem for another. For instance, we might ask ourselves are there more instances of crime in the US today than twenty-five years ago? The answer is no. Statistically, violent or property crimes per thousand citizens has fallen since the early 1990s, according to a recent Pew Research study (Gramlich). But ask the casual person on the street, and you'll find, as the Pew study found, most U.S. citizens feel there is more crime today than in the past. This answer comes from a substitution of the question asked with a different question, one that might be worded as, "have I seen more instances of crime recently?" Because it is easy to call to mind many instances of crime in our communities, given the kinds of stories that news media focus on, these limited data distort our sense of the actual data on crime, and we neglect data that counter the conclusion that there is less crime today. If the data we have available to us is what we use to make decisions, like how our students will or should react to grading, or how they feel about it, or do grades tend to motivate students, then depending on who we are and what experiences are available to us, we may often find that we have substituted a different question for the one we were trying to answer. We may only be asking, "have *I seen* grades motivate students and help them understand their progress?" This is not the same question as, "do grades motivate and help understand progress?" or even, "are grades the *best way* to motivate students in writing and English courses?"

We cannot know if our grading ecologies really help students without systematically gathering data to find out, and this starts with asking students about it first. Perhaps, we might ask this question to our own students differently to get more helpful information: What would be the best motivation for you to do the labors of the course? What would it take for you to be self-motivated to achieve the goals of our course, to work more than you are asked to? Our own educational biases as writing teachers cloud our judgment much of the time on such questions. Mine certainly has. My biases are partly why I turned to labor-based grading contracts, but they are not why I stayed with them. I gather data every quarter through labor logs, weekly reflections on our labor and the class, and my own data collection, and discuss much of it with my students. I comb through it every year. This is why I continue the practice. I see empirically and through my students' words that students prefer not to have grades, prefer to find motivation on their own, and can understand their progress in writing through words alone. Grades actually muddy these waters.

Most of us who teach writing have always loved language, loved reading, and done well enough in school to get degrees and certifications to become teachers of English and writing. We don't usually understand completely how the psychology of grades work on most of our students, students who are not like us. We often are people who were so moved by language that we wanted to teach it to others. We typically are the ones who did well in English and writing classes. Perhaps so well that we didn't have to take the kinds of writing classes we now teach. As for me, I was required to take the kinds of courses I teach, first-year writing. I barely made it through my first-year writing course at Clackamas Community College, didn't finish the same course at Linn Benton Community College the first time around. High school English wasn't much better for me. Moving within White language supremacist systems of judgment was difficult for me for a long time, even with teaches who cared and meant well. Grades always contradicted the messages I read in teachers' feedback. I persevered despite the system, not because it.

Did grades motivate me? Only to the extent that I was averse to the bad ones. I did what I needed to in order to not get a bad grade. But that is not learning, it is what educational psychologists call "performance-avoidance" and it's not the preferred stance for learners who grow. The best stance is "performance-approach," or a "focus on attaining normative competence" (Pulfrey et al. 683). Pulfrey, Butera, and Buchs show in their studies that grades cause performance-avoidance and harm students' learning. So grades may motivate some by fear, but that motivation doesn't go very far. Grades do not motivate to learn or take risks. And to be honest, grades only help students when they are perceived as rewards and praise, but real praise doesn't come with the tacit threat of punishment, which all grades do. I doubt any of my teachers meant to be malicious, but they certainly instilled fear in me, a fear of failing. Fear doesn't build intrinsic love of learning and knowledge, love of language and writing. Fear doesn't move someone to help another with a learning-problem in a course. Fear doesn't urge students to spend more time on a project because it is the right thing to do for learning something new. Fear keeps us from being hurt or punished.

Because of these dynamics, it may be useful for a teacher to ask how grades might implicitly or latently function to produce fear of failing in their classrooms. In what ways are their tacit threats that are made by the possibility of low grades? How might the assessment ecology be coercing students by fear? How might it really motivate students, not coerce them? Real motivation comes from an engaging and encouraging ecology that allows the people who are a part of it to open up, expand, help those around them, make mistakes, see their language and world as larger and larger, as endlessly possible, as always becoming (in both senses of the word). So do students need grades in a writing course to know their progress and to motivate them? No.

HOW CAN A TEACHER MAINTAIN HIGH STANDARDS WHILE USING GRADING CONTRACTS?

Another way to ask this question is: Can labor-based grading contracts make distinctions for how well students meet the objectives of particular assignments? Can they make distinctions for students' varying levels of writing skill or craft? To what extent does the quality of the labor's ultimate product factor into the assessment?

Standards, often in lists of expectations and rubrics, are reifications. We should be very cautious with how we think about and use any standard of literacy in our classrooms and schools. What are the evidence-based consequences of the use of any standard? Are they harming some students or privileging others? Is it the source of any unfairness? As I explain in Chapter 3, Lippi-Green makes a good argument for why it is nearly impossible to have standards, and as the CCCC Statement on Students Right to Their Own Language affirms, using standards of language against students amounts to one social group attempting to oppress or dominate another through judgments of language (Committee on CCCC 2–3). I make a more thorough argument about this in another place (*Antiracist* 25–75), so I won't get into those details here. But I will ask an important question to any teacher who believes in what the CCCC statement says yet feels a need to hold students to some dominant standard: What exactly do you think it means that a student has a right to the language of their nurture? What constitutes a right to one's own language in a writing classroom? Might the heart of the statement be demanding, because of the nature and consequences of grades, that students have the right to not be graded by someone else's version of language, even when those students may be attempting to gain fluency in that same version of language in that same classroom?

In one sense, standards held against students and used to dole out rewards and opportunities is a dangerously unethical thing to do. Standards-based grades are how our world and schools have become unjust. If, as most of the literature on literacy tells us, learning a dominant English means that many students of color, working-class White students, and multilingual students must reject or change their identities (Villanueva, *Bootstraps*), then holding students to some standard goes against the philosophy of labor-based grading contracts as a socially justice classroom project.

What this question often really means is: How can I as the teacher hold my students to a dominant White middle-class *habitus* as the standard of discourse in a labor-based grading contract ecology? Or how can I have my White language supremacist cake and eat it too? You cannot do this. When it comes to students meeting standards, it's not really up to the teacher. A teacher cannot hold a student to any standard by using it to grade writing. This is confusing measurement with learning (or with teaching). Often the assumption is that if we measure to a standard, we are holding students to that standard, or a particular dominant *habitus*, because it is the guide by which we say any student passes or fails the course. We think that this use of the standard makes students have to write to it. While many students may use our rubrics and other heuristics to help them write to the standard we've placed in front of them, this kind of assessment ecology mostly helps those students in striking distance to the standards. It rewards the rewarded. It only allows those who already have the closest relation to the White, middle-class *habitus* of the standard to be rewarded, and gives them the biggest share of those rewards, which starts with grades. Sarah Amed calls this aspect of the phenomenology of Whiteness "proximity," and proximities are inherited (155).

The idea of maintaining standards in this way in a classroom is an illusion. We think we are supposed to be preparing students for their futures, but we are mostly helping to maintain larger systems of oppression by maintaining a dominant, White *habitus*, that is, maintaining White language supremacy. I'm not saying we shouldn't use the biases and ways with words that we know and have been trained to use in order to respond to students' writing. I'm saying don't use *your language* as a single standard to grade students' languages because of what those grades mean outside of our classrooms, and because if we really want diverse students to succeed, then what we are saying we want is students with a wide range of proximities to our own *habitus*. Thinking in terms of standards as high and low, and as keeping them, amounts to unfair and unethical assessment practices, and usually White language supremacist ones. It limits many students' future opportunities based on language practices that they had very little choice in acquiring and that is very difficult to change in a semester or quarter.

If we believe what the linguists say, that all languages and dialects are equal in communicative value, then holding one up as the standard for communicating, because that's the way things are, or that's the version our students will need in the marketplace or their next class, reinforces a White supremacist system of raciolinguisitc oppression that is similar in function to the way sympathetic Whites in the south turned a blind eye to the evils of slavery. The truth is, similar to sympathetic Whites in the old south, we teachers benefit from the status quo, some of us more than others, even though we may be critical of the way those benefits are distributed. We have very little to gain by changing the way we think about White language supremacy unless we stop thinking about standards in terms of individuals' profit or loss, and instead see them as communal or structural, as a part of our social justice obligations.

From a pedagogical standpoint, perhaps a more communal and interconnected way of thinking about "maintaining standards" is to reframe the idea in a more critical and linguistically inclusive way. What if instead of thinking about how we should *maintain a standard*, we saw our job as *engaging students with various standards*, or understanding a dominant standard from various, equally valid perspectives in order to critique it and know its politics, understand and fight the power dynamics that it produces as a standard in other rhetorical places? These purposes allow our classrooms to offer various readings and judgments of our students' literacy performances in order to engage in dialogues about that judging, not to find the correct one, but to understand the various standards of language and communication we have in the room. This assessment work is done by deconstructing a single dominant standard as associated closely to a White racial *habitus*, not simply to mimic it, but to see it as historically created, made up of assumptions and values that are not fixed, natural, or inherently better than any other, and attached to intersectional racial formations in society. Thus, the idea that a teacher must maintain some standard of writing is counter to larger critical projects most of us promote in writing courses, and it amounts to enforcing the status quo of White language supremacy.

DO LABOR-BASED GRADING CONTRACTS MAKE STUDENTS MORE ANXIOUS OR STRESSED OUT THAN CONVENTIONALLY GRADED COURSES?

Over the years, I've had some complaints about labor-based grading contracts creating some stress or anxiety over "staying on top" of the contract or the pace of our weekly labor. Some students worry about whether they've turned everything in each week, but by the midpoint, most if not all these anxieties go away. Much of this anxiety, I'm sure, is built by years of courses that were looser about deadlines and late assignments, or they are anxious because the idea of acquiring points seems safer, more knowable, to them. They know how to behave in conventional grading systems, even if those systems create performance-avoidance and a lack of risk taking. They are so used to educational settings that put them into a performance-avoidance stance that any other stance makes them more anxious and uncomfortable. The historical weight of twelve or more years of being graded in the same ways makes for some anxiety over labor-based systems, particularly with students who have historically performed well in quality-based grading systems, who usually fit a middle-class White racial *habitus*. These students are more uncomfortable with the amount of labor they are now required to do, since in the past it often took less time and effort to get the grade they wanted. They were rewarded for being themselves, so writing was a comfortable affair, always validating, never too demanding—to invoke Amed's analysis, good grades were an inherited, racial proximity. In a labor-based grading ecology, these students may for the first time experience discomfort, have to do more work, and provide more effort in between class sessions. They may feel like they are being asked to do busy work, or that their grade is worth less because the higher grades are now accessible to more students in the class.

The best way I've found to address such concerns when they arise is to ask students about them, and let them reflect in writing, then talk it out with each other. But I also prompt them to be self-critical of their first responses. Why do you feel, I might ask, that the amount of labor I'm asking of you is too much? I'm not asking anyone in the class to do more labor than anyone else, so why are you so special? Why should you be exempt from the labor we all agreed everyone should do? Yes, this kind of question is meant to be uncomfortable, not rude or accusatory. I remind them that I ask this question compassionately, and that when we feel uncomfortable we are likely about to learn things. I also prompt them to consider our charter for compassion, that we are all in this learning-work together. So we must try to stop thinking selfishly about our own grades and our own work, but think of how that work and our grades are connected to everyone else's in the classroom. It's hard, and doesn't always work, but most at least try to understand this very difficult concept.

Most of the time, my reassurance that they are doing fine in the class and giving them updates on what I have marked for their contracts helps with the anxiety. I make a point to tend the contract each week in class, making references to it, asking if students have questions about it. The short discussions we have on our weekly labor journal freewriting in class also helps relieve some anxieties. It's often a moment when students can commiserate with one another, and realize that many are in similar situations, that the reading that week was hard for most everyone, that having little time to spend with one's family is a common concern, that juggling one's work schedule and a full course load is something everyone struggles with each week. Sometimes, I offer changes to upcoming due dates or slight alterations in the labor of the course to accommodate pervasive issues I hear. I've found that just allowing students to voice their anxieties with each other in class for five to ten minutes a week, and only responding to those issues that really need some structural changes, works the best.

217

HOW CAN LABOR-BASED GRADING CONTRACTS ACCOUNT FOR OTHER KINDS OF LABOR, LIKE EMOTIONAL LABOR, THAT SOME STUDENTS EXPERIENCE OFTEN IN SCHOOL, SUCH AS STUDENTS OF COLOR, TRANS, AND EVEN FUNDAMENTAL CHRISTIAN STUDENTS WHO LEARN IN LIBERAL CONTEXTS?

This question could be read as asking how does a contract incorporate emotional labor into the grading mechanisms of a course. I've not found ways to do this, and I'm not sure how any system can, so I'll answer it as a question about how labor-based grading contracts can facilitate an acknowledgment and discussions on the emotional aspects of learning. A group of CUNY teachers and graduate students recounted this story to me (anonymously) in a Google doc that prepared us for our online conversation, so I offer it as a way to flesh out this really good question, one that is always difficult to consider in any writing pedagogy and assessment ecology:

> A friend of mine who works at an art school (which is a PWI [predominantly White institution]) told a story the other day about a teacher whose one Black, trans student would never show up for class on the days when he knew that the conversation was going to be about race or gender. The teacher asked the student about his absences, and he explained that he didn't want to (yet again) be in the position to explain his own self-worth and life experience to a room full of (mostly) White and (mostly) cis folks—that this kind of labor was exhausting, uncompensated, and beyond the pale. I'm wondering how contracts might account for other kinds of labor: let's say, for example, the emotional labor that it can take for this student to, like, be in this school, or the kind of labor that it takes a first-gen college student to navigate new structures without the benefit of a support network that understands higher ed, or the labor involved in translanguaging. Are these things that can be "explicitly" accounted for? How so, if so?

The emotional and psychological strain and effects that the labors in writing courses asked of students, particularly ones that focus their assessment ecologies on antiracist and other social justice projects, as my contracts do, can be hard on some students. Who those students are will depend on the context, school, course, and who is in the course. But we should be mindful of who we are generally talking about. It's not usually White, middle-class students, or culturally and linguistically dominant students. The anxiety that these students may feel in certain discussions is not the same anxiety because that anxiety is abnormal for cisgender, middle-class Whites, and almost always short lived. Once the class or discussion is over, the anxiety likely goes away. This is due to their typical material existence in society and school. They are the status quo. They are not confronted daily with their Whiteness, or maleness, or cis-ness, or able-bodiedness. These subjectivities are the norm, so calling attention to them as sources of privilege and unearned power and opportunities can create feelings of defensiveness or guilt, but it is important work that needs to be done compassionately if social justice and social change is the goal. It's also important in writing classrooms, because these are the *habitus* that most literacy performances are judged against. They form in large part the standard.

For students who embody dominant *habitus*, feeling some anxiety and discomfort is good for them. It is a signal that something has gone unspoken but is now spoken, once silent and now heard. The periodic but brief moments of anxiety help Whites and other dominant subjectivities grow and become more self-aware, as long as they and everyone around them firmly understand that the classroom is a place of compassion, that the discussion isn't looking to harm anyone, but help confront the structural things that do harmed already. Part of this culture of compassion is the lack of grades and the reassurance that what the ecology expects is their labor.

Sometimes I find it helpful to frame discussions about various social justice issues as ones that produce anxiety and discomfort in a particular direction, depending on the topic and subjectivities involved. The anxiety was already there, only moving in a different direction. For instance, when we talk about ideal writing and standards as that writing that is inherently and essentially good, clear, logical, etc., many students of color and multilingual students in the room may feel anxious because they know they have been judged as failing at language in those ways in the past. This is an anxiety that often feels like self-blame and it is directed at them. But the anxiety is not purely self-imposed. It stems from the standards in the ecology and moves toward students of color. But once those standards have been identified as coming from a dominant set of arbitrary beliefs, reifications about language that might be changed, or at least understood as associated with a White racial *habitus* that confers privileges to those lucky enough to already embody it, then the anxiety changes direction. When Whites are uncomfortable in conversations about White privilege, it is good to recognize this and discuss how in the rest of our walking lives in society and other classrooms, the places you feel comfortable in, likely they do so at the expense of people of color. The anxiety is still there. It's just not directed at them, at White people.

Most of my undergraduate writing courses have consisted of mostly students of color. When you are only one of two White students in the classroom, you may feel attacked, demonized, or guilty during such discussions that are led by a teacher of color. What that scenario should reveal, I think, to the student (and perhaps the class if the student is willing to share such emotional strain) is the common emotional strain that most students of color feel in situations where the demographics are switched, which is the status quo in most other spaces in our society, and the status quo in upper division courses where White students have been the majority. It can be a compassionate moment of empathy, but one that should be recognized as unique in U.S. society and transient for the White body. Yet it is not unique, nor transient for most Black, Asian, Native American, or Latinx students. It is not transient for trans students, or disabled students.

I work hard to keep the "us versus them" language out of the classroom when discussing issues of race and racism. We also have our charter for compassion, and I remind students of the compassionate behaviors that we came up with to help us through our labors. I remind them that being uncomfortable is okay and that it means you are learning, changing, growing. That we can choose to be "brave" in moments of discomfort. However, I try to remind myself that I'm a middle-aged man, who usually has more years under his belt than most of his students, that I spent much of my life working through these issues intellectually, emotionally, and practically in my life. I try to remember that I didn't always respond to these discussions as I do today, and that I too have more to learn always, that I often only see what has been placed in front of me (WYSIATI), not everything, but more than my students (because I've had more time to see differently), that as Krista Ratcliffe reminds us, I should always be working to hear my students' ideas and concerns, even when I may feel they are immature and less thought out than my own, that they have a right to have those feelings and ideas at this moment in their lives, a right to work through them at their own paces, just as I had the right to do so at my pace. Thus my students have the right to their emotional responses to the work we do. But what no student has a right to is to harm another student, and this is the muddy, middle ground. What constitutes emotional harm? I cannot answer this question definitively.

What complicates all this is that the effects of any ecology can be uneven. The example above of the Black trans student in a predominantly White institution is not an easy situation. There's no simple solution, and many teachers may feel, rightly so, that they are unequipped to handle the conversation that is recounted. I know I still do. Having an open and humble mind about such encounters helps tremendously. Reminding myself that I need not be the savior (a habit of Whiteness) in such situations is helpful. A willingness to let go of my own goals or needs for the student in question can help me listen and ask better questions to the student. It is their education that is being negotiated, not mine. I'm not saying that we should not have expectations for our students, only that we do not need to hold on to them too tightly in moments like these. A teacher's expectation that somehow the class would benefit from the Black trans student's presence and contributions in a particular discussion or activity may be true, but it is no more important than that student's need to feel emotionally well and not overly strained by the conversation or class because they feel they get no break in their daily lives from such discussions. You, as the teacher, cannot know whether the emotional strain is simply discomfort or something more, only the student can. The teacher can ask, but only ask and wait for the student's answer. And we must do the asking very carefully, since a question from an authority figure may come off like a command.

It is comforting for me to remember that while we can prepare for many possibilities in our classrooms, we cannot prepare for all of them, and while we can want to address issues around emotional labor and strain in our classrooms, issues we know exist, we may not always be able to know beforehand if those issues will arise in this particular class with these particular students. Labor-based grading contracts that include explicit discussions about how the class will try to define their labor and engage in it mindfully and compassionately, set up conditions that are more favorable and generous in such situations as the above one. There is no clear and easy answer to this question, only a kind of wait-and-see then be-compassionate-and-let-go answer.

DOES A LABOR-BASED GRADING SYSTEM UNFAIRLY DISADVANTAGE SOME STUDENTS BECAUSE OF ITS EMPHASIS ON LABOR?

This question is similar to ones about the structural and systemic nature of privilege in contemporary society and whether using labor in grading has the ability to alleviate such injustices in the classroom. Or are we dealing with one set of systemic privileges at the expense of accentuating another set? Are the criteria by which a teacher judges labor just as embedded in systematic racism, for instance, as the criteria that have been used to assess writing quality? As many conscientious teachers understand today, many students have complex lives. My students at UW Tacoma, surely do, as did those at Fresno State. Often they work and go to school. They have other obligations, such as taking care of family. All these things take up and fragment their time during the quarter. It's unfair to ask students to quit their jobs or neglect their families to take our courses, particularly when those jobs and families may be helping them get through school. These conditions, which are becoming more typical across the US than most of us may like, create some challenges for labor-based grading contract ecologies, as they do for conventional grading systems.

As can be seen in the contract details, my labor-based contract asks students, first and foremost, to spend time doing the labor of the course. This is how you get the grade. This would seem to create some disadvantage for those students who have these other demands on their time, demands they do not fully control. It would seem to privilege a similar group of students that I've been saying traditional graded ecologies already privilege.

The problem of how much time any student can or should put into a course still exists in a conventionally graded classroom. The conditions that create such time constraints for many students come from larger structural forces in society, the rising costs of higher education, the reduction of Pell grants and other support for college, changing admission standards, increasing wealth gaps between the very rich and everyone else, the need for more students to work while going to school, among other factors. Labor-based grading contract ecologies do not create the disadvantages of limited time that many students face, but they do make this larger societal problem more present and obvious, which may fool some into believing it creates the problem. But asking for labor and using it to grade students does not cause the structural inequalities of time that students live with.

No matter the grading ecology used in a writing classroom, the same students will still face the challenges of limited time for school work. The ecology does not control the outside forces that limit students' time. At least in a labor-based grading contract ecology, we can pay better attention and account for the labor and time we are asking of students, and not hide behind standards and claims that we "don't grade based on effort." In standards-based, conventionally graded ecologies, the time required to meet some standard usually remains invisible because it isn't technically what the teacher is asking for. They are asking for quality, but what that means in reality for many students of color and multilingual students is more time than their White, middle-class peers. Privilege moves in typical directions.

It can be argued that labor-based grading contracts actually address these time issues better than conventional grading systems. In a conventional classroom where writing is graded by a standard, where one succeeds by satisfying the quality demands of a teacher, the only difference in time demands on students is how explicit those demands are to students. Usually, there is no mention of how much time some assignment will take. In fact, time on task is not a factor in the grading at all. Quality is. And this can mean that students who do not embody a White racial *habitus* in their languaging will need even more time to complete or to do well on writing assignments, but this more time spent is hidden in the curriculum, and hidden in the assessment ecology because it is unspoken and tacit. Furthermore, more time on a task does not guarantee anyone a higher grade. In the words of Eduardo Bonilla-Silva, this kind of assessment ecology produces racism without a racist teacher.

In a labor-based grading ecology time is more obvious—and I'd add: it is more honestly used in the ecology because it is explicit and negotiated, which makes it fairer and more ethical. In conventional graded ecologies, the amount of time required to get the grade you want is always unknown, but still required through its proxy in the ecology, a single judge's sense of quality. All the ecology has done is not *technically* required time on tasks to get a grade, but time in writing and reading are always required if quality of writing is used to produce grades, and likely more time is required in quality-based grading systems for many students, particularly for those students who come to the course with *habitus* other than the White, middle-class, dominant ones that are demanded in the ecology.

Hiding labor in the way conventional graded ecologies do accentuates the unfairness of the system. Meanwhile, everyone else does more labor for lower grades, and is told they just need to work harder, work like those students over there. Be like them. It is unfair. Labor-based grading contract ecologies create a clear formula for how much time is required in order to get the specific grade a student wants. If two criteria for fairness are explicitness in the pathways to the grades students seek and universal or open access to those pathways for all students in the ecology, then a labor-based grading contract ecology is fairer than standards-based grading systems, especially for students who have lots of demands on their time outside of school. In fact, by these criteria, conventional grading systems are unfair and socially unjust because they ignore the unequal amounts of time required by various students in the classroom and create pathways to course grades that are not open and accessible to everyone.

And yet, it is still possible to ask too much time of our students without considering their real-life demands on their time. I find this equally unfair. Because the amount of labor (usually defined by time on tasks and word count only) is explicit, students and teacher can mitigate the disadvantage of limited time by measuring and tending it during the semester or quarter. And because labor-based grading contracts calculate course grades by amount of labor, this justifies keeping track of and paying close attention to our labor during the quarter. One way my courses attempt to address this issue is to use our labor logs and labor journals as ways to pay attention to time on tasks and have discussions in class together about how much time we are spending on our labors, when, where, and to what effect. I always make a point to ask students frequently how well they are able to keep up with the class's pace and workload. I try hard to listen carefully to their concerns, and not suppress my own hearing of criticisms and doubt of the fairness and effectiveness of our ecology. I don't always adjust the workload, but occasionally we do. We make it a communal discussion and decision.

I also look carefully at when students are doing the labor of the class, and how they labor in their tasks. In most of the labor instructions, I include at least one step in which they must, pause in their work, and Slack something to the class.[46] I call these labor Slacks, and they give me some indications of the flow of labor in the course. If most of my students are doing their labor at the last minute, then we likely need to talk about what is causing this dynamic. Labor slacks and the reflections on their labor logs in their labor journals allows us to pay attention to how much labor we are actually doing, and address any concerns on the fly.

In the end, by being mindful of our labor, keeping track of it, measuring and tending to it in these explicit ways, we learn to appreciate what we can do in the fuller context of our lives, which means we can and sometimes do take those contexts into consideration as we move through the course and adjust how much we expect of each other. Doing all this automatically allows us to pay close attention to ways the ecology may be harming some students with time limitations on their lives outside of class and address those problems as they happen.

HOW MUCH LABOR-TIME DO YOU TYPICALLY REQUIRE IN FIRST-YEAR WRITING COURSE?

Because I have asked students to keep labor logs and because I try hard to keep track of my own practices as a teacher, I can answer this question pretty definitively. In FYW courses at UW Tacoma, where most of my students work twenty or more hours a week and go to school, my students tend to log about seven to nine hours per week of labor outside of class in a ten-week quarter. I usually assign an estimated ten to twelve hours per week of total labor. The FYW course that I discuss in Chapter 4 (seen in Table 4.2) is a typical course for me. From Table 4.2, the average total minutes of labor is 4,709.6 minutes, which comes to 7.89 hours per week of labor in a ten week period.[47] This is pretty average in any group of students over the last three years. Likely, we can adjust this figure up by about one hour, since several students do not fully complete their labor logs during the tenth week of class, nor do they include the labor put in between the tenth week and finals week, when they prepare for our final one-on-one conferences. This is likely due to the fact that once they've done the final reflective

46   As mentioned earlier, I use private communication tools, such as Slack, which function like Twitter.

47   In a more recent FYW course, the second course in our stretch sequence, the class average was 9.4 hours of labor per week (the highest was 12.35 hours/week, and the lowest was 5.68 hours/week). As of the end of week 6, my current FYW students average 8.75 hours/week of labor, while I've on average I have assigned 11.6 hours of labor.

assignment that uses the information in their labor logs, many may feel no need to continue doing the logs, or the increased stress and rush to finish the quarter pulls them away from their logs. However, these numbers are consistent with the labor logs of the class in question, and previous FYW classes. On a campus where most students work and go to school, this amount of labor each week strains them, but is doable.

Each campus will be different, and working in a semester system will affect this. For instance, at Fresno State, a semester system where few of my students worked as much as my Tacoma students, although a good portion of them were working students, the average labor I expected per week was about nine to eleven hours a week. Typically, I will tell my classes that I tend to favor the old metric of three hours of labor for every one unit of the class per week. At Fresno State, our FYW courses were four unit courses, meaning I should have expected about twelve hours of labor per week outside of class. At UW Tacoma, our courses are five units, so I should expect fifteen hours of work per week. It was more reasonable at Fresno State to get close to that number than it is at UW Tacoma because of the working conditions students tend to have. I try hard to account for these conditions, and ask explicitly about them each quarter. I'm often surprised at what students' assumptions are about how much labor for our class they expect to do or feel is most beneficial. Discussions about this topic can lead to really interesting discussions about what students assume it takes to succeed and persist in school.

One might begin such discussions by looking at a few resources on study time for college students. There are lots of such articles and resources available online, most are written for teachers. However, I don't find this a problem for students. For example, Rice University's Center for Teaching Excellence offers a detailed page about estimating appropriate time requirements for reading and writing tasks in courses. The website Statista offers statistics of average college student study time by major. Regardless of the resources you offer your students up front, my point is to begin with some evidence-based way to understand appropriate labor time requirements, and have students consider as many factors as possible, like do all courses require the same amount of time to succeed in, and what other factors in your life require your time? The answers to these questions can help you talk in more informed ways about exactly how many hours a week the labor of the class will ask of everyone.

Finally, it should be noted that labor expectations may be determined or understood in a number of ways. There is (1) the ideal labor time required for most students to succeed in a class, expressed by both the teacher and the student; (2) the actual time for individual students to do succeed in the class; (3) the estimated labor time for all work calculated and provided by the teacher; and (4) the time each student feels they have available to spend on this class in order to get what they want out of it, which may fluctuate week by week. Thus, I think, discussions about how much labor we can ask of each other on a weekly basis can be negotiated and should consider our own ideal estimations of time needed to accomplish our course goals (as a class and individually), how much time realistically each student can commit to the class, and what that will mean in terms of meeting learning goals and the minimum requirements of the grading contract.

HOW WELL DO LABOR-BASED GRADING CONTRACTS KEEP STUDENT RECORDS (GRADES) PRIVATE?

Typically, what FERPA tends to assume about students' grade information is that it is individual grades or points received for assignments turned in, and this information is confidential. No one else except the student may know about that student's personal information, unless the teacher has received from the student written permission to share the student's information with others. So a teacher would be in violation of FERPA guidelines if they posted exam or essay scores outside their office door, or called out essay grades in the class. But when there are no grades on performances, things like extra labor for A-grades are more obvious to everyone in the class. In my labor-based grading contracts, extra labor on a class presentation or doing more assessment letters for those outside one's writing group for others in the class offers ways to raise their grade, and is more obvious to everyone else in the class. This might appear to violate FERPA, since other students know that the student is doing the extra labor. But there are no grades or points for such extra work revealed to anyone. And other students do not actually know if the student in question received credit for the extra labor. To let students know their progress, or what I've got recorded in my gradebook, I either hold individual conferences periodically and tell them, or I send them an email to their university email.

Furthermore, I do not assume that knowing *that* a student is attempting extra labor is the same as knowing what credit they got for that work, or that anyone who knows this information will know if the student has met all the other labor requirements of our contract. Just because you know that a colleague in class is doing extra labor doesn't mean you know where they are at in terms of meeting our contract. There are many aspects of all classes in which students' progress and work is common knowledge or shared information in the class. And it should be this way. The assumption that other students shouldn't or cannot know the general progress of their colleagues rubs me a bit wrong. I don't mean that everyone should be in everyone else's business, or that everyone's grades are public information. I mean, knowing that a few of your colleagues are doing presentations for the class's benefit in order to raise their course grades is a good thing. It can be motivating or be a way to demonstrate good citizenship in the class.

WHAT ARE A TEACHER'S RESPONSIBILITIES TO HELP STUDENTS PREPARE FOR THE TRANSITION FROM A LABOR-BASED GRADING ECOLOGY TO THE MORE CONVENTIONAL ONES THAT ARE LIKELY IN THEIR FUTURES?

I feel very confident that labor-based grading ecologies can prepare well students for future assessment ecologies that use grades and points, ones that grade their writing. In order to prepare a student for a conventionally graded assessment ecology in the future, you do not have to grade them now. One assumption in this logic is that the main way a student will learn how to react to such grading on their literacy performances is to grade them now, to show them what kinds of grades they can expect with the level of effort they currently are putting forth in the writing. But as I argue above ("Don't some students want or need grades . . ."), grades are highly unreliable markers, especially across disciplines. So expecting a writing teacher's grading to be an accurate indicator of what that same student will get in college next year, or in sociology next semester, or biology next quarter on their writing for those very different graders, on very different writing, is unrealistic. Additionally, since grades themselves also are poor motivators and harmful to learning in a number of ways, they seem doubly bad as a method for preparing students for their future readers, even ones who will grade their writing. So the logic that preparing students for their future is to grade their writing now doesn't hold up. We should not assume that the only preparation, or even the best preparation, for students' success in future graded courses is grading their writing now.

Better preparation for future rhetorical situations, regardless of how writing is assessed in those future situations, is to offer a variety of tools for students to understand those rhetorical situations as such. One of these kinds of rhetorical tools is knowledge and experience with understanding the nature of judgment, that is, how language is judged and what the politics of that judgment is. Labor-based grading ecologies can be great preparation in this kind of criticality since they offer critical insight by working in a different ecology that conventional ones. Experiencing an alternative is the best way to gain critical insight into systems that have become naturalized and normal. One can begin to see all the things about those systems that one took for granted as natural, such as the arbitrariness of standards and the unreliability of grading as a measure of anything about writing. My ecology's focus on antiracist writing assessment, which pays close attention to the habits of Whiteness in judging language (discussed in Inoue, *Antiracist*; "Classroom Writing Assessment"), I believe, is an important tool in this kind of preparation for students.

We should keep in mind that no assessment ecology can, by itself, prepare students for the future ecologies they will be in. Partly, we don't know what those ecologies will be. Partly, we aren't those readers and graders ourselves. Partly, we aren't asking them to write in those disciplines and contexts, nor are we usually a member of those discourse communities. And partly, preparation for future assessment ecologies is not the function of assessment ecologies. It's not what they are designed to do in most cases. They are designed to measure and rank students. That's it. Measuring and ranking do not prepare students for anything. They may get students used to being ranked, but that isn't the same as being prepared to succeed in a new writing assessment ecology. So even in a labor-based writing assessment ecology, students must engage in practices that help them think through the ways that those future ecologies function. One really good way is to compare those ecologies' features and elements to the present, labor-based one. My students do this work in our discussions of dimension-based rubrics, the negotiation and renegotiation of our grading contract, our weekly labor journals, and through our problem-posing letter activities. These periodic reflective activities become more potent as preparation tools when situated in a gradeless context because that context makes students' ideas, judgments, and thinking more open to risk taking and disagreement.

HOW MIGHT LABOR-BASED CONTRACT GRADING FIT WITH THE IDEAS OF UNIVERSAL DESIGN?

This has been a growing concern of mine in my courses. I'm not sure if more students with registered or identified learning and other disabilities are more willing to be identified or ask for accommodations today than fifteen or twenty years ago, or if there is a higher frequency of college students with such disabilities, but I notice more students with disabilities today. This could also be a product of my own growing awareness of disability. A good assessment ecology, one that is socially just in every way, should be self-consciously designed to meet the principles of universal design. According to the National Center on Universal Design for Learning, universal design for learning (UDL) is defined in the Higher Education Opportunity Act of 2008 (HEOA) as:

> a scientifically valid framework for guiding educational practice that:

(A) provides flexibility in the ways information is presented, in the ways students respond or demonstrate knowledge and skills, and in the ways students are engaged; and

(B) reduces barriers in instruction, provides appropriate accommodations, supports, and challenges, and maintains high achievement expectations for all students, including students with disabilities and students who are limited English proficient.

The three key principles that help define UDL are: (1) "provide multiple means of representation," or offer information and learning to students in a variety of ways; (2) "provide multiple means of action and expression," or offer a variety of ways to do the learning; and (3) "provide multiple means of engagement," or offer a variety of reasons why students should do or engage with the learning asked of them (National Center for Universal Design). I'll avoid my own personal uneasiness with placing "limited English proficient" students with students with disabilities, since this isn't the place to discuss those issues. However, I do feel that the core assumptions of UDL are safe assumptions, that designing curricula for those on the margins and borderlands also meets the needs of those who dwell in the middle of the ecology.

In terms of the scholarship and impressive work being done around UDL and disability studies, I am still learning and perhaps most excited about ways it may help improve labor-based grading contracts. I feel I have a lot to learn and perhaps to alter in my own practices. As of now, I understand labor-based grading contract ecologies agreeing well with UDL principles. In fact, I think, in some ways, it encourages teachers and students to collaboratively interrogate and discuss such questions. For instance, the contract negotiations at the opening and midpoint of the course can be explicitly framed to engage students with the three principles of UDL, asking them: What means of representation of materials will they be able to use most effectively? What ways of learning writing and reading practices will they find most effective or engaging? What kinds of reasons for learning and doing the labor of the course will they find most engaging? What kinds of reasonable accommodations can the course make for those who feel they will have trouble meeting the labor demands of the class while still maintaining the expectations of the course? These discussions can lead to a conscious designing of course materials and methods that draw on the ideas revealed in the negotiation, even including them in the contract itself.

Students may not immediately know their answers to these questions, or may have limited answers in the first week of the course, so it is a good idea to ask again at the midpoint renegotiation. A teacher should be careful to be sensitive to students' privacy and unease with sharing potentially personal information with the class as a whole. I find it best to begin such discussions about revising our contract or making labor instructions and class lessons more accessible and engaging by asking for responses in writing and in private. This allows me to see if there are any potentially embarrassing or private information that students may feel uncomfortable sharing or that may compromise them in class. If so, I compile lists of ideas from the entire class for discussion, instead of attributing specific ideas or comments to individual students. We use these ideas to form our revisions or decide on the most universal ways to do our work together.

Weekly labor log or journal entries might also be used to periodically prompt discussion around UDL principles by asking students to reflect upon their labor practices from personal, experiential ways. Taking stock in the best and worst ways their learning practices have been working each week. For instance, weekly labor log entries, or periodic informal reflections, might ask students: what means of representation of materials have they been able to use most and least effectively that week? What ways of learning writing and reading practices have they found most and least effective or engaging that week? What kinds of reasons for learning and doing the labor of the course have they found most and least engaging? Having a brief discussion with them in class about such quick prompts can offer the teacher lots of information to alter the course on the fly, which is how I have framed such discussions in my classrooms.

One common UDL concern about labor-based contracts is their attention to weekly, and almost daily, labor activities, all of which must be turned in on time and in the fashion asked. Some have suggested that strict schedules like those often found in my assessment ecologies can disenfranchise students who have difficulties with executive function. Executive function is a set of competencies that are associated with the prefrontal cortex and deal with long-term planning, impulse control, managing time, setting long term goals, monitoring success, and modifying strategies. Joyce Cooper-Kahn and Laurie Dietzel define the cognitive concept as: "a set of processes that all have to do with managing oneself and one's resources in order to achieve a goal. It is an umbrella term for the neurologically-based skills involving mental control and self-regulation" (Cooper-Kahn and Dietzel).

A strength I feel that labor-based grading contracts have is to negotiate with students labor needs that are flexible enough to provide appropriate affordances for a range of learners, even those with difficulties around executive function. Beyond reflecting on such difficulties and helping students look for ways each can work with their own unique challenges with the labor expectations of the course, one might use the list of executive functions by the psychological researchers Gerard A. Gioia, Peter K. Isquith, Steven C. Guy, and Lauren Kenworthy as a heuristic for testing and designing one's curriculum and contract expectations. These researchers offer a list of eight executive functions, which I quote below from Cooper-Kahn and Deitzel. Teachers and their students, if time permits, can use this list to consider how a course's assessment ecology, even if it is not a labor-based grading contract ecology, accounts for students with executive function issues, and is universally designed. For instance, one might ask: how does the ecology (the grading contract, for instance) provide guidance and multiple methods for helping students who may need it along each of these executive functions as they pertain to the labors of the course?

- **Inhibition**—The ability to stop one's own behavior at the appropriate time, including stopping actions and thoughts. The flip side of inhibition is impulsivity . . .
- **Shift**—The ability to move freely from one situation to another and to think flexibly in order to respond appropriately to the situation . . .
- **Emotional Control**—The ability to modulate emotional responses by bringing rational thought to bear on feelings . . .
- **Initiation**—The ability to begin a task or activity and to independently generate ideas, responses, or problem-solving strategies . . .
- **Working memory**—The capacity to hold information in mind for the purpose of completing a task . . .
- **Planning/Organization**—The ability to manage current and future-oriented task demands . . .
- **Organization of Materials**—The ability to impose order on work, play, and storage spaces . . .
- **Self-Monitoring**—The ability to monitor one's own performance and to measure it against some standard of what is needed or expected . . .

The National Center for Learning Disabilities offers this list of common activities that require executive functioning:

- make plans
- keep track of time
- keep track of more than one thing at once
- meaningfully include past knowledge in discussions
- engage in group dynamics
- evaluate ideas
- reflect on our work
- change our minds and make mid-course and corrections while thinking, reading and writing

- finish work on time
- ask for help
- wait to speak until we're called on
- seek more information when we need it

The more I think about executive function and my experiences in my classrooms, the more I'm convinced that there is a bigger problem with this particular cognitive function in many students. Or perhaps, today's issue is that Millennials may do these kinds of cognitive tasks in a different way than generations before them, like mine. Thus one way my own labor-based grading ecology has adapted to helping students with the executive functioning demands of our classroom is to use labor instructions, not assignment sheets that are essentially a prompt or description of the assignment and its expectations, and provide such instructions as early as possible.

Labor instructions are step-by-step process instructions that focus on minimum time spent on each step, what a student should do, and what is produced. Focusing on labor, on the steps it takes to complete a labor task, on the time each step requires, and what the outputs should be, are ways to help guide students in executive functioning. To aid in time-management, I provide an overall estimated time a student will spend on the labor activity. Every week I also give students all the labor instructions, due dates, and estimated times for each labor in a list on our course website for the upcoming week. This helps them see what is ahead for the next fourteen days and the time expected of them for the labors of the course. Labor Slacks in most instructions also offer practice at self-monitoring by consciously paying attention to their labor practices and feelings.

Finally, I think it is important to note that my own emphasis on mindfulness and contemplative practices in my classroom and in all labor instructions is not inconsequential here. One thing I read into UDL's principles is its concern for how explicit classrooms are concerning the nature of the learning, how that learning happens in the labors and actions of students, and why students are engaged or not. Labor-based grading contracts offer an easy way to make such elements of one's assessment ecology explicit and a topic of discussion and negotiation. And my own response as a teacher with grading contracts has been to consciously incorporate methods that guide students along UDL's three principles, often unknowingly, testing the waters along the way and adapting as we go along in the quarter or semester. The above list of tasks that require executive function also offers a kind of heuristic that can prompt teachers and students to inquire, discuss, and change on the fly the ecology so that more students have fair and equitable access. There are no guarantees, but the use of a labor-based grading contract seems to offer an exigence for such discussions with students.

HOW ETHICAL IS IT TO ADVOCATE FOR LABOR-BASED GRADING CONTRACTS WHEN MANY FACULTY MEMBERS WHO TEACH WRITING ARE IN VULNERABLE POSITIONS?

This is a tough one, in part because it requires a lot of local and private knowledge that I cannot have if my response is going to be applicable to any given reader. But I'm often asked about this issue. What I can say is that each teacher must decide this question considering the real issues they face around tenure, promotion, job security, concerns and perceptions of grade inflation in their department or school, and student evaluations. Is using labor-based grading contracts a risk to a vulnerable teacher? Maybe, but less so than one would think; then again, who you are and what institutional position you hold matters in this. I have male privilege, but I'm also a person of color. I've worked mostly at four-year, teaching-intensive universities with relatively lighter teaching loads than many others.

The one thing that I know for sure is that my relationships with my students dramatically improved and deepened when I moved from conventional grading to a hybrid contract, and all the questions and concerns about the contract evaporated when I moved to a labor-based grading contract. My student evaluations improved also, now being quite high. While I do not want to make this as a promise to other teachers, I can say that since I have used grading contracts, which began in 2004, I have had no grade complaints or students coming to me or my department to complain or inquire about their course grades, during or after the semester or quarter was over. Most of those courses and students were located in schools that served primarily working-class, students of color: Southern Illinois University, Edwardsville; California State University, Fresno; and University of Washington Tacoma. In short, grading contracts have benefited me as a teacher, not hurt me. No chair, or dean, or provost has come to me accusing me of bad teaching. I have been tenured and promoted, all the while being quite vocal about my use of grading contracts.

At a philosophical level, a teacher might also consider the ethical threshold as a teacher of literacy that they will not cross. Grading diverse students' literacy performances is my threshold. It is simply unethical of me to do so, knowing what I know and have experienced as a student and teacher. Knowing the research on the harm that grades inflict on all students and their motivation to learn, knowing about grades' unreliability, knowing about the heuristics of judgment that cause us to make bad fast decisions, knowing of the almost universal racial implicit bias that is seemingly hardwired into our brains, knowing about the structural racism and White language supremacy connected to standards, knowing about the linguistics scholarship that shows the equality of all languages and dialects in terms of communicative effectiveness and their abilities to allow their users to think critically and creatively, and knowing the clear statements by our national professional organizations, such as the CCCC statement on Students Right to Their Own Languages and the NCTE's Conference on English Education's position statement on Beliefs about Social Justice in English Education, I as a writing teacher and conscientious citizen who cares about his students as people and language users, cannot grade their written performances based on so-called quality, knowing all that that means when situated in any school context. In short, to me, it is quite clear, but this clarity has come over time and with much concentrated study. It has also come from my own experiences in school. My job is not worth having if it means that I teach it unethically and do more harm than good. Grading by a standard, in my estimation, does more harm than good in writing courses.

I do not pretend to think that this position or judgment of the situation is universal. I also do not pretend to know the various economic and social pressures that many teachers face. Perhaps many writing teachers, such as adjuncts in colleges and teachers in public schools, feel this is a Sophie's choice. You are damned if you do and damned if you don't. Your teaching hands are forced to do things you don't want to do, that you know does harm. This may be, and it likely is a hard choice to make for anyone. But this question isn't about how do we assess student writing in order to keep our jobs, or feel good about what we do, or even to forgive ourselves for doing what we do. The question is about what is the ethical thing to do.

While I cannot answer it here definitely, only you can answer this for yourself in your context, I can offer the ethical paradox as clearly as possible, which may mean it makes us uncomfortable with what we have as our choices—this uncomfortability can push us to make unexpected changes in the systems we work within. The question, I think, assumes a false binary, but one that is often enough a part of the decision to use or not use grading contracts. What I mean is that this question assumes that we have an either-or choice to make. Either we protect the vulnerable teacher by using conventional grading systems, or we protect the vulnerable students by using contracts. Putting aside the fact that in any given situation, one would need to determine in some reasonable way how vulnerable the teacher and students really are (who stands to lose more and how is "more" decided?), we might also see this as a false-real binary. It is a real binary in the sense that this may be the choice that some teachers have, but it is also false in that the society and educational systems we work in have created it because they assume things like standards. Our educational systems make such things falsely binary. They give us only this either-or choice. Why cannot we protect both the vulnerable teacher and the vulnerable students? Why cannot our assessment ecologies do both things? And why aren't methods that protect our vulnerable students also seen as ones that protect vulnerable teachers in predatory educational systems that take advantage of them? I think, even if one starts very small, we can together change such systems, little by little. Those changes may start by seeing the false-real binary many of us have in front of us.

CHAPTER 7.

HOW EFFECTIVE CAN LABOR-BASED GRADING CONTRACTS BE?

Any conscientious teacher will want to know just how effective can labor-based grading contracts be in a writing or English course? This last chapter attempts to answer this question, and "effectiveness," as I hope you will see, is a deceptively complex concept to determine. There are a number of kinds of data one might measure in order to make arguments of how effective any writing assessment ecology is. One might use final course grades, judgments of final course portfolios, student perceptions of learning, the amount of output or writing done in the course, student attitudes about writing or their own writing at the end of the course, how well students do in later writing-intensive courses (determined by course grades, authentic writing from those courses, or other external measures), retention rates in the university after the course, how students use or employ writing as a practice after the class, among numerous other things. The point is: There are many ways to measure effectiveness, and the data one collects and analyzes to come to some conclusions about the effectiveness of a classroom's assessment ecology should match the assessment ecology's goals and primary purposes. Put another way, how any teacher (or program) finds out how effective grading contracts are will be dictated by what they believe evidence for effectiveness of contracts are in the classroom, or what the teacher believes effectiveness means. So in some ways, this question is deceptively difficult to answer. Asking the question seriously, should allow a teacher or WPA to consider what exactly their definition of effectiveness of an ecology can or should be, and what measures or data they might use to make arguments about effectiveness.

As will be clear in my discussion in this chapter, one cannot separate a labor-based grading contract from the rest of the classroom's assessment ecology, so I tend to use the two terms synonymously, speaking of labor-based grading contracts or contract ecologies as synonymous. This means that this chapter is really about understanding the effectiveness of labor-based grading contract ecologies as a whole. As the previous chapters attest to, one cannot simply insert a labor-based grading contract in a course that is otherwise no different from a conventionally graded course. In all assessment ecologies, there are many moving parts. They are complex systems (Inoue, *Antiracist* 86–92).

It should be clear that the goals of a course's assessment ecology can be different from its course learning goals. Course learning goals may be used to understand how effective a course is at achieving a number of curricular things that will vary from program to program. The goals I speak of in this chapter are best used to understand how well a labor-based assessment ecology is working, if one accepts them as I've discussed them in this book. Additionally, as you'll see, some or all of these ecological goals could be used as course learning goals too, but I am speaking of them in this chapter as assessment ecology goals, or the goals I have for determining the effectiveness of a labor-based assessment ecology.

Therefore, in this chapter, I begin by briefly discussing what effectiveness is for an assessment ecology, then why I use the noncognitive literature to help me formulate the five ecological goals that I then discuss as ways to understand a labor-based grading contract ecology's effectiveness. When discussing each goal, I attempt to offer a rationale for the ecological goal as one that can help define effectiveness in some way for a labor-based grading contract ecology, then offer several ways to measure that goal (possible evidence from the ecology), which come from my own ecologies. I mean for this chapter to be useful to both individual writing teachers and writing program administrators tasked with assessing effectiveness of writing programs. I do not think it is necessary that all labor-based grading contract ecologies have all five goals I discuss, but they are ones I use to help me collect evidence and make arguments (often to myself) about effectiveness.

UNDERSTANDING EFFECTIVENESS FOR LABOR-BASED GRADING CONTRACT ECOLOGIES

What does it mean to say that a labor-based grading contract ecology is effective? Do grade distributions explain effectiveness in such ecologies? Do ratings on portfolios explain effectiveness? Do students' opinions about writing explain effectiveness? Do students' confidence levels about themselves as writers explain effectiveness? Does the amount of labor in reading and writing tasks during the semester or quarter explain effectiveness? Any of these kinds of evidence can be compelling, however, I caution teachers and administrators. If your primary ways of seeing the effectiveness of labor-based grading contract ecologies is by measuring how close students' writing is to a predetermined, dominant Discourse, a standard, that is, to a White racial *habitus*, you haven't understood why labor-based grading contracts are important for all students, nor why I find them important for socially just, equitable, and inclusive writing classrooms.

In "Grading Contracts: Assessing Their Effectiveness on Different Racial Formations," I offer three measures of effectiveness of labor-based grading contracts that I use to understand the different degrees of effectiveness contracts had on different racial formations in my writing program at California State University, Fresno, which also situated those courses in a directed self-placement program. They are: "(1) the quantity of work produced, (2) the quality of writing produced in class, and (3) student reactions to and acceptance of the contract itself" (82). I formulated this three-pronged approach from the literature on grading contracts in writing studies (discussed in Chapter 2), which is limited and has no actual studies of effectiveness. I still find these three measures useful for external audiences as an argument for the effectiveness of many labor-based grading contract ecologies, either at the program or classroom level. Using such a three-pronged approach to understanding a contract ecology's effectiveness may not fit every writing course. More important, since that study, I've found other more nuanced ways that account for effectiveness just as well or better.

The above three kinds of evidence do not tell you how to answer the question: *What makes my labor-based grading contract ecology effective for the students I work with in my classroom?* What does effectiveness mean in your kind of assessment ecology with your students and your course's specific goals? Knowing the terrain of possible answers to this question can help a teacher decide whether a labor-based grading contract system is right for them, and the kinds of evidence necessary to explain its effectiveness to themselves, their students, and others. Effectiveness for labor-based grading contract ecologies, like all assessment ecologies, is determined by the specific learning goals the course attempts to promote. That is, an assessment ecology is only effective if it can be argued it achieves the goals for which it was designed.

A writing teacher should have good reasons for grading the way they do, or using grades the way they do, and those reasons should be evidence-based, and continually checked. Why do you give the grades you do? Why do you use the methods you use to produce course grades? Why do you think those methods help the students in front of you? How do those methods for grading help students achieve the course's learning goals? What evidence do you have to help you answer these questions? The point is, your goals for using labor-based grading contracts, like any grading ecology, should be explicit so that you know what kind of evidence will help you understand how effective the assessment ecology is at doing what it was designed to do. If half your students fail, it may be that your grading ecology is doing exactly what it is designed to do, even though failing half your class may not be one of your own goals. Because labor-based grading contracts circulate labor in the ecology as a way to calculate course grades, assessing the effectiveness of them makes a teacher have to confront the multiple ways that dominant White *habitus* already regulate all of our typical outcomes, standards, and assumptions about what makes a grading practice effective.

Too often, the presence of a dominant White *habitus* is the measure of effectiveness of an assessment ecology. That is, when we see a student producing such writing, we tend to think all is okay with that student. The course is working for them, and by default, so is the assessment ecology. But is it? Is that student working hard, challenging themselves, engaging with the material? Are they doing less than they could, or as much as they should? Are they just going through the motions? Are your methods of grading helping the student accomplish the goals of the course or are your grades simply rewarding them for who they are or what they already can do? Or maybe, your grades are just measuring and ranking students, which will privilege students with a White racial *habitus*, and harm student who do not embody it. Can that kind of ecology be called effective? Can an ecology be called effective if the teacher does not need to be concerned about what students are doing, how they are laboring to learn, and only concerned about the products submitted for a grade?

This leads to other effectiveness questions that may not seem like ones. Is your ecology punishing other students for who they are? Is it punishing students who are other than the ones who embody the ideal *habitus* that your standards and grading practices use to grade so-called quality? Can an assessment ecology be called effective if it punishes, accidentally or not, an expected group of students—that is, if punishment in the ecology is unevenly distributed among the social groups that make up that course?

I do not mean to oversimplify classroom labor dynamics, as Chapter 3 demonstrates. I realize that a teacher should not assume that all or most of their students who come to the classroom embodying a White, middle-class, racial *habitus* are not engaging enough or laboring enough—my discussion of Goal #5 (below) will demonstrate one way that I can see this. I also think it is too simple to say that all students who do not match such *habitus* are hard-working and doing all they can in the course. But I do think that grading by a standard encourages those students who already can reproduce that standard to do just enough to achieve the grade they want, and not much more. There are few rewards or encouragements structured into conventional quality-based grading ecologies that invite students to do more labor, effort, or learning than is necessary for the "A." An ecology is not effective when this happens pervasively if learning is the goal.

Grades on assignments also do not encourage students to think, feel, or behave in ways that orient them toward learning or growth, a sign of an effective assessment ecology. Grades often encourage a fixed mindset, one that is opposed to a more beneficial growth mindset, as described in psychological studies.[48] And this

---

48 Much of the psychological research on growth mindset (Dweck; Dweck et al.) reveals how important and influential a person's notions about ability are to their development in any domain. For instance, Anindito Aditomo found that university students with higher measurable growth mindset about their academic ability in a challenging Statistics course performed better than their peers when experiencing setbacks and challenges (215–16). In another study, growth

harms those students who can already produce standardized writing by keeping them from really working hard, really learning all they can, just as much as it harms those students who are not rewarded for their extra efforts because they cannot yet produce such standardized writing. Thus effectiveness, as you'll see in the rest of this chapter, has mostly to do with understanding students' laboring and noncognitive domains practiced by students. These are measures of effectiveness because they last longer and are more flexible for their unknowable futures.

As discussed in Chapter 6 (see the question, "To what extent can labor-based grading contracts address learning or course objectives or outcomes?"), I agree with Chris Gallagher's concerns about narrow learning outcomes, preferring more open concepts, such as goals or consequences. I think of the difference between goals and outcomes like this. An outcome is a destination that you want every student to get to in a course, a specific place, which is predetermined, *a priori*, regardless of who ends up in the course or how hard anyone works. This location must be decided beforehand, then judged by someone. And who do you think those people are statistically speaking in the US? What training did they get and what language, what *habitus*, do they need to succeed and be in the position to make such decisions about outcomes in writing? And therein lies the White language supremacist dangers of using outcomes to determine an ecology's effectiveness. One can measure the effectiveness of an outcome by who is judged to be at the specific destination that the outcome describes. In writing courses, this is typically done by judging writing products for their quality, or comparing them to a single White standard encapsulated in the outcome—but really this comparison is one judge's comparison to *their own* conception of the outcome, no matter how it is articulated.

Take the way decisions are made in the National Football League when referees must determine the placement of a ball or whether a foot was out of bounds. The need for instant replay protocols demonstrates the problems with knowing exactly where someone is located in the field of play. It is always a matter of the perspective of the viewer/camera/referee/judge. Ask a differently located teacher about where a particular student is located relative to their notions of a predefined outcome and their vantage point relative to the student, and you get a different answer for each teacher. The back judge and the line judge in football see the playing field differently because they are located in different places on the gridiron, and each sees different players differently because those players are located in different places on the field. This is why the game needs a back judge and a line judge positioned in different places on the field, and not just one judge. But we usually only have one judge in classrooms. In football, where the play ends, and where a foot is located

---

mindset was shown to have a positive effect on academic achievement in low-income students in Chile (Claro et al.).

is not an objective fact, but a subjective judgment based on where the judge is judging, and the game is designed around this fact of subjective judgment by using multiple judges and instant replay. Students' and teachers' linguistic, cultural, racial, gendered, and social locations in the classroom are also differently located, and create different judgments of the same text, and yet we have but one judge, located by necessity in one location, then we ask that judge to determine how effective their classroom was.

And there are many other reasons why such judgments by teachers are not just idiosyncratic and inconsistent but racist and White supremacist in effect. In Chapter 2, I explain Richard Haswell's articulation of categorization theory that psychologists have used to theorize the way holistic judgments are made. Categorization theory reveals why such judgments of student writing are not only a comparison to some fictionalized construction in the judge's head, but that that fictionalized construction is not only idiosyncratic and vulnerable to inconsistency, but will be determined by the White racial *habitus* acquired through White texts and authors that the judge has in their head because of the training that they could get in school. How many Latinx or Black or Native American authors did you read in school, in college, who talked about your disciplinary subject, say writing pedagogy? Furthermore, implicit racial bias (a version of confirmation bias) (Banaji and Greenwald), and stereotype threat (Steele; Steele et al.), discussed in Chapter 4, and Daniel Kanhman's studies of the WYSIATI and availability heuristics our brains use to think fast (and make lots of errors), discussed in Chapter 6 (see, "Don't some students want or need grades"), each provide further reasons to be very suspicious of trying to measure the effectiveness of learning in a writing classroom by anyone's judgments of other people's writing, particularly when we know that students and teachers embody by necessity different *habitus*.

There are other reasons to be cautious about using a single person's judgments of language to decide grades in diverse classrooms. In *Outliers*, Malcolm Gladwell reviews the research on patterns of aggression historically in communities in Kentucky, as well as the aggression exhibited by many people from the southern US. These studies show that southerners can be more easily turned aggressive than people from other areas of the country. Social scientists Richard Nisbett and Dov Cohen dubbed the source of such aggression, "the culture of honor," which Gladwell cites. Gladwell concludes his chapter on these studies by considering the source of various patterns of judgment and behavior in society. He says, "Cultural legacies are powerful forces. They have deep roots and long lives. They persist generation after generation, virtually intact, even as the economic and social and demographic conditions that spawned them have vanished, and they play a role in directing attitudes and behavior that we cannot make sense of our world without them" (144–45).

He calls these conditions that affect decision making and judgment, "the steady accumulation of advantages," explaining that "when and where you were born, what your parents did for a living, and what the circumstances of your upbring all make a significant difference in how well you do in the world" (175). While he avoids such discussions, Gladwell provides a way to see how racial implicit bias and particular ways that WYSIATI and the availability heuristics are a part of larger, racist and White supremacist social patterns in the US, how they will affect the success of students of color in schools, that it matters that just a few generations ago most Blacks were slaves, that just a few generations ago, Whites owned everything, decided everything, including what counted as ideal speech and writing, and that such social patterns are historically durable, in the same ways that Omi and Winant describe racial formations as historically dynamic, in the same ways that Bourdieu discusses the durability of *habitus*.

Not so ironically, in a footnote, Gladwell offers more proof of the socio-cultural, durable inheritance of behavior by illustrating it with language spoken by Appalachians, taken from David Hackett Fischer's research, concluding that "whatever mechanism passes on speech patterns probably passes on behavioral and emotional patterns as well" (175). If we know anything about language and rhetoric, from Gorgias to Protagoras, from Burke to Perelman and Albrechts-Tyteca, from Lakoff to Vico, it is that our words are epistemological in nature. To understand and make sense of our worlds is to make words about them and share them. With words come attitudes and behaviors, biases and logics. So racism and White supremacy, because they are in our past, in our educational structures, in our words, from Kindergarten to college, and in our academic disciplines' values and discourses, they—racism and White supremacy—remain with us, even as we denounce them. It is no wonder it is so difficult to escape White language supremacy in schools and society, so hard for Black students or indigenous students to even get to college. Therefore, measuring the effectiveness of writing assessment ecologies by predefined outcomes is the best recipe for White language supremacy in today's schools, even when teachers, administrators, and others explicitly disavow such a thing.

Learning goals, on the other hand, are broader and describe not a location but a direction, and often the speed or method of traveling in that direction. So exactly where one stops at the end of the semester is unknown, but the direction they are headed and the way in which they travel along that direction can be measured and determined. It is evidence of the direction and methods of traveling that I discuss in this chapter as evidence of effectiveness of labor-based grading contract ecologies. There may still be questions of judgment and perspective, but there will be fewer of them, and they usually are less important in determining how effective the ecology has been for any given student, and have a significantly smaller impact

243

on any student's opportunities for learning and success in the course. The exact destination of any student in the ecology is not as important as the directions they are headed, and the speeds at and methods by which they travel on the landscape.

DEFINING THE NONCOGNITIVE IN LABOR-BASED GOALS

Because of these reasons, I articulate my course's purpose and learning goals, but not particular learning outcomes. It is the student-determined directions and methods of travel that I'm most interested in understanding when trying to make arguments about the effectiveness of my assessment ecologies, not the specific locations at which my students may end the course. My goals are dictated, then, by the central purpose of my labor-based grading contract ecology. I will not defend this purpose, in part because I think it is self-explanatory, and because I do not hold it up for all writing teachers to adopt, rather I show it so that you can understand how the goals I offer below work toward a larger course purpose that can accommodate individual students' purposes and goals for taking the course. The larger purpose I offer may be articulated as:

> The purpose of this writing course is to encourage students to engage in a willingness to labor in mindful and meaningful reading and writing practices that lead them toward an awareness of language (and perhaps its politics) in a compassionate and safe environment that makes the course's opportunities for learning and all grades attainable by all students, no matter where they come from or the version of English they use.

My labor-based grading contract ecologies work from pedagogical assumptions that place noncognitive competencies above cognitive ones, which tend to need an exclusionary standard by which to measure them, among other problems that I've discussed elsewhere (Inoue, *Antiracist*). Equally important, noncognitive competencies feed cognitive ones. To labor in the spirit that the grading contract asks of students, I believe, can build noncognitive competencies, which I explain below. I wish to note that my use of noncognitives as competencies assumes that everyone has the ability to practice and develop what the psychological literature tends to refer to as noncognitive "traits" or "skills." I assume any non-cognitive competency or trait is along a continuum and is itself a process that is practiced by all students to some degree. In my discussion below, I refer to noncognitive traits or skills when referring to the literature that uses those terms, but I use noncognitive competency when referring to their application to the labor-based grading contract classroom because "competency," for me, suggests a process-oriented set of practices that everyone has access to.

The literature on noncognitive traits (Bowles and Gintis; Farkas; Gutman and Schoon; Zhou) argues strongly that noncognitive traits are more important to student future success in and outside of school than any cognitive skills students might acquire in college.[49] Some have even found stronger links between noncognitive traits and school decisions and attendance, as well as wages in the labor market after college, than cognitive ability (Heckman et al. 477–78). Some noncognitive traits (i.e., "conscientiousness" and "future-orientation") have been shown to determine whether college students attend classes/lectures and spend additional time studying (Delaney et al. 189). Research has also shown how noncognitive traits are associated with cognitive skills and academic outcomes more generally (Bowles and Gintis; Farkas; Heckman et al.; Lleras). Thus, noncognitive competencies appear to be one good way to articulate goals for a writing course, particularly since they map closely to labor by being practices and processes that students do.

In a UNESCO report on noncognitive skills, Kai Zhou explains noncognitive traits as: "the 'patterns of thought, feelings and behaviours' (Borghans et al., 2008) that are socially determined and can be developed throughout the lifetime to produce value. Noncognitive skills comprise personal traits, attitudes and motivations" (2). While acknowledging the contested nature of the concept of noncognitive skills, Gutman and Schoon offer this definition of them in learners:

> The term "non-cognitive skills" is used to contrast a variety
> of behaviours, personality characteristics, and attitudes with
> academic skills, aptitudes, and attainment. The concept
> was introduced by sociologists Bowles and Gintis (1976) to
> focus on factors other than those measured by cognitive test
> scores. They highlighted the role of attitudes, motivation and
> personality traits, rather than academic skills, as determinants
> of labour market success. Their findings have been reinforced
> by more recent studies, which have demonstrated the signif-
> icant role of non-cognitive skills (i.e., attitudes, motivation
> and personal characteristics) over and above cognitive skills in
> shaping labour market outcomes, social behaviour and health
> (Farkas, 2003, Heckman et al., 2006). (7)

So the practices and processes that noncognitive competencies refer to also have associated with them certain attitudes, feelings, and behaviors. As Gutman and

---

49   Borghans et al. offer a detailed footnote (#3 on page 973) that lists various studies since Bowles and Gintis' work in the mid-1970s that associate noncognitive traits to earnings. They also summarize much of the research on noncognitive traits' predictive power in the article.

Schoon's definition suggests, we might understand the difference between cognitive and noncognitive competencies in the same way that we differentiate between deduction and induction, by the direction of their logical movement and the nature of the conclusions made.

In writing courses, cognitive traits are often treated as outcomes or products that students produce. This means the value of student products, and therefore the value of student writing, is determined by cognitive competencies that are predefined, like a major premise in a syllogism, or an assertion (what Aristotle calls an *apophansis*) that a current instance is judged against in order for the syllogism to be valid. In *Prior Analytics* (I.2, 24b18–20),[50] Aristotle discusses deduction, but it is the nature of the logical movement, a move from a predefined assertion, like an outcome or standard in a writing course that is critical to see here. In a syllogism, then, the conclusion is based on a comparison of a new or present instance of writing to the *a priori* assertion (*apophansis*), a standard, or outcome. The key to the difference is the predetermined, *a priori* nature of the assertion, standard, or outcome. In writing courses, this predetermined assertion is based on cognitive competencies that align with White middle-class *habitus*.

In inductive logic, there is no *a priori* assertion before the present instance being considered. The present instance of, say, writing from a student, is not compared to some predefined outcome or standard to determine its quality or legitimacy. Instead, inductive logic is open-ended, and so are noncognitive competencies. We don't know how something like engagement or persistence will manifest itself, but we do know that these noncognitive competencies manifest in a wide range of practices and outcomes, many of which lead to success in a number of ways. These outcomes are always unique to some degree. What is not unique is their source, the noncognitive competency, the practices, attitudes, and behaviors. Thus, one observes noncognitive competencies more than judges them (against some standard), and this forms the induction. This means that noncognitive competencies, if used as goals in a writing course, will not tell us what students will produce exactly, as much as indicate the competencies students can practice activating in the course to produce what they do. Thus students' abilities to meet particular goals (or directions) are the best way to determine effectiveness of labor-based grading contract ecologies, and noncognitive competencies have shown to be a good, well-researched way to articulate such goals.

The most influential articulation of noncognitive traits is the "Big Five," which are: openness to experience, conscientiousness, extraversion, agreeableness, and neuroticism (or emotional stability) (Costa and McCrae 258; Borghans et al.;

---

50   A good overview of Aristotle's logic and how he defines and discusses deduction is offered by Robin Smith in the *Stanford Encyclopedia of Philosophy*.

Gutman and Schoon 7). These are not the only articulations of noncognitive traits, but arguably the most used and influential in the research to date. For the purposes of articulating goals for labor-based grading contract ecologies, I argue that there may be at least one more noncognitive competency useful to understanding learning and development: *a willingness to labor*. This noncognitive, as I define it, draws on three existing noncognitive traits studied already, creating a new noncognitive. In my courses, if students can demonstrate a willingness to labor, then my labor-based grading contract ecology has been effective.

The three noncognitive traits that a willingness to labor draws on are engagement, coping or resilience, and metacognitive strategies. And so, a willingness to labor, as a noncognitive competency, can be defined as a process of engagement that may start as simply satisfactorily doing the labor or work required in a course, but becomes a process of mindful, reflective labor that includes a desire or readiness to do that labor satisfactorily, despite setbacks and difficulties. In the past, I've called this a willingness to labor, "laboring to learn" instead of laboring to earn a grade (*Antiracist* 193–94). Here I attempt to theorize a willingness to labor through the research on noncognitive competencies.

Thus the overarching goal of labor-based grading contract ecologies, for me, is to get students to practice a network of interlocking, noncognitive competencies (engagement, coping and resilience, and metacognition), which I think of as a *willingness to labor*—that is, if all goes well, the particular goals that tend to regulate my labor-base grading contract ecologies encourage students to practice a willingness to labor, which are articulated primarily in Goals 1–3 below. This means that in order for me to understand how effective or successful my assessment ecology is, I must collect and consider evidence of a willingness to labor first and foremost. The design of my ecology, then, incorporates ways to do this, which have equal if not more benefits for my students.

GOAL 1: TO ENGAGE IN CONSISTENT, MINDFUL, AND MEANINGFUL PRACTICES

Gutman and Schoon place engagement under the umbrella term of "perseverance," and distinguish it from "grit" (17). They explain:

> Engagement involves how students behave, feel, and think regarding their commitment to academic tasks, activities, or school more generally (Fredricks et al., 2004), while grit refers to a trait-level perseverance and passion for long-term goals which is related to Conscientiousness (Duckworth et al., 2007).

A willingness to labor, then, is not just an intention or knowledge set. Since it involves engagement, it is also action, laboring that affects behavior and behavior that affects laboring. This dialectical relationship between the intention of the student and their labor provides for beneficial behaviors, feelings, actions, and commitments. On one hand, it is a stance that affects the way a student approaches any labor asked of them in a course, allowing them to at least do the labor, even if they don't care for it, or find it interesting at first. On the other hand, it is laboring itself, which over time, changes the way the student thinks and feels about that labor, helping them find meaning and significance in it. Fredricks, Blumenfeld, and Paris explain that most conceptions of engagement as a noncognitive trait have three forms, or three kinds of engagement by students: (1) behavioral, such as following rules, asking questions, paying attention, and participation in school-related activities (62); (2) emotional, which "refers to students' affective reactions in the classroom, including interest, boredom, happiness, sadness, and anxiety," as well as identification with the classroom, peers, and/or teacher (63); and (3) cognitive, which tends to refer to a student's investment in learning, "self-regulation, or being strategic," for instance, "a desire to go beyond the requirements, and a preference for challenge" (63).

Thus asking students how they feel about a particular assignment or session of labor is vital to helping students notice and perhaps control or shape their engagement in a course. Early in each quarter or semester, I often pose the question: Why do you find particular activities or topics of interest more engaging than others? Why do you have the interests you do? What I want students to grapple with is how our interests and engagement in particular topics, for instance, have a dialectical relationship with the practices and activities that are associated with those topics. It is a chicken-and-egg question. Students might say they are interested in football or softball because they played these sports in high school. So I ask, why did you play them in high school? Did your playing create interest? How can you know you are interested in football or softball before you begin playing it? Noticing such feelings and attitudes toward the work of a course, during or after one does it, exercises metacognitive strategies, which I'll say more about below, but it also helps students notice when and how they are becoming engaged.

And engagement can look and feel different at various times in the course, for various activities, and to different students. Engagement is not always happy and exciting feelings about an activity or topic, nor is it always a sense of losing track of time in an activity. It can be boredom or fatigue, struggle or tension and anxiety. Engagement should be understood in nuanced ways and discussed with students as a full range of emotions, feelings, thoughts, behaviors, and actions. Much of our weekly labor and mindfulness journal entries and discussions revolve around describing, naming, and talking through the ways we were engaged and how those feelings, thoughts, and actions help us or change the way we do our labors and our willingness to labor in the future for the course. The first two dimensions of three-dimensional labor in Chapter 3 (the *how* and the *that* dimensions of labor) provide reflective ways (prompting) to help students habitually access their ways of engagement in the course.

The most important thing in labor-based grading contract ecologies that I've cultivated over the years is not that students produce some ideal text or Discourse, or perform in some way that matches a preferred *habitus*, but that they engage mindfully and meaningfully in the practices of producing texts, which includes circulating those texts among readers, acting as readers themselves, and processing feedback from readers. This first goal, then, boils down to laboring at reading and writing practices in self-conscious ways. Asking students to labor in particular ways for certain amounts of time and simultaneously paying attention to that labor are the central actions of this goal. The assumption is that with the right amount of time and labor, any student will learn as much as they can. But it is possible that one can go through the motions and get very little out of a practice, so this goal also asks for mindful labor.

Being mindful and understanding one's labors as meaningful—i.e., full of meaning—are interconnected qualities of labors and often take time to cultivate. When a student sees their labor as meaningful, such as writing an essay for a class, they are aware—they notice things that have meaning, significance, or usefulness to them. Meaning is developed through self-conscious and reflective stances that they have engaged in during their writing labors or thought about afterwards. As I discuss in Chapter 3 as three-dimensional labor and mindful labor, this often means the labor of writing is done in a self-conscious way—that is, done while simultaneously realizing *that* the student is laboring at something in particular ways, at a particular time, under particular circumstances. Noticing such things in or after the writing labor accumulates meaning and value for the student, but it is very difficult to quantify how much meaning is accumulated or what it looks like (its nature). Reflective writing can offer a window into a student's mindful practices, but it needs to be done frequently throughout the semester, since consistency and repetition are important to cultivating mindful *habitus*.

What evidence in the course might there be of achieving this goal? The most direct evidence may be to measure the amount and/or consistency of labor done, then cross-reference that labor with some measure of mindfulness and meaningfulness. There are a few ways that seem most direct to me, but each have their problems. Chief among these problems is that most kinds of data on student labor are student-reported, and could be considered too subjective or inconsistent to be useful for determining an ecology's effectiveness. Students can fudge self-reported numbers, even unintentionally, but a teacher can still use them to determine the ecology's effectiveness.[51] The important thing is that you have to decide if you trust your students. If you do, then self-reporting information, such as labor logs and labor journals, will be enough evidence to make arguments about your ecology's effectiveness along this goal, but if you are using such data to make arguments to other stakeholders outside your classroom, then you'll have to decide what those audiences feel are strong evidence and/or how to frame any evidence used.

As one quick and surely incomplete example, consider a recent, writing course of mine. There were fourteen students enrolled in this first-year writing course, all first-year students in their first quarter of college. Most of the class worked outside of school. As a way to compare, consider the average combined labor accumulated by the bottom three (Latino, two White females), the middle three (Latino, Black female, White male), and the top three students (Latina, White female, White male). All students were between the ages of 18–20 years old.

Table 7.1. Average combined labor accumulated in a recent writing course by the top three, middle three, and bottom three students

	Total Labor (hrs)	Avg. Weekly Labor (hrs)	Avg. Reading Engage-ment	Avg. Writing Engage-ment	Overall Engage-ment	Avg. Final Course Grade
Top Three	82.03	8.20	3.23	3.89	3.56	4.0 (A)
Middle Three	69.77	6.98	2.98	3.45	3.21	3.7 (A-)
Bottom Three	42.28	4.22	3.23	3.03	3.13	2.6 (B-)

Let me emphasize that I am only identifying the amount of labor accumulated in the course when I identify them as top, middle, and bottom, as can be seen in the total and average weekly labor figures in Table 7.1 (first two columns). Those numbers determine bottom, middle, and top performers by amount

51   This is, of course, not the same as using these same measures to determine whether students have met a labor-based grading contract's obligations—as discussed in Chapter 4, I do not suggest using any self-reporting of labor (e.g., their labor logs) by students as a way to determine meeting contract obligations and thus determining grades.

of labor recorded in their labor logs. All students represented above met the minimum labor requirements of the contract and passed the course. The engagement ratings used a simple scale of 1–5, with 5 as most engaged and 1 as not engaged at all that students provided for each session of labor recorded in their labor logs.

What I find most helpful in determining consistent engagement in labor are the average and total labor hours accumulated by students. As mentioned before, the more a student labors in my contract ecologies, the higher the final course grade a student achieves, so the top three receive higher grades than the middle, and the middle higher than the bottom (the default grade for meeting our contract was a B, or 3.1).[52] In the five unit course represented above, I assigned students an average of eight to ten hours of labor outside of class each week of the ten-week quarter.[53] While I did not use labor-logs to determine course grades, the average weekly labor in their logs shows that the top performers were able to meet these labor targets. And since engagement in writing labors are almost always higher than reading labors, I often use writing engagement ratings as one initial measure of engagement in the class (keeping in mind that this does not mean that a student had to like all labor to be deeply engaged in it), but even taking an overall engagement rating in this case shows an ascending set of ratings, with the top performers recording a higher average engagement rating. This is a typical distribution of grades and labor in my first-year writing courses. As the table shows, the more labor a student did, the more engaged they said they were, and our contract rewarded them with higher course grades—keeping in mind that I do not use labor logs to determine whether students meet our contract.

And how effective along this goal is my assessment ecology at helping my students of color? Is it socially just? How do students of color do? When I separate the data from Table 7.1 by race of student, students of color do more labor, and are engaged at the same rates as their White peers. The average total labor recorded for the quarter for the five White students represented in Table 7.1 was 56.71 hours, while the same average for the four students of color was 74.67. That's an average of almost 2 hours more labor each week that my students of color did. This places the students of color between the middle and top groups in Table 7.1, and the White students between the middle and bottom group.

---

52   The University of Washington uses a grading system that only allows a teacher to input numerical course grades of 0.0 or 0.7–4.0. You can see the scale on the university's website (https://www.washington.edu/students/gencat/front/Grading_Sys.html).

53   As one more reference point, in a more recent FYW course, one conducted after this one, the average labor per week of all students in that course was 9.40 hours and the average overall engagement rating was 3.10.

Keep in mind that most of the students of color in this sample were in the middle and bottom groups.[54]

And what about average overall engagement? The White students recorded an average of 3.43 overall engagement and the students of color a 3.40. No difference. In terms of labor hours recorded, these numbers suggest that the ecology was effective at getting students to engage in the amount of labor I'd hoped for all students (eight to ten hours per week), with my students of color seeming to do more than my White students. In this way, I see my labor-based assessment ecology helping my students of color achieve as much or more labor than my White students, with equal engagement. Keep in mind the discouraging and unrewarding histories my students of color likely had in their past English and writing classrooms.

As I mentioned above, mindful, consistent labor makes for more meaningful labor, so seeing how much labor students accomplish in a semester or quarter is not enough to really understand how effective an ecology has been at achieving this goal. For now, I wish to point out that the mere act of paying attention to when, how long, where, and how engaged one is in their labors of the course through keeping a labor log and using frequent reflections on one's labor (see the section, "Three-Dimensional Articulation of Labor" in Chapter 3) is one way to see consistent, mindful laboring. So the fact that (1) all these students kept labor logs and labor journals consistently during the ten-week quarter; that (2) generally speaking, the more labor a student recorded the higher they rated their engagement in their labor; and (3) that students of color out-labored their White peers; all suggest that the labors were both consistent and mindful, and perhaps more so for my students of color. In the third goal below, I'll offer evidence from these students' labor journals and reflective writing in the course, but here, I'm suggesting that a teacher might measure the effectiveness of this first goal by looking at the data in labor logs and the presence of frequent, student reflections in the course.

But in order to confirm that any of the labor above is more than going through the motions, students must somehow engage with it in mindful ways, assessing what they were doing and how they were feeling. In their weekly labor and mindfulness journals that we write for just five minutes each week, I ask them to reflect upon one session of labor and explain how they were engaged with it. One of the students in the top performing group, T1 (White female), illustrates a typical kind of modest change in mindful laboring. A few weeks into the quarter, she writes:

---

54   I should also note that most of the White students in this sample completed their labor logs up to week 9, so their lower numbers could be accounted by this fact. However, as I'll discuss below in Goal 2, this trend may be just as important in understanding effectiveness of the assessment ecology.

the assignment I was most productive on was my precis. I really focused on it this week and tried hard to make it sound good, while still following the outline and having only five sentences. I wrote this in my room while I was in bed listening to some soft music. The session was engaging for me because I was in a time crunch with trying to get my assignment done before work, so I really had to focus on it and get it done so I wouldn't have to come home and finish it before I went to sleep.[55]

T1 focuses on the time crunch that is created because of her work schedule. She associates engagement in the labor with how much time she has to complete that labor before she heads off to work. Her engagement is product-centered, dictated by the goal of finishing the job. Just a few weeks later, she reflects on a similar labor session:

I worked hard on meeting the requirement for the drafts and trying to give everyone in my group a good and thorough review of their papers. I did this by reading their drafts carefully and explaining how their papers made me feel and by focusing on the two aspect[s] of the rubric that they wanted me to focus on. I needed to take breaks between everyone's papers so I wouldn't lose my mind and become uninterested, so I guess by doing this it took me longer to get this assignment done. I also was distracted by my phone with texts and notifications I was getting, so I think while I do assignments I should probably turn my phone off or put it on Do Not Disturb so I can focus on what I am supposed to be doing a little easier.

Now, T1 becomes more strategic in her laboring. She notices when she's losing focus when reading her colleagues' drafts, takes a break, and returns to the labor with new focus. What now seems to construct her engagement in her labors is her focus, her sense of being interested in the work and her colleagues' papers. She recognizes when she is interested and even finds a new practice to help her, turning her cell phone on "Do Not Disturb" so she is not interrupted. This new articulation of her labor is centered on not a product, like getting the assignment done, but on doing the labor in a focused and interested way.

While I do not wish to make too much of these numbers, nor suggest some correlation between the change in laboring habits that T1 shows in her reflec-

---

55   I do not edit any student writing offered in this chapter, except on a few, rare occasions for readability purposes.

tions, I do wish to point out that all three groups found the writing labor of the class engaging to some degree. All the students in each of the three groups above offered similar kinds of reflections, with a gradual shifting in their reflections over the quarter in the directions that T1 illustrates. They generally moved away from product-oriented, get-the-job-done goals for their labor sessions, and toward finding interest and focus, and noticing particular feelings arise during labor sessions (not always good or happy feelings).

Many of these changes may have been nudged by my prompting in class, which emphasizes describing a labor session, reflecting on how engagement was experienced, felt, and created in the session of labor, then finding something that the session teaches them for their future labor practices (discussed in Chapter 3). This prompting tends to call our attentions to several aspects of engagement in labors: (1) that engagement is not always happy or easy, but can also be feelings of difficulty and struggle; (2) that engagement can be created by consciously arranging one's body, laboring environment, or circumstances; and (3) that engagement is not a random occurrence that surprises us (it doesn't just happen to us), but something we might plan or construct in a premeditated fashion.

Finally, I've found more recently that engagement is a good initial topic of discussion to have with students, particularly since I'm asking them to rate their engagement on a scale of 1–5. In the past, I've simply given them the scale and a general guideline for each rating, such as: 1 = very low; 2 = low; 3 = neutral; 4 = high; and 5 = very high. But this scale doesn't account for the nuance that I'm describing above, nor the nuance in reflections and journal entries. So opening a discussion early on to define what each student might observe or account for in their labor sessions, then make note of what those feelings and experiences are somewhere, and frequently returning to the definition of engagement may offer students more nuanced, and perhaps more internally consistent, ways of recording and reflecting up engagement.

Table 7.2 offers various kinds of evidence that I find useful in determining a labor-based grading contract ecology's effectiveness along this first goal, which might be gathered at the end of a semester or quarter, as well as examined with students at the midpoint of the term or semester. As Chapter 3 explains, such data can be useful for students themselves to reflect upon at strategic points in the semester or quarter. Table 7.2 links particular prompts or questions to the data in labor logs. The reflections students produce might do a number of things beyond provide the teacher with student-generated evidence for the degree of effectiveness of the ecology. For instance, journal reflections can help students analyze or make sense of the numbers, looking empirically at their engagement through total labor time in the class, average engagement ratings, or how those numbers change during the course of the semester or quarter.

Table 7.2. Kinds of evidence for engagement in consistent, mindful, and meaningful practices

Data from Labor Log	Questions About Data
Amount of minutes/ hours of labor accumulated in the course	How much labor do you ask of/assign students each week? How close do students come to this target? How much labor has been reading sessions and how much writing sessions? Are there differences among various identifiable groups in the class (e.g., race, gender, generation of student)?
Average minutes/hours of labor per week of the semester/quarter	How much labor does each student average each week? What differences in averages are there among identifiable groups in the class? How consistent are the weekly averages across the quarter or semester? Are there differences between identifiable groups? How do you account for these differences?
Average engagement ratings of labor sessions	What are the average reading, writing, and overall engagement ratings for all students? What differences do you see between identifiable groups? Do overall or group average engagement ratings stay consistent across the quarter or semester? How do you account for any differences?
Comparisons of amount of labor to engagement ratings	Considering just the labor sessions that students rated highest (5) and lowest (1 or 2) in engagement, what is the average amount of total labor (or average amount of time per session) in identifiable groups? How does the amount of time compare to the mean (average) or the median (student who represents the exact middle value) of the entire class?

GOAL 2: TO CONSCIOUSLY LABOR AND WORK TOWARD RESILIENCE

This second goal of my labor-based grading contract ecologies centers on the noncognitive competencies of coping and resilience. Coping and resilience have been used interchangeably in the noncognitive literature, however, they are distinct concepts, "reflect[ing] distinct aspects of successful development and adaptation" (Compas et al. 89). Gutman and Schoon explain, "resilience and coping are both concerned with how individuals respond to stress, [but] they are conceptually distinct. Coping involves skills that people use when faced with specific difficulties, whereas resilience is a process which follows the exercise of those skills" (27). Lazarus and Folkman explain coping as "constantly changing cognitive and behavioral efforts to manage specific external and/or internal demands that are appraised as taxing or exceeding the resources of the person" (141). When one successfully copes with stressful or difficult situations, one becomes more resilient, willing to continue to exercise coping strategies in the future. Resilience, then, is a process of "positive adaptation despite the presence of risk" (Gutman and Schoon 27) through coping behaviors. I think of coping as the root noncognitive competency in coping and resilience. Thus, coping strategies and behaviors lead to resilience, or positive adaptation to stressors, risk, and difficulties. Often coping in my class is simply laboring in ways we've asked of each other.

While coping is the root noncognitive competency and resiliency is the process of successful coping, I see these two noncognitives together. For my ecologies, coping and resilience are a linked process of "purposeful responses" that move toward a sticking to tasks and labors and eventual success in tasks or goals in some way (Gutman and Schoon 27) that is recognizable to some degree by the student. Compas et al. offer this definition of coping, which I think is useful for understanding coping and resilience as a single process in a willingness to labor:

> conscious volitional efforts to regulate emotion, cognition, behavior, physiology, and the environment in response to stressful events or circumstances. These regulatory processes both draw on and are constrained by the biological, cognitive, social and emotional development of the individual. An individual's developmental level both contributes to the resources that are available for coping and limits the types of coping responses the individual can enact. (89)

Thus everyone enters a given writing course with different experiences and coping competencies, all of which are built upon during the present course. These coping competencies allow the person to regulate their emotions, cognitive abilities, behaviors, their psychology, and the environment around them. In their meta-analysis of 124 articles that studied coping, 165 independent samples, which included 33,094 participants in studies between 1980 and 2004, Connor Smith and Flachsbart identified two broad forms of coping, "approach" or engagement, and "avoidant" or disengagement (Connor Smith and Flachsbart 1081). Coping, then, appears to come in at least two forms, engaging with stressors in some way or avoiding them. The literature is clear that avoidance coping strategies have detrimental or negative effects on people and their abilities to become resilient (Barlow, Allen, and Choate 219–21), while approach or engagement coping has positive effects, helping people become more resilient through difficulties.

In their study on positive effects due to approach coping strategies after participants went through mindfulness-based interventions, Cousin and Crane explain these two kinds of coping strategies:

> Engagement strategies include responses that are oriented
> towards the stressor or one's reactions to it, such as problem
> solving, seeking for social support, or acceptance (i.e., coming
> to live with the stressor). Disengagement strategies, on the
> contrary, include responses that are oriented away from the
> stressor or one's reactions to it, such as avoidance (i.e., trying
> to avoid facing the problem, or the thoughts or emotions
> related to it) or denial. By encouraging awareness of one's
> experience in its entirety and acceptance of thoughts and
> affective states whatever their form may be (Segal, Williams &
> Teasdale, 2012 [sic]), mindfulness meditation prevents disen-
> gagement from difficult experiences when they arise. (435–36)

While I'll say more about mindfulness and metacognitive strategies in Goal 3, it is important to note the close association in the psychological literature on coping. Metacognition and awareness, in the above case through meditation and mindfulness practices, appear to offer approach coping strategies. In other words, people who went through an eight-week mindfulness-based intervention (a course) gained approach coping strategies, and reduced avoidant ones (Cousins and Crane 443). These changes in coping strategies were statistically significant, and resulted in positive effects on participants. In part because they practiced noticing their responses to stress and difficulty and their coping behaviors, participants found more effective coping strategies.

Ultimately, approach coping, if it is engaged in with some degree of conscious awareness, is an integral part to a willingness to labor. It explains a stance or orientation that a student moves toward in the labor-based assessment ecology, one that does not avoid labor or difficulties, but one that becomes oriented toward difficult or challenging labor and problems, in part through awareness. My assumption is, and I could be wrong, that many students, particularly those most harmed by past writing assessment ecologies, have a higher frequency of using avoidant coping strategies, like not doing enough work in a course, starting late or procrastinating on assignments, or not engaging fully in class activities, reading, or writing assignments.

Evidence of the effectiveness of the ecology along this goal can be seen in similar ways as the first goal. Students engage in approach coping practices, first, by simply doing the labor asked of them without the pressure of grades of quality on their writing. As mentioned in Chapters 3 and 4, the labor instructions I

257

provide for each reading or writing assignment reminds students in its opening description, purpose, and goals statements that what I'm mostly asking them to do is labor in particular ways, to be in the labor, not to finish something and turn it in, even though they will do that (see Appendix D for example labor instructions). I reinforce coping strategies by asking students to pause for a minute in their labor processes, assess what they've just done, how they've done it, and what they may be feeling, then Slack/tweet that to the class. Often, simply noticing what one has accomplished can be a coping practice, a tacit validation that shows the student, "yes, I am doing this, and I can do this work."

Gradually over the course of the term, I shape the prompts for these labor tweets to help students try out at least two other approach coping practices. First, I ask them to reframe the current work (if it is difficult work). *Reframing* could be altering how one thinks about the current work, rearticulating the goals one sets for the labor, or consciously changing one's values that are linked to the labor at hand. For instance, when reading a difficult or dense text, one with a lot of theory or new terms and ideas in it, I may ask students to pause at some difficult point in the reading (e.g., "after reading page 39, pause and tweet . . ."), spend two or three minutes to reframe their goals for reading the next few pages of the text. If we started our reading with the goal of understanding to summarize the text, I might suggest at this point that a student now read the next few pages in order to tweet a short poem or haiku using at least two or three words/terms that are new to them from those pages.

The second coping practice I offer in labor Slacks/tweets is to simply notice and accept their current feelings about the present work in a non-judgmental way (e.g., "I'm bored," or "this is confusing to read"), affirming that their feelings about their labor does not mean they cannot do the work or are a bad student, reader, or writer. We might call this coping practice *acknowledging feelings*. It is one way to remain embodied as we do otherwise intellectual work. The tweet might be taking a picture of a page of the text, and telling us how they felt while they read that page. The point I try to help them see is that their feelings do not dictate their success in laboring, in coping and being resilient. The labor tweets and reflective moments around our labor, such as the labor logs, help us further notice how we are coping, and through noticing, students can build more approach coping competence, which leads to resilience. Because approach coping practices are so vital to laboring toward resilience, thus to the larger noncognitive of a *willingness to labor*, I reiterate these four teaching practices:

- **Focus assignment instructions on the process of labor** to accomplish and the amount of time on task, words to write or read, and not on some standard of quality

- **Integrate mindful pauses** in labor processes to help students notice what they have done, how they did it, and what they are learning.
- **Ask students to reframe the labor** or work at hand by rearticulating it in a different genre, to a different audience, or from a different perspective from the ones they started with.
- **Integrate ways to acknowledge students' feelings** about the labor at hand, allowing students to voice in some way their emotional responses to the work of the course.

The assumption is that most students, once they stop getting grades and other external motivators to guide their labor, they must replace those motivations with others. Approach coping practices are the ones I focus on. The previous examples of journal entries by T1 illustrate a more qualitative way to see evidence of coping in the ecology. T1 shows how she's not only able to stay in the labor by noticing how she is coping with the challenges of getting her labor done (e.g., she takes breaks to maintain focus in her reading), but also how she invents new ways to cope (i.e., to turn her cell phone to "Do Not Disturb").

M1, a Latina student from the middle group, reflects in her labor and mindfulness journal around the same time in the quarter (around week 6–7), showing coping in subtle but similar ways. M1 reflects:

> One labor session that i felt the most interesting and engaging for me was the extra three precis, even though they weren't required to do i felt like doing 5 wasn't really enough for me to understand our texts and what we read. While writing these i was in my bed chillin with criminal minds in the background as usual, but unlike our other precis these ones seemed easier to do. I didn't have to pause or mute my show like i usually do to focus on these and instead writing them just seemed to flow this time around. I feel like it was more productive because it wasn't really required. I didn't start thinking about "well do i really have to do these?" instead i found myself more engaged and interested also because I didn't have a specific reading i had to write about. I intend to use this motivation during the precis with my dramatic revision so that my writing can flow like they did with this labor.

M1's reflection appears at its face to show less explicit coping with the labor of the class. Instead of consciously adjusting her environment or behaviors to try to change her engagement in the writing of her precis, she relies on whatever feelings arise. In this case, they happen to help her because these precis were extra labor (done to get a higher course grade). M1 just notices and hopes she can keep up this kind of engaged labor. She notices what helps her focus or stay engaged in the activity, but has a vaguer sense than T1 of how to control her future labor sessions, or does not discuss how she might. While not as explicit as T1, M1's reflection still shows coping through noticing her engagement, and acknowledging her feelings as she labors. She was chillin in her bed, engaged and interested in the work, and she notices that she's not thinking, "well, do I need to do these?" She acknowledges this as a feeling ("I feel like . . .").

Furthermore, when I look at M1's actual labor accumulated by week in the quarter next to T1's actual labor, and B1 (a Latino student in the bottom performing group), some interesting patterns appear that suggest consistent coping and resilience behaviors by M1.

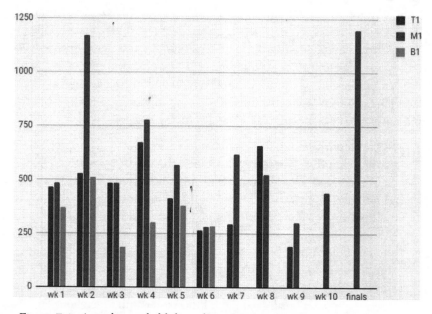

Figure 7.1. Actual recorded labor of T1, M1, and B1 by week of the quarter.

One coping strategy I've been suggesting is the simple act of noticing one's behavior, then recording it in labor logs (that's a signal of noticing). T1 didn't record her labor for the final week or during finals week, and B1 neglected to record his labor from weeks 7 on. Meanwhile, M1 records her labor through finals week. One way to read these data is to see the effects of M1 noticing her labor. They help her cope and be resilient to the end of the quarter. One confirmation of this is the amount of labor she records. Her labor did not decrease at the end of the quarter. In fact, it ramped up. All three students had similar labor patterns during the quarter, but M1 consistently recorded more labor than her peers.

She was able to stay in the labors, which allowed her to do more, and continue recording her labor.

And based on the higher amount of labor recorded by the students of color in this sample, M1 (Latina) is not an anomaly when it comes to coping and resilience. M2 (Black female) shows a similar pattern in her labor by week. She recorded 8.5 hours, 7.67 hours, and 16 hours of labor in the final three weeks of the quarter (weeks 9–10 and finals), a ramping up of labor. Meanwhile T3 (Latina) recorded 8.08 hours, 7.75 hours, and 6.67 hours in the same weeks of the quarter. While not a ramping up, it is a consistent recording to the end of the quarter. The only White student who completed his labor log to the end of the quarter was in the top group, T2, and he recorded 15 hours, 10 hours, and 5.17 hours in the final weeks—a ramping down. The same trend that T1 seems to be headed toward in Figure 7.1. All the other White students in the sample stopped recording their labor sessions in about week 9, where T1 stops. While this does affect the labor totals, it shows a trend. Is it possible that the act of completing the labor logs to the very end is a coping strategy that works well for students of color?

I want to emphasize that the actual numbers are less important in labor logs, since I don't think it is wise to compare exact numbers between individual students. Averages of identifiable groups (and the whole class) and general patterns (trends), such as those easily seen in Figure 7.1, are more useful in considering effectiveness of the ecology. Maintaining and ramping up in labor suggests successful coping and resilience strategies. Not being too focused on the numbers keeps a teacher from using one group's averages as a criterion by which all other groups in the class are judged effective or not. However, I do have a target number of hours per week I shoot for since I have identify estimated labor time on all labor instructions, so I do use this as a general guideline to understand whether I'm asking too much for a particular class or not enough labor during the quarter. Knowing how much on average you were asking students to labor each week during a term can be a useful criterion by which to gauge how effective the ecology was along Goal 1 and provides a guideline for reading labor log data for evidence of coping and resilience (Goal 2).

Many of the students in this class worked, and some had family obligations, while others only went to school, having more time to spend on school work. These factors changed what students can record, and may have actually enhance their coping competencies, since they needed more useful ones to succeed in school under heavier schedule obligations. During our discussions of our labor log entries in the middle of the quarter, around week 6, we changed the number of estimated labor each week from around twelve to around nine hours. Regardless of the actual numbers for any given class, a teacher might expect that the more students labor, generally speaking, the higher the likelihood that there are successful approach coping practices present in that group of students. The more labor recorded, and the longer they keep their labor logs also suggest coping and resilience practices.

Table 7.3 offers various kinds of evidence that may help understand how effective an ecology has been along this goal.

Table 7.3. Kinds of evidence of coping and resilience

Evidence of Coping and Resilience	Questions About Data
Amount of minutes/hours of labor accumulated in the course	How many students in the class were able to come close to or exceed the labor goals (in total mins/hours) that were agreed upon for the quarter/semester? What do students say about why they did or could not meet those labor targets? What approach coping practices did students try and say were helpful to them in accomplishing more labor? Do students complete their labor logs to the very end of the term?
Average minutes/hours of labor per week of the semester/quarter	What was the average total labor (mins/hours) for each student per week? How many students consistently achieved the labor goals (in hours/mins) each week? What do students say in weekly labor journals causes their labor time to dip below the minimum expectations? What coping strategies did students employ to maintain consistent labor week by week?
Average engagement ratings of labor sessions	How many students achieve 3 or better average engagement ratings? What do students say in journals that those ratings mean each week? Are their engagement ratings consistent over time or change? How well were students able to separate their feelings about labor from their sense of being successful in accomplishing the labor required of them?
Students' reflections on coping strategies	When asked periodically, what do students say about how they cope with the labor expected of them in the course? How closely do they say they follow the labor instructions given for assignments? Why do they deviate from them? Do they describe deviations in labor practices as approach or avoidance coping strategies?

Eli Review, a web-based, student, peer-review program that manages feedback and revision cycles for drafts, offers other kinds of data on the fly that tell stories about student intensity of work and engagement, much of which is determined by amount of words produced in feedback, number of comments made on peers' drafts, and the number of their comments that are judged effective or helpful by writers receiving feedback. If read in the right ways, this data too could tell something of coping and resilience. But as of the writing of this book, Eli Review only accounts for feedback processes, so it cannot say anything about coping or resilience, for instance, in any other labors of the course, like reading or even drafting and revising one's own drafts. Still, technologies that offer such data on the fly can be helpful in discerning such coping (Goal 2) or engagement (Goal 1) practices during a semester or quarter.

GOAL 3: TO PRACTICE METACOGNITIVE STRATEGIES FOR UNDERSTANDING ONE'S LABOR PRACTICES

While metacognitive competencies are a part of Goals 1 and 2, it is important for me to measure metacognition as a separate ecological goal. This means as a teacher, I attempt to gather evidence just to assess how effective the ecology is at encouraging students to practice metacognitive strategies as a way to understand their labor practices. In Chapter 3, I discussed labor as a three-dimensional, mindful practice, which maps most closely to the noncognitive literature on metacognitive strategies. Metacognitive strategies are those that involve a number of learning processes, such as goal-setting, planning, problem-solving, reflecting on one's strengths and weaknesses, monitoring progress, and making decisions about certain tasks and practices (Gutman and Schoon 22). Paul Pintrich provides a distinction between various definitions and models of metacognition in the psychological studies of it. There are those that focus on "knowledge of cognition" and those that focus on "the processes involving the monitoring, control, and regulation of cognition" (219).

In his overview of the literature around assessing metacognition in learning environments, drawing on Flavell's work on metacognition and cognitive monitoring, Pintrich offers a three-part model for metacognition. Metacognition, he says, involves, first, "strategic knowledge" about "general strategies for learning, thinking, and problem-solving" that tend to work across various domains and disciplines (220). For example,

> Strategic knowledge includes knowledge of the various
> strategies students might use to memorize material, to extract
> meaning from text, and to comprehend what they hear in

classrooms or what they read in books and other course materials. Although there are a large number of different learning strategies, they can be grouped into three general categories: rehearsal, elaboration, and organizational (Weinstein & Mayer, 1986). (Pintrich 220)

The second part to Pintrich's model is "knowledge about cognitive tasks," which include information about particular tasks' difficulty and other cognitive tasks required within a larger task. Knowledge about cognitive tasks is understanding the "what," "how," "when," and "why" of particular cognitive tasks (Paris et al. 296–98; qtd. in Pintrich 221). This knowledge helps a student use particular strategies and knowledge in particular situations for particular purposes. In writing classrooms, we often help students with rhetorical awareness and reading texts rhetorically, which are treated as cognitive abilities, but Pintrich's model explains that those cognitive abilities move into, or share, noncognitive domains, likely those cognitive competencies become noncognitive over time as a practice becomes "second nature" or habit (or as I've said here and elsewhere, as it becomes *habitus*). Finally, Pintrich identifies accurate "self-knowledge" about one's strengths and weaknesses as the third element in his model (Pentrich 221).

So if labor is to be mindful in the ways that I discuss in Chapter 3, then another way to explain the three dimensions of that mindful labor is to see those dimensions of labor as places to exercise metacognitive practices. The nature of these practices, what they activate or exercise in students, is at least three things:

1. strategic knowledge and knowledge about learning, thinking, and problem-solving;
2. knowledge about specific cognitive reading and writing tasks (the what, how, when, and why of tasks); and
3. accurate self-knowledge (strengths and weaknesses) about one's own reading and writing labors.

As you might guess, just keeping a labor log and journal offers evidence of each of these metacognitive dimensions, but it's the nature of that evidence and what students do that often matters most in understanding how effective a learning environment is along this kind of dimension. Having accurate self-knowledge about one's reading and writing labors (or understanding clearly the way others judge or would judge one's writing, for instance) is one thing, but using accurate self-knowledge strategically for planning and problem-solving in the future is another. Guided reflection is often required to make such knowledge usable or transferrable.

And so, reflection and metacognitive practices tend to make the habitual, our unseen or unheard practices and dispositions, seen and heard. Doing so gives a writer more control over their dispositions, providing knowledge of how to use them strategically, and perhaps change some of them. One way to think of this movement from cognitive to noncognitive is to think of it as a metacognitive process that pays attention to our labors and feelings during and after our labors. In labor-based grading ecologies, metacognitive practices often focus on the processes of labor and the attending attitudes and feelings experienced with them in order to build approach coping strategies and engagement, which allow students to stay in labor longer and have more opportunities to understand their labor in all three dimensions.

Reflections on one's labor, both as one is laboring and afterwards, then become evidence of metacognition. In fact, the act of recording one's labor is an act of metacognition, particularly in a labor log that requires the student to notice various features that construct their labor sessions, such as duration of the session, date and time of day, description of the labor, where the session of labor takes place, and engagement ratings. Pausing to record such data after each session is a metacognitive practice, just as labor tweets in the middle of a labor process are. Thus evidence of metacognition is not just written reflections, although those are important, but the data recorded by the student on their sessions of labor for the class.

Additionally, there has been much discussion in writing studies about the usefulness of metacognition for learning to write. In composition studies, the literature on reflection, and most notably Kathleen Blake Yancey's work (*Reflection*; *A Rhetoric*), offer writing teachers ways to think about metacognition in literacy classrooms. Yancey explains that in the different literatures on metacognition and reflection, these two concepts are defined differently as learner practices. Yancey says that metacognition is "thinking about thinking associated with planning, self-monitoring, and self-regulation," while reflection is oriented to self-assessment activit[ies] occurring at the end of a learning cycle, though capable of prompting a new one" (*A Rhetoric* 6). In order to practice metacognition, she explains that most models say that students should engage in processes of monitoring and control, thus they usually take on a pattern like this:

- assess the task at hand, taking into consideration the task's goals and constraints;
- evaluate their own knowledge and skills, identifying strengths and weaknesses;
- plan their approach in a way that accounts for the current situation;

- apply various strategies to enact their plan, monitoring their progress along the way;
- reflect on the degree to which their current approach is working so that they can adjust and restart the cycle as needed. (Yancey, *A Rhetoric* 7; Ambrose et al. 191–99)

Thus, in the psychological and educational literature, metacognition is a process of monitoring and controlling how one goes about doing the labors of learning, while reflection is the final step in the larger processes of metacognition. The kind of reflection that writing teachers tend to think of as metacognition, then, is just the last step in the above five-step process that is always happening, if a student is exercising metacognition along the way. To be clear, for my purposes in this chapter, metacognition occurs *in the labors of learning*, and is exemplified in the labor log, while reflection happens *after the labors of learning* but focuses its attention on those labors, and is exemplified in the labor journal and other formal reflection documents.

Of course, this is not the only way in which reflection has been defined. The two most influential figures for Yancey's work on reflection are John Dewey and Donald Schon. Dewey says that "reflective thought" is based on "active, persistent, and careful consideration" (qtd. in Yancey, *A Rhetoric* 7; Dewey 6), so it could be argued that Dewey is thinking about reflective thought as a part of a larger process of metacognition, perhaps similar to the one identified in the educational literature by Yancey. Schon's work on reflection among practitioners in professional settings explains reflection in at least two ways, as "reflection in action" (Schon 28) and as "reflective transfer" (Schon 97). Again, Schon also appears to be thinking about reflection as a part of an ongoing process that happens as one practices and that changes or "transfers" new ideas, practices, strategies, and competencies, which occurs afterwards. Yancey's own three kinds of reflections in writing classrooms is the most influential in writing circles and draws on Dewey and Schon. She defines three kinds of reflection for writing classrooms:

- *reflection-in-action*, the process of reviewing and projecting and revising, which takes place within a composing event;
- *constructive reflection*, the process of developing a cumulative, multi-selved, multi-voiced identity, which takes place between and among composing events; and
- *reflection-in-presentation*, the process of articulating the relationships between and among the multiple variables of writing and the writer in a specific context for a specific audience (Yancey, *Reflection* 200).

One might view Yancey's three kinds of reflection in writing courses as a loose overlay to the five-step process of metacognition mentioned above, with a more focused consideration on what happens to the learner in the reflection process. That is, Yancey's model focuses on the nature of the reflective discourses and practices that occur in the processes of learning to write. So her model actually is more labor-oriented, and reveals the nature of the changing reflective stances a student moves in and out of.

Yancey's three reflection practices also can be mapped to the metacognitive processes of learning that I've discussed already. Reflection-in-action is the metacognitive processes of monitoring and control that occur in the first four steps of Ambrose et al.'s model (above), cited by Yancey, and is equivalent to Schon's reflection in action. This metacognition, I attempt to capture in labor tweets that occur during the processes of labor—often, I think of them as modified versions of think aloud protocols, mindful moments that help us pay attention to our labors. Constructive reflection is the in-between process of metacognition, often happening along the way in a course periodically. I see this mostly in labor journal entries when students construct and articulate versions of themselves and their labor practices. While reflection-in-presentation is the final step in the course's movement to the end of the semester or quarter. In my courses, this often occurs formally in our end-of-quarter letter of reflection that pays careful attention to our labor as a practice, which examines labor logs and journals for patterns and insights, then represents labor as a practice over the semester or quarter by the student.

There are several ways to structure a course so that it is easy to assess an ecology's effectiveness along this course goal, which may be clear already. I simply make it difficult for me to not see evidence of metacognition, since we look consistently and carefully at our labor logs, labor tweets, and labor journals, then center our final conferences on their final, formal reflections on their labor as a practice during the quarter. These final reflections on labor as a practice, as discussed in Chapters 3 and 4, offer evidence of the ecology's ability to help students become more conscious of their labors in ways that help them monitor, plan, read, and write flexibly in the future.

The students in my course example from Table 7.1 generally had trouble with articulating their labor as a practice, which isn't unusual for young, first-year writing students. But a few students in the middle category (and most in the higher performing category) were able to begin doing this. For instance, M1 (Latina) offers this reflection during week 7 of the quarter. I asked students to look at their labor logs and make some observations about their labor as a practice. She writes:

Throughout these 7 weeks of the quarter I have produced 3,510 minutes worth of labor which divides into 510 minutes per week. I spend more time and I am more engaged on the work where I have to write rather than the reading. That makes me wonder why, is it because of the reading material? Or maybe I just learn better when I can write it out rather than when I read it? I liked looking at my labor and seeing how much I actually got done over the past 7 weeks. It makes me feel better knowing I actually did work and didn't slack off like I did when I did when I was in High School.

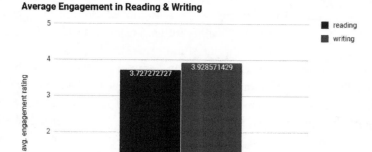

Average Engagement in Reading & Writing

Recording my labor has been very helpful in the way that I can see how much work into my assignments and see what I enjoyed doing most and what I didn't enjoy as much. What I did enjoy I obviously put more work into which means if I can find some way to be interested in whatever my assignment is than I can make it better and do better on the assignment. I plan to use that method with my other classes and assignments.

M1 does a good job here, well enough to find some useful information for her future practices. She demonstrates metacognitive practices by keeping her labor log current (so she can do this reflection) and by finding some useful patterns in her labors. In the process, she constructs in this journal entry a reflective self and description of her laboring in the course.

It is interesting to note that her average engagement ratings for reading and writing sessions are pretty close, only a difference of .2. More typically, students self-report their writing engagement at .5 or higher than their reading engagement in my courses at UW Tacoma. And since both of these engagement ratings are well above 3, her labor sessions seemed to be going well. I consider engagement ratings of 3 or higher to be good engagement. What she isn't able to talk about, but hints at in her first paragraph, is that her reading labors total only about 1/7 of her total writing labors, meaning she engaged in seven times the amount of writing labor, than reading. Granted the course is set up to be more writing heavy, but not this lopsided. More typical in this class was for writing labors to be four or five times as much as reading labors. It likely meant for M1 that she found deeper engagement when she wrote for our class and so she did more of it. Her knowing this is a good sign of metacognition about her labors. And because M1 is in the middle category of students, one could argue that this is a good sign of the ecology's effectiveness along this goal. A deeper look at the reflections of others in this category (middle category) in the class would help understand how true this is.

But understanding how effective the ecology is at getting students to engage consistently in metacognitive practices about their labor can be measured in other ways too. Counting the number of labor Slacks/tweets each student accumulated is one way. For instance, the average number of labor tweets for the high, middle, and bottom performing groups from Table 7.1 align with their other labor data. The high group averaged 29.3 tweets over the semester, the middle group, 21.6, and the low group, 16.3. If a teacher wished to use labor tweets even more strategically toward metacognitive ends, making them a more integral part of the class and every assignment, other data could be gathered to understand how effective the ecology was at achieving this goal. For example, one possible index of metacognitive practice about one's labor could be total hours of labor divided by the total estimated hours assigned, then multiplied by the total number of tweets a student sent divided by the number assigned. Since an increase in either labor hours or tweets would increase the total index number, and more tweeting or labor continues to raise the score. One could weight either side of the equation further by using a multiplier, for instance, multiplying the tweets by two. As an example, here's my metacognitive index formula:

In my example groups from Table 7.1, the metacognitive indexes for each student in each category match my sense of each student's metacognitive capacities, as demonstrated in the course and their final portfolios. For example, T2 (White male) offered a total of 31 tweets in our 10 week quarter, and logged 92.67 hours of labor, which gives him a metacognitive index of 1.28. Meanwhile, T3 (Latina) had fewer labor hours logged (88.17) but substantially more tweets (37), which increased her index to 1.45. So while T3 didn't do quite as much labor as T1, which would be measured as favorably along the first goal above, along this third goal, her labor tweets show her to be more metacognitive in the labor she did complete (she paused and tweeted more).[56]

The metacognitive index is just a crude number that may help at midpoint, for instance, in seeing quickly how a class or individual students, are doing along this dimension, perhaps showing whether a teacher might need to probe more deeply into journals or have conversations in class. If used, take it with a grain of salt. The index is just a number, a construct. But I will say that when I average each group in Table 7.1, I get consistent metacognitive indexes that match generally my senses of those groups of students in my class (top is at 1.10, middle at .77, and bottom at .31). These indexes also suggest how close to the labor hours and labor tweet targets I tried to set for them, with a metacognitive index score of 1 being perfectly met.

Is there an index number that suggests to me a student isn't doing enough along this dimension? This is hard to say. Perhaps, but one would need some criteria by which to compare these numbers. My goals in this class were always to assign between eight to ten hours of labor each week, give or take, and to ask students to do on average 2.5 labor tweets each week. So if a student did ninety hours of labor and twenty-five tweets, they would get a metacognitive index of 1. But I'm often wanting students to tweet more, since I find that tweeting is a mindful activity when done in the way I ask. So I can see myself adjusting this formula to weigh more heavily tweets, say with a multiplier of two. This would mean that tweeting is calculated as more metacognitively heavy.

I offer these details about my metacognitive index, not so that you might use it yourself, but to show how a teacher might collect such simple data in order to measure such a goal empirically, even if it says very little about the nature of the metacognitive practices circulating in the ecology. This number, then could be evidence of an ecology's effectiveness along this goal, but a poor indicator of the nature of those metacognitive practices. Since I don't use outcomes, instead more open-ended goals, I am okay with only knowing that my ecology is effective in some way.

Finally, another kind of evidence a teacher might use to make arguments about their ecology's effectiveness along this goal might be simply the number of students who completed their labor logs to the end of the course. I used to have about 30%–50% of my students not complete their labor logs to the very end of

---

56   I should note that I've experimented with this formula for metacognitive index and found other useful formulas using the same data. For instance, a simpler version is one that replaces the right-side of the present formula with just number of tweets. So a theoretically typical student doing all that is asked of them, and nothing more, would have a metacognitive score of approximately equal to the number of tweets assigned at any given moment in the quarter or semester. The higher their score, the more metacognitively engaged they are.

the course, as was the case for this course.[57] Now, I do a better job at reminding students and using the logs each week, which has translated into nearly everyone completing their labor logs to the final days of the course. Table 7.4 shows several ways to gather evidence of effectiveness for this goal, and some questions that may help a teacher investigate that data.

Table 7.4. Kinds of possible evidence of metacognition around labor

Evidence of Metacognition	Questions about Data
Labor tweets	How many labor tweets per assignment (or per week) do students do on average? How many total did they do and how many did you ask of them?
Labor logs and metacognitive indexes	How many students completed their labor logs during the semester/quarter? How many entries per week did they do on average? What is the average metacognitive index for the top, middle, and bottom groups of students (determined by amount of labor recorded in labor logs)?
Labor journals	How many students completed their labor journals (did all journal entries assigned)? How many students had longer journal entries in the final few weeks of the semester/quarter than in the first few weeks?
Formal reflection documents	How many students were able to make sense of their labor logs and journals in formal reflection documents (journals and/or letters of reflection in portfolios)? How many were able to articulate future best practices or lessons learned about their reading or writing labors in those reflection documents?

Note that I'm not asking questions about the nature of metacognition in the evidence listed in Table 7.4, but one might if a teacher wanted to know the nature of the metacognition circulating in their course, which may be important to understanding the effectiveness of metacognition in that class (if metacognitive practices are predefined). As I discuss in Chapter 6, I don't know where each of my diverse students start in my course, nor can I anticipate what their linguistic competencies will be after my class. They learn what they can, and only that. I cannot force things, nor am I willing to punish students with lower grades for being who they are. This means that my ecology's effectiveness need only

---

57   In this course, four of the twenty students did not make entries in their labor logs into November (finals week is early December). Interestingly, one of the students who completed the necessary extra labor for a 4.0 in the course was in this group, while the other three students ended up with low but passing course grades.

be measured by whether metacognitive practices, like pausing and tweeting, or reflecting each week on their labors, are being practiced consistently. The nature of that metacognition is what we discuss together as a class or student and teacher, but it need not be factored in my determination of whether my ecology is effective or not.

Furthermore, the nature of metacognition is too varied to have predetermined ideas about what all students should come to. As Tyler Richmond and I discuss, reflection likely is itself a racialized discourse, and may pose contradictions for many multilingual students and students of color who do not share a White racial *habitus* that is typically a part of reflective discourses in college classrooms (142). So I don't want to measure my ecology's effectiveness at getting students to practice metacognitive strategies by assuming a preferred White racial *habitus* in metacognition. Finally, since the grading ecology is a labor-based one, its goals, even ones that promote metacognition, are about measuring how effective the course is at getting students to labor in particular ways, without putting too many constraints on what laboring means. This allows this goal of the ecology to be open-ended and looking for new ways to do metacognition.

GOAL 4: TO SEEK AN AWARENESS OF THE POLITICS OF LANGUAGE AND ITS JUDGMENT.

This goal could easily be considered a part of the previous goal, since its focus on seeking awareness is very close to metacognition, so one might think of seeking awareness of language and its politics as a specific, focused version of metacognitive practices. However, because this goal centers on examining and questioning the power dynamics of language norms, expectations, and judgments that circulate in assessment ecologies, or systems that contain social arrangements of uneven power, I want it to be its own ecological goal. Some of these power relations come from the dominant Discourses used as standards in the assessment ecologies that students circulate in (e.g., White racial *habitus*). Some are from gender, racial, and other social dimensions of those in the ecology itself that intersect with those dominant Discourses.

Regardless of what power dynamics in language and its judgment one wishes to focus on in a classroom, this learning goal requires specific information about such politics, which for some people does not seem the purview of a writing classroom. I don't see how any writing classroom can escape politics, either in terms of pedagogy or curriculum. Politics have always defined language instruction, its history, pedagogies, and assessment practices. I've spent some time drawing out this argument historically and theoretically in classroom writing assessments (Inoue, *Antiracist*) from a racialized standpoint. But I'm not the first to explain the writing classroom or its assessment in terms of politics. To see the evidence of the politics in writing instruction, we need only look to the discussions on remediation (Rose; Otte and Mlynarczyk; Soliday) that note the historically recurring "literacy crises" that respond to various political exigencies of the time, mostly the presence of people in schools who were not there before, or who weren't noticed before. We might consider also the discussions around the politics of writing in English departments and colleges (Miller; Ohmann; Crowley; Kynard), or the historically situated politics in testing and assessment (Hanson; Faigley; Elliot; Inoue and Poe; Poe et al.). Or we might look to the discussions in assessment that explain the politics of judgment, who judges are, and where those judges get their values (Guba and Lincoln; Broad; Huot; White et al., *Assessment of Writing*; White et al., *Like a Whale*). No matter the literature one draws on, the conclusion is the same: Teaching literacy means helping students learn about the politics of literacy and how one's language is judged in the world from those politics.

How does a teacher measure a student's awareness of the politics of language and its judgment? Some theory about language, race, power, and Whiteness are needed. I will offer a condensed version of some of the discussions I use, mainly Whiteness, but there are others, and it will depend on the teacher's politics and philosophy of language, as well as the program's and its curricula. But first, I must say a few words about "awareness," an important term that is related to reflection and metacognition, and is central to the nature and methods by which this goal's effectiveness can be understood and measured.

Awareness comes from being mindful and reflective of one's practices, so this goal is interlaced with the first three above. As Yancey points out in her discussion, reflection is the final step in metacognitive processes. This means that reflective documents are often thought of as a way of articulating what has been learned through metacognitive actions and later reflecting labors. When teachers wish to assess whether a reflective document is adequate or productive, they do not sit on the shoulder of the student, watching them "reflect" as they write. We get the final product, which we then judge as the student reflecting. But it is not the actual reflecting (verb), per se. We are not looking at the act or the labor of reflecting. It is, as Yancey points out, "reflection-in-presentation," or "a public text representing the self" to a reader (*Reflection* 70). In short, we are reading and judging the noun, reflection, as an indicator of the verb, reflecting, that created the noun in front of us. We don't really know the labor of reflecting as much as we know the product in front of us as a representation of some kind of previous labor.

Furthermore, most teachers make decisions about their ecology's effectiveness at getting students to become aware of language and its politics by comparing a present student's reflection-in-presentation on such things against a set of expectations, an exemplar, or a prototype that the teacher holds in their head, three kinds of judging that I explain in Chapter 2 through Haswell's work on holistic judgments. As Catherine Fox argues about critical thinking in critical pedagogies, our typical ways of understanding this kind of goal's effectiveness in writing courses seems to require that we have an idea of what "awareness of the politics of language" is, then judge students against that idea. They have to mimic our (the teacher's) kind of awareness, says Fox (202–03), and this is a Whitely stance to take as a teacher (201–02).

While I do have my ideas about what an awareness of the politics of language and its judging looks and sounds like, I try not to use that as criteria, or an exemplar or prototype against which to judge students' performances as adequate or not. Instead, I draw on contemplative traditions, traditions that tangibly honor labor as practice done nonjudgmentally—that is, I do not use some kind of "awareness criteria" or exemplar to judge a student's practices of reflection along this goal in order to know how effective my assessment ecology has been. If students are producing reflective documents, recording their labor sessions in their labor logs, then they are doing some form of seeking awareness. How deep or to what degree are questions that have little meaning to understanding my assessment ecology's effectiveness since most of what I can read in a written product is a construction of many other elements in the ecology, in my reading practices, and in the life of that student.

Students can learn and do exactly what they can at this moment. Why would I think that my ecology is less effective because a student who hasn't yet been able to articulate the way Whiteness functions in the judgment practices of his peers, say in their feedback to him, when perhaps she has just recognized Whiteness in her world this quarter for the first time? Is it not enough to see that she is seeking? I know this sounds like I'm saying that anything written down is evidence of this goal if the student says so, but that's not quite it, and there are ways I think one can triangulate. But awareness is a stance in labor, so finding a way to measure the doing of it in labor is the most direct, yet most difficult thing.

To help explain further why I see evidence of this goal in this seemingly permissive way, it helps to understand another assumption about labor in many contemplative traditions. Unlike typical assumptions we make to judge an instance of reflection-in-presentation, contemplative traditions (Barbezat and Bush; Chodron; Hahn; Zajonc) assume that mindfulness, or a reflective stance in a practice, requires the person to first practice, and through practicing, a reflective, mindful stance is slowly acquired, yet never perfected (thus we are always practicing). This stance tends to be called "awareness." While awareness is always a goal, it is not an outcome that tells a practitioner or student that they've done the practice correctly, that they've arrived and are *aware*. Yet iron-ically, simply doing the practice is doing it correctly—one has already arrived, one is already here. There is no one way to do it, no set criteria, no exemplar, no prototypes, by which to judge one's practice as aware or not. One cannot do a practice wrong, or perfectly right, for that matter. But one can continue to work at a practice, continue exploring ways to do it, continue seeking to be-come aware—remember, we are all always becoming. Thus value distinctions, ones that hierarchize instances of reflections, for instance, have no meaning in this "non-judgmental" paradigm of judging the evidence of effectiveness for this goal. Since one can only do a practice like seeking awareness, and explore know-ing *that* they are doing it as they do it, it is the *exploring* part that is key. When students are doing the labor, if it is designed right, they are already here, seeking, becoming aware. This is what I look to find evidence of in my ecologies when I measure for this goal's effectiveness.

To measure this goal's effectiveness, I need to gather evidence of the ways students practice seeking awareness of the politics of language, likely imitating at first these reflective stances by posing questions and attempting answers, in order to notice that they are practicing posing questions. Part of this stance of awareness is focusing on noticing while practicing the stance, at first pretending to be mindful and reflective until that pretending becomes more authentic, or habitual—until their practicing becomes *habitus*. But it is unrealistic to expect students to form new *habitus* in a ten-week quarter or a fifteen-week semester, so I look only for the imitating, the initial seeking of awareness in their reflective documents, not to particular conclusions. In several other places, I discuss ways an assessment ecology might meet this goal, as recurring assessment practices that are problematizing (*Antiracist* 237–67), and as Frierian problem-posing, letter-writing activities ("Classroom Writing Assessment"). These reflective doc-uments, as instances of reflection-in-presentation, do offer ways to measure the effectiveness of the ecology at achieving this goal. I look for the presence of the seeking of awareness, not particular practices, conclusions, or insights.

So, the nature of any student's own awareness about the politics of language is that student's business. It simply is not my place to judge whether a student is right or wrong about such things, even if I likely have more information about what they may be trying to learn or understand. I'm still seeking myself. So understanding the ecology's effectiveness along this goal needs to reflect this pedagogical assumption in my ecology. Furthermore, this more humble stance toward my students' seeking awareness of the politics of language is a way to avoid Whitely habits of being the judge, peacemaker, and assuming I know what is right for all students, habits that many have already identified as Whitely habits (Pratt; Fox 201; Frankenberg; Frye 153–54), habits that Fox argues we must "disarticulate" from our assumptions about criticality in our pedagogies (204). This doesn't mean that I cannot offer my own ideas about things during the term, but in this chapter, I'm talking about assessing the effectiveness of the ecology's ability to meet this goal. So judging the effectiveness of this goal in reflections is mostly about noticing when the stance of seeking awareness occurs, without judging the nature of what the student comes to understand or articulate, even though I might make an observation or two about these things to the student during the term.

What this kind of nonjudgmental judgment by a teacher does is demonstrate one counter disposition to those of a White racial *habitus* practiced by most writing teachers. And this kind of judging, not so ironically, illustrates how to apply the theoretical insights that this goal demands students come in contact with. That is, seeking awareness of the politics of language and is judgment is a stance teachers can use to assess the effectiveness of this same goal in our ecologies. Is the seeking of awareness present? How many students are doing this regularly? So, I'm arguing that measuring the nature of the awareness is a different question from measuring its effectiveness in an ecology. Presence, for the most part, means effective, even if it is a rough measure. Measuring the nature of students' performances that might demonstrate this goal is a qualitative process that might look a lot like Broad's dynamic criteria mapping, while measuring the effectiveness of the ecology to produce such stances in labor is a matter of finding out if such seeking of awareness is present, regardless of what it looks or sounds like.

Again, I know that many will read this kind of evidence gathering as permissive and loose, perhaps even a way to lower so-called standards. In reality, it is that you've accepted one set of assumptions about what it means to measure effectiveness along such a goal, and I've accepted another set, a set of assumptions I've been attempting to make explicit. I argue that the first set of assumptions, like our schools and academic disciplines, like the dominant English promoted in society, are steeped in Whiteness and promote White language supremacy, while the latter assumptions that center around nonjudgmental judgment attempts to disarticulate those Whitely assumptions in order to form more perfect judgment practices, ones that embody the kind of critical impulses toward valuing diverse perspectives, logics, and Englishes that we say we value.

Let me put it one more way, perhaps to make you uncomfortable if you still are not convinced: If you think that you know best what your students need to know about communication and writing, about what they should be aware of in language and its politics, if you think that you can dictate the standard for such practices, that you are benevolent enough and truly have all your students' best interests at heart when deciding on and administering your standards of awareness and criticality, then you are enacting a White racial *habitus* that has been one major way schools and society have perpetuated White language supremacy. It is a reenactment of Whitely good intentions, the White savior mentality, and an unnecessary taking on of the White man's burden.

In "White Woman Feminist," Marilyn Frye, drawing on Minnie Bruce Pratt (1984), offers a list of dispositions that equate to Whiteliness, or Whitely dispositions. These dispositions might be thought of as habits of Whiteness, a White *habitus*, and they amount to the following:

- *Being a judge and peacemaker*: a disposition toward giving responsibility and punishments, being the preacher and martyr, taking responsibility and the glory.
- *Self-understood benevolence*: a disposition toward seeing oneself (and other Whitely people) as benevolent, good-willed, fair, honest, and ethical.
- *Being procedurally ethical*: a strong sense of right and wrong, usually rooted in dispositions toward forms, procedures, due process, and rules as the basis of the ethical; to be good, one acts according to the rules, which is understood as principled.
- *Authority*: a disposition toward running the show, or aspiring toward it, and a belief in one's infallible authority in most matters. (Frye 153–54; Fox 202; my emphasis)

While as the teacher, I try hard not to enact these dispositions of a White racial *habitus* in my responses to my students' writing, I also know that students may still read me as acting in such ways. This goal in the assessment ecology is designed to help the ecology discourage and disable the power of such *habitus*. But the effects are always uneven. I am still the teacher of record. I must "run the show" and distribute grades. Sometimes, I must be the peacemaker and judge, even if those roles do not mean being a preacher and martyr (I may still be read in these ways). Nevertheless, I do not have to act as if my authority is based on infallibility. I do not have to be the "preacher" every time a question is posed to me or the class. I do not have to see myself as a benevolent teacher, etc. I am simply the teacher, a man who is flawed as much as his students are, yet a man who is in a position of power, therefore must act responsibly.

I say all this to say that the effectiveness of this goal in the assessment ecology is just as much about how teachers conduct themselves as how students do. I'm tempted to say that one kind of evidence of this goal's effectiveness in an assessment ecology is how much seeking of awareness of the politics of language and its judgment the teacher is doing? Evidence of a teacher's seeking of awareness might be in things like the teacher's comments and feedback, the absence of grades and ranking of student writing and work, and a teacher's labor and mindfulness journal that focuses on questions about how that teacher is practicing such a stance of seeking awareness. Are you seeking awareness of the politics of language and its judgment, or have you figured it out already? How long did it take you to get to whatever conclusions you might make about the nature of your current awareness?

Drawing on other theories of Whiteness as well, including most notably Sarah Amed, my students and I have created a set of habits of White discourse that are pervasive in school standards for writing and in readers who judge writing by those standards. There are six habits that are most characteristic of a White racial *habitus*, which leads many teachers to feeling that their own linguistic dispositions, which are not simply linguistic but embodied, as James Paul Gee among others have argued (Young; Inoue, *Antiracist*), are the best standard by which to judge their students. These habits of Whiteness can be used to help students and teacher form practices of seeking awareness of the politics of language and its judgment. My students and I articulate them as follows:

- **Unseen, naturalized, orientation to the world**—an **orientation (or starting point) of one's body in time and space that makes certain things reachable**; assumes (or takes as universal) proximities (capabilities to act and do things) that are inherited through one's shared space; an oxymoronic haunting, leaving things unsaid/unstated for the audience to fill in and contains multiple contradictions (is ambiguous) in how it can be understood; a style of embodiment that is invisible to the person or voice; a way of inhabiting spaces that is comfortable (allows the person to "sink into the space" around the body); the space becomes an extension of the White body and its discourse in such a way that it is hard to distinguish where the White body ends and the world begins; any utterance may participate in this orientation to the world by how the utterance operates in the space (does it sink in?) and what its effects are.
- **Hyperindividualism—self-determination and autonomy** is most important or most valued; self-reliance, self-sufficiency, and self-control are important; individual rights and privacy are often most important and construct the common good; the truth is always good to hear, no matter how painful, good, or bad it may be (each individual has the right to know the truth).
- **Stance of neutrality, objectivity, and apoliticality**—assumes or invokes a voice (and body) or its own discourse as neutral and apolitical, non-racial, which might use some of the other habits to reinforce this neutral and objective stance.

- **Individualized, rational, controlled self**—person is conceived as an **individual who is rational, self-conscious, self-controlled, and determined**; conscience guides the individual and sight is the primary way to identify the truth or understanding; social and cultural factors are external constraints to the individual; meaningful issues and questions always lie within the self; individuals have problems and solutions are individually-based; both success and failure are individual in nature; failure is always attached to the individual and often seen as weakness; control of self is important, as is work and staying busy, or being industrious and productive; unsure how to cope with the uncontrollable in selves, society, or nature.

- **Rule-governed, contractual relationships**—a focus on the **individual in a contractual relationship** with other individuals; focuses on "informed consent" and negotiation of individual needs; individual rights are more important and non-political, whereas socially-oriented values and questions are less important and often political (bad) by their nature; attachment to laws, rules, fairness as sameness; the contractual regulates relationships; little emphasis on connectedness, relatedness, feeling, interconnection with others; individuals keep difficulties and problems to themselves.

- **Clarity, order, and control**—a focus on **reason, order, and control; thinking (versus feeling)**, insight, the rational, order, objective (versus subjective), rigor, clarity, and consistency are all valued highly; thinking/rationality and knowledge are non-political, unraced, and can be objective; anti-sensuality is valued, while there is a limited value of sensual experiences, considerations of the body, sensations, and feelings; a belief in scientific method, discovery, and knowledge; deductive logics are preferred; usefulness and pragmatism are important measures of value and success. (Inoue, "Classroom Writing Assessment" Appendix A)[58]

I introduce and use these habits to help students pose questions about judgments on their writing, and come up with larger questions about the nature of judgment itself. We do this periodically, often after each draft's assessment letters (feedback from peers) are circulated. If we have time, I push them to ask deeper questions in light of their own power dynamics in their writing groups, or translate their initial insights to other contexts, say another course that they must write in, one that may grade their writing.

---

58   In the past, my students and I have drawn on the following to help us build these habits of White discourse: Ahmed; Barnett; Brookhiser; Elbow ("Ranking"); Fanon; Fox ("The Evolution"); Frye; Kennedy, Middleton, and Ratcliffe; Myser; McGill; and Ratcliffe.

In the example FYW course I've been using in this chapter, we used these habits of a White discourse to explore differences in peers' judgments made on drafts at two points in the quarter. I asked students to write a letter to me about differences in a few of their colleagues' judgments made on their last draft, looking for ways that the above habits of Whiteness might be informing the way they or their peers read things. To invent the letters, I ask them to build a table with three columns based on their readings of their colleagues' assessment letters. One column has peers' judgments on their drafts (literally copying and pasting of the words from reader's assessment letters to the writer). The next column has the rubric dimension that the judgment just pasted into the previous column is speaking to or about (another copy and paste). And the third column gives the habit of Whiteness that the writer thinks most applies to the judgment. Using these tables, the letters are then written to start a short dialogue about judgment with me.

While I've been arguing that the nature of the seeking of awareness is not as important to measure in order to understand if an ecology is effective at meeting this goal, I understand the need to know the nature of such reflections. T3 offers a typical example of seeking an awareness of the politics of language and its judgment through a look at the way her group members understood one of our rubric dimensions that focused on how we use evidence in our drafts. What made her draft problematic (in a good way) to start with was that it was a poem. The assignment was to dramatically change their drafts from the last version. She chose to change her research essay into two poems, each offering a side of the debate about bullying in school. T3 writes:

> One of the main artifacts that all colleagues chose to focus
> on was, "How does the writer manage or treat evidence of all
> kinds in their argument or discussion?" When J discussed this
> artifact in her letter of assessment, she pointed out how she
> felt that my attempts were unsuccessful. "I felt this dimension
> is where you lacked in your poem. In the directions it said
> that we need at least 3 sources of evidence in your poem, I
> struggled even finding one. Early in this draft I saw that you
> tried to tie the movie "Mean Girls" into it by saying "All I
> could think about is how conflicts were handled in mov-
> ies." . . . I see what you were trying to do here by using the
> movie as a source, but it did not work for me" (J). I struggled
> reading this line because I thought that my letter beforehand
> would clear any confusion as to why there were not any sourc-
> es but at least I had tried. I thought that if I had pointed out

my own errors before hand, then maybe the readers would
be a bit more understanding that incorporating three blatant
sources into what I was writing was extremely difficult. Then
Jamerika mentioned, "I do not think it necessarily even needs
sources, but just for our requirements" (J). After reading this I
thought, "Wait." J kind of contradicted herself in a way [. . .]
Which one does she want me hook onto? Making my sources
better? Or realize that they are not even needed? S, however,
contradicted with what J had first mentioned about my sources. "I understand that as your draft was a personal invention,
there's really only minimal need for sources. Besides the necessary ones you included of course, sources really do not make
much sense in this specific context" (S). This makes sense to
me. I felt that when I first started writing that sources were
not really necessary, even though it is a requirement. But if I
want a good grade, then I need to follow those specific labor
instructions, right? [. . .]

So far here is how I have interpreted the contradictions: 1:
"Your attempt at including evidence was not successful. You
should try X, Y, and Z to make it more efficient—BUT, your
poem does not need sources anyways." 2: "Since this is a poem,
sources are not even needed." [. . .] I am at a crossroad.

[. . .] How can you successfully include sources in something
that is not a traditional essay?

What I find exemplifies this ecological goal the most in this letter is the way in
which T3 maintains a questioning attitude toward her colleagues' judgments,
trying to hear the way in which each is reasonable. She comes to a good question
that really is rooted in a sense of the politics of language, even though she cannot
articulate those politics here. How do you include sources in poems (in a way
that all readers will recognize and accept)? T3 is asking good questions that come
from judgments on her draft. While she cannot yet articulate a question about
judgment itself, she is asking about expectations and norms, which is fundamentally a question about the politics of language and its judgment, audiences and
expectations, genres and conventions. As the reader of this letter, I can respond
by helping her articulate these nascent questions as political ones, ones about
who has the power to determine the answers, under what conditions, and to
what effects in society or schools.

In T3's table, she links J's contradictory judgment, but one that ultimately
sides with the draft's requirements (that assumed a conventional paper), to the

White habit of an "Individualized, Rational, Controlled Self," explaining that "I mentioned in my letter that I struggled with including sources throughout the piece, and my subtle attempt of including a source was not viable for J." T3 associates S's judgment that centers on sticking to the genre expectations of poems with the habit of "Hyperindividualism," which she explains in this way: "[s]ince I did a personal poem, sources aren't necessarily needed. This contradicts J's point." Because the table doesn't ask her to come to some conclusion, just record observations, it helps T3 seek awareness of the politics of language, even if she doesn't articulate clearly these politics in the letter—that is, articulate the contradictions in judgments that she raises as uneven power dynamics and differences in expectations or norms that are enforced in most school assessment ecologies through the use of grades and a teacher's authoritative feedback.

The next step would be for T3 and I to talk about how these judgments, while they participate in such habits of Whiteness like an individualized, rational, and controlled self, and hyperindividualism, are not engaging in White language supremacy. Why? It is simply that J is a Black female colleague (S is a White male)? White language supremacy can be enacted through a body of color. Both do not engage in White language supremacist judgment practices because our assessment ecology keeps that from happening. How such judgments are circulated and their effects on those in the ecology matters to seeing such White habits as enactments of White language supremacy. The draft is not graded or ranked, so even if judges have engage in such White habits in feedback, as J and S seem to have in differing degrees, they are not used against T3 to force her to do something she isn't interested in doing in her writing or punish her for not doing it in the first place. She has a real revision choice, and the labor-based ecology helps her seek awareness in a safe way. This context makes the mere presence of such reflection in the letter an indication of the ecologies effectiveness along this fourth goal.

The measure I use to assess the ecology's effectiveness at this goal, then, is not what T3 and her colleagues come to understand or articulate about White language privilege. Doing so would be a Whitely act itself on my part, since I'd have to use my own notions of what students should come to understand about the politics of language, regardless of their own subject positions or goals for our course. Instead, I look for the seeking of understanding through the questioning of judgments, which she and most of her colleagues do.

In retrospect, I can see one way that I might be able to further set up the assessment ecology so that all students demonstrate such a seeking of awareness. I might add one column to the brainstorming tables that all students must complete before they can write their problem-posing letters to me. This new column might ask them to pose a question or two that each row of information reveals to them about the politics of language, or about the judgment made in that instance. As an example, consider a portion of T3's table that she submitted with her letter to me, which I've revised to include a new column (far right, "Question(s)" column) that poses a question or two about the politics of language and its judgment that might come from considering the information in that row.

Table 7.5. An example of a table that shows evidence of seeking an awareness of the politics of language and its judgment

Colleagues Judgments	Rubric Dimension	Whiteness Trait	Question(s)
"In the directions it said that we need at least 3 sources of evidence, and in this poem, I struggled even finding one . . . I saw that you tried to tie in the movie "Mean Girls" . . . I see what you were trying to do here by using the movie as a source, but it did not work for me" (J).	*How does the writer **manage or treat** evidence of all kinds in their argument or discussion?*	**Individualized, Rational, Controlled Self**—I mentioned in my letter that I struggled with including sources throughout the piece, and my subtle attempt of including a source was not viable for J.	What is "rational" or "controlled" about explicitly using a source in a poem, or even an essay? Where do these norms or expectations that J identifies in our assignment come from?
"I consider this structure to create clarity, effectiveness, etc. I understand that as our draft was personal invention, there's only minimal need for sources. Besides the necessary ones you included of course, sources really don't make much sense in this specific context" (S).	*How does the **structure** of the draft create clarity, effectiveness, or persuasion for the reader? // How does the writer **manage or treat** evidence of all kinds in their argument or discussion?*	**Hyperindividualism**—Since I did a personal poem, sources aren't necessarily needed . . . This contradicts J's point.	Where does S get his expectations about poems and sources? Why value those expectations here, ones that are "hyperidividualistic," that value mostly my voice in the poem? Does our class allow us to value them? Would another class not value them?

The exact questions are not that important for determining the ecology's effectiveness at producing this goal. Instead, it is the presence of the questions and how they link to the data in the other cells in the row of the table. It's a simpler way to see effectiveness without overly determining in a Whitely way what students should come to. Of course, this is, as I've discussed throughout this chapter, only the way a teacher would determine how effective their labor-based grading contract ecology has performed along this goal. I am not speaking to how a teacher might respond to such student reflections, or what discussions classes might have from them, or what we might learn afterwards about our ecology by looking at the nature of students' reflections on the politics of language.

Table 7.6 offers some kinds of evidence that can be useful in determining a labor-based grading contract ecology's effectiveness at encouraging this goal.

Table 7.6. Evidence of awareness of the politics of language and its judgment.

Evidence of Seeking Awareness of the Politics of Language & Its judgment	Questions to Ask of the Data
Problem-Posing reflective activities (reflection-in-presentation)	How many students complete the problem-posing activities? Do most students pose questions about judgments of their writing that look to understand how each judgment is reasonable? How many questions do students pose on average?
Tables or other observation-based heuristics	How many students complete the heuristic activities? Do most or all students make observations about White habits of discourse in judgments of their writing? Can students make observations about various *habitus* that inform judgments on writing? How many questions on average do students make?
Problem-posing journals (teacher or students)	How many journal entries does each student complete? How long are the entries on average? Do they get longer as the course goes on? Can students form observations and questions about the politics of language and its judgment in most journal entries? Do students engage in questions about White language privilege or other *habitus* in language and judgment in most or all entries of the journal?

The effectiveness of an assessment ecology along this goal can be argued often by simply counting how many students, and how often, engage in questioning the nature of the judgments of their or others' writing. As can be seen in the right column, much of how I determine such counting is by determining: (1) how many students are able to complete most or all of that kind of labor; (2) how many questions students can pose (the more present, the higher degree of effectiveness of the ecology); and (3) how many students tried to employ the theories of Whiteness and White language privilege to their labors?

When measuring for this goal in a course, a teacher should be mindful of who their students are and where they come from. Many privileged, White students will have a hard time accepting something like White habits of discourse that contribute to White language supremacy.[59] They will hear it as "reverse racism," or a personal attack. This is not a reason not to engage in such questions. In fact, it is the reason to do so. In most classrooms in which I've taught, the students are mostly students of color and working-class. Many are multilingual. So this goal is an easy one to discuss with such students, many of whom already feel oppressed by educational systems that have punished them for their language use. Such oppression usually gives a person some automatic awareness of the politics of language.

GOAL 5: TO MAINTAIN SOCIALLY JUST CONDITIONS FOR LEARNING BY ENSURING EQUITABLE OPPORTUNITIES TO RECEIVE ALL FINAL COURSE GRADES POSSIBLE.

As I discussed in Chapter 2, Rawls' notion of justice as fairness dictates that everyone in a society should have a "fair equality of opportunity" (43). In assessment ecologies in writing classrooms, this means that in order for an assessment practice to be socially just, all students in the ecology should have equal access to all of the opportunities that afford success in and from the ecology, which includes access to all of the possible course grades. Con(De)fining precisely what students should learn in a literacy learning course by judging students against a single standard or outcome, then, will exclude some students from having full access to all possible opportunities for learning, success, and grades. This does not make for a socially just assessment ecology.

As I argue at the opening of this chapter, when used to measure success of students or the effectiveness of a course, outcomes are a socially unjust means to do so, because by their nature, they are exclusionary. Measuring for this final course goal helps me attend to ensuring equal opportunities for grades to all students in my courses. While grades are not learning, they do directly affect students' latter opportunities in and out of school, so as an indication of future consequences and available opportunities in and after school, they are

---

59   One way to prepare some White students for discussions of the racial politics of language is to begin with readings on White fragility by Robin DiAngelo ("White Fragility"; *White Fragility*) and cultivating "brave spaces" for such discussions by Arao and Clemens.

important. Furthermore, grades affect the psychology of students, their attitudes and confidence levels in present and future tasks, which is another way of saying they affect students' abilities to do the labors of learning in school. Relatedly, Inman and Powell have argued that grades in writing classrooms have important affective dimensions associated with them that may determine students' abilities to learn or succeed in a classroom. They often are symbols of desire, "a reassurance of rigor" (42), or a symbol of regulation that controls behavior (44). So because they exist already in educational systems, grades are still important, perhaps through a haunting White presence outside contract graded classrooms.

Beyond my application of Rawls' theory, it is important to understand Iris Marion Young's "social connection model" for responsibility that structures social justice in a society, and in my labor-based contract grading ecologies. Young's theory is predicated on mid-twentieth century observations about individuals' social responsibilities to all of the other members of a society. She explains that "members of a whole society collectively bear responsibility for taking care of one another's old age, health care, and children, and for keeping us out of poverty" because we are all interconnected. She says, "people owe one another a certain measure of reciprocal care because of these interdependencies" (9).

In order for societies to meet these reciprocal responsibilities, we have to have social and other structures in place in order to prevent inequalities and injustices from occurring (33–34). Young's explanation of her social connection model for a responsible society works just as well for classroom writing assessment ecologies. In fact, one can hear the writing classroom in Young's description of the model:

> The social connection model of responsibility says that individuals bear responsibility for structural injustice because they contribute by their actions to the processes that produce unjust outcomes. Our responsibility derives from belonging together with others in a system of interdependent processes of cooperation and competition through which we seek benefits and aim to realize projects. (105)

So like antiracist writing assessment ecologies (Inoue, *Antiracist* 93–104), Young's social connection model for responsibility assumes that we are all interconnected because we are elements in larger structures in society that are interdependent, which makes us structurally interdependent. This interconnectedness as an explicit aspect of a classroom grading ecology is vital to antiracist projects (Inoue, *Antiracist* 104), and to assessment ecologies that attempt to help students form critical stances of judgment. We need each other if we all are to have fair equality of opportunity, and to understand that our perspectives and views are located in a universe of other perspectives and views. In order for any one person to learn and succeed, that individual requires a web of others to help them.

To help me design and assess how effective my ecology is at achieving this goal, I ask myself a simple question about my syllabus and the grading ecology I've designed, which I later ask my students at week 1 and 6 (in a ten-week quarter system) when we negotiate the grading contract together: *Does everyone in the class have an equal opportunity to get all of the possible course grades available?* Is this assessment ecology fair enough for everyone? If we think it isn't, then what rules and structures in the contract do we need to adjust or change? What structures and assignments need to change in the course? Checking students' felt sense of the fairness of a labor-based grading contract is one way to measure and ensure this goal. If students feel that the contract is fair, and they've had at least two opportunities in the quarter or semester to negotiate the terms of the contract, then there is a high probability that most or all will find it fair enough. And such negotiations are important in measuring the effectiveness of this goal. That is, another measure of this goal is whether the ecology offers these two moments in the quarter or semester to (re)negotiate the contract's details.

As Chapter 4 explains, these two moments of negotiation are important. Getting students' assent or agreement about the fairness of the contract in the first week may not be enough to ensure a contract's acceptable level of fairness. In fact, one should double-check this, since students may feel coerced into agreeing to the contract because most of the time FYW courses in college are required. Many students may not feel they can just drop the class, or contest ideas in the contract. This also means that beyond having a second, midpoint, renegotiation, I look also at grade distributions of the course after it's over. While some students may not choose to pursue higher grades in a labor-based system for a lot of reasons, there still should be more Bs and As than in conventional bell curves (or a "normal distribution"), if one assumes that more students than not will attempt more labor to get higher course grades.

To understand how I use grade distributions to help me determine how effective my grading ecologies are at this goal, it's important to understand a bit of statistics. I am by far not an expert at statistics, but one doesn't need to be an expert in order to understand grade distributions and make observations about equal opportunity in the ecology. A statistical normal distribution, or bell curve, is a distribution (of grades in this case) in which about 68% of all the grades are within one standard deviation from the mean (the average grade). This means that about 68% of the scores plotted on a graph fall on either side of the median score (the exact middle score) on the graph. About 95% of all grades fall within two standard deviations from the mean, and 99% of all grades are within three standard deviations from the mean. Figure 7.2 illustrates a typical bell curve and where the percentages of the data are relative to the median score (designated as μ in Figure 7.2).

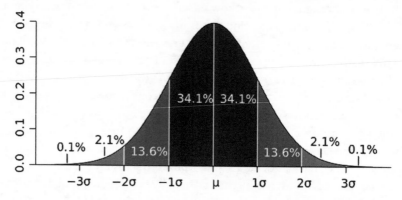

Figure 7.2. A standard bell curve, or normal distribution.

While there is much evidence to argue that in human populations many measurements do naturally result in such bell curved distributions, for example the height of men and women. However, the instrument of measuring is vital in having both highly valid and reliable results by which to create such distributions and call them accurate assessments of diverse groups of people. One can establish reliable measuring protocols and instruments to determine the height of a diverse range of people. No one disputes the length of an inch or a centimeter. The grades in writing courses, or grades on writing assignments, however, are a more difficult and disputable measurement, and the instruments (scoring guides, standards, rubrics, etc.) used to determine such grades are highly diverse and idiosyncratic since they come from and are applied by the human brain. It is difficult to establish anything like reliability in any set of grades on writing, which past research has shown.[60] Furthermore, accepting scores or grades that then get used to produce a grade distribution means we accept whatever standards of writing were used to produce those grades.

I say all this to qualify what I'm about to offer. I do not mean to suggest that course grades tell us the fairness of a grading ecology in a writing course, but they do offer some indication of unfairness. One assumption that Young makes about all social systems, such as conventional grading ecologies in writing classrooms, is that they are inherently unfair to some students, thus we must work at

---

60   As mentioned in Chapter 6 under the question of "don't students want or need grades . . ." there is lots of research that illustrates the unreliability of grades on writing in high school and college settings.

not being unfair—at not simply accepting the status quo, the standard operating procedures of grading in schools.

When I use grade distributions to help me determine how effective my ecology has been at achieving this goal, I compare my data to a simple rule. The rule is that if my course's grade distribution can show that most students who abide by the labor-based grading contract get good grades (B-/B range), then my ecology has ensured a reasonable degree of equal opportunities. While in most classrooms, a single writing teacher can determine this without the need of calculating mean grades and standard deviations (SD) of those distributions, doing so can help programs with many courses, where such eyeballing of grades and students is much harder to do. But calculating the mean grade and SD for a course can also provide a numerical way for a teacher to track their courses' assessment ecology's effectiveness at achieving this goal over time. For these reasons, I use median grades and SDs. In my context, I feel it is a reasonable goal for me to expect that 75% of all my students should achieve a course grade of 3.1 (B). This means at least fifteen of the twenty students who normally fill my FYW courses should be able to meet the contract or exceed it. That's my numerical target for an acceptable effectiveness level at this ecological goal.

I am a data hoarder on my courses and students. I have always wanted to have evidence to understand what is happening in my classrooms, so I have my course grades from two decades of teaching first year writing, and those distributions tell a story in three parts that is instructive here. Table 7.7 shows the mean grade and standard deviations for my course grades in three different periods of my teaching. These periods of teaching correspond to the way I structured my FYW courses' grading ecologies. The first two rows of data are the first two periods, and rows three and four make up the last period. The rows in the table are: (1) FYW courses during the academic years of 1998–2000, where I used conventional grades and standards; (2) FYW courses between the academic years of 2001–2004, where I was experimenting with grading systems, but not using labor-based grading contracts; (3) FYW courses between the academic years of 2005–2012, where I used labor-based grading contracts; and (4) FYW courses between the academic years of 2014–2016, where I used labor-based grading contracts at UW Tacoma.

I separate rows three and four because the nature of the courses are different enough that they are worth distinguishing. Row three represents courses in a sixteen-week semester system, while row four represents courses in 10-week quarter-based school system, my current university in the state of Washington, whose campus is mostly working-class students of color. The length of time in the ecology does seem to matter more than other ecological elements. As Chapter 3 discusses, time matters when labor is the primary measure of value and worth in an ecology. I also acknowledge that Row one represents courses from a two-year college in Salem, Oregon with a mostly White, working-class student population. Row two represents courses from a primarily White, four-year university in Washington State. Row three represents courses from a four-year regional university in southern Illinois that served a large working class, African-American population, as well as a four-year university in central California that was an Historically Hispanic Serving Institution, whose students were mostly working-class.

Table 7.7. Mean grades and standard deviation of final course grade distributions for my first-year writing courses

	Mean Grade	Standard Deviation	# of Ws or Is (percent of total)
Conventional FYW Courses (1998–2000)	1.79 (D+/C-)	1.41	15.26%
Experimental FYW Courses (2001–2004)	2.92 (C+/B-)	.79	5.56%
Labor-Based FYW Courses (2005–2012)[61]	3.18 (B)	.40	1.41%
UWT Labor-Based FYW Courses (2014–2016)	3.32 (B+)	.44	7.14% (1.79%)

The means and standard deviations in Table 7.7 do not calculate students who withdrew, dropped, or received incomplete grades, but it is worth noting the differences in each group. I've included the percentage of the entire group of W and I grades (I do not have records for those students who dropped my courses) given in the far-right column. This is one indicator of the level of unfairness in a grading ecology. When 15% of all my students registered for my FYW courses withdraw or got an incomplete (as in Row one), it suggests a higher degree of unfairness in those conventionally graded ecologies than the other ecologies represented in the table, which used different grading ecologies. I should acknowledge that there are lots of reasons for a working-class, White, mostly first-generation group of students to withdraw or get incompletes in a course. There are limitations to such data, but it is a good place to start inquiring about an ecology's effectiveness at this goal. I don't want to ignore such data, even if I might have ways of explaining the numbers.

61   I should note that from 2005 to about 2009, my grading contracts, as I discuss in Chapter 2, were hybrid contracts, but still mostly labor-based (up to the B course grade).

The differences in Ws and Is move down quite a bit as I move to experimental assessment ecologies, and finally labor-based ones. The higher percentage of Ws and Is in my UWT labor-based ecologies (7.14% in Row four) is likely skewed by my first FYW course taught at UWT in my first quarter returning to a quarter system after about fifteen years away. Both Row one and four represent ten-week quarter system courses. So in parentheses in Row four, I've included the number of Ws and Is from this group without that first class. What also skews this number is the fact that it has less data than the other rows because of the fewer FYW courses I generally teach annually at UWT.

As Table 7.7 shows, the mean grade (based on a 4.0 scale) went up over time in my FYW courses, meaning as I moved to labor-based contract grading ecologies in my FYW courses my mean grade, the average grade given, moved from a D+/C- (1.79) to a C+/B- (2.92), to a B (3.18), then to a B+ (3.32). The total movement of the average grade given was more than a full letter grade, but the differences in standard deviation (SD) I find most interesting. SD shrinks as my grading ecologies move to a labor-based system. SD tells us how much variation there is in the grades, or how dispersed the grades are in the distribution of all grades in that category on the table. So if I want to be most effective at this goal, I would need as evidence a high mean grade and a small SD, or a small spread. This will mean more students hover closer to that mean, whatever it is, if the SD is small—that is, if the spread of grades is not that dispersed.

According to Table 7.7, when I used conventional grading ecologies, about 68% of my grades were 1.41 grade points from the mean grade of D+ (1.79). In effect, 68% of all my grades were between a 3.2 (B-) and a .38 (D-/F). This also means that some within one SD of the mean grade in those classes failed the course. On a 4.0 scale, a 1.41 SD could be considered slightly dispersed, or a wider spread than expected. To give you another way to see this, in Row one's courses, if the grades were evenly dispersed, then in a class of twenty, about seven students received grades between 1.79 and .38. At UW, where we use a numerical 4.0 scale to record final course grades, 1.79 is in the middle of the C- range (1.8–1.5). This means that most students in my courses did not get high grades. In fact, if we consider the lower half of the C- range as failing, then 50% of all my students received non-passing grades. This is not an effective grading ecology at achieving equal opportunities for success.

Compare the first row to the groups with the smallest SD, the FYW courses in which I used labor-based grading contracts, or Rows three and four. In Row three, for instance, 68% of the students received between 3.58 (B+/A-) and a 2.78 (C/C+). Most students received average to higher grades, and all passed the course. A failing grade is a 1.4, so even students within two SDs of the mean passed the course with at least a 2.38 (C+) final grade. Two SDs accounts for about 95% of all students. This meets my high standard for effectiveness along this ecological goal. In my current FYW courses at UWT, represented in the fourth row, similar effectiveness numbers can be seen. Sixty-eight percent of students received between a 3.75 (A-) and 2.88 (high end of the B-). And because of the high mean grade, only about 2% of students received final grades lower than 2.0 (C). These are even better numbers, thus show a high degree of effectiveness.

If one measure of unfairness is a relatively large number of W and I grades, then another measure of unfairness might be the SD of the final course grades in a class. As you can see from my discussion, it isn't as simple as saying the smaller the SD, the fairer the ecology, since a small SD in the first row of data in Table 7.7 might still show too many students failing or struggling unnecessarily if the mean grade is low. But having a smaller SD in a course that has an average grade of 3.18 or 3.32 does appear to be a fairer ecology, if we accept a higher degree of passing students as an indirect indicator of equal access to all course grades, and really we mean equal access to higher grades, since anyone can get a low grade by doing nothing.

Based on the average grade for my labor-based grading contract ecologies in those rows (3.25) and their small SD (.42), my labor-based contract grading ecologies can be seen as highly effective at ensuring equal opportunities to receive all possible grades since about 98% of the grades given, which accounts for two SD from the mean grade, were passing grades, or 2.42 (C+/B-) or higher. In other words, the vast majority of students had access to the higher grades on the scale. Add to this the fact that these same labor-based ecologies had fewer numbers of W and I grades, dramatically fewer than my conventionally graded students. This makes for compelling evidence of a high degree of effectiveness of labor-based grading contract ecologies to ensure equal opportunities for high grades.

But looking at one's grade distributions and considering how close they are to normal distributions may not tell a teacher enough to know how effective their assessment ecology has been at ensuring equitable opportunities for all grades to all groups of students. Who gets what grades and under what conditions? Do students of color, for instance, choose not to pursue more labor than White students, generally speaking? Do some groups of students have more time constraints during the semester than others in my grading ecologies? These are difficult questions to answer that can only be figured out once a course begins, and the class meets. I find labor logs and labor journals help in my looking for such problems. But we might also look at mean grades and SDs within important racial formations.

Table 7.8 offers these data by racial formations in my UW Tacoma courses between 2014 and 2016, because I have access to these data. The data is limited, because I only teach between one to two FYW courses a year. The table does not represent a sample. Table 7.8 represents all my FYW students. Because my classrooms are racially diverse, there appears to be enough data on each racial formation to calculate means and SDs, with the possible exception of the Latinx formation, as suggested by that group's higher SD in the distribution of grades. One measure of a grading ecology that offers all racial groups equal opportunities for all course grades is a high mean grade and a small SD that is consistent with the other groups measured. In the UW system, a 1.5 is the lowest course grade that is passing in any course (C-). No student in my classes has received such a grade. In other words, if you got to the end of the quarter, you got at least a 1.6 course grade. A few have withdrawn from the class because they would not be able to get such a final grade. The number of these students is shown in the far-right column, with a percentage of the group in parentheses.

Table 7.8. The Mean grade and standard deviation in grade distributions of four racial formations in my FYW courses at UW Tacoma

Racial Formation (total students)	Mean Grade	Standard Deviation	Total # of Ws
Asian (12)	3.33	.43	1 (8.3%)
Black (11)	3.12	.51	1 (9.1%)
Latinx (7)	3.30	.87	0 (0.0%)
White (26)	3.40	.31	2 (7.6%)

How consistent is the mean grades and SDs of each group compared to the others? Are they all about the same? And do they all equate to the same number or percentage of students in each racial formation passing the class and achieving the same kinds of grades? If they are similar, then one could argue that my grading ecology is antiracist because it offers equal opportunities for success (and failure) for all racial formations in my classes. As you can see from Table 7.8, this is mostly the case. The slightly higher SD for the Latinx group could be due to its lower number of total students, since one or two students out of seven would skew this number, but I would consider this inconclusive. And yet, the Latinx numbers are not that far off. Black students still do the worst of all formations, with a slightly lower mean grade and wider spread in the SD, but even in this group, 98% (which accounts for two SDs from the mean) received a 2.1 (C) or higher final course grade. The Latinx group is also still within this same threshold, with 98% of students getting a 1.56 (C-) or higher course grade. Generally speaking, these are consistent numbers that all show 98% of students with access to higher grades and succeeding in our labor-based contract grading ecologies.

These data show me a grading ecology that is socially just, offering equitable opportunities to all for the highest grades.

CONCLUDING WITH TWO CRITICISMS

I'd like to conclude this chapter by addressing two criticisms that could be leveled against labor-based contract grading ecologies that have direct bearing on how effective some may find them. One important measure of effectiveness, no matter the ecological goals being measured, should be student reactions to the grading ecology. How do students feel and experience the grading ecology? There are a number of ways to define such a measure. Typical ways might be through end of course anonymous surveys of students that ask any of the following:

- How happy were you with the grading contract?
- How satisfied were you with the grading contract to create a fair grading environment?
- How helpful was the grading contract to your learning in the course?
- How effective did you find the grading contract for your purposes in the course?
- How effective was the grading contract in allowing you to take risks in your writing, or to learn the kinds of writing skills and practices you were hoping to?
- Do you prefer the grading contract for writing courses over conventional grading?

While each of these questions define student reactions differently, they get at much of the two criticisms that I think need consideration.

Both of the criticisms are tied to the labor component of the ecology. The first concerns criticisms of contract grading offered in Spidell and Thelin's study of hybrid grading contracts that looked at student reactions to them, published in 2006. The second is a criticism of writing classrooms that overly regulate the labor and activities of students by promoting what Soliday and Trainor call "audit culture," which is an anthropological term. Soliday and Trainor's study also uses qualitative measures of students' experiences in classrooms. I find both studies to be important works that help explain why labor-based grading contracts, at least in the ways I try to enact them (and discuss them in this book), avoid the problems of student dissatisfaction with any grading ecology, thus it's important to hear that I assume students should feel good, satisfied, and accepting of whatever grading ecology they are in. So these two criticisms are about effectiveness, since part of effective grading ecologies, for me, is how students experience them and react to them.

I should note that in another place I critique the raceless methodology used in the Spidell and Thelin study, and demonstrate a way to have a racial methodology in order that one can see and make arguments about the racialized dimensions of one's data ("Racial Methodologies"). Despite this problem with the study, Spidell and Thelin offer important insights to those contemplating the effectiveness of their own hybrid grading contract ecologies. What Spidell and Thelin's study shows is how mostly working-class White students at a Midwest university found a hybrid grading contract much like Danielewicz and Elbow's (discussed in Chapter 2) in writing courses. They make the following findings about their hybrid contracts:

1. students resented not getting grades, or not having their work quantified by grades (41);
2. the contract tended to create more anxiety over and resistance to the work in the course (43–44);
3. the contract made typically high-performing or highly motivated students feel an unfair "leveling effect" (i.e., it didn't seem fair that their hard work over drafts was counted the same as someone else's, less-than-hard work) (45);
4. students wanted more input into the construction of the contract (48);
5. the contract made the course more difficult than necessary (48);
6. there were no consistent attitudes or reactions to the contract (50–52); and
7. students had a difficult time seeing the difference between hybrid contracts and conventional grading systems (52–54).

Spidell and Thelin do not argue to writing teachers that hybrid contracts are not worth the time, instead they argue for a cautious use, one that is tempered by working closely with students, negotiating the terms of the contract, and helping engage in dialogue about their work along the way. In short, they suggest writing teachers listen to their students. A good principle. The six concerns above, which equate to the study's conclusions and title, "not ready to let go," might be seen as a criticism of the labor-base grading contracts I discuss in this book, but the ecology from which they spring are not the same as those I've been discussing. In fact, labor-based grading contracts address most of these concerns, and one could say they also offer unique conditions for deeply attending to our students, which can also address several of these student concerns.

In other places ("Grading Contracts" 88; "Racial Methodologies" 134), I show the way students from various racial formations in labor-based writing assessment ecologies at California State University, Fresno, show acceptably high levels of happiness, helpfulness, effectiveness, satisfaction, and preference (five of the kinds of student reaction questions listed earlier in this section) for mostly labor-based grading contracts in writing classes.[62] Students in labor-based contract grading ecologies do not seem to hold resentment toward the lack of grades (Concern #1 above) when they have ongoing conversations about grades, about what they mean, how they have been used against them, and their effects on students' motivations and feelings about themselves as writers. In my ecologies, our parallel discussions of compassion and caring discussed in Chapter 5 help students lose much of what Elbow describes as a "hunger for ranking" ("Ranking" 190–91, 197), which is at the heart of this first concern. But it isn't the only thing creating such a reaction to the Spidell and Thelin's hybrid contract. It is also the contradiction in philosophies of assessment at work in the hybrid contract, which I've discussed in Chapter 2.

The hybrid nature of the contracts in Spidell and Thelin's study likely had something to do with the student concerns voiced in #1, #2, #3, and #7. The fact that on many writing assignments, usually more formal assignments, the teacher would still determine the quality of the writing, as explained in their contract for an "A" grade (64). This creates a contradiction in how some grades are determined (those above a B). Leaving the teacher's judgments of quality in the grading ecology as a way to determine a crucial distinction, that between B grades and A grades, means that students still have to care about grades on every writing assignment. They might not be worried about failing so much, but if they care about getting a better grade, then they surely care about those quality judgments, the very thing that contracts are meant to mitigate. Letting the teacher's judgments of A-quality work circulate in the ecology creates this contradiction when part of the contract determines some course grades in other ways. These competing logics that produce signifiers of success and achievement (one based on labor for grades up to a "B" and one based on a teacher's judgments of quality for those above the "B") will create more anxiety and resistance to the work of the course (Concern #2)—it is easy to feel like you don't know how well you are doing when grades are left off writing until the very end of the term, when it really matters.

This same dynamic in student responses to hybrid contracts can be seen in Inman and Powell's more recent study, where students still had concerns about "where they stand" in the class (41), which the authors attribute to a deep-seated desire for grades. This desire stems from students senses that grades are "signifiers of how much work remains to be done," which is connected to their identi-

---

62   Because these conclusions come from a program with many different teachers using the same grading contract template, I cannot say that all instances of the contract were purely labor-based, likely some were hybrid. However, the mandatory training the program gave at the time to teachers on the use of contracts was labor-based.

ties in school (42). Inman and Powell argue that grades have become "affective carriers of emotion" for students, "markers of achievement" that teachers cannot (and perhaps do not want to) ignore. However, like Spidell and Thelin's study, Inman and Powell neglect to consider the hybrid nature of their contracts, and how the presence of both labor-based and quality-based decisions about progress and achievement in their study's courses might confuse students and make them anxious about how well they are doing. Neither study considers the real possibility that withholding quality judgments in an ecology until the very end of the term, when the A/B distinctions are made, would make many students feel a need for grades because they know that judgment is coming and is important still.

Thus hybrid contract ecologies create a contradiction and perhaps anxieties around it. In effect, students receive contradictory messages. On the one hand, they are told the contract is here to help you forget about grades and take risks, to just write, and do all you can to develop yourself as a writer. On the other hand, the way higher course grades are determined is the same way they always have been, by a teacher's judgment. No wonder students had a difficult time distinguishing their hybrid contract from conventional grading (Concern #7) in the Spidell and Thelin study.

According to Inman and Powell, however, it is students' affective-based desires for grades, which are needed references to their status and identity that causes such problems in students' reactions. They give a student response as an example of this need for a reference-grade as a marker of status: "[I] did not understand if [I] was average or below . . . I really do not know where I stand in this course" (40). The authors explain these comments by saying that the student understands her standing in terms of a grade, which also tells her if she is average or below (40). They suggest that it is the history of grades that creates such desires and affective dimensions within students (36–7), but they do not mention how the presence of even just A-grades that are determined differently than those below them, can cause such confusions and desires. In fact, Spidell and Thelin gesture to this problem, saying, "[w]e wonder, then, if, adhering to letter grades for different types of writing throughout the contracts—being clearer about expectations—somehow produced the discomfort or uncertainty in these classes" (42). In contrast, Labor-based grading contracts are clearer for students because they do not contain the contradiction that hybrid ones do.

It may be obvious to some that Concerns #4 and #7 are not issues in my labor-based grading contract ecologies. We have a full week and half of initial negotiations of the contract that begin with understanding what the contract is saying and how it is different from conventional grading systems, and renegotiation processes at midpoint (explained in Chapter 4). I also provide different labor instructions for all assignments, as well as ask students to be continually mindful of their labor practices. These practices keep students from confusing our assessment ecology from conventional ones (Concern #7).

But as Spidell and Thelin remind us, hearing from students directly is vital in understanding their reactions. In my own ecologies Concerns #1, #2, #3, #4, #6, and #7 do not appear to be a problem, even up to the midpoint renegotiation processes, which begin with reflections on how the contract has treated them, how they are doing in the course, and how fair they find the contract now. In the example course I've been using in this chapter, no students in the class said the contract was unfair at the end of week 5. In fact, all found it fair and had positive observations about it. Student B3 (a White female) in the Bottom performing group from Table 5.1, offers a typical reflection on the contract at this midpoint:

> At the start of the quarter I didn't really appreciate the late to class/missed days policy because it just sort of seemed unfair if there were emergencies. My dad has leukemia and gets unbelievably sick quite often, and when he is in that sort of condition he needs someone there to take care of him, my step mom works full time and often can't get out of work so i'll stay and make sure he's drinking water and getting rest. I understand now that my education should be a priority and I don't really like missing class anyway, but I have worked out with my family how my step mom can wait for me to get home and then she will go to work and I'll spend the rest of my day taking care of my dad. In my eyes the contract still seems really fair, with class only being three days a week it's pretty easy to get over being sick quickly or working it out with our professor.

> The contract still wonderfully reflects the course goals, overtime I have managed to make friends with the people in our class and I enjoy hearing their constructive criticism of my work, I genuinely value their opinions. While in high school I never really talked to many people just because I was shy and I absolutely hated group activities, but I have found that I really like doing group activities in this course, I have managed to make friends just by doing them.

> I don't believe there should be any changes made, I think everything laid out still makes sense for what we want to accomplish, the time is flying by and I think everyone in our class is managing to meet the goals well.

B3 finds the contract fair, and helping her meet her goals. She also finds the contract helping her colleagues, seeing our class in a more communal light. While she is concerned about her ill father, and offers some details that constrain her ability to come to class every day, she doesn't seem anxious about the course, or resentful about the labor involved in it. The one issue she raises is the late/missed class policy, which many other students in the class mentioned, a detail we renegotiated in the next class session. Furthermore, unlike Inman and Powell's students, she doesn't seem concerned about grades as markers of status or progress. The affective dimensions I read in her reflection have more to do with her relationships with her colleagues and their feedback on her writing, which have little to do with status and more with mutually beneficial and compassionate relationships.

T3 (Latina) also offers typical reflections on our contract that demonstrate in other ways how different our labor-based assessment ecology is from those in the hybrid contract studies. After wondering about the number of missed/late days in the contract, T3 explains:

> The contract, in my eyes, is still fair. As said in the beginning of the quarter, there are no surprises. Students know what to do in order to receive full credit. Everything is laid out for us and that is an extremely fair advantage that will only provide success rather than failure.
>
> I believe that the grading contract and the things we have done in the class so far reflect the course goals well. This is a very engaged class, we are constantly doing group work and editing and reflecting each others assignments which is what makes this class so enjoyable. In the beginning of the quarter we were all awkwardly silent towards each other and did not have much to say about the things we read or the papers we wrote. But now, we all look forward to having group discussions and getting to talk about what we read/wrote. The course goals were very specific on what Asao wanted us to accomplish and we are almost done with the quarter and finished these goals without even noticing.

Similar to B3, what appears to characterize the grading ecology for T3 is not a need for grading, nor a nagging affective desire a grade, but enjoyable relationships with colleagues. Reflections like these reveal, in my opinion, students who are at ease with the course, even if they may say that the course is a lot of work. I argue that the reason students like B3 and T3 can be so at ease in our ecology, expressing no anxiety over grades, or the leveling effect, is that the teacher's judgments of writing are not used in the ecology to determine course grades at any level. There are no contradictions of judgment, at least not in terms of calculating grades.

Perhaps the one concern above about making the course more difficult than expected by enforcing more labor than students were used to (Concern #5) might still be an issue in my version of labor-based grading contract ecologies. But it looks different in my classrooms, and I think it can be seen as positive. Spidell and Thelin offer Rachel's response to the contract as indicative of this concern, in which she says the contract makes some students "angrier" because: "If they planned on showing up, doing minimum work and passing with a C, than [*sic*] forcing them to sign a contract that says that's what they have to get is a bit crazy" (49). While Spidell and Thelin identify this comment as evidence of Concern #5, I also see it as evidence of #2. My students rarely voice such concerns, but sometimes they do. However, because I ask them explicitly about the contract's level of fairness, I believe this helps students separate the amount to work from other concerns that I think are at the heart of the "crazy" concern here, and it leads back to the contradictions in judgment that are a part of hybrid grading contract ecologies.

But I have other evidence of such conclusions. Compare Spidell and Thelin's student responses to the generally high effectiveness, happiness, and preference rates of students at CSU, Fresno for labor-based grading contracts in two consecutive academic years (2009 and 2010). Considering just the White racial formation in these data, since they may more closely match the student populations that Spidell and Thelin use, we see some evidence of what they find, but with a key difference. At CSU, Fresno, we found that 68.32% (spring 2009) and 58.24% (spring 2010) of White students preferred labor-based grading contracts, and 74.75% (spring 2009) and 76.67% (spring 2010) found them effective, while 70.30% (spring 2009) and 70.97% (spring 2010) were happy with the contracts (Inoue, "Grading Contracts" 88).

While these students had mixed feelings about the contract in open-ended comments (with 117 positive and 109 negative), there were two strong positive themes in them, concerning "'relieves pressure' (29 comments) and 'expectations and clarity' (21 comments)" (91). Labor-based grading contracts offered students relief from the pressures of grades on their drafts and provided clear expectations for course grades. These end of semester survey responses seem to match my own students' reflections, like T3 and B3 above. The other racial formations at Fresno had similar comments, with fewer mixed reactions. In fact, the Asian student population, which were mostly Hmong in our sample (who were mostly multilingual and first generation students), tended to find the labor-based contract system one that offered them "freedom to write" and "tended to express appreciation and praise for the contract's ability to keep grades off their writing and assignments" (89). Meanwhile their preference rates were also higher (81.48% in 2009 and 70.64% in 2010) (88).

These kinds of programmatic findings suggest, at least for many students of color, that labor-based grading contracts do not cause the concerns that Spidell and Thelin see in their mostly White, Midwestern students. But the bigger difference, I believe, is not the racial subject positions of the students, but the presence of the contradiction in judgment in the ecology that affects various groups differently, but still negatively. More recently in my own classrooms, if Table 7.8 is any indicator, even White racial formations find success in properly designed labor-based grading contract ecologies.

The second criticism that could be made about labor-based grading contracts and the way I've argued their effectiveness in this chapter, centers on discussions of "audit culture" and the regulation of labor in writing courses made by Mary Soliday and Jennifer Seibel Trainor.[63] Drawing on student interviews of juniors, Soliday and Trainor wanted to understand how students experienced their writing intensive courses. They found that the regulation of writing tasks tended to create mixed feelings in students (half the students experienced regulation negatively, and half positively) around a lack of freedom to exercise agency and make decisions about their writing (134). Taken from their student interviews, the authors explain regulation: "they [students] felt regulated when confronted with assignments dominated by mandates and rules, lists of 'do's and don'ts,' required steps, and rubrics that 'must be' followed in order to meet assignments" (126). They link notions of regulation by students in their study to the anthropological concept of "audit technologies," which "are not 'neutral' 'practices' but 'instruments for new forms of governance and power'" (127). They do not deny the need for certain kinds of regulation in schools, but feel that "regulation has become too powerful" (127).

Soliday and Trainor sum up some of their findings:

> When students perceived that their writing was regulated, they tended to equate writing with assessment, ascribing rhetorical exigency to rules and steps mandated in prompts [. . .] affect[ing] how students negotiated complexity; how they related to their teachers and peers; and how they described their authorship. Conversely, when students saw writing in terms of doing and making, they ascribed rhetorical exigency to composing or to disciplinary content and purpose. These students moved beyond instrumental views of writing, imagining themselves as authors with professional

---

63   I thank Jonathan Hunt for bringing this criticism to my attention.

expertise. (129)

Inman and Powell also discuss Soliday and Trainor's concerns about audit culture and regulation in their grading contract classrooms. They see evidence of audit culture in the ways that grading contracts tend to limit teachers' abilities to control students' behaviors through grades (45–46). Teachers in their study simply could not use grades to reward or punish, and this troubled them. This led to a felt problem for some teachers. They explain: "The course contract, in their initial experiences, blurred the lines of their [teachers'] roles in passing judgment on student writing, on their identities as judges and juries of writing. And there were concerns that they, as the people who sanctioned these students, would be judged as ineffective teachers by the institution" (47). This anxiety over a lack of regulation by teachers, I think, speaks more to the Whitely *habitus* those teachers embody, than a problem with assessment ecologies that have no grades in them. As I discussed earlier in this chapter, a White *habitus* often brings with it a set of dispositions toward being an authority and judge over others, and a sense of benevolence about one's judgments. I hear this *habitus* in Inman and Powell's teachers' desires to grade.

However, with my use of labor logs and labor instructions that are primarily process instructions, or step-by-step processes that lead students through reading and writing labors of the course, it is easy to see how regulation is a part of my ecologies. The question that I think Soliday and Trainor want us to ask is, what kind of regulation is occurring and what effects does it have on students' agency as writers?

It is important to first note that Soliday and Trainor's study is of juniors in writing intensive courses, not writing courses taught by trained compositionists. While I'm sure there are good teachers of writing in other disciplines, their training is limited, and they may not know or be able to apply many of the best practices that the field of writing studies holds. They also define agency in part by how closely a student takes on the *habitus* of one's discipline, which is an unrealistic expectation to place on FYW students, most of whom may not know what they want to do yet, or may not have picked a major. Agency in writing decisions for FYW students likely should be defined differently.

Despite these caveats, two things seem clear about the kind of regulation or audit technologies to which Soliday and Trainor refer and that have negative effects on student agency in writing. The kind of regulation set up in these negative assessment ecologies sends messages to students that writing is an assessment, a test of knowledge or ability, and that writing has mandated rules and steps to follow, which likely will be graded. So the nature of the regulation is to control the nature of what students produce. The audit technology is a check-list that allows the teacher to account for information learned or tasks completed. It is lists of to-do's, which include items in a draft that are listed on rubrics and prompts (to be graded). Students know what this kind of regulation is attempting to do: control the products or outcomes of their learning. But as my discussion of why I based effectiveness on noncognitive goals shows, the audit technologies in my courses do not regulate the products of students' labors. It regulates their labors, and allows them to determine what those labors create and even mean to them.

In Soliday and Trainor's study's conclusions, they describe the more agentive students, the ones that they say take on writing as "craft" by experiencing it as a "subtle relationship between skill and creativity, rules and imagination" (129). Furthermore, this craft model also tended to be encouraged in courses that set up writing as a "sketch design," or as "a 'kind of bounded openness'" that encourages students "to connect technical craft to the imagination," meaning in most cases writing was not equated to assessment, yet procedures were still given clearly (136). Writing tasks, the labor of writing, then, in their study, was articulated by students as "doing and making." I'm not sure I could explain the heart of labor-based contract gradings any better than to say that it frames reading and writing practices as "doing and making." It keeps them as verbs, not nouns. And vital to doing this is making sure that writing is not equated to assessment. It is not an opportunity to be tested, but a chance to do something and make something. If most of this book has not made this argument in detail, then I don't think I'm able to make it.

CODA.

ASSESSING ENGLISH SO THAT PEOPLE STOP KILLING EACH OTHER

"Is it possible to teach English so that people stop killing each other?"
Ihab Hassan asked my group of teaching assistants in 1968. We are still
trying to come up with an answer.

—O'Reilley, "Exterminate," p. 143

I close this book with Mary Rose O'Reilley's invocation of Ihab Hassan's question for several reasons. The short 1989 article in which O'Reilley offers the above is a kind of rumination on her teaching life to that point, which began in the 1960s. She asks, "how did I get here," and invokes Jerry Farber's infamous article and book, *The Student as Nigger*, which I open with in Chapter 1. So in one sense, O'Reilley brings me full circle back to Farber and problematizing grades in the writing classroom. The question above is prompted by a growing cynicism in her own teaching, and a sense that "young people in the profession know rather little about the history of what, to some of us in mid-career, is still 'the new pedagogy'" ("Exterminate" 143). The new pedagogy she speaks of is loosely the student-centered classroom and discussions of power relations in the classroom, pedagogies that look to give up power, pedagogies that agree with many of labor-based grading contracts' basic assumptions.

As I'm sure you've figured out by now, labor-based grading contracts can offer students in writing classrooms the chance not just to redirect the way power moves in the classroom, but to critique power, and that begins by making obvious how power usually moves and who controls it. Labor-based grading contracts show us that in writing classrooms, power can move, not through standards and teacher's judgments of student writing—although teachers still judge writing—but through students' own labors. While they de-emphasize a dominant, White, academic, discursive standard, they may make learning such a standard easier for many students if writing with less anxiety and the ability to take more risks in writing is linked to such learning. But mostly, I promote labor-based grading contracts because they can encourage assessment ecologies that value multiple Discourses and allow students to maintain their right to their own Discourses in the English writing classroom. I promote them because they make learning a dominant White racial Discourse problematic (in the Freirean sense), offering conditions in the classroom that allow diverse *habitus* and judgments to sit side by side in tension, allowing students to question and critique that dominant Discourse while paradoxically having the choice to learn it or something else. I promote them because they work against White language supremacy by offering conditions for counter hegemonic discussions about language and judgment, and allow for alternative ways of languaging that provide students with flexible, rhetorical practices that can help them in their futures. Ultimately, I promote them because they create sustainable and liveable conditions for locally diverse students and teachers to do antiracist, anti-White supremacist, and other social justice language work, conditions that are much harder to have when writing is graded on so-called quality or by some single standard, and when students' labors are not fully recognized and valued. These conditions, conditions that I believe are fairer for raciolinguistically diverse students, open the writing classroom to ask similar questions that Hassan and O'Reilley do. And they start with standards controlled by teachers.

Do standards in English writing classrooms kill people? Hmm. Maybe a better question is this: In a world of police brutality against Black and Brown people in the US, of border walls and regressive and harmful immigration policies, of increasing violence against Muslims, of women losing their rights to the control their own bodies, of overt White supremacy, of mass shootings in schools, of blatant refusals to be compassionate to the hundreds of thousands of refugees around the world, where do we really think this violence, discord, and killing starts? What is the nature of the ecologies in which some people find it necessary to oppress or kill others who are different from them, who think or speak or worship differently than them? All of these decisions are made by judging others by our own standards, and inevitably finding others wanting, deficient. People who judge in these ways lack practices of problematizing their own existential situations. They lack an ability to sit uneasily with paradox.

I don't mean to suggest that there are not some cases where a person is simply mentally ill or an anomaly, the exceptions to the norm. I'm saying there are far fewer of those cases than we may think. If literacies are bound up not just with communication but with our identities and the social formations that people find affinity with, if literacy is bound up with how we understand and make our worlds, then a world with literacy classrooms that use singular standards to determine progress and grades of locally diverse students, a world that holds every student in the classroom to the same standard regardless of who they are or where they came from or what they hope for in their lives, is a world that tacitly provides and validates the logics of White supremacy. It is a world that promotes White language supremacy. It is a world that validates the use of a dominant *habitus* to make similar kinds of judgments of people elsewhere outside of school.

Our students learn how to judge their world by the practices of judgment they experience as they move through their worlds. Experiencing standards over and over in classrooms validates by repetition the practice. If standards are always applied and people are ranked based on them, if people are denied things because of them in dispassionate ways through the first twelve or sixteen years of one's life—the crucial literacy learning years—then I think it is easier to justify judging everyone, no matter the subject or decision, circumstance or situation, by a single standard, unproblematically, and those judgments lead, if one pushes the logic far enough, to killing.

So, how do we teach English so people stop killing each other? Perhaps, we might ask, how do we judge language so that people stop killing each other? That, I think, is the real question. This is the exact problem that I argue labor-based grading contracts explicitly addresses in writing classrooms, the problem of grading locally diverse students, the paradox of teachers who are by necessity steeped in a White racial *habitus* while many of their students are not, the problem of how to help students and teacher confront and discuss bravely the racialized politics of language and its judgment. Yes, if we can confront such paradoxes in the judgment of language, in the judgments of *habitus* through our *habitus*, then maybe some of the killing may stop.

O'Reilley concludes her article: "The point is, you can't just put your chairs in a circle and forget about the human condition" (146). I wish I could say that this good conclusion was on my mind over most of the last fifteen years as I developed my version of contracts, but it wasn't. It has only been in the last five or six years that I've understood how important it is to account for the human condition, that is, the material conditions, the embodied conditions of learning in various, diverse bodies who inhabit different places in our larger community. This human condition is implicated in any writing classroom where a group of locally diverse (or homogenous) students come together to read, write, and engage. And what is more critical to the human condition, as Hannah Arendt reminds us, than labor, work, action. No matter how one wishes to define these terms, they reference people toiling, exerting, struggling, trying, suffering, succeeding, and failing. They reference making and historicizing, building for others, not just for ourselves. Laboring, which may be a good synonym for suffering in the writing classroom, is quintessentially the human condition.

Ten years after O'Reilley wrote the above article, she revisited her teaching in *Radical Presence: Teaching as Contemplative Practice.* In its opening chapter, she says, "I would like to ask what spaces we can create in the classroom that will allow students freedom to nourish an inner life" (3). What she means by an inner life are contemplative practices that might offer students learning and something else, something human, perhaps something that acknowledges their unique human conditions. What she offers in the book are beautiful ruminations and contemplative practices from her classroom, deep listening, paying attention, being still enough to notice, standing in radical presence. Here's how O'Reilley describes the practices of deep listening from her classroom:

> it deals with the whole rather than with the parts: it attends not to the momentary faltering but to the long path of the soul, not to the stammer, but to the poem being born. It completes the clumsy gesture in an arc of grace. One can, I think, *listen someone into existence*, encourage a stronger self to emerge or a new talent to flourish. (21)

What strikes me about O'Reilley's contemplative pedagogy is its compassion and its potential for growing the patience in teachers that is needed when we confront students who are different from us, who do not look, or sound, or come from the same places as we do, or want the same kinds of things for themselves as we do. Her pedagogy is one that asks us to listen deeply to our students, cultivating enough grace to allow for their seemingly clumsy gestures, their momentary faltering in words, so that their poems, or papers, or new selves, can be born. Labor-based grading contracts offer conditions, for such compassionate pedagogies to work, pedagogies that can, I think, listen many students into existence. Or rather, labor-based ecologies, ones fundamentally focused on the three dimensions of laboring, ones that do not use a dominant White standard of language to rank students, provide an encouraging and compassionate place for us to *attend* to our students, for students to *attend* to each other and themselves. Attending is more than an auditory metaphor. It is more fully embodied and compassionate. It includes a vital part of what I hear O'Reilley asking us to consider in our pedagogies: the material conditions of learning, living, languaging, and laboring. Attending includes the bodily, which is also about presence—being present for ourselves and others. It is about paying attention to this still moment, acknowledging the emotional and intellectual dimensions of it, and about beholding that which is becoming in front of us all the time. I believe, labor-based grading contracts help cultivate assessment ecologies in which students have more ability and more opportunity to be radically present, to be here in this moment, the only moment any of us have, and just practice.

In 1997, Fred McFeely Rogers, the acclaimed host and originator of "Mr. Rogers' Neighborhood,"[64] the public television show for children, receive a life-

---

64   *Mr. Rogers' Neighborhood* first aired in 1968 and recorded its final shows in 2000. By the time, Mr. Rogers had finished, he had been awarded four Emmys and forty honorary degrees and had recorded 896 episodes of his TV show ("Fred Rogers").

time achievement award at that year's Daytime Emmys. In his now famous and short acceptance speech, he asked the audience for a favor: "All of us have special ones who have loved us into being. Would you just take, along with me, ten seconds to think of the people who have helped you become who you are. Ten seconds of silence." I cannot think of a more compassionate way to articulate the way each of us becomes who we are today and who we will be tomorrow. But to see it, to see the loving into being, requires what Mr. Rogers asks of us, what O'Reilley asks, that we attend others into being, that attending is an act of love as much as it is of grace, and loving helps others become. As I reflected in Chapter 1, we are all *becoming*, in all the ways that that word can mean. I was loved into being because I was becoming. I was a beautiful brown boy, a becoming brown boy in a dark world of White supremacy and racism with just enough people around me to attend me into being, and it is my obligation to return that attending and loving, first to those who loved me into being, then to others who are not me, my students and colleagues, all of whom are becoming themselves. Is there anything more important? Is there a better answer to Hassan's and O'Reilley's question?

While I realize that some of our students, perhaps even some of us teachers, may not characterize our childhoods as places in which people around us loved us into being, but maybe we might imagine a classroom in which this could be true. A present and future that is becoming. We might think of the assessment ecologies we cultivated with our students as places that invite us, urge us, move us to love our students and their writing labors into being, to attend to them without ranking.

To attend to others into existence, to act in compassionate ways, and to be radically presence are the same practices. They are labors of loving and learning, of living and growing. To love is to attend, to deeply listen to another who is not like us, to be present for them, and to do so on their terms, not to change them into our image of middle-class Whiteness, or some other *habitus*, but to simply do so because they, like us, are becoming. Love-attending is a practice of radical presence. It is not easy. But our students are here. We are here. It is now. We have no other moment but now. Really attending deeply means sitting with another in their relative suffering, being compassionate, without conditions, like our mothers and grandmothers, fathers and grandfathers, our brothers and sisters often do, or did, or could have in a more perfect world.

In a recent FYW course, the second in our stretch sequence, one of my students offered a description of his past literacy experiences, hinting at what our class' labor-based grading contract gave me. He is African American, with parents from Africa, but he was raised in the US. I leave his "stammers" and "clumsy gestures" to urge you to attend deeply right now, right here.

My experience in the past with literacy hasn't been positive; when I was as young as I can remember when it came to writing or reading I just wouldn't do it, I didn't like it. Like in elementary school, reading especially was always reward- ed. During those schooling days logging our reading for the school week was a requirement; however, if we read long enough or read a challenging book we'd earn points and could trade them in for candies, toys and electronics. But I soon compared myself to other people because of the expensive things they got from their points, which in turn I saw as them being extremely proficient at reading. So what I did was take a bunch of challenging books that were above my level and stressed myself meaninglessly over them and putting myself down because no matter what I tried, I couldn't read at the level of my peers. It all just became some silly game to me. My younger self was thinking "I only play games that I like so I'm just not gonna go a deal with that", and for the longest time that's what I've seen it as, something that I just don't want to partake in. So I gave up. Gave up on trying to be like everyone else, and until recently only ever saw reading as a chore. This goes the same for writing too. Whenever I had to do it, it was just boring. Was always told to close read the literature, look for devices and methods in the writing. You don't know how many times from a teacher I've heard "look for the literary de- vices the author uses to convey their purpose." Sure it was a of learning about literature, but I thought it was a superficial way of learning; could never apply what was taught towards my own endeavors because I felt what was taught was so shallow.

Now, it isn't so bad thanks to this class when I started it in the winter quarter, it got me used to reading and writing, espe- cially writing.

When I sit in the presence of my student's words, when I try to listen deeply, when I stop placing any of my expectations on him for this writing, I don't have to ask or urge him to find more meaning than the final sentence, than the simple fact that our labor-based grading contract ecology "got me used to reading and writing." That is something, given his past experiences. He is becoming right in front of me, and I'm lucky enough to witness it.

But this doesn't mean I cannot dialogue with him, ask more questions, and do so in an environment that rewards this extra labor. I can model a way to compassionately attend him into being, and he might return that attending to me or his peers. But he will surely see an alternative to the standards-driven, White language supremacist classroom that I'm arguing does so much harm in and out of school. He will get chances to problematize the judgments of language and consider the ways our *habitus* function in systems of judgment like those in schools, like White supremacist ones in the larger society. Such an ecology, such a writing classroom, assesses writing so that people might stop killing each other by seeing difference not as a threat or as wrong but as another becoming. Yes, I have flimsy evidence for such a claim, but if I'm going to have faith in anything that will stop the killing, and violence, and discord in the world, I'd like it to be our loving and compassionate attending to each other.

WORKS CITED

Adam, Barabara. *Time*. Polity, 2004.

———. "The Timescapes Challenge: Engagement with the Invisible Temporal." *Researching Lives Through Time: Time, Generation and Life Stories*. Barbara Adam, Jenny Hockey, and Paul Thompson. Edited by Rosalind Edwards. Timescapes Working Paper Series, no. 1. Jun 2008. http://www.timescapes.leeds.ac.uk/assets /files/timescapes/WP1-Researching-Lives-Through-Time-June-2008.pdf. Accessed 31 Jul. 2017.

———. *Timescapes of Modernity: The Environment and Invisible Hazards*. Routledge, 1998.

Adebayo, Bob. "Cognitive and Non-Cognitive Factors: Affecting the Academic Performance and Retention of Conditionally Admitted Freshmen." *Journal of College Admission*, no. 200, 2008, pp. 15–21.

Aditomo, Anindito. "Students' Response to Academic Setback: 'Growth Mindset' as a Buffer against Demotivation." *International Journal of Educational Psychology*, vol. 4, no. 2, 2015, pp. 198–222.

Ahmed, Sara. "A Phenomenology of Whiteness." *Feminist Theory*, vol. 8, no. 2, 2007, pp. 149–68.

Alim, H. Samy, et al. *Raciolinguistics: How Language Shapes Our Ideas about Race*. Oxford UP, 2016.

Allen, James. "Grades as Valid Measures of Academic Achievement of Classroom Learning." *The Clearing House*, vol. 78, no. 5, May/June, 2005, pp. 218–23.

Allison, Libby, et al., editors. *Grading in the Post-Process Classroom: From Theory to Practice*. Heinemann, 1997.

Althusser, Louis. "Ideology and Ideological State Apparatuses (Notes towards an Investigation)." 1970. Translated by Andy Blunden. *Lenin and Philosophy and Other Essays*. Monthly Review Press, 1971.

Ambrose, Susan A., et al. *How Learning Works: Seven Research-Based Principles for Smart Teaching*. 1st ed., Jossey-Bass, 2010.

Anderson, Geoff., et al. *Learning Contracts*. Kogan Page, 1996.

Anson, Chris. "Response and the Social Construction of Error." *Assessing Writing*, vol. 7, 2000, pp. 5–21.

Arao, Brian, and Kristi Clemens. "From Safe Spaces to Brave Spaces: A New Way to Frame Dialogue around Diversity and Social Justice." *The Art of Effective Facilitation: Reflections from Social Justice Educators*, edited by Lisa M. Landreman, Sylus, 2013, pp. 135–50.

Arendt, Hannah. *The Human Condition*. 2nd ed., 1958. U of Chicago P, 1998.

Aristotle. *Prior Analytics*. Trans. A. J. Jenkinson. *Internet Classics Archive*. http://classics .mit.edu/Aristotle/prior.html. Accessed 10 Dec. 2017.

Association for Psychological Science. "Brain Can Be Trained in Compassion, Study Shows." https://www.psychologicalscience.org/news/releases/compassion-training.html#. Accessed 8 Jun 2017.

Ault, B. A. "*Oikos* and *Oikonomia*: Greek Houses, Households and the Domestic Economy." *British School at Athens Studies*, vol. 15, 2007, pp. 259–65.

Banaji, Mahzarin R., and Greenwald, Anthony G. *Blindspot: Hidden Biases of Good People*. Delacorte Press, 2013.

Baraka, Imamu Amiri. *Home*. William Morrow & Co., 1966.

Barbezat, Daniel P., and Mirabai Bush. *Contemplative Practices in Higher Education: Powerful Methods to Transform Teaching and Learning*. Jossey-Bass, 2014.

Barlow, David H., et al.. "Toward a Unified Treatment for Emotional Disorders." *Behavior Therapy*, vol. 35, no. 2, 2004, pp. 205–30.

Barnett, Timothy. "Reading 'Whiteness' in English Studies." *College English*, vol. 63, no. 1, 2000, pp. 9–37.

Batchelor, Stephen, et al. "Understand, Realize, Give Up, Develop." *Tricycle Magazine*. Fall 2017. https://tricycle.org/magazine/understand-realize-give-develop/. Accessed 01 Aug. 2017.

Bauman, Marcy. "What Grades Do for Us, and How to Do Without Them." *Alternatives to Grading Student Writing*, edited by Stephen Tchudi, NCTE, 1997, pp. 162–78.

Bear, George G., et al. "Rewards, Praise, and Punitive Consequences: Relations with Intrinsic and Extrinsic Motivation." *Teaching and Teacher Education*, vol. 65, 2017, pp. 10–20.

"behold, v." *OED Online*. Oxford UP, Mar. 2017. http://www.oed.com/view/Entry/17232. Accessed on18 Apr. 2017.

Belanoff, Pat. "The Myths of Assessment." *Journal of Basic Writing*, vol. 10, no. 1, 1991, pp. 54–66.

Berlin, James A. *Rhetoric and Reality: Writing Instruction in American Colleges, 1900–1985*. Studies in Writing and Rhetoric, Southern Illinois UP, 1987.

Berte, Neal R. *Individualizing Education through Contract Learning*. University: U of Alabama P, 1975.

Blackstock, Alan, and Virginia Norris Exton. "'Space to Grow': Grading Contracts for Basic Writers." *TETYC*, vol. 41, no. 3, Mar. 2014, pp. 278–93.

Blankenship, Shortie McKinney. *The Effects of Regular Grading and Contract Grading on College Students' Achievement, Performance, and Preference for Grading Systems*. 1977. Ohio State University. Ph.D. dissertation.

Bleich, David. "What Can Be Done About Grading." *Grading in The Post-Process Classroom: From Theory to Practice*, edited by Libby Allison, et al. Boynton/Cook Publishers, 1997.

Bonilla-Silva, Eduardo. *Racism Without Racists: Color-Blind Racism and The Persistence of Racial Inequality in The United States*. Rowman and Littlefield Publishers, Inc, 2003.

Borghans, Lex, et al. "The Economics and Psychology of Personality Traits." *Journal of Human Resources*, vol. 43, no. 4, 2008, pp. 972–1059.

Bourdieu, Pierre. *The Logic of Practice*. Translated by Richard Nice. Stanford: Stanford UP, 1990.

———. *Outline of a Theory of Practice*. Translated by Richard Nice. Cambridge UP, 1977.

Bowles, Samuel, and Gintis, Herbert. "*Schooling in Capitalist America* Revisited." *Sociology of Education*, vol. 75, no. 1, 2002, pp. 1–18.

Bowman, Joel. P. "Problems of the Grading Differential." *The Journal of Business Communication*, vol. 11, no. 1, 1973, pp. 22–30.

Broad, Bob. *What We Really Value: Beyond Rubrics in Teaching and Assessing Writing*. Utah State UP, 2003.

Brookhiser, Richard. "The Way of the WASP." *Critical White Studies: Looking behind the Mirror*, edited by Richard Delgado and Jean Stefancic, Temple UP, 1997, pp. 16–23.

Brown, Philip Melvin. "An Examination of Freire's Problem-Posing Pedagogy: The Experiences of Three Middle School Teachers Implementing Theory into Practice." 2013. University of Georgia, Ph.D. dissertation.

Brubaker, Nathan D. "Negotiating Authority in an Undergraduate Teacher Education Course: A Qualitative Investigation." *Teacher Education Quarterly*, vol. 36, no. 4, Fall 2009, pp. 99–118.

Burke, Kenneth. *Language as Symbolic Action: Essays on Life, Literature, and Method*. University of California P, 1966.

Charnley, Mitchell. V. "Grading Standards Vary Considerably, Experiment Shows." *Journalism Educator*, Oct. 1978, pp. 49–50.

Charter for Compassion International. Charter for Compassion. 2017. https://charter forcompassion.org/.

Center for Compassion and Altruism in Research and Education. "Compassion." http://ccare.stanford.edu/research/wiki/compassion-definitions/compassion/. Accessed 02 Jun 2017.

Chödrön, Pema. *How to Meditate: A Practical Guide to Making Friends with Your Mind*. Sounds True, 2013.

Claro, Susana, et al. "Growth Mindset Tempers the Effects of Poverty on Academic Achievement." Proceedings of the National Academy of Sciences of the United States of America, vol. 113, no. 31, 2016, pp. 8664–68.

"comely, adj." *OED Online*. Oxford UP, Dec. 2016. http://www.oed.com/view/Entry /36857. Accessed on 8 Mar. 2017.

Committee on CCCC Language Statement. "Students' Right to Their Own Language." *College Composition and Communication*, vol. 25, no. 3, 1974, pp. 1–18.

Compas, Bruce E., et al. "Coping With Stress During Childhood and Adolescence: Problems, Progress, and Potential in Theory and Research." Psychological Bulletin, vol. 127, no. 1, 2001, pp. 87–127.

Conference on English Education. "Position Statement on Beliefs about Social Justice in English Education." Originally published Dec. 2009. http://www.ncte.org/cee /positions/socialjustice. Accessed 17 May 2017.

Connor-Smith, Jennifer K., and Celeste Flachsbart. "Relations Between Personality and Coping: A Meta-Analysis." *Journal of Personality and Social Psychology*, vol. 93, no. 6, 2007, pp. 1080–1107.

Cooper-Kahn, Joyce, and Laurie Dietzel. "What is Executive Functioning?" LD Online: The Educators' Guide to Learning Disabilities and ADHD. Published 2017. http://www.ldonline.org/article/29122/. Accessed 30 May 2017.

Costa, Paul T., and Robert R. McCrae. "From Catalog to Classification: Murray's Needs and the Five-Factor Model." *Journal of Personality and Social Psychology*, vol. 55, no. 2, 1988, pp. 258–65.

Cousin, Gaëtan, and Catherine Crane. "Changes in Disengagement Coping Mediate Changes in Affect Following Mindfulness-Based Cognitive Therapy in a Non-Clinical Sample." *British Journal of Psychology*, vol. 107, no. 3, 2016, pp. 434–47.

Crancer, Joanne, et al. "Contract Systems and Grading Policies." *Journal of Nursing Education*, vol. 16, no. 1, Jan. 1977, pp. 29–35.

Crowley, Sharon. *Composition in the University: Historical and Polemical Essays*. U of Pittsburgh P, 1998.

Danielewicz, Jane, and Elbow, Peter. "A Unilateral Grading Contract to Improve Learning and Teaching." *CCC* vol. 61, no. 2, 2009, pp. 244–68.

Davidson, Richard. "Studies on Compassion." Video. Uploaded on 21 Oct. 2016. https://youtu.be/il7W3A8uRxk. Accessed 7 Jun 2017.

Dead Prez. "They Schools." *Let's Get Free*, Loud Records, 2000.

Delaney, Liam, et al. "The Role of Noncognitive Traits in Undergraduate Study Behaviours." *Economics of Education Review*, vol. 32, 2013, pp. 181–95.

Dewey, John. *How We Think: A Restatement of the Relation of Reflective Thinking to The Educative Process*. D.C. Heath & Co., 1933.

Diederich, Paul B. *Measuring Growth in English*. NCTE, 1974.

DiAngelo, Robin J. *White Fragility: Why It's so Hard to Talk to White People about Racism*. Beacon Press, 2018.

———. "White Fragility." *International Journal of Critical Pedagogy*, vol. 3, no. 3, 2011, pp. 54–70.

Dobrin, Sidney I. *Postcomposition*. Southern Illinois UP, 2012.

Duckworth, Angela L., et al. "Grit: Perseverance and Passion for Long-Term Goals." *Journal of Personality and Social Psychology*, vol. 92, no. 6, 2007, pp. 1087–1101.

Duffy, John. "The Good Writer: Virtue Ethics and the Teaching of Writing." *College English*, vol. 79, no. 3, Jan. 2017, pp. 229–50.

Dulek, Ron, and Annette Shelby. "Varying Evaluative Criteria: A Factor in Differential Grading." *The Journal of Business Communication*, vol. 18, no. 2, 1981, pp. 41–50.

Dweck, Carol S. *Mindset: The New Psychology of Success*. Random House, 2006.

Dweck, Carol S., et al. "Motivational Effects on Attention, Cognition, and Performance." *Motivation, Emotion, and Cognition: Intgrative Perspectives on Intellectual Functioning and Development*, edited by D. Y. Dai and R. J. Sternberg, Lawrence Erlbaum Associates, 2006, pp. 41–56.

"economy, n.". *OED Online*. Oxford UP. 2015. http://www.oed.com/view/Entry/59393. Accessed 09 Aug. 2017.

Ekman, Paul. "Darwin's Compassionate View of Human Nature." *JAMA*, vol. 303, no. 6, 2010, pp. 557–58.

Elbow, Peter. "Grading Student Writing: Making It Simpler, Fairer, Clearer." *New*

Directions for Teaching and Learning, vol. 69, 1997, pp. 127–40.

———. "Ranking, Evaluating, Liking: Sorting Out Three Forms of Judgment." *College English*, vol. 55, 1993, pp. 187–206.

———. "Taking Time Out from Grading and Evaluating While Working in a Conventional System." *Assessing Writing*, vol. 4, no. 1, 1997, pp. 5–27.

Elbow, Peter, and Belanoff, Pat. *Sharing and Responding*. 3rd ed., McGraw-Hill, 1999.

Elliot, Norbert. *On a Scale: a Social History of Writing Assessment in America*. Peter Lang, 2005.

Engels, Friedrich. *The Principles of Communism*. 1847. Moscow: Progress Publishers, 1999, https://www.marxists.org/archive/marx/works/1847/11/prin-com.htm. Accessed 09 Aug. 2017.

Ericsson, K. Anders, and Pool, Robert. *Peak: Secrets from the New Science of Expertise*. Houghton Mifflin Harcourt, 2016.

Ericsson, K. Anders, et al. "The Role of Deliberate Practice in the Acquisition of Expert Performance." *Psychological Review*, vol. 100, no. 3, 1993, pp. 363–406.

Faigley, Lester. *Fragments of Rationality: Postmodernity and the Subject of Composition*. U of Pittsburgh P, 1992.

"failure, n." *OED Online*, Oxford UP, Jan. 2018, www.oed.com/view/Entry/67663. Accessed 30 Jan. 2018.

Fanon, Frantz. *Black Skin, White Masks*. Pluto Press, 1986.

FAO, IFAD, UNICEF, WFP and WHO. *The State of Food Security and Nutrition in the World 2017*. Building resilience for peace and food security. www.unicef.org. FAO, 2017. Accessed 6 Feb. 2018.

Farber, Jerry. *The Student as Nigger: Essays and Stories*. Contact Books, 1969. http://disciplinedminds.tripod.com/student-as-nigger.pdf. Accessed 28 Dec. 2018.

Farkas, George. "Cognitive Skills and Noncognitive Traits and Behaviors in Stratification Processes." *Annual Review of Sociology*, vol. 29, no. 1, 2003, pp. 541–62.

Fischer, David Hackett. *Albion's Seed: Four British Folkways in America*. Oxford UP, 1989.

Flavell, John H. "Metacognition and Cognitive Monitoring: A New Area of Cognitive-Developmental Inquiry." *American Psychologist*, vol. 34, no. 10, 1979, pp. 906–11.

Foucault, Michel. *Discipline and Punish: The Birth of the Prison*. 1975. Translated by Alan Sheridan, Vintage, 1995.

Fox, Catherine. "The Race to Truth: Disarticulating Critical Thinking from Whiteliness." *Pedagogy: Critical Approaches to Teaching Literature, Language, Composition, and Culture*, vol. 2, no. 2, 2002, pp. 197–212.

Fox, Renee. "The Evolution of American Bioethics." *Social Science Perspectives on Medical Ethics*, edited by George Weisz, Kluwer Academic Publishers, 1990, pp. 201–17.

Frankenberg, Ruth. *White Women, Race Matters: The Social Construction of Whiteness*. U of Minnesota P, 1993.

Fredricks, Jennifer A., et al. "School Engagement: Potential of the Concept, State of the Evidence." *Review of Educational Research*, vol. 74, no. 1, 2004, pp. 59–109.

"Fred Rogers." *Wikipedia, The Free Encyclopedia*. Wikipedia, The Free Encyclopedia, 28 Dec. 2018. Web. 28 Dec. 2018.

Freeman, Kathleen. *Ancilla to the Pre-Socratic Philosophers*. Harvard UP, 1966.

Freire, Paulo. *Pedagogy of the Oppressed*. 1970. Translated by Myra Bergman Ramos, Continuum, 2005.

Frye, Marilyn. "White Woman Feminist." From *Willful Virgin: Essays in Feminism*. Crossing Press. 1992. *Feminist Reprise*. http://feminist-reprise.org/2017/06/marilyn -frye-on-whiteliness/. Accessed 3 Jul. 2016.

Gallagher, Chris. "The Trouble with Outcomes: Pragmatic Inquiry and Educational Aims." *College English*, vol. 75, no. 1, Sept. 2012, pp. 42–60.

Gates, Henry Louis. *The Signifying Monkey: A Theory of Afro-American Literary Criticism*. New York: Oxford UP, 1988.

Gee, James Paul. "Literacy, Discourse, and Linguistics: Introduction." *Journal of Education*, vol. 171, no. 1, 1989, pp. 5–17.

Gensler, Harry J. *Ethics and the Golden Rule*. Routledge, 2013.

Gladwell, Malcolm. *Outliers: The Story of Success*. 1st ed., Little, Brown and Company, 2008.

Goetz, Jennifer L., et al. "Compassion: An Evolutionary Analysis and Empirical Review." *Psychological Bulletin*, vol. 136, no. 3, 2010, pp. 351–74.

Goldberg, David Theo. *Racist Culture: Philosophy and the Politics of Meaning*. Blackwell Publishers, 1993.

Goleman, Daniel. "Wired For Kindness: Science Shows We Prefer Compassion, and Our Capacity Grows With Practice." *Washington Post*. Jun 2015. https://www.wash ingtonpost.com/news/inspired-life/wp/2015/06/23/wired-for-kindness-science -shows-we-prefer-compassion-and-our-capacity-grows-with-practice/?utm_term =.4ae78178ef8b. Accessed 7 Jun 2017.

Gould, Stephen Jay. *The Mismeasure of Man*. W. W. Norton and Company, 1981.

Graham, Daniel W. "Heraclitus." *Internet Encyclopedia of Philosophy*. http://www.iep .utm.edu/heraclit/#H3. Accessed 26 Jul. 2017.

Gramlich, John. "5 Facts about Crime in the U.S." Pew Research Center, 21 Feb. 2017, http://www.pewresearch.org/fact-tank/2017/02/21/5-facts-about-crime-in -the-u-s/.

Greenfield, Laura. "The 'Standard English' Fairy Tale: A Rhetorical Analysis of Racist Pedagogies and Commonplace Assumptions about Language Diversity." *Writing Centers and The New Racism: A Call for Sustainable Dialogue and Change*, edited by Laura Greenfield and Karen Rowan, Utah UP, 2011, pp. 33–60.

Greenwald, Anthony G., and Linda Hamilton Krieger. "Implicit Bias: Scientific Foundations." *California Law Review*, vol. 94, no. 4, 2006, pp. 945–67.

Grimm, Nancy. *Good Intentions: Writing Center Work for Postmodern Times*. Heinemann, 1999.

Guba, Egon G., and Yvonna S. Lincoln. *Fourth Generation Evaluation*. Sage Publications, 1989.

Gutman, Leslie Morrison, and Ingrid Schoon. *The Impact of Non-Cognitive Skills on Outcomes for Young People*. Literature review for Institute of Education, University of London; Education Endowment Foundation. https://educationendowmentfoun dation.org.uk/public/files/Publications/EEF_Lit_Review_Non-CognitiveSkills.pdf. Accessed 2 Dec. 2017.

"habit, n." *OED Online*. Oxford UP, Dec. 2016. http://www.oed.com/view/Entry /82978. Accessed on 15 Feb. 2017.

Hacker, Andrew. "Liberal Democracy and Social Control." *The American Political Science Review*, vol. 51, no. 4, 1957, pp. 1009–26.

Hahn, Thich Nhat. *Peace is Every Step: The Path of Mindfulness in Everyday Life*. Bantam, 1991.

Hall, Stuart. "Race, The Floating Signifier." Video and transcript. Media Education Foundation. http://www.mediaed.org/transcripts/Stuart-Hall-Race-the-Floating -Signifier-Transcript.pdf. Northampton, MA, Media Education Foundation, 1996.

Hamp-Lyons, Liz, and William Condon. *Assessing the Portfolio: Principles for Practice, Theory, and Research*. Hampton, 2000.

Hannaford, Ivan. *Race: The History of an Idea in The West*. The Woodrow Wilson Center Press, 1996.

Hanson, F. Allan. *Testing Testing: Social Consequences of the Examined Life*. U of California P, 1993.

Harris, Cheryl I. "Whiteness as Property." *Harvard Law Review*, vol. 106, no. 8, 1993, pp. 1707–91.

Hartwell, Patrick. "Grammar, Grammars, and the Teaching of Grammar." *College English*, vol. 47, no. 2, 1985, pp. 105–27.

Hassencahl, Fran. "Contract Grading in the Classroom." *Improving College and University Teaching*, vol. 27, no. 1, Winter 1979, pp. 30–33.

Haswell, Richard. "Rubrics, Prototypes, and Exemplars: Categorization Theory and Systems of Writing Placement." *Assessing Writing*, vol. 5, no. 2, 1998, pp. 231–68.

Heckman, James J., et al. "The Effects of Cognitive and Noncognitive Abilities on Labor Market Outcomes and Social Behavior." *Journal of Labor Economics*, vol. 24, no. 3, 2006, pp. 411–82.

Hoffman, Martin L. "Is Altruism Part of Human Nature?" *Journal of Personality and Social Psychology*, vol. 40, 1981, pp. 121–37.

Horner, Bruce, et al. "Language Difference In Writing: Toward a Translingual Approach." *College English*, vol. 73, no. 3, 2011, pp. 303–21.

Huot, Brian. *(Re)Articulating Writing Assessment for Teaching and Learning*. Utah UP, 2002.

Ignatiev, Noel. *How the Irish Became White*. Routledge, 1995.

Inman, Joyce Olewski, and Rebecca A. Powell. "In the Absence of Grades: Dissonance and Desire in Course-Contract Classrooms." *College Composition and Communication*, vol. 70, no. 1, 2018, pp. 30–56.

Inoue, Asao B. "A Grade-less Writing Course That Focuses on Labor and Assessing." *First-Year Composition: From Theory to Practice*, edited by Deborah Coxwell-Teague and Ronald F. Lunsford, Parlor Press, 2014, pp. 71–110.

———. *Antiracist Writing Assessment Ecologies: Teaching and Assessing for a Socially Just Future*. The WAC Clearinghouse and Parlor Press, 2015.

———. "Articulating Sophistic Rhetoric as a Validity Heuristic for Writing Assessment." *Journal of Writing Assessment*, vol. 3, no. 1, 2007, pp. 31–54.

———. "Classroom Writing Assessment as an Antiracist Practice: Confronting White Supremacy in the Judgments of Language." *Pedagogy: Critical Approaches to Teaching Literature, Language, Composition, and Culture*, vol. 19, no. 3, forthcoming.

———. "Community-Based Assessment Pedagogy." *Assessing Writing*, vol. 3, no. 9, 2005, pp. 208–38.

———. "Friday Plenary Address: Racism in Writing Programs and the CWPA." *WPA: Writing Program Administration*, vol. 40, no. 1, 2016, pp. 134–54.

———. "Grading Contracts: Assessing Their Effectiveness on Different Racial Formations." *Race and Writing Assessment*, edited by Asao B. Inoue and Mya Poe, Peter Lang, 2012, pp. 79–94.

———. "Racial Methodologies for Composition Studies: Reflecting on Theories of Race in Writing Assessment Research." *Writing Studies Research in Practice: Methods and Methodologies*, edited by Lee Nickoson, and Mary P. Sheridan, SIUE Press, 2012, pp. 125–39.

———. "Theorizing Failure in U.S. Writing Assessments." *Research in the Teaching of English*, vol. 48, no. 3, Feb. 2014, pp. 330–52.

Inoue, Asao B., and Mya Poe. *Race and Writing Assessment*. P. Lang, 2012.

Inoue, Asao B., and Tyler Richmond. "Theorizing the Reflection Practices of Female Hmong College Students." *A Rhetoric of Reflection*, edited by Kathleen Blake Yancey, Utah State UP, 2016, pp. 125–45.

Jacobson, Matthew Frye. *Whiteness of a Different Color: European Immigrants and the Alchemy of Race*. Harvard UP, 1998.

Jolls, Christine, and Cass R, Sunstein. "The Law of Implicit Bias." 94 Calif. L. Rev. vol. 94, no. 4, 2006, pp. 969–96.

Jones, James M. *Prejudice and Racism*. 2nd ed., McGraw-Hill, 1997.

Kahneman, Daniel. *Thinking, Fast and Slow*. Farrar, Straus, and Giroux, 2011.

Keltner, Dacher. "The Compassion Instinct." *The Greater Good Magazine*. Originally published on 01 Mar. 2004, http://greatergood.berkeley.edu/article/item/the_com passionate_instinct. Accessed 02 Jun 2017.

———. "Dacher Keltner on the Evolutionary Roots of Compassion." Video. Uploaded 28 Jun 2012. https://www.youtube.com/watch?v=3qrShIMtYJU. Accessed 08 Jun 2017.

———. "TEDxBerkeley—Dacher Keltner—04/03/10." Video. Uploaded 19 Jun 2010. https://www.youtube.com/watch?v=KsFxWSuu_4I. Accessed 02 Jun 2017.

Kendi, Ibram X. *Stamped From the Beginning: The Definitive History of Racist Ideas in America*. Nation Books, 2016.

Kennedy, George A. *A New History of Classical Rhetoric*. Princeton UP, 1994.

Kennedy, Tammie M., Joyce Irene Middleton, Krista Ratcliffe. editors. *Rhetorics of Whiteness: Postracial Hauntings in Popular Culture, Social Media, and Education*. Southern Illinois UP, 2017.

Kirschenbaum, Daniel S. and Sheryl Wetter Riechmann. "Learning with Gusto in Introductory Psychology." *Teaching of Psychology*, vol. 2, no. 2, 1975, pp. 72–76.

Knapp, John V. "Contract/Conference Evaluations of Freshman Composition." *College English*, vol. 37, no. 7, 1976, pp. 647–53.

Knowles, Malcolm S. *Using Learning Contracts*. 1st ed., Jossey-Bass, 1986.

Kohn, Alfie. "The Case Against Grades." *Educational Leadership*, Nov. 2011, pp. 28–33.

———. *Punished by Rewards: The Trouble with Gold Stars, Incentive Plans, A's, Praise, and Other Bribes*. Houghton Mifflin Company, 1999

Kolln, Martha, and Hancock, Craig. "The Story of English Grammar in United States Schools." *English Teaching: Practice and Critique*, vol. 4, no. 3, 2005, pp. 11–31.

Kruse, Louise C., and Diane M. Fager Barger. "Development and Implementation of a Contract Grading System." *Journal of Nursing Education*, vol. 21, no. 5, May 1982, pp. 31–37.

Kynard, Carmen. *Vernacular Insurrections: Race, Black Protest, and the New Century in Composition—Literacies Studies*. SU NY Press, 2013.

LaHaye, Laura. "Mercantilism." *The Concise Encyclopedia of Economics*. 2nd ed., http://www.econlib.org/library/Enc/Mercantilism.html. Accessed 12 Aug. 2017.

Lathan, Rhea Estelle. *Freedom Writing: African American Civil Rights Literacy Activism, 1955–1967*. NCTE, 2015.

Lazarus, Richard S., and Folkman, Susan. *Stress, Appraisal, and Coping*. New York, Springer Pub. Co., 1984.

Leahy, Richard. "Writing Made Possible: A Contract Approach." *Improving College and University Teaching*, vol. 28, no. 4, Fall 1980, pp. 155–57.

Lévi-Strauss, Claude. *Introduction to the Work of Marcel Mauss*. 1950. Translated by Felicity Baker. Routledge & Kegan Paul, 1987.

Levitin, Daniel J. *This Is Your Brain on Music: The Science of a Human Obsession*. Dutton, 2006.

Lilius, Jacoba M., et al. "Compassion Revealed: What We Know About Compassion at Work (And Where We Need to Know More)." *The Oxford Handbook of Positive Organizational Scholarship*, edited by Kim S. Cameronand Gretchen M. Spreitzer, Oxford UP, 2011.

Lippi-Green, Rosina. *English with an Accent: Language, Ideology, and Discrimination in the United States*. Routledge, 2012.

Lleras, Christy. "Do Skills and Behaviors in High School Matter? The Contribution of Noncognitive Factors in Explaining Differences in Educational Attainment and Earnings." *Social Science Research*, vol. 37, no. 3, 2008, pp. 888–902.

Macnamara, Brooke N., et al. "Deliberate Practice and Performance in Music, Games, Sports, Education, and Professions: A Meta-Analysis." *Psychological Science*, vol. 25, no. 8, 2014, pp. 1608–18.

Mandel, Barrett. "Teaching without Judging." *College English*, vol. 34, no. 5, 1973, pp. 623–33.

Marrou, Henri, I. *A History of Education in Antiquity*. Translated by George Lamb. U of Wisconsin P, 1956.

Marshall, Max. "The Floating Technique: Teaching Without Grades." *Improving College and University Teaching*, vol. 8, no. 1, Winter 1960, pp. 23–29.

Marx, Karl. *Capital: A Critique of Political Economy, Volume I.* 1867. Progress Publishers. 1999, https://www.marxists.org/archive/marx/works/1867-c1/index.htm. Accessed 09 Aug. 2017.

———. *Grundrisse: Foundations of the Critique of Political Economy.* 1939–1941.Translated by Martin Nicolaus. Penguin. 1973, https://www.marxists.org/archive/marx/works/1857/grundrisse/. Accessed 09 Aug. 2017.

———. *Theories of Surplus-Value.* Progress Publishers. 1863. Retrieved from https://www.marxists.org/archive/marx/works/1863/theories-surplus-value/. Accessed 09 Aug. 2017.

Matsuda, Paul. Kei. "The Myth of Linguistic Homogeneity in U.S. College Composition." *College English*, vol. 68, no. 6, 2006, pp. 637–51.

Mcallister, Margaret. "Learning Contracts: An Australian Experience." *Nurse Education Today*, vol. 16, no. 3, 1996, pp. 199–205.

McGarrell, Hedy M. "Self-Directed Learning Contracts to Individualize Language Learning in the Classroom." *Foreign Language Annals*, vol. 29, no. 3, 1996, pp. 495–508.

McGill, David, and John K. Pearce. "British Families." *Ethnicity and Family Therapy*, edited by Monica McGoldrick, et al., Guildford Press, 1982, pp. 457–79.

Miller, Susan. *Textual Carnivals: the Politics of Composition.* Southern Illinois UP, 1991.

Milroy, James, and Leslie Milroy. *Authority in Language: Investigating Standard English.* 4th ed., Routledge, 2012.

Mosco, Vincent. *The Political Economy of Communication.* 2nd ed., Sage Publications, 2009.

Myser, Catherine. "Differences from Somewhere: The Normativity of Whiteness in Bioethics in the United States." *The American Journal of Bioethics*, vol. 3, no. 2, 2002, pp. 1–11.

National Center for Learning Disabilities. "Executive Function Fact Sheet." 2008. http://www.ldonline.org/article/24880. Accessed 30 May 2017.

National Center on Universal Design for Learning. "About UDL." 26 Mar. 2015, http://www.udlcenter.org/aboutudl. Accessed 30 May 2017.

Negowetti, Nicolw E. "Implicit Bias and the Legal Profession's 'Diversity Crisis': A Call for Self-Reflection." *Nevada Law Journal*, vol. 15, 2015, pp. 930–1631.

Newcomb, Lawrence Howard. *The Effect of Contract Grading on Student Performance.* 1973. Ohio State University, Ph.D. dissertation.

Nichols, Andrew, et al. *Rising Tide II: Do Black Students Benefit as Grad Rates Increase?* The Education Trust, Mar. 2016, https://edtrust.org/wp-content/uploads/2014/09/RisingTide_II_EdTrust.pdf.

Nisbett, Richard E., and Dov Cohen. *Culture of Honor: The Psychology of Violence in the South.* Westview Press, 1996.

Ohmann, Richard M. *English in America: A Radical View of the Profession.* Oxford UP, 1976.

Omi, Michael, and Howard Winant. *Racial Formation in the United States.* 3rd ed. Routledge, 2015.

O'Reilley, Mary Rose. "'Exterminate . . . the Brutes'—And Other Things That Go Wrong in Student-Centered Teaching." *College English*, vol. 51, no. 2, 1989, pp. 142–46.

———. *Radical Presence: Teaching as Contemplative Practice*. Boynton/Cook Publishers: Heinemann, 1998.

Otte, George., and Rebecca Mlynarczyk. *Basic Writing*. The WAC Clearinghouse and Parlor Press, 2010.

Paris, Scott G., et al. "Becoming a Strategic Reader." *Contemporary Educational Psychology*, vol. 8, no. 3, 1983, pp. 293–316.

Perelman, Chaim, and L. Olbrechts-Tyteca. *The New Rhetoric: A Treatise on Argumentation*. Translated by John Wilkinson and Purcell Weaver. U of Notre Dame P, 1969.

Pintrich, Paul R. "The Role of Metacognitive Knowledge in Learning, Teaching, and Assessing." *Theory Into Practice*, vol. 41, no. 4, 2002, pp. 219–25.

Plato. *Cratylus*. 360 B.C.E. Translated by Benjamin Jowett. *Internet Classics Archive*. http://classics.mit.edu/Plato/cratylus.html. Accessed 26 Jul. 2017.

Plutarch. *Plutarch's Lives, Translated from the Original Greek, with Notes and a Life of Plutarch*. By Aubrey Stewart and George Long. George Bell & Sons. 2004/[1894]. Retrieved from https://www.gutenberg.org/files/14033/14033-h/14033-h.htm #LIFE_OF_PERIKLES. Accessed 09 Aug. 2017.

Poe, Mya, et al., editors. *Writing Assessment, Social Justice, and the Advancement of Opportunity*. The WAC Clearinghouse and The UP of Colorado, 2018.

Polczynski, James J., and L. E. Shirland. "Expectancy Theory and Contract Grading Combined as an Effective Motivational Force for College Students." *The Journal of Educational Research*, vol. 70, no. 5, 1977, pp. 238–41.

Postman, Neil. *Amusing Ourselves To Death: Public Discourse in the Age of Show Business*. 20th Anniversary edition. 1985. Penguin, 2005.

Powell, Pegeen Reichert. *Retention and Resistance: Writing Instruction and Students Who Leave*. Utah State UP, 2013.

Pratt, Minnie Bruce. "Identity: Skin Blood Heart." *Yours in Struggle*, edited by Elly Bulkin, et al., Long Haul Press, 1984.

Prendergast, Catherine. *Literacy and Racial Justice: the Politics of Learning after* Brown v. Board of Education. Southern Illinois UP, 2003.

Pulfrey, Caroline, et al. "Why Grades Engender Performance-Avoidance Goals: The Mediating Role of Autonomous Motivation." *Journal of Educational Psychology*, vol. 103, no. 3, 2011, pp. 683–700.

Ratcliffe, Krista. *Rhetorical Listening: Identification, Gender, and Whiteness*. Southern Illinois UP, 2005.

Rawls, John. *Justice as Fairness: A Restatement*. Belknap P of Harvard UP, 2001.

Reeves, Arin N. *Written in Black and White: Exploring Confirmation Bias in Racialized Perceptions of Writing Skills*. Yellow Paper Series. Nextions, 2014.

Reichert, Nancy. "Practice Makes Perfect: Contracting Quantity *and* Quality." *TETYC*, vol. 31, no. 1, Sept. 2003, pp. 60–68.

Ricardo, David. *On the Principles of Political Economy, and Taxation.* 1817. J. McCreery Printer, 2010, http://www.gutenberg.org/files/33310/33310-h/33310-h.htm. Accessed 09 Aug. 2017.

Rice Center for Teaching and Learning. "How Much Should We Assign? Estimating Out of Class Workload." 11 Jul. 2016. http://cte.rice.edu/blogarchive/2016/07/11/workload. Accessed 12 Jun. 2018.

Richardson, Elaine. *PHD to Ph.D.: How Education Saved My Life.* New City Community Press and Parlor Press, 2013.

Riddell, Tom, et al. *Economics: A Tool for Critically Understanding Society.* 9th ed., Prentice Hall, 2010.

Robinson, Ken. "RSA ANIMATE: Changing Education Paradigms." *Youtube*, upload by The RSA, 14 Oct. 2010, https://www.youtube.com/watch?v=zDZFcDGpL4U. Accessed 28 Dec. 2018.

Roediger, David R. *The Wages of Whiteness: Race and the Making of the American Working Class.* Rev. ed., Verso, 2007.

Rosch, Eleanor. "Principles of categorization." *Cognition and Categorization*, edited by Eleanor Rosch and Barbara B. Lloyd, Erlbaum, 1978, pp. 26–48.

Rose, Mike. *Lives on the Boundary. The Struggles and Achievements of America's Underprepared.* The Free Press, Macmillan, Inc., 1989.

Rowland, Robert, and Deanna F. Womack. "Aristotle's View of Ethical Rhetoric." *Rhetoric Society Quarterly*, vol. 15, no. ½, Win-Spr 1985, pp. 13–31.

Sackrey, Charles, et al. *Introduction to Political Economy.* 7th ed., Dollars & Sense, 2013.

Sale, Maggie. "Call and Response as Critical Method: African-American Oral Traditions and *Beloved*." *African American Review*, vol. 26, no. 1, 1992, pp. 41–50.

San Juan, E., Jr. *Racism and Cultural Studies: Critiques of Multiculturalist Ideology and the Politics of Difference.* Duke UP, 2002.

Schön, Donald. *Educating the Reflective Practitioner.* Jossey-Bass, 1987.

Scott, Tony. *Dangerous Writing: Understanding the Political Economy of Composition.* Utah State U P, 2009.

Segal, Zindel V., et al. *Mindfulness-Based Cognitive Therapy for Depression.* 2nd ed., New York, Guilford Press, 2013.

Seppala, Emma. "Loving-Kindness Meditation." *Greater Good In Action.* http://ggia.berkeley.edu/practice/loving_kindness_meditation. Accessed 7 Jun 2017.

Shiffman, Betty Garrison. "Grading Student Writing: The Dilemma from a Feminist Perspective." *Grading in the Post-Process Classroom*, edited by Libby Allison, et al., Heinemann, 1997, pp. 58–72.

Shor, Ira. "Critical Pedagogy Is Too Big to Fail." *Journal of Basic Writing*, vol. 28, no. 2, 2009, pp. 6–27.

———. *Empowering Education: Critical Teaching for Social Change.* U of Chicago P, 1992.

———. "Monday Morning Fever: Critical Literacy and the Generative Theme of Work." *Freire for the Classroom: A Sourcebook for Liberatory Teaching*, edited by Ira Shor, Heinemann, 1987, pp. 104–21.

Simon-Thomas, Emiliana R. "Three Insights from the Cutting Edge of Compassion Research." *The Greater Good.* 7 Sept. 2012. http://greatergood.berkeley.edu /article/item/three_insights_from_the_cutting_edge_of_compassion_research. Accessed 7 Jun 2017.

Smalls, Krystal A. "Flipping the Script: (Re)Constructing Personhood Through Hip Hop Languaging in a U.S. High School." *Working Papers in Educational Linguistics,* vol. 25, no. 2, 2010, pp. 35–54.

Smith, Adam. *An Inquiry into the Nature and Causes of the Wealth of Nations.* 1776. Random House, Inc., 2000, https://www.marxists.org/reference/archive/smith -adam/. Accessed 09 Aug. 2017.

Smith, Robin, "Aristotle's Logic," *The Stanford Encyclopedia of Philosophy,* Spring 2017 ed., Edward N. Zalta (ed.). https://plato.stanford.edu/archives/spr2017/entries /aristotle-logic/. Accessed 10 Dec. 2017.

Smith, Steven. "Loving-Kindness Meditation." The Center for Contemplative Mind in Society. http://www.contemplativemind.org/practices/tree/loving-kindness. Accessed 7 Jun 2017.

Smitherman, Geneva. *Black Talk: Words and Phrases from the Hood to the Amen Corner.* Revised Edition. Houghton Mifflin, 2000.

———. "'God Don't Never Change': Black English from a Black Perspective." *College English,* vol. 34, no. 6, 1973, pp. 828–33.

———. *Talking and Testifying: The Language of Black America.* Wayne State UP, 1977.

Soliday, Mary. *The Politics of Remediation: Institutional and Student Needs in Higher Education.* U of Pittsburgh P, 2002.

Soliday, Mary, and Jennifer Seibel Trainor. "Rethinking Regulation in the Age of the Literacy Machine." *CCC,* vol. 68, no. 1, Sept. 2016, pp. 125–51.

Solórzano, Daniel G., and Tara J. Yosso. "A Critical Race Counterstory of Race, Racism, and Affirmative Action." *Equity and Excellence in Education,* vol. 35, no. 2, 2002, pp. 155–68.

———. "Critical Race and LatCrit Theory and Method: Counter-Storytelling." *Qualitative Studies in Education,* vol. 14, no. 4, 2001, pp. 471–95.

———. "Critical Race Methodology: Counter-Storytelling as an Analytical Framework for Education Research." *Qualitative Inquiry,* vol. 8, no. 1, 2002, pp. 23–44.

Spidell, Cathy, and William H. Thelin. "Not Ready to Let Go: A Study of Resistance to Grading Contracts." *Composition Studies,* vol. 34, no. 1, Spring 2006, pp. 35–68.

Starch, Daniel, and Edward C. Elliott. "Reliability of the Grading of High-School Work in English." *The School Review,* vol. 30, no. 7, Sept. 1912, pp. 442–57.

Statista. "Number of hours college students spent studying per week in the United States, by major 2011." https://www.statista.com/statistics/226433/college-student-study-hours-by-major-2011/. Accessed 12 Jun 2018.

Steele, Claude E. *Whistling Vivaldi: How Stereotypes Affect Us and What We Can Do.* W. W. Norton and Company, 2010.

Steele, Claude E., S. J. Spencer, and J. Aronson. "Contending with Group Image: The Psychology of Stereotype and Social Identity Threat." *Advances in Experimental Social Psychology,* edited by M. P. Zanna, Academic Press, 2002, pp. 379–440.

Stelzner, Sara Latham. "A Case for Contract Grading." *The Speech Teacher*, vol. 24, Mar. 1975, pp. 127–32.

Stoddard, Lothrop. *The Rising Tide of Color Against White World-Supremacy*. Charles Scribner's and Sons, 1921.

Sue, Derald Wing. *Overcoming Our Racism: The Journey to Liberation*. Jossey-Bass, 2003.

———. *Race Talk and the Conspiracy of Silence: Understanding and Facilitating Difficult Dialogues on Race*. Wiley, 2015.

Swaminathan, Nikhil. "Why Does the Brain Need So Much Power?" *Scientific American*, 28 Apr. 2008. https://www.scientificamerican.com/article/why-does-the-brain -need-s/. Accessed 3 Aug. 2017.

Taylor, Hugh. "Student Reaction to the Grade Contract." *Journal of Education Research*, vol. 64, no. 7, Mar. 1971, pp. 311–14.

Tchudi, Stephen. "Introduction: Degrees of Freedom in Assessment, Evaluation, and Grading." *Alternatives to Grading Student Writing*, edited by Stephen Tchudi, NCTE, 1997, pp. ix-xvii.

Thaiss, Chris, and Terry Myers Zawacki. *Engaged Writes and Dynamic Disciplines: Research on the Academic Writing Life*. Boynton/Cook, Heinemann, 2006.

Trimbur, John. "Composition and the Circulation of Writing." *CCC*, vol. 52, no. 2, 2000, pp. 188–219.

Veblen, Thorstein. *The Theory of the Leisure Class*. Houghton-Mifflin, 1973/[1899].

Villanueva, Victor, Jr. "Blind: Talking about the New Racism." *The Writing Center Journal*, vol. 26, no. 1, 2006, pp. 3–19.

———. *Bootstraps: From an American Academic of Color*. NCTE, 1993.

Volosinov, V. N. *Marxism and the Philosophy of Language*. 1973. Translated by Ladislav Matejka and I. R. Titunik. Harvard UP, 2000.

Weaver, Richard. *The Ethics of Rhetoric*. Hermagoras Press, 1985.

Weber, Max. *The Protestant Ethic and the "Spirit" of Capitalism and Other Writings*. 1905. Penguin Books, 2000.

Weinstein, C. E., and R. Mayer. "The Teaching of Learning Strategies." *Handbook of Research on Teaching*, edited by Merlin C. Wittrock, Macmillan, 1986, pp. 315–27.

Weng, Helen Y, et al. "Compassion Training Alters Altruism and Neural Responses to Suffering." *Psychological Science*, vol. 24, no. 7, 2013, pp. 1171–80.

White, Edward M., et al. *Very Like a Whale: the Assessment of Writing Programs*. Utah State UP, 2015.

White, Edward M., William Lutz, and Sandra Kamusikiri, editors. *Assessment of Writing: Politics, Policies, Practices*. Modern Language Association of America, 1996.

Williams, Joseph M. "The Phenomenology of Error." College Composition and Communication, vol. 32, no. 2, May 1981, pp. 152–68.

Williams, Raymond. *The Country and the City*. New York, Oxford UP, 1973.

———. *Marxism and Literature*. Oxford UP, 1977.

Wolvin, Andrew D., and Darlyn R. Wolvin. "III. Contract Grading in Technical Speech Communication." *The Speech Teacher*, vol. 24, Mar. 1975, pp. 139–42.

Yancey, Kathleen Blake. *Reflection in the Writing Classroom*. Utah State UP, 1998.

———. Editor. *A Rhetoric of Reflection*. Utah State UP, 2016.

Young, Iris Marion. *Responsibility for Justice*. Oxford UP, 2011.

Zajonc, Arthur. *Meditation as Contemplative Inquiry: When Knowing Becomes Love*. Lindisfarne Books, 2009.

Zak, Frances, and Christopher C. Weaver, editors. *The Theory and Practice of Grading Writing: Problems and Possibilities*. SU NY Press, 1998.

Zarzeski, Marilyn Taylor. "The Use and Benefit of Flexible Student Contracts." *Issues in Accounting Education*, vol. 13, no. 3, Aug. 1998, pp. 585–94.

Zhou, Kai. *Non-Cognitive Skills: Definitions, Measurement and Malleability*. Background paper for 2016 Global Education Monitoring Report. 2016. http://unesdoc.unesco.org/images/0024/002455/245576E.pdf. Accessed 2 Dec. 2017.

GRADING CONTRACT FOR FIRST YEAR WRITING

Class:

Imagine that this wasn't an official course for credit at UWT, but instead that you had seen my advertisement in the newspaper or on the Internet, and were freely coming to my home studio for a class in cooking or yoga. We would have classes, workshops, or lessons, but there would be no official grading of omelets or yoga poses, since letters and numbers would be meaningless in those scenarios. But we all would learn, and perhaps in an encouraging, fun, and creative environment. In considering this course and that home studio scenario, we might ask ourselves three questions: Why are grades meaningless in that home studio setup? How do grades affect learning in classrooms? What social dynamics does the presence of grades create? In both situations, instructors provide students or participants with evaluative feedback from time to time, pointing out where, say, you've done well and where I, as the instructor, could suggest improvement. In the home studio situation, many of you would help each other, even rely on each other during and outside of our scheduled meetings. In fact, you'd likely get more feedback from your peers on your work and practices than in a conventional classroom where only the teacher is expected to evaluate and grade.

Consider two issues around grades. First, using conventional classroom grading of essays and other work to compute course grades often leads students to think more about acquiring grades than about their writing or learning; to worry more about pleasing a teacher or fooling one than about figuring out what they really want to learn, or how they want to communicate something to someone for some purpose. Lots of research in education, writing studies, and psychology over the last 30 or so years have shown overwhelmingly how the presence of grades in classrooms negatively affect the learning and motivation of students. Alfie Kohn (2011), a well-known education researcher and teacher of teachers, makes this argument succinctly. To put it another way, if learning is what we are here for, then grades just get in the way since they are the wrong goals to strive for. An "A" doesn't build a good bridge for an engineer, nor does it help a reporter write a good story, or a urban planner make good decisions for her city. It's the learning that their grades in school allegedly represent that provides the knowledge to do all that they need to. And so, how do we make sure that our goals aren't about grades in this class, but about learning to write?

Second, conventional grading may cause you to be reluctant to take risks with your writing or ideas. It doesn't allow you to fail at writing, which many suggest is a primary way in which people learn from their practices. Sometimes grades even lead to the feeling that you are working *against* your teacher, or that you cannot make a mistake, or that you have to hide part of yourself from your teacher and peers. The bottom line is, failure at writing is vital to learning how to write better. And we have to embrace our failures, because they show us the places we can improve, learn, get better—and these are the reasons we are in college! Grades on our work and writing do not allow us to productively fail. They create conditions that mostly punish failure, not reward it for the learning opportunity it can and should be.

As you might already notice, what I'm arguing for here is a different kind of classroom, and even education. Sir Ken Robinson (2010), a well-known education researcher, makes the argument in a TED talk that typical schooling, with grades and particular standards, is an old and mostly harmful system that we've inherited, but now needs to change. One harmful aspect of this old system is that it assumes everyone is the same, that every student develops at the same pace and in the same ways, that variation in skills and literacies in a classroom is bad. It is clear the opposites of these things are more true. For all these reasons, I am incorporating a labor-based grading contract to calculate course grades in our class.

I offer this first draft of a contract that focuses on the responsibilities we'll assume, not the things to which someone else (usually the teacher) will hold you accountable. The pedagogical shift I'm suggesting is in part a cultural one, one that I would like you to control. Therefore, we will try to *approximate* the evaluative conditions of a home studio course. That is, we will try to create a culture of support, or rather a *community of compassion*, a group of people who genuinely care about the wellbeing of each other—and part of that caring, that compassion, is doing things for each other. It turns out, this also helps you learn. The best way to learn is to teach others, to help, to serve. So we will function as collaborators, allies, as fellow-travelers with various skills, abilities, experiences, and talents that we offer the group, rather than adversaries working against each other for grades or a teacher's approval.

Do not worry. You will get lots of assessments on your writing and other work during the semester from your colleagues and me. Use these assessments (written and verbal) to rethink ideas and improve your writing and practices, to take risks, in short to fail and learn from that failing. Always know that I will read everything and shape our classroom assessment activities and discussions around your work, but you will not receive grades from me. Sometimes, I will not even comment directly on your work, except in class when we use it or discuss it. I want you not only to rely on your colleagues and yourself for assessment and revision advice, but to build strategies of self-assessment that function apart from a teacher's approval.

Therefore the default grade for the course is a "B" (3.1). In a nutshell, if you do all that is asked of you in the manner and spirit it is asked, if you work through the processes we establish and the work we assign ourselves in the labor instructions during the quarter, if you do all the labor asked of you, then you'll get a "B" (3.1) course grade. It will not matter what I or your colleagues think of your writing, only that you are listening to our feedback compassionately. We may disagree or misunderstand your writing, but if you put in the labor, you are guaranteed a B (3.1) course grade. If you miss class (do not participate fully), turn in assignments late, forget to do assignments, or do not follow the labor instructions precisely, you will get a lower course grade (see the final breakdown grade table on the last page of this contract).

"B" GRADES

You are guaranteed a course grade of "B" (3.1) if you meet all of the following conditions.

- **Participation.** You agree to **fully participate in at least 84%** (26 of 31) of our scheduled class sessions and their activities and assignments, which means **you will need to be present in class, as most activities cannot be done before or after class and require your colleagues to compete.** So, you cannot miss more than 5 class sessions. Usually, attendance in class equates to participation. **NOTE:** Assignments not turned in because of an absence, either ones assigned on the schedule or ones assigned on earlier days in class, will be late, missed, or ignored (depending on when you turn it in finally, see the Guidelines #4, #5, and #6 below)

  Any absence due to a university-sponsored group activity (e.g., sporting event, band, another class field trip, etc.), military-related absences (e.g., deployment, work, duty, etc.), or documented illness will be considered independently of the above attendance policy, as long as the student has FIRST provided written documentation as soon as they are aware of the days they will be absent. This will allow us to determine how he/she will meet assignments and our contract, despite being absent. This may include absences due to illness that has a medical/doctor's note confirming the illness. Each of these circumstances will be determined on a case-by-case basis in consultation between the student and me (Asao) in a manner that is fair to all parties involved.

- **Lateness**. You agree to come on time or early to class. Walking into class late 1–2 times in a quarter is understandable.
- **Sharing and Collaboration**. You agree to work cooperatively and collegially in groups. This may be the easiest of all our course expectations to figure out, but we should have some discussions on what we expect from each other.
- **Late/Incomplete Work**. You agree to turn in properly and on time all work and assignments expected of you in the spirit they are assigned, which means you'll complete all of the labor instructions for each assignment. During the semester, you may, however, turn in a few assignments late. The exact number of those late assignments is stipulated in the table on the last page of this contract, which we negotiate. **Late or incomplete work is defined as any work or document due that is turned in AFTER the due date/time BUT within 48 hours of the deadline.** For example, if some work (say a written reflective piece) was due on Thursday, February 15 at 11:59 pm, that piece must be turned in by 11:59 pm on Saturday the 17th.
- **Missed Work**. If you turn in late work **AFTER the 48 hours** stipulated in Late/Incomplete Work, then it will be considered "missed work," which is a more serious mark against your grading contract. This is due to the fact that all assignments are used in class when they are due, so turning in something beyond 48 hours after it is due means it is assured to be less useful, and its absence has hurt your colleagues in class (since they depended on you to turn in your work for their use).
- **Ignored Work**. You agree not to ignore any work expected of you. Ignored work is any work unaccounted for in the quarter—that is, I have no record of you doing it or turning it in. My sense is that ignoring the work so crucial to one's development as a learner in our community is bad and unacceptable, so accumulating any "ignored work" will keep you from meeting our contract expectations (see table in Breakdown of the Main Components Section).
- **All Work/Labor and writing** needs to meet the following conditions:
  - *Complete and On Time*. You agree to turn in on time and in the appropriate manner complete essays, writing, or other labor assigned that meet all of our agreed upon expectations. (See Late/Incomplete Work for details on late assignments). This means you'll be honest about completing labor that asks particular time commitments of you (for example, "write for 20 minutes," etc.).
  - *Revisions*. When the job is to revise your thinking and work, you will reshape, extend, complicate, or substantially clarify your

ideas—or relate your ideas to new things. You won't just correct or touch up. Revisions must somehow respond to or consider seriously your colleagues' assessments in order to be revisions.

◦ *Copy Editing*. When the job is for the final publication of a draft, your work must be well copy edited—that is, you must spend significant time in your labor process to look just at spelling and grammar. It's fine to get help in copy editing. (Copy editing doesn't count on drafts before the final portfolio or first drafts).

KNOWING WHERE YOU STAND

This system is better than regular grading for giving you a clear idea of what your final grade looks like at any moment. If you are doing everything as directed and turning things in on time (no matter what anyone says), you're getting a B (3.1). As for participation in class, you'll have to keep track of it, but you can check with me at any time. I'll tell you what I have recorded.

IMPROVING YOUR CONTRACTED GRADE

The grade of B (3.1) depends primarily on *behavior* and *labor*. Have you shown responsible effort and consistency in our class? Have you done what was asked of you in the spirit it was asked? Higher grades than the default, the **grades of 3.4, 3.7, or 4.0**, however, require *more labor that helps or supports the class* in its mutual discussions and examinations of rhetoric or the myths of education, literacy, and identity. In order to raise your grade, you may complete as many of the following items of labor as you like (doing three gets you a 4.0). Each item completed fully and in the appropriate manner will raise your final course grade by .3. The first and last items may be done twice, each counting as a separate labor.

- **Extra Précis-Responses (2 total extra):** At particular times in the quarter, you can do extra précis-Responses. You must complete a total of two extra ones in order for this extra labor to count as enough extra labor for the .3 course grade bump. Each extra precis-response is due the day we have scheduled to discuss those readings.
- **Labor Journal Essay (2 total):** At week 7 and 10, you may write an essay that looks back at your labor journal entries as a record of your labors toward learning in this class. This essay will be about 3–4 pages long and be written directly to me (Asao), but the class likely will read them too in order to learn from your own discussion of your learning.
- **A Bigger Project:** For each project we do, you can opt to do more labor on it at each phase of invention, research, drafting, and revision.

This mostly means more research and sources incorporated into the culminating artifact, and the related documents that help you build your drafts, such as our annotated bibliographies, which we will do before the project is drafted. See our syllabus's "Extra Labor" section for complete details on this labor.

- **Extra Assessments (3 extra formal ones)**: You may do three extra assessments for three different colleagues not in your original writing group. You must do one extra assessment letter for each project (i.e., projects 1 and 2), and one extra portfolio assessment at the end of the quarter. So this extra labor must be planned from at the beginning of the quarter. These assessment letters will follow the same labor instructions as the normal ones you'll do.

- **A lesson/activity/handout**: These handouts are on a topic and material that you research for the class's benefit and will need at least 2 weeks lead time, working with me (Asao) on the materials. While we'll determine together the scope your lesson, the main elements of your labor will be to produce: (1) a 1–2 page handout for the class's benefit in our writing and thinking; (2) some outline for our in-class activity that introduces your handout; and (3) a short reflective essay to me (Asao) of about 1–2 pages (300–600 words) on what you learned in the process of doing this labor and what you feel the class stands to gain from the lesson you offered us.

- **Some other labor that benefits the class** and our mutual learning of rhetoric, language diversity, and academic writing. Do you want to write about and report to us on a cultural event related to the class? Or maybe you would like to read an article for us and summarize some of its findings or ideas that you think will help us do our work in class? If you have an idea, come to me (Asao) early. We will plan it, while making sure the amount of labor is commensurate with the other items above.

Thus, for every item you complete on the above list, your contracted grade will **improve by .3 grade points**. So if you meet the conditions for a B-contract (3.1), then your grade can improve in the following ways:

- **1 item** completed = course grade of **3.4**
- **2 items** completed = course grade of **3.7**
- **3 items** completed = course grade of **4.0**

If you are working toward a C-contract (2.1) or lower, the same .3 movement up the grade latter applies by completing 1–3 items on the list above. You may even do more than three items and continue to raise your grade by .3 per item. Your course grade, then, equates to a 2.4, 2.7, 3.0, 3.3, respectively.

BREAKDOWN OF THE MAIN COMPONENTS

Below is a table that shows the main components that affect your successful compliance with our contract.

	# non-Partic Days	# of Late Assigns.	# of Missed Assigns.	# of Ignored Assigns.
A (4.0)	5	5	1	0
B (3.1)	5	5	1	0
C (2.1)	6	6	2	0
D (1.1)	7	7	3	1
E (0.0)	8	8	4	2

Gimme/Plea. I (Asao), as the administrator of our contract, will decide in consultation with the student whether a gimme is warranted in any case. The student must come to me (Asao Inoue) as soon as possible, usually before the student is unable to meet the contract (before breaching the contract), in order that he/she and I can make fair and equitable arrangements, ones that will be fair and equitable to all in the class and still meet the university's regulations on attendance, conduct, and workload in classes. **You may use a gimme for any reason, but only once in the semester.** Please keep in mind that the contract is a public, social contract, one agreed upon through group discussion and negotiation, so my job is to make sure that whatever agreement we come to about a plea will not be unfair to others in class. A gimmie/plea does not allow you to ignore any work expected of everyone in the class. A plea is NOT an "out clause" for anyone who happens to not fulfill the contract in some way; it is for rare and unusual circumstances out of the control of the student.

Exemplary labor. If by our final meeting conference (end of quarter), **you miss no classes (participate in all activities), have no late, missed, or ignored assignments, and do not use a gimme**, then you will earn an extra .4 (equal to one item on the advanced contract) to your final course grade. This rule is meant to reward those students who engage in all the labor of the course in the fullest spirit asked of them and demonstrate themselves to be exemplary class citizens.

By staying in this course and attending class, you accept this contract and agree to abide by it. I (Asao) also agree to abide by the contract, and administer it fairly and equitably.

APPENDIX B.

SAMPLE CHARTER FOR COMPASSION

Taken and modified from: The Charter for Compassion, https://charterforcompassion.org/charter/charter-overview.

The principle of compassion lies at the heart of all religious, ethical, and spiritual traditions, calling us always to treat all others as we wish to be treated ourselves. Compassion impels us to work tirelessly to alleviate the suffering of our fellow creatures, to dethrone ourselves from the center of our world and put another there, and to honor the inviolable sanctity of every single human being, treating everybody, without exception, with absolute justice, equity, and respect.

It is also necessary in both public and private life to refrain consistently and empathically from inflicting pain. To act or speak violently out of spite, chauvinism, or self-interest, to impoverish, exploit or deny basic rights to anybody, and to incite hatred by denigrating others—even our enemies—is a denial of our common humanity. We in this class acknowledge that we have failed to live compassionately to some degree.

We therefore pledge to do all that we can, knowing we'll fail on occasion, to restore compassion to the center of our lives (at least in this course and during this quarter) and attempt to engage with our colleagues in this course with compassion. This means we will work to think first of others, their benefit, their well-being, and their learning, knowing that others are compassionately working for our benefit. We will strive to see our interdependence and interconnectedness, and labor for one another.

The following specific actions and behaviors we pledge to do in order to encourage and adopt a compassionate stance toward our colleagues in this class:

Overall
- Act toward and speak to others as you would want them to do for you if the roles were reversed
- Take responsibility for the effects of your words and actions on others, even when your intentions were not to cause them harm

Listening
- Listen attentively and intently (with intention to understand) first, using eye contact, and forming an opinion after you fully understand their point of view

- Be open minded toward others' ideas and understanding of their backgrounds
- Pay attention to your body Language (try not to be defensive)
- When you're uncomfortable, speak up and tell others, so they know

Responding

- Mindfully respond to others' ideas (acknowledge someone's ideas before presenting your own)
- Vocally affirm that you respect and empathize with those around you
- Use a calm and collected tone of voice; be careful with your word choice; avoid aggressive language, and don't use harsh words
- Encourage compliments and be nice to others
- Aim to educate

APPENDIX C.

SAMPLE LABOR LOG

You can access the most recent version of the labor log that I give to my students to use before the first day of each course online (http://tinyurl.com/y7e6rpms). It is a Google Sheets, which has formulas and graphs. The formulas also use links to another online spreadsheet that I use to keep track of all labor numbers. Using such interconnectivity in the spreadsheets can take some time to figure out, so I suggest starting with just having students use the spreadsheets as logs.

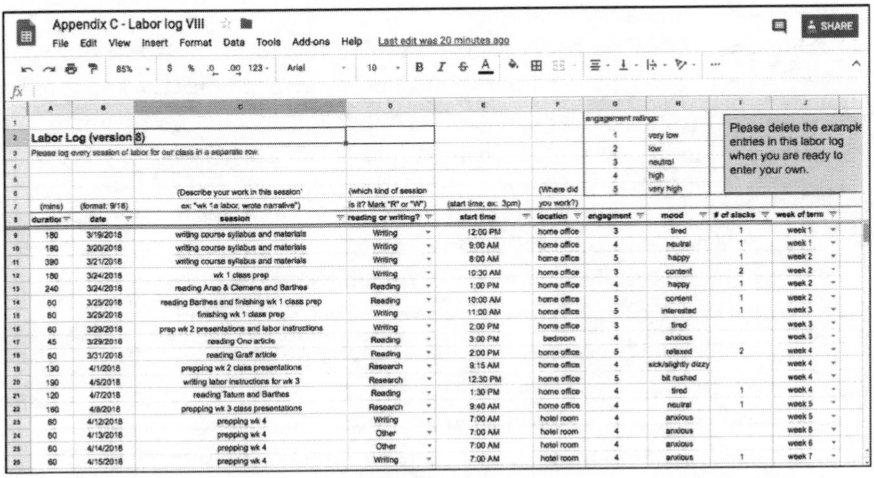
Appendix C - Labor log VIII

File Edit View Insert Format Data Tools Add-ons Help Last edit was 20 minutes ago

SHARE

Labor Log (version 8)

Please log every session of labor for our class in a separate row.

engagement ratings: 1 very low; 2 low; 3 neutral; 4 high; 5 very high

Please delete the example entries in this labor log when you are ready to enter your own.

(mins)	(format: 9/18)	(Describe your work in this session' ex: "wk 1a labor, wrote narrative")	(which kind of session is it? Mark "R" or "W")	(start time; ex: 3pm)	(Where did you work?)				
duration	date	session	reading or writing?	start time	location	engagment	mood	# of slacks	week of term
180	3/19/2018	writing course syllabus and materials	Writing	12:00 PM	home office	3	tired	1	week 1
180	3/20/2018	writing course syllabus and materials	Writing	9:00 AM	home office	4	neutral	1	week 1
390	3/21/2018	writing course syllabus and materials	Writing	8:00 AM	home office	5	happy	1	week 2
180	3/24/2018	wk 1 class prep	Writing	10:30 AM	home office	3	content	2	week 2
240	3/24/2018	reading Arao & Clemens and Barthes	Reading	1:00 PM	home office	4	happy	1	week 2
60	3/25/2018	reading Barthes and finishing wk 1 class prep	Reading	10:00 AM	home office	5	content	1	week 2
60	3/25/2018	finishing wk 1 class prep	Writing	11:00 AM	home office	5	interested	1	week 3
60	3/29/2018	prep wk 2 presentations and labor instructions	Writing	2:00 PM	home office	3	tired		week 3
45	3/29/2018	reading Ono article	Reading	3:00 PM	bedroom	4	anxious		week 3
60	3/31/2018	reading Graff article	Reading	2:00 PM	home office	5	relaxed	2	week 4
130	4/1/2018	prepping wk 2 class presentations	Research	9:15 AM	home office	4	sick/slightly dizzy		week 4
190	4/5/2018	writing labor instructions for wk 3	Research	12:30 PM	home office	5	bit rushed		week 4
120	4/7/2018	reading Tatum and Barthes	Reading	1:30 PM	home office	4	tired	1	week 4
160	4/8/2018	prepping wk 3 class presentations	Research	9:40 AM	home office	4	neutral	1	week 5
60	4/12/2018	prepping wk 4	Writing	7:00 AM	hotel room	4	anxious		week 5
60	4/13/2018	prepping wk 4	Other	7:00 AM	hotel room	4	anxious		week 6
60	4/14/2018	prepping wk 4	Other	7:00 AM	hotel room	4	anxious		week 6
60	4/15/2018	prepping wk 4	Writing	7:00 AM	hotel room	4	anxious	1	week 7

Figure C.1. Screen capture of Labor Log Version 8 from Google Sheets.

Each session of labor is recorded in a row of data in the labor log, so each column asks for a small bit of information about each session. While I'm often tweaking the columns of data I ask students to record in their logs, these data have been the most stable over the last few years:

- Duration (in minutes)
- Date of session
- Description of session
- Type of session (e.g., reading, writing, research, or other)
- Start time of session
- Location of session
- Engagement rating (1–5)

- Number of Slacks/Tweets
- Week of term/quarter/semester

See the screen capture of what my most current labor log looks like as of this writing, and how I've filled it in for my own labor, as a way to demonstrate.

LABOR INSTRUCTIONS FOR DRAFTING YOUR PERSONAL NARRATIVE

Due by Wed, Sept. 26 at 11:00 a.m.
Canvas Post in forum: wk 1 - narratives
Slack channel: #wk1-narratives
Estimated labor time: 230 minutes total

These labor instructions will lead you through a process that develops your personal narrative, which you'll use to introduce yourself to the class and explain your personal writing goals for the quarter. While it is small, it is very important to your success in the class. Our syllabus explains this assignment as:

> **Personal Narrative (1):** For the first day of class, you'll write a personal narrative that does two things. First, it introduces you to the class in your own words, and second, it discusses what your goals are for this course. This narrative should focus on details and specifics, showing us a kind of picture of you as a reader and writer or student, or as a language user. You decide how you wish to introduce yourself to us. Focus on these two questions: Who are you as a reader and writer, as a language user? What do you hope to accomplish in this course this quarter? This should be a short, 1–2 page (300–500 words) narrative only, posted on Canvas (in the "wk 1 - narratives" forum) by our first class session. As with all labor, there will be labor instructions for this work.
>
> I assess all personal narratives the same. You may earn full credit (i.e., you've done the assignment according to its expectations), or no credit (i.e., you haven't met the expectations of the assignment or posted it on time)

PURPOSE AND GOALS

Our purpose for this labor is to introduce ourselves to our colleagues in class and consider the most important personal goals for this class that you would like to accomplish. The goals for the following labor process are:

- To brainstorm and draft an introduction to our colleagues in class
- To draft a set of personal reading and writing goals that you can work toward during the quarter

DO NOT FORGET: Start your labor logs now! Please log all your labor sessions in your labor log on G'drive. This is required for every labor session of this class.

PROCESS

Please read completely the labor process below first, then follow each step carefully to get full credit for doing this assignment.

1. **Find a quiet spot** where you can do your work in peace and be completely in the present moment for yourself and your colleagues. Be mindful of places where there's too much background noise, even if you feel you're accustomed to it. You want to be able to do your work uninterrupted and in peace and quiet. This will allow you to focus better and do the work below more thoughtfully and mindfully.

2. **Read our handout on Reading as a Mindful Practice**, which explains not only how to read more deeply any text, but how to prepare to do that kind of work. Follow the instructions in that document as you read it. It will take you to other short texts. We'll use this practice in all our reading done this quarter. This will take about **20 minutes**.

3. Sit comfortably in your chair, rest your hands in your lap or to your sides, and close your eyes. Feel your body, your toes, your hands, your chest, your stomach. Then **do a mindful breathing practice** for 3 minutes. The key is to notice each breath and how it feels in your throat, or nose, or body. Just notice it without judging yourself. Breathe in and say in your mind, "in." Then breathe out and say in your mind "out." If your mind wonders, notice those thoughts. Do not judge yourself. Do not follow them or pursue them. Just observe them. It is normal for our minds to wander and be active. Just notice the wondering and gently bring your attention back to your breath. Use an online meditation timer to help you keep track of your time. Spend **3 minutes** in this mindful practice.

4. **Make a planning document for your personal narrative**. While you may make a plan, you can deviate from that plan when you actually begin drafting, but it's always good to have a plan when writing. To plan, I'd like you to do some brainstorming of ideas. Start by listing or writing some ideas about some experiences that you've had with either reading or writing for school or outside of school, whichever seems most important for you to tell us about. You decide. Spend at least **20 minutes**, but take

longer if you need it. It is the time in the activity that is most important, not what the planning document looks like or how detailed it is. Focus your attention on the following three lines of questioning when brainstorming or prewriting. **Be sure to have notes on three sets of questions** (you'll need them below).

- What experience with reading or writing have you had that seems typical, or important to you for some reason? What happened? How did you experience that labor of reading or writing? What are the main characteristics of the experience? Where and when did it happen? What does that experience tell you about yourself?

- What goals do you hope to accomplish in this course, a first-year writing course for UWT? Why these goals? Do any of them match our program's goals for class on pages 1–2 of our syllabus? What goals of yours seem particularly about you as a reader and/or writer? Why?

- What do you anticipate will be a challenge in this course in meeting your personal goals? Why will those challenges be challenges for you this quarter? What do you plan to do to overcome those challenges?

5. **Pause for a few minutes to notice what you've done**. In order to be more mindful of what we are doing and learning in our class, I will ask us often to pause in our labors and post a Slack message (like a tweet). This will help you do your labor more mindfully by asking you to pause for a minute and pay attention to what you are doing and how you are feeling about it. This is how you can be more conscious of what and how you are learning stuff. And it makes you a better learner! So for this first time, **take a picture of your planning document and post that picture in Slack in the Channel #wk1-narratives. With the picture, tell us how you are feeling about your narrative.** If you are doing this on a laptop or computer, to post, click on the "+" in the correct channel, then click "your computer," and select the picture you took. You'll be prompted to add a message. If you are doing this in the Slack app on your phone, it's even easier. Tap the picture icon at the bottom of the screen in the appropriate channel. Don't forget to add a note about how you're feeling about your narrative. Make sure we can read clearly your planning document in the picture. This should take **1 minute**.

6. **Draft** your personal narrative using the planning document you just created. **Choose one reading or writing experience** to focus on. Tell us about it, then talk to us about how and why you feel it represents you as a reader or writer. Try to offer some questions that the experience and

its details raises for you and your literacy(ies). What questions about language, literacy, or your literacy does this experience reveal to you? End your narrative with a separate, thoughtful paragraph about your goals for this class (TCORE 101). List your goals. **Try to have 4–5 real goals** (but you could have more), with some being about you as a reader and some about you as a writer. Drafting this narrative may take between **2–3 hours**, but it could take longer, and will be between **300–600 words** in length. The more time you spend, the more you will get from the labor. So give yourself time, and multiple sessions of drafting, if possible. Here are the two main parts of your narrative that are most important for us (and you) and make it complete:

- What reading or writing experience from your past exemplifies you as a reader or writer?
- What are your own personal learning goals for this course (TCORE 101)? Why those? How do you plan on accomplishing them?

7. Now, before you finish your narrative, **go to its beginning and make a new, first paragraph**. This will be a short, maybe 1 or 2 sentence paragraph. These sentences will be your opening and greeting to us, and your chance to help us identify key aspects of your identity, and help us identify you in the right ways, ways you feel most comfortable with. Tell us how we can identify and reference you in class. For instance, what is your name? What gender and pronoun do you most identify with and use to reference yourself? What racial designation and ethnic group do you most find affinity with? Do you speak or use more than one language?

8. Keep in mind that ethnicity and race are not the same thing, but they often correlate. Think of ethnicity as the culture you identify with, like Irish or Chinese, while race is a much broader term that tends to signal other things in U.S. culture, which we'll talk about. Racial designations come in about 4–5 categories: Black, White, Asian, Pacific Islander/Polynesian, Latinx, and Native/Indigenous Peoples. If you identify as a mixed-race person, then you may tell us that too. Here's an example of this welcoming set of sentences, using my identifying information:

> Hello, my name is Asao B. Inoue. I am a cisgendered
> Asian male, who prefers the pronouns "he/him." My father
> was Japanese from Hawaii and my mom is combination of
> Greek, Scottish, and English, as best our family can say. I
> was raised speaking only English in my household.

343

9. Please understand that this part of your narrative is not meant to out anyone or cause undue emotional trauma. It is meant to help us be clear and explicit about who we are and how we'd like others to know us.

10. Finally, **give your narrative a title**, something that matches the center of the narrative. What short, snappy title can you give this narrative that encapsulates what you want us to know about you as a colleague and perhaps what you hope to accomplish in the course? While the title may come to you quickly, give yourself at least **1–2 minutes** to make a good one. Make sure to use the title in your Canvas posting.

11. **Post** your personal narrative in the discussion forum on Canvas, wk 1—narratives. Post it by Wed, Sep 26 at 11:00 am. We will read these out loud on the first day of class to introduce ourselves to each other. I'll do one too.